Sugamo Prison, Tokyo

Sugamo Prison, Tokyo

*An Account of the Trial and Sentencing
of Japanese War Criminals in 1948,
by a U.S. Participant*

JOHN L. GINN

McFarland & Company, Inc., Publishers
Jefferson, North Carolina, and London

> The present work is a reprint of the library bound edition of Sugamo Prison, Tokyo: An Account of the Trial and Sentencing of Japanese War Criminals in 1948, by a U.S. Participant, *first published in 1992 by McFarland.*

LIBRARY OF CONGRESS CATALOGUING-IN-PUBLICATION DATA

Ginn, John L, 1928–
  Sugamo Prison, Tokyo : an account of the trial and sentencing of Japanese war criminals in 1948, by a U.S. participant / by John L. Ginn.
    p.   cm.
  Includes bibliographical references and index.

  ISBN 978-0-7864-6762-4
  softcover : 50# alkaline paper ∞

  1. War crime trials—Japan. 2. Tokyo Trial, Tokyo, Japan, 1946–1948. I. Title.
  JX5438.8.G56 2012
  341.6′9′026873052—dc20   92-50424

BRITISH LIBRARY CATALOGUING DATA ARE AVAILABLE

© 1992 John L. Ginn. All rights reserved

No part of this book may be reproduced or transmitted in any form or by any means, electronic or mechanical, including photocopying or recording, or by any information storage and retrieval system, without permission in writing from the publisher.

Front cover design by David K. Landis
(Shake It Loose Graphics)

Manufactured in the United States of America

McFarland & Company, Inc., Publishers
  Box 611, Jefferson, North Carolina 28640
  www.mcfarlandpub.com

For all the American soldiers
who served at Sugamo Prison,
both living and deceased

CONTENTS

Acknowledgments	ix
Introduction	xi
The Prison	1
The Prisoners	
Class A	15
Classes B and C	33
The Trials	
Class A	37
Classes B and C	56
The Sentences	
Class A	121
Class C	137
The Executions	177
The Americans	195
Reflections	241
Appendix A: Names of the Accused	247
Appendix B: Potsdam Declaration	259
Appendix C: IMTFE Charter	261
Appendix D: Full Text of MacArthur's Review of the War Crimes Sentences	267
Appendix E: Sugamo Prison Roster, 1945–1952	268
Bibliography	289
Index	293

ACKNOWLEDGMENTS

John L. Ginn in 1948

I am especially indebted to my wife, Jan, a workaholic who has supported my effort with constructive criticism, patience, and long hours before a word processor that beeps every time a Japanese name or word is entered into it.

Special thanks to the men of Sugamo—listed in the American section—who contributed some excellent information and photographs; and to Max Rutzer and Taura Nelson of Image Processor, Inc., of Walla Walla, Washington, who, in performing a commercial service, went far beyond the call of duty.

My thanks, too, to Robert L. Burr, director of the Crosby Library at Gonzaga University in Spokane, Washington; and to Susan Akers, Jan Cronkhite, and the staff of the Walla Walla County Library who found and obtained old, scarce books needed for my research.

Finally, I am grateful to Glenn Hinsdale of Bothell, Washington, who edited this book and provided some sound advice. He is not only a close friend but has the rare ability to make insults sound like compliments. It often takes several weeks for the insultee to realize that they weren't.

INTRODUCTION

Never in the history of the human race has any event affected more people of all nationalities than World War II. Tens of millions were destroyed in battle. Tens of millions were slaughtered because of religious beliefs or ethnic backgrounds. Tens of millions were wounded mentally or physically or both. The war touched every human who survived it: Not only were their lives changed, however; the lives of the millions born since World War II continue to be affected by it.

Large and small cities were leveled, nations torn apart. Historians and statisticians differ on the precise figures; however, almost all of them agree that about fifty-five million people perished during World War II. Hideous instruments of destruction were invented. Some that are being perfected even now include nuclear weapons; biological warfare; long-range, virtually radar-proof bombers; sonar-proof submarines; and laser-guided missiles.

The war touched every continent on earth. It required mobilization of manpower and matériel and cooperation and coordination among nations of a quality and quantity inconceivable to most experts even today.

The war between the United States and Japan was extraordinary and unique. It began with an excellently coordinated surprise display of air and sea power by the Japanese at Pearl Harbor and ended with the most lethal air raids in history by the Americans.

Never before had such large armies been transported through thousands of miles of oceans to do battle on hostile islands, supplied and supported only by planes and ships. As a naval conflict, it was unmatched in history. More battles were fought and more ships sunk than in all other twentieth-century naval battles combined. Never before had air and sea power depended on each other so completely for survival.

There are hundreds of books about the magnitude of this war; there are volumes describing major battles, humbling defeats, and specific navy, army, marine, and air force engagements. There are diaries by POWs and fighting men from both sides. There are war atlases and encyclopedias. Practically everything known about World War II has been written and rewritten. Nevertheless, new facts and information continue to appear, to the consternation of some who wish that history could be a more exact science.

The war with Germany and its allies ended on May 7, 1945, and the war with Japan ended on August 14, 1945, both in unconditional surrender. This book begins with the end of the war that involved the United States and Japan.

Long before Pearl Harbor, Japanese military leaders schemed and plotted to bring about war and expand outward to obtain more territory and natural resources. In September 1931, they provoked an incident in Mukden, Manchuria, by bombing the South Manchurian Railway. The Japanese Kwantung army, stationed in Manchuria, had secretly installed heavy guns and used this incident to start war without permission or sanction from the Japanese government. They did not declare war but attacked suddenly and without warning, killing thousands of unsuspecting Chinese soldiers. Within a short time they occupied all of Manchuria. Thereafter the Japanese army was completely out of control, and anyone in the Japanese government who tried to place restraints on the Kwantung army was likely to be assassinated. Among those who were killed were premiers, advisers to the emperor, and the Lord Keeper of the Privy Seal and other government ministers.

In July 1937 the Kwantung army clique staged another incident — at the Marco Polo Bridge, near Peking that brought about full-scale hostilities with China. The Japanese were conducting unauthorized military maneuvers in the area around the bridge. They claimed that Chinese troops had fired on them and that a Japanese soldier was missing. Another sneak attack on Chinese troops took place, with heavy loss of life on the Chinese side.

The Japanese military clique used Manchuria and China for multiple purposes in their preparations for the upcoming world war, especially as tactical and strategic training grounds for their top generals and troop leaders. Later, when the militarists began drug trafficking in Manchuria and China, they were able to use these countries to finance their military operations. In addition, their counterparts in Tokyo were bringing pressure to bear for the buildup of planes, ships, and munitions.

Military clique leaders within the Japanese army and navy were determined to have a war, were preparing themselves for it, and by December 1941 believed they were ready for it.

By mid-July 1945 the Japanese had been defeated in the war they initiated with surprise attacks on December 7, 1941.* However, the Japanese military leadership refused to accept defeat. The Americans had not yet released the atomic bomb, the most destructive weapon ever created in the history of mankind.

The Japanese navy had been defeated at Midway Island and in the Battle of Leyte Gulf. Their army had been defeated in Okinawa, the Philippines, and many smaller islands. Over Japan, U.S. bombers were searching for worthwhile targets. Practically everything of value to the Japanese war effort had been destroyed. People were literally beginning to starve.

But the military leaders still believed that victory could be achieved through one last big battle, by throwing every available man, woman, and child into a suicidal attack on the invading forces. They were depending on the Japanese Bushido code, which values honor over death, and Japanese willingness to fight until death in kamikaze suicide attacks.†

On July 26 the Allies warned Japan that it faced surrender or total destruction. Terms of the surrender were based on the Potsdam Proclamation and called for the demobilization of Japanese military forces, Allied occupation of Japan, elimination of the military clique, and trials for war criminals. The military leaders did not accept those terms and by their silence rejected them.

Contrary to popular belief, the nuclear bombings of Hiroshima on August 6 and Nagasaki on August 9, 1945, did not bring the war to an end. On August 8 the Soviet Union, in violation of a nonaggression pact with Japan, declared war and invaded Manchuria. This, at least as much as the nuclear bombs, broke the confidence of the military. The Japanese were hoping to use the influence of the Soviet Union in making peace with the United States and its allies.

The Japanese prime minister and foreign minister called an emergency meeting with Emperor Hirohito on August 9. (The emperor did not govern but exercised sovereignty and reigned over the Japanese nation.) He listened to both sides of the argument, letting his ministers and statesmen make the final decision. He often left such conferences

---

On that date they seized the Bund international settlement in Shanghai; and attacked Kota Bharu, a British protectorate on the east coast of Malaya; southern Thailand, Singapore, Guam, Hong Kong; and, of course, Pearl Harbor.

†*In 1570 a Mongol emperor with an invasion fleet set sail for Japan. It appeared that Japan would be easily defeated, but a typhoon sank and dispersed the Mongol fleet. The Japanese were convinced that the storm had been created by the gods and named it* Kamikaze, *or "divine wind."*

without speaking. In this meeting, however, after listening to both the war and peace factions, the emperor ignored tradition and custom and called for the acceptance of the Potsdam Declaration and agreed to the Allied demands. He told his stunned leaders: "The time has come when we must bear the unbearable." The meeting adjourned.

Almost immediately the military once more began plotting to continue the war. Even the emperor's words were not enough to stop them, although the foreign minister did let the Allies know that Japan was preparing to surrender.

A coup attempt began at once. The militarists determined to fight on and remove from power—by assassination or other means—the defeatist leaders who were influencing the emperor. This came to the attention of the premier, and another imperial conference was called on August 14.

The emperor again ignored tradition and informed his leaders that Japan would be destroyed if the war was not stopped. He declared that he could not allow that to happen whatever his own fate might be, and that he was willing to go before his people on radio. When he left the conference, most of the twenty-four leaders were weeping.

The next day the "sacred voice of the emperor" set a precedent unimaginable to most Japanese: It spoke directly to the Japanese people, telling the public what was actually happening and terminating the war by accepting the Allies' surrender terms unconditionally.

In the meantime the Japanese government, still ruled by the military, was using every precious minute to destroy any records that could possibly be harmful to them.

On August 16 the Allies formally accepted Japan's surrender. On September 2 the official documents were signed by Japanese leaders in Tokyo Bay, aboard the battleship *Missouri.*

Gen. Douglas MacArthur planned for the Eleventh Airborne Division to land at Atsugi Airfield on August 23. The Japanese quickly informed him that government authority over the armed forces was not yet complete and that they needed more time to bring radical forces under control. The general agreed and set August 26 as the new date. However, a storm prevented the main landing of occupational troops until August 30.

For the Russians the war with Japan was over after only twenty-four days. It lasted fourteen years for the Chinese, and almost four for the Americans, British, and Dutch.

THE PRISON

Sugamo Prison no longer exists except in official American and Japanese records, and in the memories of those who served time there as prisoners or guards. In its place now is a very expensive housing and shopping complex named Sunshine City, the location of the tallest building in Japan. In one corner of this complex is a small park where a large stone marks the location of the prison's gallows. A message in Japanese reads "Pray for Eternal Peace."

Compared to other Japanese and American prisons, the life span of Sugamo was a short one. Constructed in the early 1920s and demolished in 1971, it was the best-constructed and most modern prison in Japan. The Japanese copied the architecture of Sugamo from some of the better European prisons.

Located approximately six miles north-northeast of the Imperial Palace, near Ikebukuro Station in Toshima Ku, in Tokyo, Sugamo Prison was initially used for holding political prisoners. "Political" included anyone the members of the military clique believed could interfere with their war goals. Into this category fell Communists, dissenters, spies, and anyone else whom the military felt should be imprisoned—for practically any reason. In 1938 a leader of the Tokyo-Yokohama Communist group, Shinichi Matsumoto, was picked up in a police roundup of suspects and kept in Sugamo Prison for a year without a hearing or trial. Many of Japan's leading publishers and journalists spent time in Sugamo for writing or publishing ideas detrimental to the aims and goals of the military.

The prison was virtually untouched by the war, but almost everything surrounding it was destroyed by bombs. A small portion of the medical ward was partially destroyed by the near miss of an incendiary bomb in early 1945. It was repaired by the American occupation forces late in 1945.

While under Japanese control, the prison was a single compound covering about six acres, enclosed by a thick, twelve-foot-high, reinforced concrete wall. The Japanese guards who served at the prison also lived

Main gate of Sugamo. (Courtesy Lloyd Oler)

within the compound. There they had their living quarters, kitchen, eating area, and minimal recreation facilities. The guards were supervised by a prison governor.

The occupation forces began rounding up suspected Japanese war criminals early in September. While Army troops were readying Sugamo Prison, other troops from the Thirty-fifth AAA group, reinforced with two batteries from the 579 AAA, were guarding war criminal suspects at Omori Prison—designated as XI Corp Stockade 2. This prison, much smaller than Sugamo, was located on Omori Island—land reclaimed from Tokyo Bay. During the war, this facility had been a notorious POW camp for Americans.

On December 8, 1945, the overcrowded Omori prisoners were transferred to Sugamo Prison—known then as XI Corp Stockade 1. The two batteries of troops serving at Sugamo provided guard duty and security around the clock.

In March 1946, administration and control of Sugamo Prison was assigned to 8th Army with headquarters in Yokohama. Lt. General Robert L. Eichelberger was the Commander.

One of the first prisoners to be processed into Sugamo Prison was Hideki Tojo. Ironically, the date and time listed on Tojo's basic personnel

The Prison

Administration Building, Sugamo Prison. (Courtesy John L. Ginn)

record was 14:40, December 8, 1945. This was exactly the same local time that Ambassador Nomura was sent into Secretary of State Cordell Hull's office in Washington, D.C., in December 1941 to present Japan's final negotiation.

The prison's administration building was centrally located on the south side. It consisted of six long wings, of which five were three-story tiers of cells, and one a two-story tier. It was provided with exercise and labor yards, service areas, a laundry, and an execution building. There was also a smaller building, known as the Blue Prison, within this compound for women prisoners. Under Japanese administration, Sugamo was never fully occupied by prisoners.

The Japanese did execute prisoners, however. Two of the more important were Richard Sorge, a German spying for the USSR, and Hotsumi Ozaki, one of his top people. Ozaki was a Japanese citizen. Numerous others in this spy ring were discovered, tried, and imprisoned throughout Japan.

Sorge was an insider with the Germany Embassy, posing—with certified credentials—as a German correspondent. He provided two top German newspapers with many articles that pleased both the Germans and the Japanese. He had the complete confidence of Germany's ambassador, Gen. Eugen Ott, while he set up a ring of spies that covered China, Indochina, Manchuria, the Philippines, Korea, and virtually all

Ex-Premier General Hideki Tojo

of Japan's Far East conquests. Sorge provided the Soviet Union with thousands of coded messages, keeping the Russian government completely informed of Japanese military actions and plans.

Sorge and Ozaki were hanged on November 7, 1944. Other members of the spy ring were imprisoned for terms of varying lengths. Some later perished in other prisons for lack of medical attention, and some were released when the American occupation forces liberated Japanese prisons.

Other spies executed at Sugamo included five American agents. In July 1943 William J. Donovan, director of the Office of Strategic Services (OSS), sent a six-man team into Japan as part of a B-29 bombing mission. They parachuted from the plane at night over Honshu, equipped with transmitters, Japanese currency, rations, and weapons. The Japanese soon realized that spies were reporting their convoy and troop movements to the Allies. Japan lost five ships in one convoy and four troop transports in another. Military units searched the countryside and eventually caught five of the OSS agents. They were taken to Sugamo, interrogated, and executed by hanging later in November 1944 — the same month as Sorge and Ozaki. (The sixth agent was never caught and continued to transmit ship movements to the U.S. military. After the war he came in from the cold and served as a colonel with the occupation forces.)

Sugamo held about sixty political prisoners when the Eighth Army

Sugamo Prison execution building. (©Dr. Walter Hood, all rights reserved.)

troops took command. They were released because there were no reasons to keep them. Also, room was needed for suspected war criminals.

The Japanese had developed a technique for hanging people that appears to have been more humane than methods used elsewhere. A cone-shaped wooden block, fitted above the noose, was stabilized by rubber washers. This cone served to render the prisoner unconscious a millisecond before his neck was broken. These blocks were found at Sugamo when the occupation forces arrived and were used for most of the executions resulting from trial sentences handed down by the International Military Tribunal for the Far East Command (IMTFE).

On occupying Sugamo Prison, the Eighth Army provided almost five hundred troops to staff it. By mid-1947 the roundup of war criminals had netted approximately two thousand prisoners and protected witnesses.

Ironically, two of the prisoners brought to Sugamo were Procurator General (former Justice Minister) Tsusei Iwamura; and Justice Minister Hiromasa Matsuzaki. (A procurator general has about the same authority in Japan as the attorney general in the United States.) In the past both of these prisoners had had supervisory control of the prison, and both were well aware of the painstaking efforts taken to make it escape proof.

An outer compound, encompassing about twelve acres, was built around the inner one, enlarging the prison area by 100 percent. The outer boundary was protected by a ten-foot-high, fourteen-strand, barbed-wire fence. The wire fence surrounding the outer compound was not there to prevent the escape of prisoners but to prevent the Japanese from stealing coal and food from the Americans. (During the early years of the occupation there was an abundance of cold and hungry Japanese citizens.)

This compound contained all the amenities and facilities the U.S. Army strives to bestow on its personnel. These included Quonset huts for quarters; a mess hall and post exchange; officers' and enlisted men's clubs; and a post theater and baseball and football fields. The football field also served as a track for exercising and a parade ground for troop formations and ceremonies. There was an orderly room for the records and files of all personnel serving at Sugamo; a bowling alley (the first in Japan); an armory; a motor pool; a snack bar; and a Red Cross Service Club at which monthly or bimonthly dances were held and at which GIs could play Ping-Pong tournaments, checkers, and chess matches.

Improvements to the prison itself began almost immediately after the Americans arrived. On the priority list were the heating, cooling, and ventilation systems and repairs to the medical facilities. The prison took on a new look as both the exterior and interior were painted with brighter colors. The grounds were landscaped, trees and shrubbery planted, and new buildings erected. Some of the improvements created confusion among the prisoners because they were required to move from one cellblock to another without explanation while repairs and improvements were made.

In 1948, when the war crimes trials were being concluded, security was strengthened with guard towers, jeep patrols, and a main gate manned twenty-four hours a day by double guards. There were also special details to watch and guard the prisoners inside the prison and to transport Class A prisoners to Tokyo by bus, and Class C prisoners to Yokohama by army bus or truck, to be tried.

Class A war criminals were those accused of "crimes against peace"—namely, the planning, preparation, initiation, or waging of a declared or undeclared war of aggression; or a war in violation of international law, treaties, agreements or assurances; or participation in a common plan or conspiracy for the accomplishment of any of the foregoing.

Class B criminals were those charged with conventional war crimes—

Back view of Sugamo, showing cellblocks. (Courtesy John L. Ginn)

namely, "violations of the laws or customs of war." Such violations included but were not limited to murder, ill treatment, or deportation to slave labor or for any other purpose of the civilian population of, or in, occupied territory; murder or ill treatment of prisoners of war or persons on the seas or elsewhere; improper treatment of hostages; plunder of public or private property; and wanton destruction of cities, towns, or villages or devastation not justified by military necessity.

Class C criminals were those accused of "crimes against humanity"— namely, murder, extermination, enslavement, deportation, and other inhumane acts committed during Japan's war with China and World War II or persecutions on political or racial grounds in execution of, or in connection with, any crime within the jurisdiction of the tribunal, whether or not in violation of the domestic law of the country where the crimes were perpetrated. Leaders, organizers, instigators, and accomplices participating in the formulation or execution of a common plan or conspiracy to commit any of the foregoing crimes were deemed to be responsible for all acts performed by any person in the execution of such plans.

In August 1947 the U.S. Army newspaper, *Stars and Stripes Review,* published the following article about Sugamo Prison and its operation:

> Sugamo Prison, a network of modern, well-landscaped buildings of pale tan concrete, stands in a Tokyo residential section which has been reduced to ashes and wastelands by wartime incendiary bombing. It stands as an example to the world both of American justice and of humane, efficient prison management.

Here the Provost Marshal Section of Lt. General Robert L. Eichelberger's Eighth Army has confined the 1,100 Japanese nationals accused or convicted of war crimes. Many former PW guards and army generals, civilians and politicians are serving sentences ranging from a few months to life imprisonment at hard labor. But the majority are awaiting trial. Of these, many will be released without trial and others may be acquitted. Although new suspects are constantly being found and brought to the prison, it is expected that all prisoners will be either tried or released by early next year.

The prison was originally built by the Japanese during the decade leading up to the war. Here prisoners awaited trials during months and often years of physical privation and brutal treatment from guards. Two years ago Eighth Army Provost Marshal Section took it over for temporary confinement of war crime suspects.

Today, from the outside, only high walls and watch-towers betray the purpose of these buildings. The windows, even the walls of the buildings, are clean. Trees and carefully cultivated gardens surround the buildings, with a large vegetable garden at one end of the premises.

The interior displays a recent paint job and the cleanliness of a hospital. Prisoners are required to scrub their cells several times a week, and to keep them in order at all times. Each cell contains a table and chair, electric light, straw floor mat, and a covered lavatory.

The prisoners themselves are in good health. They wear clean uniforms which are washed and ironed by a laundry on the premises.

The prison staff goes beyond mere accommodation of basic physical needs in trying to arrange for the prisoners a decent life.

Prisoners are encouraged to practice religion. Christian services are conducted for them, and a Buddhist altar with a Japanese priest in attendance is available to them.

The Chaplain, Captain John A. Ryan, has obtained through the Red Cross many books written in both English and Japanese and has set up a rotating library for the prisoners. Although few of them can speak or understand (oral) English, most can read and write it.

Humane treatment of war crime suspects does not imply softness or inefficiency. Each soldier has well defined duties, which he must carry out correctly. A thorough system of guards has prevented even an attempted escape from the prison. Prisoners eat, work, or exercise at specified times. The complex machinery of prison operations functions with precision.

The staff follows careful procedures to prevent spread of disease. Every incoming prisoner is inoculated against the same diseases as is the American soldier entering the theatre. He receives a thorough physical examination and any necessary medical attention. A doctor remains on duty 24 hours a day in case of emergency.

The mess personnel observe rigid regulations to ensure sanitation. The kitchen is kept immaculate. The Japanese workers are required to take showers and to don clean uniforms every morning before starting work.

Colonel Francis W. Crary of St. Louis, Missouri, commanding officer, considers that the success of Sugamo depends upon the character of the men operating it. He desires discipline and prompt, precise performance of duty from them. But he especially wants them to live up to democratic ideals. He operates the prison on the principles that a man is not guilty until convicted and even then remains a human being.

Mr. E. L. Carr, noted author, sums up one's impression of the prison as follows:

> The first impression a visitor gets of Sugamo Prison, Tōkyō—where the Japanese charged with war crimes are imprisoned—is one of tremendous, purposeful, and kindly alertness on the part of the U.S. officers and men charged with guarding the prisoners. They seem interested in their work, fully conscious of the possibilities of mistakes, and yet there is no sign of the arrogance and cruelty which stained the records of Japanese and Nazis alike. Every conceivable precaution is taken to be sure that Tojo and his accomplices meet their just deserts, but the routine of confinement is accomplished without whipcracking or torture chambers. A visit to Sugamo makes one proud of democracy, and even prouder of the men it breeds.

In 1948 a prisoners' vegetable garden was established in the inner, and later in the outer, compound. This not only assisted greatly in providing better meals to the prisoners but markedly improved morale among them. Some of the prisoners had served time in other Japanese prisons. They told their guards that Sugamo was being operated in an improved and more humane manner than they had ever experienced before.

There were still many who complained about one thing or another, however. One frequent complaint was about the difference in the financial status between the American guards and the prisoners. They could see the Americans smoking at will and eating whenever they were hungry, while for the prisoners, both tobacco and food were rationed. Although the Americans were improving the conditions at Sugamo, they had no intention of allowing the prisoners to fare better than the Japanese civilian population.

Within the administration building was a large, centrally located meeting room. This room, converted into a chapel, or religious room, was used by both the prisoners and the Americans. The Americans used it on Sundays, and the Japanese used it during the week or whenever the appointed prison Buddhist priest, Dr. Shinsho Hanayama, decided to

Lonnie B. Adams. (Courtesy Lonnie B. Adams)

conduct religious services or perform last-rite ceremonies. Some American soldiers were married and others had their children baptized in this chapel.

Shortly before the Korean War began, an American officer, Capt. Lonnie Adams, was assigned to Sugamo as prison officer. After meeting with his top NCOs and the leading inmates, he determined that prisoner morale was very low. He requested and received permission from the commanding officer to allow the prisoners more time in the exercise yards outside their cells, and improvements were made in the weekly Sugamo newspaper.

When the Korean War began in 1950, there was a shortage of soldiers at hand. This deficit was partially made up with GIs stationed at various military installations throughout Japan. At Sugamo the officers were reduced from forty to seven and the enlisted men from more than four hundred to less than one hundred. All executions of condemned war criminals had been completed by April 7, 1950. Shortly after that, prisoners serving terms were beginning to be paroled. At this time the Japanese penal system began replacing some of the GIs with Japanese guards.

Captain Adams called a meeting of prisoners and told them of his manpower shortage and that he had two choices: He could either lock them up and keep them locked up, or they could elect to govern themselves.

They quickly told him that they could govern themselves without any problems. They did so, and there were no major disciplinary problems.

Some of the inmates volunteered to assist in any way with the Korean conflict, including combat. Three hundred were put to work at a large hydroponic farm near Tokyo and greatly increased vegetable production. Other inmates volunteered to work on a project constructing wooden pallets for the war effort and consistently surpassed the production goals initially set by Captain Adams and later by themselves.

At the same time Captain Adams was making life more bearable for the prisoners. The prison hospital was enlarged, an X-ray machine and X-ray technician were put in place, along with a medical laboratory and facilities for tuberculosis patients. A school was built, and an education program was begun. Dr. Tochima, the Buddhist priest who replaced Dr. Hanayama, greatly assisted Captain Adams in organizing the school. Classes were conducted in automobile mechanics, library science, the abacus, art, photography, tatami- and shoemaking and repair, and English.

As the American medical personnel at Sugamo were phased out for the Korean War effort, Japanese doctors and medical technicians were brought in. There was even an obstetrician on duty. Sugamo was about halfway between several large American housing complexes and Tokyo, and after many pregnant American wives couldn't make it into Tokyo in time for delivery, arrangements were made to have a qualified doctor at the prison hospital. He was kept relatively busy.

Room was also found for a prison library, and donations of books reached five thousand by 1950. A goldfish pond and an aviary were established, with the Japanese people donating fish and birds in abundance. An entertainment program was initiated to bring theater productions to the post theater. Sumo wrestling matches were conducted on the football field in the outer compound, and track meets and May Day exercises were attended by the majority of the inmates.

During the first year of the Korean War, many Korean and Chinese spies serving as maids, waiters, waitresses, and clerks were arrested near American military headquarters buildings and in nearby hotels and restaurants throughout Japan. Sugamo received sixty women prisoners, whom Captain Adams confined in Blue Prison. At that time he was using Japanese women as prison matrons, but later these were replaced by matrons from the federal penal system in the United States. Male spies were housed in cellblock 5, guarded by incoming Japanese replacement guards. These prisoners were tried and sentenced or acquitted.

In September 1951 all the foreign nationals being held at the Eighth

Fred Barwise. (Courtesy Fred Barwise)

Army Stockade were transferred to Sugamo. The "Big Eight" stockade was located about five miles southeast of Sugamo, and before the end of the war it had been called Toyotama Prison. The transfer involved almost three hundred prisoners, who were confined in number one cell block. These prisoners were held until shortly after the peace treaty with Japan was signed, at which time they were transferred to a Japanese prison south of Yokohama. They were mostly Korean and Chinese. However, there were some Filipinos, Indonesians, and other Orientals convicted of murder, robbery, rape, petty theft, and dealing in narcotics. Many of them were on narcotics at the time of their transfer. At Sugamo they went through drug withdrawal cold turkey and without medical aid.

When the Japanese peace treaty was signed in September 1951, the Japanese were in almost total control of the prison. They were gradually moved in and trained to run Sugamo Prison as American personnel were transferred out. They were in complete control by May 1952. The numbers of prisoners released on parole increased. By 1956 the total number of war criminals was down from more than 2,000 to 383. These were all long-term prisoners convicted of the most serious offenses. By December

1958 Sugamo's doors and gates were closed, the remaining prisoners pardoned, and its official use as a prison ended. There was no ceremony, no newspaper notice, and no photographs.

The last officer to leave Sugamo was Capt. Lonnie B. Adams, Jr. He reported: "You would never have known that the prison had changed over from the Americans to the Japanese unless you had actually been there."

There are no records of anyone ever escaping from Sugamo while it was under U.S. military jurisdiction. Slightly more than 2,000 war criminals and protected witnesses were held there for varying periods of time. There were several suicides and several attempted suicides.

Sugamo served two distinct functions during its existence. It held mostly political prisoners after its construction, and after the end of World War II, it held primarily war criminals — and their accomplices — who had caused the political prisoners to be imprisoned.

In 1971 the prison was purchased from the Japanese government for 17.7 million dollars by the Japan Urban Development Company. In its place rose a housing and shopping complex, relieving pressure on a congested area of Tokyo.

Sgt. Fred Barwise from Florida, an ex-GI from Sugamo on his way from the States to Vietnam, stopped in Tokyo for several days in 1971. He decided to pay a visit to his old stomping grounds. He reports: "I went out to see Sugamo, and the wrecking ball was set up and demolishing the walls. However, the NCO Club, theater and most of the buildings near the main gate were intact. I turned around, walked out the main gate, and thought to myself: 'Fred, you could very well be the last Sugamo GI to see Sugamo.'"

THE PRISONERS

Class A

The United Nations War Crimes Commission (UNWCC) was established in London in mid-1943 primarily to prepare for the prosecution of Axis war criminals. However, it also coordinated the worldwide amassing of evidence and data relating to Japanese war crimes. This commission published a white paper recommending that suspected Japanese war criminals be arrested by the United Nations for trial before an International Military Tribunal for the Far East (IMTFE). Without citing names, the members of the commission specifically referred to those in authority in the government and the military and in the financial and economic affairs of the Japanese Empire.

Thus it became the responsibility of the IMTFE to determine who among the leaders of Japan had promoted the waging of aggressive and unprovoked war and prescribed oppressive occupation policies and rule by terror tactics in various territories. The responsibility for forming the IMTFE was assigned to the Supreme Commander for the Allied Powers (SCAP), and General MacArthur was being pressured by the Allied press to round up and prosecute war criminals even before his headquarters was fully established and the occupation forces secured.

When it came to taking orders, MacArthur was one of a kind. He usually did follow them, but often in his own way and according to his own schedule. He received orders from the State-War-Navy Coordinating Committee (SWNCC) to keep names of war criminal suspects secret until they were arrested, and to divide the suspects into three groups—Class A, B and C. These instructions also stated: "You will take no action against the Emperor as a war criminal." MacArthur was further instructed to arrest all those suspected of war crimes beginning with "the period immediately preceding the Mukden incident on September 18, 1931."

At Mukden, Manchuria, eight days before that date, the Japanese had secretly placed two huge, heavy-artillery pieces within their compound.

One was aimed at the Seventh Chinese Brigade Barracks and the other at the Mukden airfield. The Japanese military clique had been planning this action for some time. Several miles away a bomb was planted on the tracks of the South Manchurian Railroad near the Chinese barracks. At 10:00 P.M. on the evening of September 18, the bomb exploded, providing the necessary excuse "to bring order" by sending troops in to seize Mukden. At 10:30 the artillery opened up on the Chinese while Japanese troops attacked the city.

By morning Mukden was in Japanese hands. The army clique had just made one of its first and most important moves in taking control of the Japanese government. At the request of the cabinet, the army commander ordered the Kwantung Army to limit its hostilities. The army simply ignored those instructions and took all of Manchuria, the military clique in Tokyo providing all the assistance they needed. Several of the Class A war criminals played direct roles in the Mukden incident, which led to the war with China and eventually to the war with the United States and its allies.

By the middle of September 1945, SCAP made its first move in the roundup of suspected war criminals. Thirty-nine suspects were ordered detained at Sugamo Prison. Among the first suspects were Hideki Tojo and his Pearl Harbor–era cabinet. Even though Tojo had his private doctor instruct him as to the exact location of his heart, he failed in his attempt to commit suicide. As the American and Japanese police approached his house he shot himself. The bullet missed his heart by a fraction of an inch. Fast American action and some GI blood saved his life. (Some other suspected war criminals succeeded in committing suicide.)

By November, MacArthur had a fairly complete master list of war crimes suspects. Among those indicted were seven Kwantung Army generals, a former minister of communications, three former premiers, and twenty-two others. It was December 6 before orders were issued for the detention of Prince Fumimaro Konoye, who was drafting a new, more democratic constitution, and Marquis Koichi Kido, another trusted adviser of the emperor.

Even though MacArthur had been instructed to keep the names secret until the suspects had been placed in detention, the general neglected to do so. His orders to the Japanese police charged with making the arrests were to apprehend Class A war crime suspects and have them report to Sugamo within ten days. This gave the suspects ample opportunities to commit suicide and thereby escape trial. Vice Adm. Takijiro Onishi, creator of the Kamikaze forces; War Minister Korechika Anami; Gen. Shigeru Hondo, leader of the Kwantung Army military clique and planner of the Mukden incident that started the war with China; Field Marshal Hajime Sugiyama; Gen. Shizuichi Tanaka, the Eastern Army commander who helped break up acts of disorder by troops at the Imperial Palace before the emperor's surrender speech; Kumihiko Hashida, former minister of education; Chikahiko Koizumi, former minister of welfare and army surgeon general; and Prince Konoye all elected to commit suicide.

Koizumi would definitely have been questioned about medical and biological experiments on live prisoners and Chinese civilians. Prince Konoye took potassium cyanide and left a note stating: "I have made many political mistakes since the China incident for which I am responsible, but it is unbearable for me to be tried before an American court as a war criminal." Konoye had been premier on three occasions and was held in great esteem by the Japanese and Americans alike as a man of high intelligence. He was close to the emperor and was being groomed by the Americans to play a key role in postwar Japan. His suicide caused MacArthur some embarrassment and brought out the worst of tempers among the Allies, especially the USSR. (Konoye had been an acknowledged enemy of Communism.)

Although there are no accurate records as to how many of the top, middle, and lower grades throughout the Japanese military committed suicide at the end of the war, some estimates are as high as two to three thousand.

All the Allies that fought the Japanese were clamoring for a rapid roundup and trial of the Japanese war criminals. By the end of the war there was evidence of mass atrocities to prisoners of war throughout the Japanese Empire, and brutality to both civilians and prisoners in all areas that had been occupied by the Japanese. These atrocities shocked people of all civilized nations. It seems remarkable that today most of those responsible for the Japanese atrocities have been forgotten.

The Class A war prisoners who were tried and sentenced by the eleven judges of the IMTFE were:

Gen. Sadao Araki (1877-1966). From 1927 Araki was a high-ranking military officer. He was promoted to full general in 1933. An energetic proponent of the army policy of political rule in Japan and military expansion and aggression abroad, he was minister of war from 1931 to 1934, served on the Supreme War Council from 1934 to 1936, and was minister of education in 1938-39. In this last position he promoted the army policy of preparing for wars of aggression by inflaming the warlike spirit of the young men of Japan through speeches and control of the press. While education minister, he reorganized the Japanese school system to train boys under a rigid, military-style program.

As a senior adviser to the cabinet in 1939–40, he helped to formulate the military policy of enriching Japan at the expense of its neighbors. He both approved and championed army policies in Manchuria, to separate that territory from China, create a Japanese puppet government there, and place its economy under the rule of Japan. The Japanese puppet state of Manchukuo was set up in 1932. Araki also supported army efforts in Jehol, a province in northeastern China that was incorporated into Manchukuo by the Japanese in 1935. General Araki was an arrogant, egotistical man who referred to the war with China as "a gift of the gods." After Pearl Harbor he was a close, important adviser to Premier Tojo.

Gen. Kenji Doihara (1883–1948). At the beginning of the period under review by the IMTFE (September 18, 1931, through September 2, 1945), Doihara was a colonel in the army. By April 1941 he had attained the rank of general. Before the Manchurian action, he spent eighteen years in China and was the army's specialist on the subject. He was intimately involved with the initiation and advancement of the war of aggression against China and Manchuria, and with the development of Manchukuo.

Doihara was commander of the Kwantung Army from 1938 to 1940, a member of the Supreme War Council from 1940 to 1943, and army commander in Singapore in 1944–45. He worked in close cooperation with other leaders of the military clique in the planning, development, and execution of military actions to bring East and Southeast Asia under Japanese control. With his knowledge of China and his talent for intrigue, he became intensely involved in the army's drug trafficking in Manchuria. Later he ran cruel and inhumane POW camps in Malaya, Sumatra, Java, and Borneo. Food and medicine were available that could have been used to relieve the horrible conditions suffered by prisoners in the POW camps. These supplies were withheld by a policy for which Doihara was responsible.

Col. Kingoro Hashimoto (1890–1957). As an army officer, Hashimoto joined the military clique and its conspiracy to wage aggressive war early in the 1930s. He held extreme views and advocated the expansion of Japan by seizing Manchuria by force. He was an ardent believer in government by military dictatorship.

Hashimoto was commander of an artillery regiment during the "Rape of Nanking" in 1937. He spent most of his time plotting the assassination of those hindering the army clique's plans. He was a principal in many activities of the conspirators, which ultimately suppressed the democratic elements in Japan. In October 1931 he was a major plotter in a plan to overthrow the cabinet and establish one that would support the conspirators. He was a prolific publicist and contributed to the success of the conspirators by inciting the people's appetite to possess Japan's neighbors.

Hashimoto was also privy to the plot of May 1932, which resulted in the assassination of Premier Tsuyoshi Inukai, who promoted democracy. Hashimoto's publications and the activities of societies he founded were devoted to the destruction of democracy and the founding of a form of government more favorable to the use of war to expand Japan's realm. During this period he became director general of the Imperial Rule Assistance Association. In fact, he claimed some of the credit for the seizure of Manchuria and for Japan's leaving the League of Nations. He was a racist in the true sense of the word.

Field Marshal Shunroku Hata (1876-1962). Hata was a member of the Supreme War Council in 1937; commander of the China Expeditionary Force in 1938 and 1941-44; and minister of war in 1939-40. Favoring Japanese domination of East and Southeast Asia, he exerted significant influence on government policy. To reach this objective, he approved the abolition of political parties, to be replaced by the Imperial Rule Assistance Association.

From March 1941 until 1944, as commander in chief of forces in China, he continued to wage war. As inspector general of military education — one of the highest active posts in the Japanese army — he continued to wage war against China and the Western powers.

In 1938 and again from 1941 to 1944, while in charge of forces in China, his soldiers committed atrocities on a grand scale. Either he was aware of these atrocities and took no action to prevent them, or he was completely indifferent and made no efforts to know whether orders for the humane treatment of both prisoners of war and civilians were obeyed.

Baron Kiichiro Hiranuma (1867-1952). Hiranuma was a member of the Privy Council from 1924 to 1939; a founder and president of Kokuhonsha, a right-wing patriotic society, from 1926 to 1928; premier in 1938; minister of home affairs in 1940; minister without portfolio in 1940-41; and president of the Privy Council in 1945.

A nobleman, a monarchist, and a major political element in Japan over many years, Hiranuma was one of the early proponents of war but in 1943 became disillusioned and changed his mind. He then participated in a secret plan to sue for peace.

Baron Koki Hirota (1878-1948). Hirota was ambassador to the Soviet Union from 1928 to 1931, foreign minister from 1933 to 1936, and premier in 1936-37. While he was foreign minister and premier, the Japanese gains in Manchuria were being consolidated. In 1936 his cabinet formed the National Policy of Expansion in East and Southeast Asia. This policy eventually led to the war between Japan and the Western powers in 1941.

He was a protégé of Mitsuru Toyama, founder of the Black Secret Society, and became the "godfather" of Japanese politics in the 1930s. During his tenure of office, he was a forceful leader and both an originator and supporter of aggressive plans adopted and executed by the military and various cabinets.

As foreign minister, he received reports of the atrocities conducted in Nanking from December 1937 — immediately after the Japanese entered the city — through February 1938. Reports also came from Nanking through Red Cross officials and others over many months, and the matter was taken up by the War Ministry. Hirota was either derelict in his duty by not insisting before the cabinet that immediate action be taken to stop the atrocities, or he failed in other actions available to him to get the same results. He was content to rely on reassurances while thousands of murders, rapes, and other atrocities were being committed.

Naoki Hoshino (1892-1978). Hoshino was chief of financial affairs in Manchukuo from 1932 to 1934; director of general affairs (chief civilian officer) in Manchukuo in 1936; chief minister without portfolio in 1940-41; and chief cabinet secretary from 1941 to 1944.

When Tojo became premier, he selected Hoshino to be his secretary general and asked him to help select his cabinet. Hoshino was in the decision-making group that decided that war with the Western powers was preferable to pulling Japanese troops out of China. He directed the financing of the Japanese occupation of Manchuria through the army's drug trafficking there. He was a fanatical hard-liner on Japanese expansion and drafted the declaration of war against Great Britain and the United States.

Gen. Seishiro Itagaki (1885-1948). Itagaki was vice-chief of staff of the Kwantung Army in 1936-37; minister of war in 1938-39; chief of the army general staff in 1939; commander in Korea in 1941; a member of the Supreme War Council in 1943; and commander in Singapore in 1945.

He assisted in engineering the so-called "Mukden incident" as a pretext for military action and played a principal part in the intrigues that brought about the creation of the puppet state of Manchukuo. As vice-chief of staff of the Kwantung Army, he was also active in establishing puppet regimes in Inner Mongolia and northern China. When fighting began in China at the Marco Polo Bridge near Lukouchiao, about ten miles southwest of Peking, in July 1937, he was sent to China, where he served as a division commander and promoted military expansion.

While minister of war in the Hiranuma cabinet, he became a strong advocate of an unrestricted military alliance between Japan, Germany, and Italy.

He was arrogant, cruel, and without compassion when dealing with prisoners and civilians in China, and with the prisoners of war in POW camps under his jurisdiction in Singapore, Borneo, Java, Sumatra, Malaya, and the Andaman and Nicobar Islands. The conditions for POWs in these areas were horrible. Food and medical supplies were so strictly rationed that deaths occurred daily in large numbers. He made no attempts to rectify the situation, even though food and medicine were available.

Okinori Kaya (1889–1977). Kaya was a civilian, appointed councilior of the Manchurian Affairs Bureau in 1936; vice minister of Finance in 1937–38; adviser to the Finance Ministry in 1938; a member of the Asian Development Committee in 1939; president of the North China Development Company from 1939 to 1941; and finance minister in the Tojo cabinet from 1941 to 1944.

Kaya was an early and strong advocate of the selling of opium to the Chinese to finance the expense of the occupation. He plundered Chinese industry and exploited their natural resources for the Japanese war effort. He arranged financing for the Siam-Burma Railroad and assisted in setting the time schedule for its completion with the full knowledge that civilian and POW laborers were constructing it. He was also aware of the atrocious conditions that existed in these labor camps.

Marquis Koichi Kido (1889–1977). Kido was a member of the emperor's household with the position of chief secretary to the Lord Keeper of the Privy Seal from 1930 to 1936; education minister and welfare minister in 1937–38; minister of home affairs in 1939; and Lord Keeper of the Privy Seal from 1940 to 1945.

In 1937 Kido adopted the views of the conspirators and devoted himself wholeheartedly to their policies and the pursuit of war with China. He was intent on the complete Japanese military and political control of that country.

Kido was a high-ranking politician respected by both the military and the emperor. He became Emperor Hirohito's closest adviser and confidant during the war. He was also an ardent diarist. After the war the diary he had kept while in positions of power became an encyclopedia of information for prosecutors during the Tokyo trials of war criminals.

Gen. Heitaro Kimura (1888–1948). Kimura was an army officer engaged in administrative work for the War Ministry. This culminated in his becoming vice minister of war from 1941 to 1943. Later he was appointed councillor of the Planning Board and councillor of the Total War Research Institute. He became commander in chief of the Burma Area Army, a post he kept until the surrender of Japan in 1945.

While with the War Ministry, he helped plan the China war and the surprise attacks leading to war with the Western powers. He approved the use of POW and civilian slave labor. As commander of military forces in Burma, he was fully aware of the dreadful conditions and numerous deaths attached to the construction of the Siam-Burma Railroad. He was also responsible for not restraining his troops from committing numerous atrocities on the Burmese civilian population.

Gen. Kuniaki Koiso (1880–1950). Koiso joined the conspiracy of the military clique in 1931 by participating as one of the leaders of the "March Incident," staged to overthrow the Hamaguchi government and put in place a government favorable to the occupation of Manchuria. Thereafter he played a leading role in the development of Japanese plans for expansion from August 1932 to 1934, when he was appointed chief of staff of the Kwantung Army.

Koiso was army commander in Korea from 1935 to 1938; minister of overseas affairs in 1939; governor-general in Korea from 1943 to 1944; and premier in 1944–45.

While chief of staff, he went beyond the scope of his normal duties by advising on political, economic, and military matters to further Japan's expansion plans in Manchuria and Jehol. Later he took part in the direction of the war with China, in the beginning of the occupation of French Indochina, and in the negotiations intended to obtain economic concessions from the Netherlands East Indies. During this same period he advocated a plan for Japan to "advance in all directions."

Koiso was one of the more important members of the Japanese military clique that gained complete control of Japan in the 1930s and 1940s. He became known as the "Tiger of Korea" for his brutal treatment of Korean civilians.

Gen. Iwane Matsui (1878–1948). Matsui was a senior officer in the Japanese army, becoming a general in 1933. He was Emperor Hirohito's personal appointee to the Geneva Disarmament Conference from 1932 to 1937 and commander in chief of the Central China Area Army, which included the Shanghai Expeditionary Force and the Tenth Army in 1937–38. With these troops he captured the city of Nanking on December 13, 1937.

However, Chinese military forces had withdrawn before the fall of Nanking, so the occupation was of a defenseless city. There followed a three-month succession of absolutely unbelievable atrocities committed by the Japanese troops on the civilian population. There were wholesale massacres and individual murders, rapes, looting, and arson. Thousands of women were raped, approximately one hundred thousand civilians were murdered, and millions of dollars' worth of property were stolen or burned. On December 17, at the height of the atrocities, Matsui made a victor's entry into the city and spent a week there. From his own observations and the reports of his staff, he must have been aware of these atrocities. Daily reports of these events were made to the Japanese diplomatic representatives in Nanking, who in turn reported them to Tokyo. Matsui did nothing to stop or alleviate ongoing atrocities against the Chinese people. In 1938 he retired and ceased to play an active role in the military.

Yosuke Matsuoka (1880-1946). A civilian, Matsuoka was Japan's chief delegate to the League of Nations in 1933; president of the South Manchurian Railway from 1935 to 1939; and foreign minister in 1939-40. He was also a vigorous public speaker and the author of pugnacious articles in favor of the military's expansion policy. He was an admirer of Hitler, Stalin, and Mussolini and formulated the Axis alliance with Germany and Italy and the nonaggression pact with Russia. He did not live to stand trial. He died of tuberculosis in 1946.

Gen. Jiro Minami (1874-1955). Minami was the minister of war in 1931; a member of the Supreme War Council from 1931 to 1934; commander of the Kwantung Army from 1934 to 1936; governor-general of Korea from 1936 to 1942; and a member of the Privy Council from 1942 to 1945. Like most other generals in the Japanese army, he had attended the Japanese Military Academy and served in the Sino-Japanese War of 1895.

Minami was an early advocate of rule by military might and at all times was a warmonger in the army clique that planned aggressive, unprovoked war in Manchuria and China, and later with the Western powers in other areas of Asia. He was a firm believer that "international law should be interpreted from the viewpoint of executing the war according to our own opinion" and in the so-called Greater East Asia Co-prosperity Sphere.

Minami ruled Japan's Korean conquest with an iron fist and during that assignment had American and British POWs brought to Korea and paraded through the streets to show the population that the Japanese were a superior race.

Gen. Akira Muto (1892–1948). Muto was vice-chief of staff of the China Expeditionary Force in 1937; director of the Military Affairs Bureau from 1939 to 1942; army commander in Sumatra from 1942 to 1944; and army chief of staff in the Philippines in 1944–45.

Muto commanded the Second Imperial Guards Division in northern Sumatra from April 1942 until October 1944. Widespread atrocities were committed in the area occupied by his troops. Prisoners of war and civilian internees were starved, neglected, tortured, and murdered. Civilians were massacred on a large scale.

In 1944 Muto became chief of staff to Yamashita in the Philippines and held that post until the Japanese surrender. He was in a strong position to influence policy, yet here again a reign of massacre and other atrocities was perpetrated by his troops on the civilian population. His POWs and civilian internees were routinely starved, tortured, and murdered.

Adm. Osami Nagano (1880–1947). Nagano was delegate to the Naval Disarmament Conference from 1931 to 1933; navy minister in 1936–37; fleet commander in 1937; navy chief of staff in 1941; and naval adviser to the emperor in 1944. Like many other Japanese of high military rank, he served in the foreign ministry early in his career. Nagano was naval attaché to the Japanese Embassy in Washington, D. C. He was the chief planner of the sneak attacks on Pearl Harbor, Hong Kong, Kota Bharu, Manila, and other areas.

On January 5, 1947, partway through his trial, Admiral Nagano died of bronchial pneumonia at the 361st U.S. Army Hospital. On the death of the sixty-eight-year-old admiral, his American counsel made public a letter written by Nagano in which he "regretted that the Americans had not been informed of the attack on Pearl Harbor — perhaps by two minutes" — and that the attack had been a mistake. Previously he had revealed that he opposed the alliance with Germany, war against the United States, and that Japan should have gotten out of China, where it was engaged in a no-win situation.

A young reporter at the trial, Arnold Brackman,* sent a note to the defendants during a lunch break, asking for their reactions to Nagano's death. Tojo expressed sorrow, "especially because the world could not hear from the Admiral's own mouth of the true position of the Japanese Navy." Foreign Minister Togo added that in a conversation with Nagano shortly before his death, he had stated that he "would reveal, on the stand, the true story of Pearl Harbor." The youngest defendant among the Class

---

Brackman later published a book, detailing the trials of the Class A prisoners, titled The Other Nuremberg.

A suspects, Gen. Kenro Sato, wrote in his diary that Nagano had died at Sugamo of "maltreatment" and that "a window had broken in Nagano's cell. The Admiral had covered it with a newspaper to block out the cold air, but a guard tore off the cover and, despite repeated requests, the window was not repaired. Nagano contracted pneumonia."

The windows at Sugamo were hinged in the middle and could be opened or closed by pulling or pushing an arm on the bottom. Steel bars, about four inches apart, were on the inside. Due to moisture, atmospheric pressure, and temperature changes, the windows were difficult to close at times. If the prisoner wasn't careful, the window would slam shut. Nagano, a large and fairly strong man for his age, did exactly that. He broke three panes of glass. This occurred at 9:30 P.M. when the prison engineer and Japanese workmen were at home and several miles from Sugamo. The duty officer called and asked the engineering officer to repair it. He was informed that it would be done the first thing in the morning when he came to work. Paper was put over the broken panes but came loose during one of the coldest nights of the winter. The engineering officer received a royal chewing-out from Sir William Webb and General MacArthur's chief of intelligence, Maj. Gen. Charles A. Willoughby.

Adm. Takasumi Oka (1890–1973). Oka was chief of the Naval Affairs Bureau from 1940 to 1944 and vice minister of the navy in 1944. He was another chief planner of the surprise attacks by Japanese naval forces in December 1941. In the planning stages of war against the United States and its allies, Oka wanted to destroy sea power and all bases that could possibly be used for a counterattack "by the positive employment of forces" in the Australian and Hawaiian areas.

Later in the war, while in charge of the Naval Affairs Bureau, he issued orders for the transport of allied POWs and civilian slave laborers aboard the "hellships" on which survival conditions were practically nonexistent: Thousands died in the cramped holds from lack of air, sanitation facilities, food, and medicine.

Oka also believed that if the survivors of torpedoed Allied ships were killed, it would hinder the Allied war efforts, since these men couldn't be easily or quickly replaced. He issued orders to shoot them while they were in the water. He administered several prisoner-of-war and civilian internee camps on Pacific islands, where the conditions closely resembled those on his "hellships."*

Dr. Shumei Okawa (1886–1957). Okawa, a civilian, was the major force behind the growth of the Japanese militarists in the 1930s. A

See Case 154 in the Class C trial section.

revolutionary fanatic, Okawa was a racist, terrorist, propagandist, and author of numerous publications. He believed in government by military dictatorship and advocated the regimentation of the Japanese people for a war of Asian conquest.

He was the leading planner of several assassination attempts on premiers, one of which was successful — Premier Inukai in 1932. He was fully involved in three abortive coups d'état against cabinets that were in conflict with policies espoused by the militarist and right-wing fanatics.

Okawa could speak five languages and during his education had become interested in Japanese history. He grew more and more nationalistic and was a member or leader of several secret societies and political intrigues, one of which was to seize Manchuria in preparation for war against the United States and other Western powers. He played a leading role in the Mukden incident and was the strongest advocate of Japan's "Strike South" faction.

On the opening day of the trials of Japanese war criminals, he created a sensation by hitting Tojo on the head several times. Taken to the 361st Station Hospital for psychiatric examination, he proved to have advanced syphilitic meningoencephalitis. One psychiatrist felt that he was insane; the other — a Japanese — believed that he was sane. He did not stand trial but was not allowed to leave the hospital.

On December 31, 1948, a week after the executions of the condemned prisoners, Okawa was declared sane and released from the psychiatric hospital. He died nine years later from a heart attack.

Gen. Hiroshi Oshima (1886–1975). Oshima was an army officer engaged in the diplomatic field. He was first military attaché to the Japanese Embassy in Berlin and was later promoted to ambassador to Germany. He served in Berlin until the war ended. Oshima was a firm believer in Hitler and Nazism and exerted his energies to advance the plans of the ruling military clique in Japan.

While assigned to Germany as military attaché, he often went over the ambassador's head in his dealings with Foreign Minister Joachim von Ribbentrop in an effort to get Japan involved in a full military alliance with Germany. On his appointment as ambassador, he continued to pursue his goal of creating a treaty that would align Japan with Germany and Italy against the Western powers and thus complete the Hirota policy.

Oshima was one of the leading conspirators and consistently supported and promoted the goals of the military leaders in Japan. He became intimate with Hitler, Himmler, Göring, and Ribbentrop and organized an abortive plot to assassinate Stalin. Many Japanese considered Oshima to be "more Nazi than the Nazis."

The Prisoners

Gen. Kenro Sato (1895-1975). In 1937 Sato, a member of the Military Affairs Bureau, was promoted to lieutenant colonel. In addition to his normal duties, he was appointed an investigator of the Planning Board. Later, he became secretary of the Planning Board.

The Konoye cabinet presented the General Mobilization Law to the Diet in February 1938. Sato was appointed as an "explainer" of the law and made a speech before the Diet supporting it.

In February 1941 Sato was appointed chief of the Military Affairs Section of the Military Affairs Bureau and was promoted to major general in October. In April 1942 he attained the important post of chief of the Military Affairs Bureau. He held this post until 1944.

After the sneak attack on Pearl Harbor, Sato claimed: "Japan would dictate peace terms in the enemy capital." In 1944 he became an army commander in Indochina. In this position he issued orders affecting the transportation and treatment of prisoners of war and civilian internees, many of whom worked — and died — as slave laborers on the ill-fated Siam-Burma Railroad. Sato took no action to rectify complaints and protests about the behavior of his troops toward these prisoners.

Mamoru Shigemitsu (1887-1957). Shigemitsu was ambassador to China in 1931-32, vice minister of foreign affairs from 1933 to 1936; ambassador to the Soviet Union from 1936 to 1938; ambassador to Great Britain from 1938 to 1941; and foreign minister from 1943 to 1945. He was a career diplomat who held very important positions in the militarist-controlled government of the 1930s and the early 1940s.

Before 1943 Shigemitsu repeatedly gave the Foreign Office advice that ran counter to the policies of the military clique. By 1943 he was fully aware that as far as Japan was concerned, the country was engaged in a war of aggression. He knew that the policies of the conspirators had caused the war and indeed had often advised that they should not be put into effect. Nevertheless he played a principal part in waging that war until he resigned on April 13, 1945.

It is most unlikely that Shigemitsu would have ever been brought to trial by the Americans had it not been for the USSR's insistence that he be indicted. While he was foreign minister, the Allies transmitted protest after protest to the Japanese Foreign Office regarding inhumane treatment of prisoners, refusal to permit the protesting powers to inspect POW camps, refusal to permit the representatives of the protesting powers to interview prisoners without the presence of a Japanese witness, and failure to provide information about the names and locations of prisoners. All the protests went unanswered or were answered only after months of unexplained delay.

Shigemitsu and General Umezu signed the instrument of surrender aboard the battleship *Missouri* in Tokyo Bay in 1945. Shigemitsu served only two years in prison, reentered politics, and was appointed foreign minister again in 1954.

Adm. Shigetaro Shimada (1883-1976). Shimada was vice chief of the naval staff from 1935 to 1937 and commander of the China fleet in 1940. In October 1941 he became eligible for the post of navy minister, an office he held in the Tojo cabinet until August 1944. For six months (February to August 1944) he also held the post of chief of the naval general staff.

Shimada was a strong supporter of the militarists and authorized the navy's surprise attacks in December 1941. He played a key role in all decisions made by the conspirators in planning and launching those attacks. After war was declared, he played a principal role in waging it.

Some of the worst massacres and murders of prisoners — and of survivors of torpedoed ships — were committed by members of the Japanese navy in the Pacific islands. Those immediately responsible ranged in rank from admiral down. It is inconceivable that Shimada had no part in responsibility for these murders, or that he did not know that they were being committed. He failed to take adequate steps to prevent them.

Toshio Shiratori (1887-1949). Shiratori was director of the Information Bureau of the Foreign Ministry from 1930 to 1933; minister to Sweden from 1933 to 1937; ambassador to Italy from 1938 to 1940; and adviser to the foreign minister from August 1940 to July 1941.

Shiratori entered the Japanese diplomatic service in 1914 and became prominent as chief of the Foreign Office Information Bureau. In that position he justified Japan's seizure of Manchuria to the world's press. Early in the implementation of Japan's expansion plans, he was expressing views on matters of policy that received consideration at high official levels. Early on, he advocated that Japan should withdraw from the League of Nations and supported the establishment of a puppet government in Manchuria.

While minister to Sweden, he drafted letters expressing his view that Russian influence should be expelled from the Far East, by force if necessary, before the Soviet Union became too strong to be attacked. He was also of the opinion that any foreign influence that might be harmful to Japanese interests should be excluded from China and that Japanese diplomats should support the policy of the military. He showed himself to be a wholehearted believer in an aggressive war.

Returning to Japan, he published articles advocating a totalitarian government in Japan and an expansionist policy for Japan, Germany, and

Italy. While the alliance between these nations was being negotiated, he was assigned to Rome as ambassador to Italy. There he collaborated with Oshima, ambassador to Germany, in support of the conspirators who insisted on a general military alliance with those countries. He went to the extreme of refusing to comply with the instructions of the foreign minister, who wanted a more limited alliance. Both Shiratori and Oshima threatened to resign if the conspirators' wishes were not met.

Returning to Japan, Shiratori conducted a propaganda campaign advocating all the aims of the conspirators—that Japan should attack the Soviet Union, ally itself with Germany and Italy, determine action against the Western powers, create a "new order," and seize the opportunity offered by the European war to advance south and attack Singapore.

Shiratori became ill in 1941 and resigned his position with the Foreign Office.

Gen. Teiichi Suzuki (1884–1984). A lieutenant colonel and member of the Military Affairs Bureau in 1932, Suzuki became a major general in 1937. He was chief of the China Affairs Bureau from 1938 to 1941, president of the cabinet Planning Board and minister without portfolio from 1941 to 1943, and adviser to the cabinet in 1943–44.

Suzuki was an active member of the conspiracy. After the assassination of Premier Inukai in May 1932, he reported that similar acts of violence would occur if new cabinets were organized under the existing political leadership. The objective was to secure a government that would support the conspirators' aim against China.

During his assignment with the Military Affairs Bureau, he insisted that the Soviet Union was the enemy of Japan and assisted in the preparations then being made to wage aggressive war against the USSR.

After becoming a major general, he was one of the organizers and head of the political and administrative divisions of the Asia Development Board. Here he actively furthered the exploitation of the areas in China that were occupied by Japan. He was involved with Japan's drug marketing in China and promoted the use of civilians and POWs as slave labor.

When the second Konoye cabinet was formed to complete the military domination of Japan, and to implement the move to the south, Suzuki became minister without portfolio and one of the councillors of the Total War Research Institute. Then Konoye replaced Hoshino with Suzuki as president of the Planning Board. Suzuki held this position until the fall of the Tojo cabinet on July 19, 1944. As president of the Planning Board and minister without portfolio, Suzuki regularly attended the meetings of the liaison conferences leading to the initiation and waging of aggressive wars against the Western and Allied powers.

Suzuki lived to be one hundred years old and died of heart failure in 1984. He was the last of the Class A war criminals. He was released on parole from Sugamo in 1955 and was granted a full pardon in 1958.

Shigenori Togo (1884–1948). Togo was ambassador to Germany in 1937; ambassador to the Soviet Union in 1938; and foreign minister in 1941–42 and in 1945. From the date of his first appointment until the outbreak of the Pacific War, he participated in the planning and preparation for war. He attended cabinet meetings and conferences and agreed with all decisions adopted.

Togo was a career diplomat who was removed from his post as ambassador to Germany due to his hostility toward the Nazis. After the outbreak of the Pacific War, he collaborated with other members of the cabinet over its conduct as well as the waging of war in China. He was involved in peace negotiations with the United States before the attack on Pearl Harbor.

He stated that he joined the Tojo cabinet on the assurance that every effort would be made to bring the negotiations with the United States to a successful conclusion. He also stated that from the date of his taking office, he opposed the army and was successful in obtaining concessions that enabled him to keep the negotiations going. However, when the negotiations failed and war became inevitable, instead of resigning in protest he continued in office and supported Japan's wars of aggression. He claimed that to do otherwise would have been cowardly.

Togo resigned in September 1942 over a cabinet dispute about the treatment of occupied countries.

Gen. Hideki Tojo (1884–1948). Tojo was chief of the Manchurian Secret Police in 1935; councillor of the Manchurian Affairs Bureau in 1936; chief of staff of the Kwantung Army in 1937–38; vice minister of war in 1938; minister of war from 1940 to 1944; and premier from 1941 to 1944. As premier he was also head of the Ministry of Foreign Affairs, Home Affairs, and Education.

When Tojo became chief of staff of the Kwantung Army in June 1937, he joined the ranks of the conspirators and was a principal in practically all their activities. He planned and prepared for an attack on the Soviet Union, recommended further expansion in China in order to free the army from anxiety about its rear in the proposed attack, and assisted in organizing Manchuria as a base for that attack. There was never a time thereafter when he abandoned his determination to launch such an attack if a favorable opportunity should occur.

In May 1938 he was recalled from the field of combat and occupation in China to become vice minister of war. In addition to that assignment, he held numerous other appointments so that he played a prominent part in practically every aspect of the mobilization of the Japanese people and economy for war. He adamantly opposed any suggestion of a peaceful compromise with China.

Tojo became minister of war in July 1940, and thereafter his history is the history of the successive steps in which the conspirators planned and waged wars of aggression against Japan's neighbors. He was the principal leader in making plans and in the waging of all wars. He believed in and furthered the aims of the military clique with ability, persistence and resolution.

He became premier in October 1941 and kept that post until July 1944. As war minister and premier, he maintained the belief that the national government of China should be conquered, so the development of China's natural resources could become Japan's.

Tojo was head of the War Ministry, which was in charge of the care of prisoners of war and civilian internees in the theater of war, including the supply of billets, food, medicine, and hospital facilities. Above all, he was the head of government, charged with continuing responsibility for the care of all prisoners. The inhumane treatment meted out to the prisoners was well known to Tojo and he took no measures to punish offenders or to prevent similar offenses from occurring in the future. His attitude toward the Bataan Death March provides the key to his conduct toward these captives. In 1942, he was aware of conditions of that march and that numerous prisoners had died as a result of those same conditions. When he was in the Philippines in 1943, he made perfunctory inquiries about the march but took no action and no one was punished. He explained later that a commander of a Japanese army in the field is given a mission, in the performance of which he is not subject to specific orders from Tokyo. Thus the head of the Japanese government knowingly and willfully refused to perform the duty of enforcing the laws and customs of war.

Early in the war Tojo issued instructions that prisoners who did not work should not eat. In the construction of the Siam-Burma Railroad, specifically designated for military purposes, no proper arrangements were made for billeting and feeding prisoners or for caring for those who became ill in that miserable climate. He learned of the barbaric conditions to which the captives, who were virtually slaves on the project, were being subjected and sent an officer to investigate. The only action taken was the trial of one company commander for the ill-treatment of prisoners.

Nothing was ever done to improve conditions. Deficiencies, diseases, starvation, and lack of medical care continued to kill off the prisoners until the completion of the project.

Statistics relating to the high death rate from malnutrition and many other causes — including beatings and torture — in prisoner-of-war camps were discussed at conferences over which Tojo presided. The shocking condition of the prisoners in 1944, when Tojo's cabinet was replaced, and the enormous number of prisoners who had died from lack of food and medicine are positive proof that he did not take proper measures to care for them.

Extreme measures were taken at the highest levels of the Japanese government, navy, and army to prevent knowledge of the mistreatment of prisoners from reaching the outside world. Tojo was responsible for those measures.

Gen. Yoshijiro Umezu (1882–1949). Umezu was a section chief of the general staff from 1931 to 1934; commander of the China Expeditionary Force in 1934; vice minister of war from 1936 to 1938; commander of the Kwantung Army from 1939 to 1944; and army chief of staff in 1944–45. He was an inside member of the military clique within the army.

While Umezu was commander of Japanese troops in northern China from 1934 to 1936, he continued the Japanese aggression in that country. He established a pro-Japanese local government and, under threat of force, compelled the Chinese to enter the Ho-Umezu Agreement of June 1935. This, over a period of time, limited the power of the legitimate government in China.

During his tenure as vice minister of war, the national policy plans of 1936 and the plan for important industries of 1937 were decided on. These were strictly army plans and were a primary cause of the war in the Pacific between Japan and the United States and its allies.

When fighting in China broke out again in July of 1937 as a result of the Marco Polo Bridge incident, Umezu knew and approved the plans of the conspirators to carry on the war with China. He was a member of cabinet planning boards as well as numerous commissions that contributed to the formulation of the aggressive plans of the clique and the preparations necessary to execute them.

Umezu was a humorless warmonger who earned the nickname Ivory Mask while he was commander of the Kwantung Army in Manchuria. Toward the end of the trial, he was hospitalized with cancer. Umezu's defense attorney did not make an opening statement, and he did not take the stand in his own defense. Thus ended the trial of a general of the Japanese army in China and chief of the army general staff — the position he held when he suffered his worst humiliation by being the officer who formally surrendered the Japanese forces aboard the *Missouri*.

Classes B and C

Between the end of the war and the beginning of the occupation, there was a nationwide military effort to destroy records of atrocities. Despite this action, however, some records survived. Then, too, numerous officials believed that the militarists were responsible for the state of affairs in Japan at the end of the war and willingly provided the Americans with substantial records.

One of the best sources of information leading to the roundup of Class B and C war criminals was the surviving prisoners of war and civilians interned by the Japanese military forces. Their information and the subsequent investigations caused almost two thousand indicted suspects and protected witnesses to be held at Sugamo Prison. The roundup of war criminals in 1945-48 resulted in the most crowded conditions of the prison's existence. This condition was constantly being relieved, for several reasons. Many prisoners were released due to lack of evidence. Some were acquitted, a very few committed suicide, some died from diseases they had contracted, and some were executed. By late 1951 there were 1,349 war criminals remaining at Sugamo and these numbers continued to decline—primarily due to paroles—until the peace treaty was signed.

The 980 suspected war criminals held at Sugamo and tried at Yokohama by the Eighth Army Military Tribunal were mostly Class C suspects.

Approximately thirty Class B war criminals were tried in Yokohama after the war. These offenders were mostly high-ranking officers whose troops committed atrocities. Most of these suspects were held at Sugamo. Some Class B war criminals were held and tried in Manila. One was Lt. Gen. Masaharu Homma, an amateur playwright and leader of the pro-British-American minority in the army. On November 6, 1941, he was ordered to conquer the Philippines with the Fourteenth Imperial Army. As a general, Homma was usually behind schedule in accomplishing his military objectives and became an embarrassment to the Japanese High Command early in the war.

Another Class B war criminal tried in Manila was Lt. Gen. Tomoyuki Yamashita. On November 6, 1941, he received orders to invade and conquer Malaya and Singapore with the Twenty-Fifth Imperial Army.

Yamashita, the "Tiger of Malaya," was a heavyset, bull-necked general whom Tojo did not fully trust. In 1929 he supported General Ugaki's plan to reduce the army by several divisions. He was also accused of not being tough enough on the Philippine people late in the war.

Overall, at Yokohama and throughout the Allied Military Tribunals in the Far East (and in other areas formerly occupied by the Japanese), a total of 4,200 Class C offenders were accused of atrocities. Many were tried in China, the Philippines, and other battle areas. All those who were arrested in Japan were tried at Eighth Army Headquarters in Yokohama, Japan, commencing on December 27, 1945.

These former army, navy, and civilian employees attached to the Japanese military had been directly involved in committing some of the most abominable and barbaric atrocities in the history of civilized mankind.

The Western mentality and morality found it extremely difficult to match the prisoners' personalities to their past records as soldiers or sailors in the Imperial Forces. The American guards found them to be intelligent, docile, interesting, and often humorous. Most of them wanted to learn English and had their own methods for getting the guards to talk to them. One prisoner asked his guard what would happen if he hit a Japanese citizen. The guard told him that he would be court-martialed and would probably have to spend several months in the Eighth Army stockade. The prisoner replied: "That is very bad. All I did was cut off the head of a British soldier, and I got forty years."

Another prisoner was left behind while out on a work detail about ten miles from Sugamo. When he was discovered missing, a guard detail was sent to search for him. They found him four miles from the prison, rapidly walking back. He said that he didn't want to be late for supper.

As the roundup of war criminals continued, several female prisoners were arrested and confined to the Blue Prison. The most important of these was the woman known as Tokyo Rose. Her name was Iva Toguri until she married Phillip D'Aguina, a Portuguese born in Japan. She was an American citizen and, basically, that's all she wanted to be. A native of Los Angeles, she had just celebrated her twenty-fifth birthday when she sailed to Japan to care for a sick aunt at the request of her father. Because of a rushed departure, she failed to obtain a U.S. passport and became stranded in Japan when the war started.

In August 1943 she was ordered to take a part-time job at Radio Tokyo in the English-Language Program, whose goal was to demoralize U.S. troops. Arrested on September 18, 1945, she spent a year in Sugamo's

Tokyo Rose leaving Sugamo for the United States. *From left to right:* Sgt. George Stepneck, Tokyo Rose, Capt. Francis McCormick. (Courtesy John L. Ginn)

Blue Prison before being released for lack of evidence in support of any charge as either a Class B or C war criminal.

She was arrested again when she returned to the United States. "She was pre-tried by the press and convicted before the trial," charged Masayo Duus, who thoroughly researched the case of Tokyo Rose three years before publishing her book on the subject. Duus claimed: "The judge sentenced the legend of Tokyo Rose." Iva Toguri was convicted of treason in 1949 and sentenced to ten years in prison, fined ten thousand dollars, and stripped of her citizenship. By the time she was sentenced, she had already spent more than two years in prison and more than three "living in Hell" in Japan, where she was considered an "enemy alien."

There were fourteen women on Radio Tokyo's "Zero Hour." Iva was the only Nisei—American-born Japanese—and the only one accused of treason. She broadcasted no more than what was written for her by the radio staff. Imprisoned American officers convinced her that she could assist the Allies by voicing subtle absurdities and nuances that the Japanese couldn't understand. These same officers later testified in her defense at her trial in San Francisco in 1949.

Many ex-GIs feel that Tokyo Rose actually performed a service to her country. Dog tired and sweating out dark nights of tension on Pacific islands, they found something to laugh about when she went on the air. She knew so little about troop psychology that she entertained as many or more troops as she aggravated.

Iva Toguri was pardoned by President Gerald Ford in January 1977. She had served six and a half years in prison but lived as a woman without a country for almost three decades before her citizenship was restored. It was indeed a disgraceful miscarriage of justice.

The two other women sharing Blue Prison with Tokyo Rose were accused of Class C war crimes but were released for lack of evidence supporting the charges against them.

The Class C male war criminals held at Sugamo for trial and sentencing are listed alphabetically in appendix A. These same prisoners are listed by court docket number in the chapter "The Sentences." Since there are so many of them, only various groups will be discussed there.

THE TRIALS

Class A

The trial of the major Japanese war criminals in Tokyo never received the worldwide attention that the Nuremberg, Germany, trials did in 1945-46. The indicted and accused Nazi leaders were well known, both in Europe and in the United States. Their names were familiar and pronounceable.

By the end of the war with Japan, the Americans were totally fed up with war, the loss of loved ones, and the struggle to reach that stage in their lives. Everyone involved in World War II was shocked and appalled by the Holocaust, the mass murder of Jews and other peoples, and at the atrocities committed against both prisoners of war and civilians throughout the Far East. The world at large was demanding that war criminals be tried and that justice be rendered to men gone mad.

The trial of the Class A war criminals in Japan was the longest continuous trial in history. It lasted for two years and ninety-eight days, beginning on May 3, 1946, after nine months of preparation, and ending on November 12, 1948. The IMTFE rendered individual verdicts to each of the twenty-six accused.

The one name that Americans most associated with the war was that of Tojo. Other Japanese names that were somewhat less familiar were those of Emperor Hirohito and Admiral Yamamoto. But Hideki Tojo, ex-general, ex-minister of war, and ex-premier, was the focal point of the upcoming trial. How could Sadao Araki, Kenji Doihara, Kingoro Hashimoto, Kiichiro Hiranuma, and other similar names possibly be of interest to people who had seldom heard them and had trouble pronouncing them? Once the war was finally over, Americans wanted to find ways to forget it — and that is precisely what we did. A twenty-seven-month-long trial greatly assisted our memory loss.

If the American people had had any idea of the extent of the Japanese conspiracy, scheming, plotting, treachery, and assassinations that went into the attempt to justify their invasions, conquerings, occupation, and rule by terror between 1931 and 1945, the names of most of the accused war criminals would have been as familiar as those of the Nazi leaders.

There were other trials of Japanese war criminals before and during the Class A trial in Tokyo and the Class B and C war crimes trials in Yokohama. Some of these, as we have seen, took place in the Philippines, where a five-man U.S. Military Commission held the first major Japanese war crimes trials after WWII in Manila. General Yamashita, commander of all Japanese forces in the Philippines, was tried in October 1945, convicted, and, on December 7, sentenced to death. Also convicted was General Homma, the commander of troops who forced Filipino and U.S. prisoners of war into the Bataan Death March.

The government of the Philippines tried 169 accused Japanese war criminals, convicted 133, and executed 17. Trials conducted by U.S. Military Tribunals in the Marianas and other Pacific combat areas resulted in 113 convictions.

During 1945 and 1946, Nationalist Chinese courts convicted 504 Japanese war criminals. Britain convicted 811; Australia, 644; the Netherlands, 969; and France, 198.

The Soviet Union apparently believed in doing things differently. It entered the war against Japan on August 8, 1945, between the nuclear bombings of Hiroshima and Nagasaki, in violation of a nonaggression pact, attacking the Japanese in large force in Manchuria and surrounding areas and continuing to batter them for awhile even after they surrendered unconditionally. Practically the entire Kwantung Army was captured. It has been estimated that more than 375,000 Japanese soldiers and civilians were killed or enslaved between 1945 and 1950. There are no records of trials or proceedings against them by the Russians.

A total of 92 executions of Class A, B, and C war criminals resulted from the U.S. military trials in the Philippines, the Marianas, other Pacific islands, and the IMTFE trial in Tokyo. Only 7 of those executed were Class A war criminals.

The Allied trials were made public. All testimony was transcribed, and the accused were provided every opportunity to defend themselves. A large number of those brought to trial were acquitted and released. The trials were covered by a small army of national and international news correspondents.

The Class A war criminals were tried in an elaborate courtroom, hastily constructed by the occupation forces, in the former auditorium of the Japanese War College. Taken over by the War Ministry during the war, the college was located on a hill near the center of Tokyo known as Ichigawa Heights. (Like Sugamo, it had been spared during the bombings of Tokyo.) The courtroom was finished with wood paneling. There were huge, bright klieg lights for movie and still photographers and glass compartments for press and radio representatives and translators. All these efforts resulted in a glaring, showy setup that was intended to be dramatic. When the weather warmed up the lights became a real problem—the building was not air-conditioned until midway through the trials, and the courtroom became almost unbearably warm. The long mahogany bench for the eleven judges was elevated to a commanding level, which on first appearance seemed to be excessively high. Across the room, in front of the judges, was a plain, three-tier compartment for the prisoners. Near the center of the 110-by-80-foot room was the witness box, which stood alone in the English style, with long benches and tables nearby for the court attendants and lawyers.

Official spectators were seated in soft, comfortable chairs behind a railing near the front of the room and equipped with earphones that could be adjusted to the language of their choice. English and Japanese were the principal languages spoken and translated. However, there were times when Russian and Chinese were used.

On the opening day of the IMTFE trial, everyone in the occupation who was "somebody" was in the official spectator area, including MacArthur's young son, Arthur. In the rear of the courtroom was a somewhat-cramped spectator balcony for the Japanese spectators, whom the occupation authorities had assumed would be the principal audience.

Into the bright lights, glare from the glass cubicles, and generally theatrical atmosphere came twenty-four of the twenty-six Class A prisoners. Dressed in a variety of clothing and wearing an equally different range of facial expressions, they all looked quite old and tired as they took their assigned seats. They had breakfasted early and had been transported from Sugamo in a U.S. Army bus with paper-covered windows, led and followed by MPs in Jeeps.

These Class A war criminal suspects had been held in Sugamo since their arrests, isolated from the rest of the suspects. In general they were a polite, obedient, docile group of old men—vastly different from the days of their military command over the government and people of the Japanese Empire.

The proceedings were delayed for about an hour because two of the accused, being flown in from a prison in Bangkok, had been detained. They were Seishiro Itagaki—the arrogant, ruthless terror of Southeast Asia—and Heitaro Kimura—who approved the use of slave labor for the Siam-Burma Railroad in which thousands of POWs and civilians perished.

At 11:13 A.M., after postponing the proceedings for about an hour, the judges decided not to wait any longer. (Itagaki and Kimura didn't arrive until 2:30 P.M.)

The trial itself resulted from a meeting, conducted in Cairo in 1943, among the heads of state of the United States, Great Britain, and China. The joint decision reached at that meeting was made public in December. "The three great allies are fighting this war to restrain and punish the aggression of Japan." This decision was defined more clearly two years later in item 6 of the Potsdam Declaration, which states: "There must be eliminated for all time the authority and influence of those who have deceived and misled the people of Japan into embarking on world conquest," and in item 10: "We do not intend that the Japanese shall be enslaved as a race or destroyed as a nation, but stern justice shall be meted out to all war criminals, including those who have visited cruelties upon our prisoners."* This item brought the United States and its Allies much trouble and put the fear of Buddha into the Japanese military forces shortly before the surrender—especially those who knew they had committed atrocities and other war crimes.

With this and other Allied-decreed legal authority, SCAP approved and published a charter on January 19, 1946, that authorized and directed the activities of the IMTFE. The charter was a prototype of that employed by the military tribunal for the Nuremberg trials in Germany and repeated some of that exact language. The IMTFE charter cited Tokyo as the permanent seat of the tribunal and called for SCAP to appoint six to eleven members from names provided by the signatory nations on the surrender document, and by India and the Philippines. It also provided the format for the organization, quorum, voting procedure, and other operational matters before the IMTFE. The tribunal was granted the power "to try and punish Japanese war criminals who ... are charged with offenses which include crimes against peace." These charges were outlined along with conventional war crimes and crimes against humanity.†

The tribunal ruled out many of the counts against the defendants since there was some degree of redundancy and a lack of sufficient evidence to justify a finding on others. Counts 2–26, 28, 30, 34, and 37–53 were eliminated. The charges, with their corresponding numbers, applied in the trials, were:

**See text of the Potsdam Declaration in appendix B.*
†*See charter, appendix C.*

1. Leaders, organizers, instigators, or accomplices in the formation and execution of a common plan or conspiracy to wage wars of aggression, and war or wars in violation of international law.
27. Waging unprovoked war against China.
29. Waging aggressive war against the United States.
31. Waging aggressive war against the British Commonwealth.
32. Waging aggressive war against the Netherlands.
33. Waging aggressive war against France (Indochina).
35–36. Waging war against Russia.
54. Ordered, authorized, and permitted inhumane treatment of prisoners of war and others.
55. Having deliberately and recklessly disregarded their duty to take adequate steps to prevent atrocities.

The charter specified that the tribunal was not to be bound by the technical rules of evidence. Any evidence it found to have probative value was admissible, as were "all purported admissions of statements of the accused." It provided the tribunal with power "to impose upon the prisoners, on conviction, death or other punishment" it determined to be fair and just. General MacArthur was designated to have reviewing authority. The only cases that reached his office for review, however, were those in which a death sentence was imposed. He could reduce but not increase sentences.

An eleven-judge tribunal was selected by SCAP, with Sir William Webb as president. A big, charismatic man of fifty-nine, Webb had been a distinguished member of the Australian bar since 1913 and chief justice of Queensland from 1940 to 1946. Until the IMTFE trial Sir William had never sentenced a man to death in all his years as a judge.

The judges and prosecutors selected by the countries representing the IMTFE were:

Australia
   Sir William Webb, judge
   A. J. Mansfield, prosecutor
Canada
   Edward Stuart McDougall, judge
   H. G. Nolan, prosecutor
China
   Ju-ao Mei, judge
   Che-chun Hsiang, prosecutor

France
   Henri Bernard, judge
   Robert Oneto, prosecutor
India
   Radha M. Pal, judge
   Govinda Menon, prosecutor
Netherlands
   B. V. A. Roling, judge
   W. G. F. Boegerhoff Mulder, prosecutor

New Zealand
    Erima Harvey Northcroft, judge
    R. H. Quilliam, prosecutor
Philippines
    Delfin Jaranilla, judge
    Pedro Lopez, prosecutor
Soviet Union
    Ivan M. Zaryanov, judge
    S. A. Golunsky, prosecutor
United Kingdom
    Lord Patrick, judge
    Arthur Comyns-Carr, prosecutor
United States
    Maj. Gen. Myron C. Cramer, judge
    Joseph B. Keenan, prosecutor

Most of the judges had colorful though solid backgrounds. The judge first selected to represent the United States was John P. Higgins, who proved to be an embarrassment to the IMTFE. He was chief justice of the Massachusetts State Supreme Court and a relative nonentity compared to the other IMTFE representatives.

Joseph B. Keenan, the chief prosecutor, wrote to the Truman administration: "Lest there be a misunderstanding, the Superior Court of Massachusetts, being local in its jurisdiction and intermediate in rank, does not in the eyes of others reach the dignity of the U.S. District Court." Eventually Higgins was replaced by General Cramer.

Another embarrassment on the judges' bench was the Russian representative, Zaryanov. In violation of the existing nonaggression pact, Russia had attacked Japan two days before the unconditional surrender, an issue that was not resolved during the trial. In addition the reports of what Russia had done and was currently doing to the imperial armies it had captured in Manchuria, China, and North Korea were making headlines in the Japanese news during the trial.

Since the trial was international in scope, every effort was exerted to make it a fair one. General MacArthur signed a special proclamation establishing the IMTFE in January 1946 and issued Special Order No. 20 establishing the charter governing its actions on April 26, 1946. Despite these efforts, the prosecution had a distinct advantage. It was fully assisted by SCAP, and each nation involved provided an associate prosecutor, who worked under Joseph Keenan. He revealed the extent of the prosecution's case on opening day by reading a statement twice as long as the indictment (which ran to seventeen pages and fifty-five counts). There were thirty-seven pages, with an additional forty of supporting appendixes. With the support of SCAP, the prosecution was able to select a full administration team of stenographers, secretaries, translators, clerks, and other essential personnel from MacArthur's headquarters for the long, difficult trial.

Most of the Class A war criminal suspects at Sugamo were quick to obtain defense counsel. Three Japanese attorneys played important roles in organizing the defense. Ichiro Kiyose, even though purged by SCAP as an ultrarightist with military leanings, was a very capable and astute defense attorney. He had served in the prewar Diet for eight terms and was to become Speaker of the House after the peace treaty was signed in 1952. Kenzo Takayanagi, a Harvard Law School graduate, prepared numerous briefs for the defense. He was extremely intellectual and served with distinction. The third member was eminent scholar Somei Uzawa, president of Meiji University, and renowned in the legal arena. Uzawa told a press conference: "I hold Tojo responsible for the war, but he should still get a fair trial." He was unanimously chosen by the defendants to be chief of the defense when the trial began. Kiyose, who was his deputy, told reporters: "Tojo's case is defensible," and "No single individual or group of individuals could be responsible for a conflict of the magnitude of the Pacific War."

At the beginning of the trial, the defense was disorganized. Keenan appealed to Washington to send twenty attorneys to Tokyo to assist. A request was made by SCAP for a search through the occupation forces for military personnel capable of assisting the defense counsel. On May 17, 1946, two weeks after the trial began, fifteen defense attorneys arrived from Washington. A number of Japanese attorneys had been engaged by the suspects, and six American attorneys already in Japan joined the defense. One, Capt. Beverly Coleman, a U.S. naval officer and a lawyer in civilian life, was appointed chief of the defense team. John W. Guilder, another navy man, was selected to be assistant chief of defense.

The diversity of charges against the suspects rendered the defense practically incapable of acting as a unit. Coleman and Guilder attempted to organize the defense team so that they would not be working against each other. The growing army of defense attorneys arriving from the U.S. had different ideas, however. The Supreme Commander of the Allied Powers continued to refrain from supplying the defense with the logistic support that Coleman considered adequate. Coleman and Guilder called on MacArthur to discuss the problem. When they were unable to obtain what they believed to be the necessary assistance from MacArthur, they submitted their resignations. Despite these problems the Japanese accused were all provided with adequate counsel during the trial.

Meanwhile Keenan's prosecutors were keeping long hours, deciding who among almost ninety Class A suspects at Sugamo Prison should stand trial. The men stationed at Sugamo referred to them as "major" war criminals, and the Class B and C prisoners as "minor" war criminals. The difficult task of selecting those to indict was put in the hands of the prosecutor's Executive Committee, chaired by Arthur Comyns-Carr. The committee wanted to limit the number of defendants and agreed that each nation represented in the IMTFE should indict two Class A suspects.

Shortly after the list was thought to be complete, the Russians arrived. Filing into Tokyo were the Russian judge, I. M. Zaryanov; S. A. Golunsky, the associate prosecutor; and fifty lawyers, clerks, interpreters, cooks, gardeners, chauffeurs, and many others whose sole purpose appeared to be to occupy space. Since General MacArthur had greatly restricted the Soviet authority in the occupation, they intended to be noticed in the IMTFE trials. Later information from the American Intelligence Service proved that at least fifteen members of the group were in the Russian Intelligence Service.

Golunsky read the list of the accused and informed Keenan that he was authorized to name two additional suspects. He then surprised the prosecution by naming the two Japanese officials who had signed the unconditional surrender documents — Foreign Minister Shigemitsu, former ambassador to Russia, and General Umezu, a former commander of the Kwantung Army in Manchuria. Umezu was the last chief of staff of the Japanese army, and the prosecutors had given much thought to his arrest, but Shigemitsu had already been selected to testify as a witness for the prosecution. Both were arrested and sent to Sugamo Prison to await trial.

The twenty-eight original defendants listed as Class A war criminals were arraigned before the IMTFE on May 3, 1946. They had been selected from the hundreds of military and civilian leaders arrested and questioned early in the occupation. Among the accused were nineteen military professionals and nine diplomats. The military leaders had gained control of the Japanese government in the late 1920s. Therefore the Allies had in custody most of the men primarily responsible for nearly twenty years of Japanese aggression. The Allied case was based on the premise that fewer than thirty leaders had been successful in turning the Japanese nation into a single military machine directed by a military dictatorship bent on expansion and conquest.

The original twenty-eight Class A suspects had been carefully selected from a total of eighty-four suspected war criminals being held at Sugamo. The basic idea was similar to that of the Nuremberg trials — to set an example. The Amerians realized that there was no possible way to try all the war criminals. The Japanese as well as the German war criminals merely changed clothes and walked off into the crowds. A Japanese could easily change his first, last, or entire name. As to the unknown millions of atrocities that had been inflicted on the Chinese people, mostly civilians, the Allies could have brought war crimes charges against practically the entire Kwantung Army.

Copies of the indictment and the charter for the IMTFE were given to each defendant. The indictment was a detailed and documented case against the twenty-eight leaders. It consisted of forty-three typed pages and an appendix citing forty-seven treaties, conventions, protocols, and other international agreements that the indicted had allegedly violated. It contained very harsh language. It charged the defendants with promoting a scheme of conquest; planning and initiating aggressive wars in China, the United States, the British Empire, the Netherlands, and other areas; crimes against peace, conventional war crimes, and crimes against humanity in violation of the Hague Accords and the Geneva Conventions. They were also charged with murdering, maiming, and mistreating prisoners of war and civilians; with plundering and destroying cities and towns, far beyond any military necessity; and with mass murder, rape and torture. Anyone listening to the charges would have expected to see a group of savages wearing heavy chains sitting in the chairs of the accused, not merely a group of old men in rumpled clothes.

Along with the indictment Joseph Keenan issued a press release that stated: "It is high time, and indeed was so before this war began, that the promoters of aggressive, ruthless war and treaty-breakers should be stripped of the glamour of national heroes and exposed as what they really are—plain, ordinary murderers."

The extremely long and often boring trial recapped, in sober legal terminology, a crowded era of Japanese history. The record of conquest began in the 1920s, with the war in China, and ended with the nuclear blasts in 1945. The history was peppered with extreme cruelty and indifference to human life, elements abhorrent to the Western sense of morality. The prosecution coped with crimes against humanity that ranged from the planned brutality used by the emperor's Kempeitai police to break the will and spirit of Allied and Asian prisoners, to the uncontrolled hysteria that destroyed Nanking and Manila in an orgy of rape and murder. The anticipated impact of this information on the Japanese people never occurred, due to the cumbersome legal requirements of presenting it. They became bored and then irritated by the constant reminders of their guilt. By the end of the long trial, some of these feelings turned into sympathy for these broken old men.

The prosecution went into details of Japan being practically as enslaved as the territories it occupied, due to the people's lack of opposition to military rule. After the militarists gained control of the government during the 1930s, they established an elaborate system for controlling the people. They created the Kempeitai and used it to suppress and oppress the people and to encourage warlike and combative sentiments. The Kempeitai considered themselves agents of the emperor. They were very similar to the Gestapo in Hitler's Germany and the KGB in Stalin's Russia.

On May 6 the court opened to hear the accused plead. All pleaded not guilty to the charges against them. One of the first attorneys to speak for the defense was U.S. Army Maj. Ben Bruce Blakney. He attacked the jurisdiction of the IMTFE. He charged that since all the judges were Allied nationals, "a legal, fair, and impartial trial is denied to the accused." He asked why the accused were not being tried by judges from neutral nations. Blakney then expounded on the theory that "war is not a crime." He espoused this theory until Joseph Keenan, red faced, took the podium to launch his rebuttal. His prose almost attained the color of his face, and he closed with a parting shot suggesting that "it would be necessary to wait until man landed on Mars in order to find some neutral nations or people to come and sit upon judgement of those responsible for aggressive war."

(Shintoism, Japan's primary national religion, also played an important role in military aggression. Shinto combined ancestor worship, patriotism, and a strong conviction that the emperor, the people, and the soil were sacred. Its main features were emperor worship and self-sacrifice. The emperor was believed to be a direct descendant of the Sun Goddess. Shintoism became the official state religion and served Japan's military all too well. Shinto beliefs held that a man killed in combat for his emperor and country became a god himself, and if he died seven times he reached Nirvana. During the Amerian occupation, the importance of this religion was greatly diminished through the efforts of SCAP.)

Naturally, much attention was centered on the Pearl Harbor attack. In fact, too much emphasis and time were wasted. The prosecution would have made its point more accurate by stating that Japan's aggression had been a planned military operation, and by describing *all* the events that occurred on December 7, 1941. At 12:45 P.M. *Japan time,* Japanese troops seized the Shanghai Bund. At 1:40 P.M. Kota Bharu, on the east coast of Malaya, was attacked. At 3:05 P.M. Sigora and Patani in southern Thailand were attacked. At 3:20 P.M. Pearl Harbor was attacked. At 4:20 P.M. Ambassador Nomura delivered a "war note" to Secretary of State Cordell Hull. At 5:20 P.M. a British gunboat was sunk in China. At 6:00 P.M. Singapore was attacked from the air. At 8:05 P.M. Guam was attacked, and at 9:00 P.M. Hong Kong was attacked. At 11:40 P.M. Emperor Hirohito issued an Imperial Rescript declaring war on Great Britain and the United States.

The attack on Kota Bharu was a clear case of aggressive war without warning, in violation of international law. Kota Bharu was a small port on the northeast coast of the Malay Peninsula. The British and Indian forces fought bravely to defend it. Maj. Gen. Arthur Percival, the British commander of Malaya and Singapore, testified by affidavit before the IMTFE that, "at Kota Bharu we were wiped out almost to the last man." It is important to note here that the Japanese and British were not involved in negotiations regarding Kota Bharu or any other British protectorate when the Japanese attacked. The Japanese launched a prearranged attack without *any* notice or warning. This was a more distilled form of sneak attack than Pearl Harbor. Nevertheless, the IMTFE spent little time on the other attacks and proceeded to concentrate on Pearl Harbor.

From time to time during the trial, there arose the subject of trying the emperor as a war criminal. Australia in particular wanted him in court, but then, most of the Allies wanted him in the lineup at one time or another. Early in the trial, the Soviets clamored for his arrest. Finally General MacArthur warned the Allies that if the emperor was brought to trial, it would be "absolutely essential" to bring an additional one million troops into Japan. In fact, President Truman discussed this subject with Winston Churchill and sought his advice about whether or not to try the emperor. In Truman's opinion the decision was a political, not a military one. MacArthur knew six months before the trial that President Truman and Prime Minister Churchill had definitely decided not to bring the emperor to trial. MacArthur was in full agreement with that decision.

In one respect the emperor *was* in the IMTFE trial, however. His closest confidant and adviser, Marquis Kido, was the only Class A war criminal sentenced because of his relationship to the emperor. Kido kept an accurate, detailed series of diaries containing dates, names, and places of every important political and imperial meeting and event from January 1, 1930, to December 15, 1945. Kido voluntarily informed the IMTFE of the existence of these voluminous diaries. Keenan's staff referred to the diaries as "the working Bible of the prosecution and the key to all further investigations."

The emperor was also represented in court by a blood relative: Prince Morimasa Nashimoto, a seventy-one-year-old member of the royal household, was extremely popular in Japan. He had taken part in the Russia and China wars and held the rank of field marshal. His arrest created a great deal of consternation among the Japanese, and for the first time the Japanese government intervened, making a formal request to MacArthur for a postponement of the prince's arrest. The reply from SCAP was that no special consideration would be made for members of the imperial house.

The trial was slowly moving forward. But if anything could go wrong to delay it, it did—much more than anyone could have imagined.

After Keenan delivered the opening statement for the prosecution, he left Tokyo for Washington for several weeks. There was speculation as to why he left at this critical moment. (Some thought that he might be trying to solve a drinking problem.) While he was absent, several of the American prosecutors made an appointment with MacArthur in an effort to replace Keenan. Their chief complaints centered around his bullying tactics, drinking, effusive methods, and his egocentricities. MacArthur apparently either did not believe them or had a high enough regard for Keenan's organizational skills to overlook them. No action by SCAP was taken, and the issue was not brought up again during the trial. On his return Keenan found out about the scheme and became even more scathing.

Even at this early stage of the trial, the defense lawyers were facing interservice rivalry. Not only was Coleman's group of navy lawyers at odds with members of other branches of the service, they were becoming rivals in defense of their clients as well. In an effort to resolve this problem, an emergency meeting of the defense attorneys was convened. Nothing was resolved, and Coleman and Guilder made an appointment with MacArthur, at which time they asked to be transferred to other duties. MacArthur blew a few fuses, but on June 5 Coleman and the entire naval defense team were transferred. By June 16 the defense teams were reorganized, with George Yamaoka, a well-known Japanese American bilingual attorney, filling Coleman's role.

The judges also had their share of problems. On June 8, Judge Delfin Jaranilla arrived in Tokyo to represent the Philippines. The next day he attended a party where he met David Smith, the American attorney who was counsel for Koki Hirota, the close-mouthed ex-premier. Smith discovered that Jaranilla had been in the Bataan Death March and had been a prisoner of the Japanese for a year. The following day Smith and Hirota's Japanese counsel, Tadashi Hanai, drafted a motion suggesting "the disqualification and personal bias of the Philippines Judge." Smith and Hanai were both graduates of Georgetown University Law School. Both argued that since the Bataan Death March was part of the evidence for the prosecution, Jaranilla "maintain[ed] a personal bias and prejudice against their defendant" and that Hirota therefore "[would] not be able to obtain a fair and impartial trial." Webb informed these defense counselors that the bench had "no power to set aside an appointment by General MacArthur" and that "if a judge retired voluntarily at this period, it is going to create a long delay in the trial and it would be unfair to the other judges."

During the next session Webb reported: "This tribunal is now fully constituted for the first time." By then John Higgins, the U.S. judge, had learned of Keenan's fiery cables to Washington regarding his appointment. Apparently someone in the group that had earlier visited MacArthur in an attempt to remove Keenan had the desire to embarrass him. The attempt failed because an embarrassed and humiliated Higgins notified Washington of his resignation before Keenan had a chance to think about it. They in turn asked Keenan to notify MacArthur and inform him that Maj. Gen. Myron C. Cramer "was available to replace him immediately." However, this claim was inaccurate, and MacArthur pleaded with Higgins to stay on the bench for an additional week until Cramer could arrive. Naturally, when General Cramer arrived on July 22, the defense attorneys filed motions challenging his presence. At 3:15 P.M. on that day, Judge Webb announced: "The tribunal, by a majority, holds that General Cramer, the American representative, is eligible to sit as a member of this tribunal." The motion was dismissed.

A major problem that prolonged the trial became apparent very early, beginning in one of the first stages of the prosecution's attempt to prove the police-state mentality existing in Japan in the 1930s. Hyoe Ouchi, a professor at Tokyo University, had been purged—along with eight others on the faculty—for criticizing the military invasion of China in 1937. Ouchi and others from the university had been detained at Sugamo Prison for eighteen months. During the cross-examination, the defense countered with blatant delaying tactics. For example, when Ouchi mentioned a law passed in 1939 making military training compulsory, Defense Attorney Kleiman asked: "You have just used the word, 'passed'; by that do you mean passed by the Diet?" Kleiman continued to ask similar questions until testy Sir William Webb, in a loud voice, said: "I can not allow this to go on. . . . If you are going to have every i dotted and every t crossed in this case we will never finish." Other defense lawyers would serve the bench with motions—most of them invalid—at the drop of a hat. Some wanted to get into a dialogue regarding the Japanese Constitution and to engage in debates about the legality or illegality of the charges. Almost every line of questioning was met head-on by dramatic legal maneuvering. The never-ending, long-winded legal interruptions often turned into contests of wills, personalities, and mentality between the bench, the prosecutors, and the defense. All too often the same ground would be covered again and again.

Another prime difficulty had to do with Japanese — quite possibly the most difficult language on earth to translate accurately into English. One of the changes made in the attempt to expedite the proceedings involved modifying Rule 66 of the tribunal's Rules of Procedure, which held that "a copy of every document intended to be used in evidence by either the prosecution or the defense will be delivered to the accused or his counsel." The prosecution explained that "a 300 page book in Japanese took thirty translators ten days to render into English and that out of the entire book the prosecution might only have to introduce a paragraph or a page." There wasn't enough photographic equipment in occupied Japan to handle work required by the court. (It should be remembered, too, that in 1946 there were no photocopy machines.) Naturally the defense fought the modification of Rule 66. However, the bench overruled the objection and added that the use of affidavits by witnesses would also save additional time.

The prosecutors were united in their goal to prove to the world that Japan had engaged in aggressive wars on a large scale in disregard of treaties and conventions, and that the country's leaders had put aside the customs of war in practice. However, the defense had twenty-eight individual cases to protect. Whenever any important witness testified, nearly every defense counsel, both American and Japanese, wanted to cross-examine him on behalf of their individual clients. The judges worked out a plan by which only one lawyer for each side could conduct the examination.

What the IMTFE needed most was a president who was a dynamic and diplomatic leader. Sir William Webb was neither. Yet another delay was caused by the natural politeness of the Japanese. A Japanese defense attorney taking the floor would begin: "With the permission of the President of the Tribunal, I would like to submit testimony addressing the subject in the following categories" — a process that would continue for several minutes. Webb finally stopped this custom by telling the Japanese defenders exactly how to address the bench in order to save time. Other Japanese counsel had a knack for making a question into a speech that could have confounded the patience of Job.

Then there were the "shouting generals": In the Japanese army, both officers and noncoms bark orders to those under them. Naturally, the higher the rank of the soldier, the more experience he had in barking orders. In the novel *Shogun*, by James Clavell, which became a movie, the shogun, with his combination snarl-bark-and-growl method of giving orders, has a remarkable similarity to the generals testifying before the IMTFE. In the Japanese army, officers could slap noncommissioned soldiers at will. They, in turn, slapped those of lower rank whenever they felt like doing so. No help for the poor civilian, dog, or whatever, who got in the way of a battered private!

Maj. Gen. Kikusaburo Okada, chief of the War Ministry's Planning Section, was one of the first witnesses to testify. His answers to the simplest questions shook the building. Webb bristled and said: "He is not addressing the Japanese Army now." Several other generals began in the same eardrum-popping manner until Webb managed to get them under control. These witnesses did not provide the defense with much assistance. They took up much time, and several probably did more harm than benefit to their defense.

At about this time, the verdicts were reached at the Nuremberg trials. On October 1, almost eleven months after the trial of Nazi war leaders had begun, the four-nation tribunal returned its verdicts. They sentenced twelve to the gallows, seven to imprisonment for terms of ten years to life, and acquitted three. The prosecution had fought hard for death sentences for all the defendants. For the first time in history, political and military leaders had been tried and convicted for waging aggressive war. It proved that, in world opinion, aggressive war is "the supreme international crime." Reichsmarschall Hermann Göring committed suicide two hours before he was to be executed. He ingested potassium cyanide and died before the prison doctor could reach him. A correspondent from the *London Times* reported that Hitler's deputy "for a day made sport of Nuremberg."

Orders from SCAP were issued to Sugamo Prison for the immediate tightening of security on the Class A war criminals. The prison's commanding officer, Col. Dana C. Schmahl, began a regime of security that made life more difficult and embarrassing for both prisoners and guards. At Sugamo's infirmary the teeth of all Class A defendants were X-rayed for poison implants. The cells were searched at different times, sometimes daily, while the prisoners stood naked, facing a wall. Each morning those going to Ichigawa Heights for trial were guarded at all times while shaving and showering. After dressing, they were taken into a room where they disrobed. They were then taken to another room and issued a different set of clothes. Only then were they taken to the army bus for transport to the trial. This bus was guarded by one Jeep full of military police leading the way and another following. After the day's trial, they were returned to Sugamo in the same fashion, led to a room where they disrobed and were given an embarrassing head-to-toe body search, and moved to another room where they dressed in their prison garb for the evening and night. This was repeated daily until the conclusion of the trial.

Security was also tightened at the main gate, guard towers, and throughout the prison. An individual guard was assigned to each of the Class A suspects. The prisoner was required to sleep facing the cell door, which had been removed, with his face and hands exposed. A light in each cell was kept on twenty-four hours a day, at great discomfort to the prisoners.

The defense set up a new howl of protest at the tightened security measures. It stated: "While we have no desire whatever to interfere or make any recommendations respecting security measures, we do wish to call the Tribunal's attention to the fact that part of the measures appear to us to be unreasonable and closely connected with a fair trial to the accused."

By mid-December, the prosecution was focusing on the atrocities suffered by the Allied POWs and civilian slave laborers. Details of the suffering and deaths resulting from forced slave labor, lack of food and medicine, torture, beatings, and murder were recorded in the IMTFE chronicles. Emphasis was placed on some of the more important areas and crimes committed under Japanese occupation—the Bataan Death March, atrocities in the Philippines, the "Rape of Manila," the "Rape of Nanking," the Siam-Burma Railway, and the "hellships" used to transport prisoners of war. Everyplace captured by the Japanese was ruled by terror.

The testimony of surviving witnesses about these atrocities was shocking not only to the court but also to the defendants. Most of them, after listening to the testimony, began to fidget, cup their ears, remove headphones, and look as if they needed to go to the restroom en masse. The statistics of the number of deaths in areas of Japanese occupation pointed to one main fact—Japan's rule by terror was a planned method of genocide, as barbaric as the Nazi Holocaust. Pedro Lopez, the Philippines prosecutor, provided evidence showing that 131,028 murders had been committed during the Japanese occupation and stated: "Hundreds suffered slow and painful death in dark, foul, and lice-infested cells for whom quick, scientific mass extermination in a lethal gas chamber at ... Dachau would have been a welcome alternative."

On January 24, 1947, Carlisle Higgins, an American assistant prosecutor, made the announcement: "Mr. President, the prosecution will now rest." This announcement presented the defense with renewed energy to confound the court with an abundance of new motions. There were motions for a mistrial, attacks on the jurisdiction of the tribunal, and motions for dismissal of the individual cases against the accused. After some more showboating by Webb, each of the motions was dismissed on February 3. The bench then granted a three-week recess so that the ninety-six Japanese and twenty-three American attorneys who composed the defense team could prepare their cases.

The defense started off badly. Not everyone on the defense team agreed with the opening statement, and the situation continued to deteriorate. The defense proved to be weak and at times provided amusement to the court. The barking generals didn't help matters. There were too many statements from prominent Japanese military officers such as: "I firmly believe that violence, plunder, and the like absolutely did not occur," and, referring to the conflict with China: "We became very popular with the people." Gen. Isau Yokohama testified that his orders were to "love the people" in China. The two most frequently used answers to questions from the prosecution were "I don't know" and "I don't remember." The Japanese witnesses, in an effort to explain themselves, testified interminably. Webb complained: "It is a Japanese weakness to express themselves in great length and it's difficult to control it, but the indulgence of this weakness has a devastating effect on the paper and ink supply. We have consumed one hundred tons of mimeograph paper and a vast quantity of ink and we are facing a shortage of both." There seemed no way to stop the waste of material and time in processing documents.

Some of the judges believed that the defense was unnecessarily prolonging the trial. It has since come to seem evident that they were doing exactly that. World events were shaping up for a showdown between Communism and democracy, and the defense was hoping that the showdown would make it easier for the Japanese militarists to justify their actions.

The Russians and Webb crossed swords frequently regarding excessive presentations of testimony and documents. Webb explained the democratic process of allowing all the evidence available for the defense. V. Berezhkov, a commentator for Moscow's *New Times*, complained:

> The major Japanese war criminals will die a natural death long before the International Military Tribunal passes its verdict. The defense has literally showered the Tribunal with documents of all kinds with the idea of confusing and protracting the trial, yet Sir William Webb, who does not miss an opportunity to complain of delays, is himself in a large measure responsible for the dilatoriness of the proceedings. Instead of

ruling out statements of the defense counsel which are extraneous to the trial, he willingly allows them on the floor.

The defense phase of the trial was going from bad to worse, and several factors assisted in its downward slide. One was Arthur Comyns-Carr. A master at producing important missing documents to counter equitable defense testimony, he did this time and again, devastating the defense. Another was the time-consuming clashes of personality between Webb, seemingly hostile defense counsels, the Russians, and Chief Defense Counsel Blakney. To top this off, the defense's interpreters, translators, typists, and clerks were in short supply and had an overwhelming workload. Counsel and staff worked around the clock on occasion, and on all weekends and holidays. Twice in April they required a week of recess to process papers, and by mid-June the defense collapsed altogether. William Logan appealed to the bench for a six-week recess. After the usual haggling, Webb granted the request. On August 4, when the tribunal reconvened, the defense began justifying the Japanese action in the Pacific. Frank Tavenner, the associate prosecutor, probably summed up the defense efforts when he asked: "Should we ask the defense if they plan to show the United States attacked Japan at Pearl Harbor?" After much counterpunching, the defense failed to make it appear that the Americans had been the chief cause of the war.

On December 26 the defense of Tojo's actions during the war began. Ichiro Kiyose read the opening statement, which contained many stock phrases such as: "Japan had neither planned nor prepared beforehand for the war against the United States, Britain, and the Netherlands"; "In China, Japan had entertained neither territorial ambition nor the idea of economic monopoly"; "Tojo neither gave orders for, tolerated, nor connived at any inhumane acts"; and "Japan's attack on the Anglo-American powers had been provoked by the Allied Nations." Throughout the trial Tojo wore the same plain, brown khaki uniform. The jacket had a high collar, always buttoned to the top. With tight lips, a bald head, and slightly oversize glasses, he looked defiant but confident and relaxed. He produced a 250-page affidavit that was his justification to the world for his decisions and actions. This paper did absolve the emperor from all responsibility, however, as Tojo took full blame, declaring: "The full responsibility for the Pacific War rested on the Cabinet and High Command and was absolutely not the responsibility of the Emperor." There was not even a small note of regret for any of the military actions in China, treatment of POWs, civilian slave laborers, nor for the millions of dead. He did say, however, that he blamed himself, as premier, for defeat.

Joseph Keenan decided to conduct the cross-examination personally, in spite of the fact that he had previously selected John Fihelly, former chief of the Criminal Division of the U.S. Attorney General's Office, to do so. This action on Keenan's part accomplished two things immediately. He got rid of one of his best prosecutors, and he made the defense happy. They didn't think that Keenan was qualified for the task. He later proved them correct. He was crude, abrupt, and sanctimonious with Tojo—to the point that he became an embarrassment to the prosecuting team. By this time Keenan had a total of 340 lawyers and American and Japanese staff working for him. Even though he wasn't properly prepared, he still made some points in the cross-examination. Tojo said: "I really didn't know that the Japanese fleet had sailed for Pearl Harbor and even though I met the Emperor several times in early December, I did not discuss the impending strike at Pearl Harbor. I spoke with him on greater matters than that, on war itself, as a whole, which included that matter."

On January 12, 1948, it was announced that the defense had no further evidence. At this time there should have been great rejoicing from everyone involved in the IMTFE trial, but this was not to be. The bench, departing from Anglo-American customs of law, ruled to admit all rebuttal evidence that had important or probative value. This ruling turned the courtroom into a three-month-long combat zone for lawyers on both sides. New evidence was entered by the prosecution; new directives, notes of meetings, and diaries were made available. The defense argued that much of this new evidence was unreliable and based on hearsay and gossip. On February 10 the bench moved the court into the mitigation phase. After more arguing, it was another month before the defense concluded its summation. On April 6, 1948, the IMTFE convened and Webb announced that the court "reserves its judgement and adjourns" until a time to be announced later.

On November 4 the court reconvened to read the judgment. Three of the accused Class A war criminal suspects were absent due to sickness. Shiratori was suffering with tuberculosis, Umezu had cancer, and Hiranuma had viral pneumonia. Webb read the verdict. It took him eight days to read the more-than-twelve-hundred-page document to the court.

The trial alone provided a transcript of almost fifty thousand pages. A total of 414 witnesses testified during the trial and 779 affidavits and depositions were provided by others. Some 4,336 exhibits were submitted as evidence. It may have been a blessing that the Japanese military destroyed most of the incriminating evidence in the time between the agreement to the surrender and the beginning of the occupation.

The courtroom was again crowded, braced, and quiet when the IMTFE announced the sentences on November 12, 1948. One by one, as their names were called, the prisoners arose in the glare of camera lights to hear their fate. Sir William Webb, looking stern and inflexible, read the tribunal's findings and sentence for each of the accused quickly and then waited impatiently for the next prisoner to rise. All the ex-leaders of the Japanese military tried to preserve a mask of indifference, but some were unsuccessful.

Classes B and C

Following the authorization by SCAP on December 5, 1945, the commanding general of the U.S. Eighth Army, Robert L. Eichelberger, began appointing military commissions to try Class B and C war crimes cases, mainly in Yokohama. The commissions at Yokohama tried 371 cases — a total of 1,002 defendants. They acquitted 183, sentenced 119 to death by hanging, 60 to life imprisonment, and the remainder to prison terms of varying lengths.

The military tribunals usually consisted of five military officer teams with legal backgrounds. They assigned investigators, interpreters, interrogators, prosecutors, and clerical assistance. Each suspected war criminal was provided with at least one American and one Japanese defense attorney. They could arrange to have their own defense counsel if they preferred to do so. Affidavits, records, witnesses, and testimony from friends, fellow soldiers or sailors, and themselves would be heard by the tribunal. In many cases the suspect had admirals, generals, and religious leaders to plead on their behalf.

As in the IMTFE trial, the tribunals went to great lengths to assure that the trials were legal and fair. In March 1949 several U.S. senators reviewed the trial process for the Class C war criminals and commented: "War crime trials should be conducted in the same spirit of justice as prevailed under General MacArthur in the Pacific. We want to be sure that the judicial system used is as good in this country as was used in the Pacific. There was nothing improper in the conduct of the trials of Japanese war criminals, although many there were convicted and executed."

The Office of the Judge Advocate General, Eighth Army, examined each case to determine if the tribunal had committed any legal errors of disadvantage to the accused. The reviewer developed a synopsis of all facts and an opinion and recommendation for approval or disapproval of the tribunals's findings. The judge advocate then examined the review and the record of the trial and added his own opinions and recommendations or his concurrence with the reviewer's findings. The review was then routed to the commanding general for final action. A death sentence required confirmation by SCAP. This last process saved the lives of seventy condemned Japanese war criminals. Fifty-one trials involved findings of "not guilty" and were not reviewed.

In addition to the trials in Yokohama, other Class B and C trials took place in Shanghai, Manila, the Marianas, and other Pacific battle areas. The U.S. Navy also tried a number of war criminals on Kwajalein in the Marshall Islands, and on Guam.

Other nations also conducted war crimes trials following the war. The Australians convicted 644 Japanese war criminals, Britain more than 800, the Dutch 969, and France convicted 198 in Indochina.

Class C prisoners were taken in U.S. Army buses to Eighth Army Headquarters in Yokohama for their trials. The first trial began on December 18, 1945, and the last one ended on October 3, 1949. The trials were conducted before, during, and after the IMTFE trial in Tokyo. The Tokyo trial was one trial with twenty-five defendants, whereas the Yokohama trials consisted of 371 separate cases dealing with more than one thousand defendants. Although the Yokohama trials were conducted by military officers, they were under orders from Douglas MacArthur, in his position as SCAP in the Far East, and were sanctioned by the IMTFE.

Since the Far East Command Policy Decision of April 3, 1946, defined the term *war crimes* in three rather broad categories, more detailed explanations follow to assist the reader. Charges against Class C suspects were in these categories:

1. Violations of the laws and customs of war.
2. Atrocities committed against prisoners of war.
3. Subordinates allowed to commit atrocities against prisoners of war.
4. Atrocities ordered against prisoners of war.
5. Medical treatment and/or supplies necessary for survival withheld.
6. Illegal trials and executions of prisoners of war.
7. Desecration of the dead.
8. Medical experiments on prisoners of war.
9. Murder of prisoners of war.
10. Vivisection performed on prisoners of war.
11. Falsifying records pertaining to prisoners of war.

There follows a presentation of selected cases showing the range of war crimes committed by the Class C prisoners. Because of the number of cases and the amount of duplication in the types of cases tried, only a few will be discussed here. The rolls of microfilm obtained from the National Archives, after being transcribed onto paper, amounted to 5,469 pages—far too much for use in one book. Some of the trials deal with one individual while others include numerous suspects, all of whom were involved in the same multiple atrocities committed against specific individuals or groups. Most of the Class C trials were concluded in two or three days, although those involving a large number of accused often took from one to eleven months.

CASE 1

Tatsuo Tsuchiya, age twenty-eight. He was a former corporal in the Japanese army, wounded in combat and discharged. After recovering, he was assigned to Mitsuchima Prisoner of War Camp in Honshu, Japan, as a civilian guard also in charge of clothing and supplies. Before joining the army, he was a farmer and mat maker.

Charges. Violations of the laws and customs of war. Between November 1942 and September 1945, while at Mitsuchima POW Camp, committed atrocities against prisoners of war. On March 5, 1943, he, jointly with seven other guards, beat Pfc. Gordon Teas, an American POW, to death. On November 2, 1944, he, jointly with three others, beat Sgt. Gerald Lundquist. Between November 1942 and May 1944 he beat Private First Class Kolilis, Major Cory, and Private Vigil; forced prisoners to beat each other; and misappropriated and withheld Red Cross supplies.

For the Prosecution. The prosecution's case rested largely on affidavits and other written statements. These were strongly contested by the defense until the prosecution provided documents to show that "enemy belligerents" are not entitled to the protection of the U.S. Constitution and presented a Supreme Court decision to make the point.

The accused was represented by an individual Japanese civilian counsel in addition to the regularly appointed defense counsel.

The commission heard three POWs, Sergeant Lundquist, Private Kolilis, and Private Vigil, who were victims of the camp guards, testify to the treatment they received. One prisoner stated that the accused was, "particularly vicious and took a sadistic delight in beating men with anything that came into his hands." Sergeant Lundquist personally described beatings administered to him by the accused and other guards.

For the Defense. Tsuchiya and five other Japanese testified in his behalf. Nakajima Sudeo, commander of the camp; Haruni Kawate, errand boy for the CO; and Yokichi Nishima, Yoshiki Matsusaki, and Tomatsu Kimura, guards at the camp, testified that Tsuchiya was "very gentle and considerate," "had no authority to punish prisoners," "treated prisoners strictly with fairness," and "executed his duty faithfully and well." In his testimony Tsuchiya stated that he treated the prisoners "fairly and squarely and looked after the protection and interest of them." He never knew the names of the victims since they were addressed by numbers. He categorically denied committing the various forms of abuse and mistreatment of prisoners with which he was charged.

Court Opinion. The commission found the evidence sufficient to prove the accused guilty on four of the eight specifications, and that the record contained competent evidence to prove, beyond a reasonable doubt, the charges against him.

Sentence. Life imprisonment at hard labor.

CASE 15

Yaichi Rikitake, was tried from March 7 to March 22, 1946. He joined the Imperial Army in 1905, was commissioned in 1917, and retired in May 1933. He was recalled to duty in March 1944 and was assigned as commander of POW Camp Number 3 in Kukuoka, Japan. Rikitake was sixty-two years of age, which was unusual for a camp commander.

Summary of Evidence. From March 6, 1944, until August 15, 1945, the accused failed to provide proper medical care for prisoners who were sick or injured by refusing them the use of medicines and surgical instruments available at the camp. American medical officers were helpless to treat sick prisoners and were often required to perform operations with hacksaws and other crude tools even though proper medical instruments were supplied by the Red Cross and were found stored in the camp warehouse at the end of the war. Prisoners were required to perform heavy work even when they were diseased and unfit to perform any work. As a result many prisoners died during the accused's tenure as commander.

Prisoners were required to live and work in inadequate clothing, which resulted in many of them contracting fatal pneumonia. Additional clothing was available and was found stored in the warehouse subsequent to the surrender. Three days each month prisoners were permitted to exchange worn-out clothes. A Japanese guard stood at the exchange line and regularly beat and mistreated those prisoners who appeared. In time the prisoners preferred to go without rather than be subjected to the beatings. Rikitake observed these beatings at the exchange line but did nothing to prevent them.

Prisoners were beaten daily by the guards, with fists and with bamboo sticks. They were also required to stand at attention for long periods of time, to stand in cold water, and to have water thrown on them during the winter months. The accused not only did nothing to stop his guards from beating the prisoners, but he personally slapped or hit them with his fists.

Cash, Woodall, and Armitage, American POWs, were severely beaten by guards and given the "water cure." The beatings were administered with clubs, and each of them was knocked to the ground several times. The water cure is a form of torture in which a prisoner is tied to an object, such as a stretcher, which is propped against a wall so that the victim's head is lower than his body. Water is then forced into his nostrils until he loses consciousness. Afterward he would be revived and beaten again. Hot pokers and lit cigarettes were applied to various parts of Cash's body.

In December 1944 Onella, Wheeler, and two other POWs were caught playing cards in their quarters in violation of orders. They were stripped of their clothing, taken in front of the guardhouse, and forced to hold weights over their heads for several hours while they suffered a severe beating. They were struck and kicked about the legs and groin, then had cold water thrown on them.

In February 1945 two American and two Dutch POWs were found with food that they had purchased from a Japanese civilian. All four were stripped and forced to stand for three hours in a tank of water deep enough that they had to stand on their toes in order to breathe. They were then put in the guardhouse, where they received regular beatings, for several days.

In February 1945 Wheeler was required to work while he was sick and running a high fever. He collapsed on the job and died two days later.

While Rikitake was camp commander the prisoners were frequently punished collectively for infractions of rules committed by individuals. This punishment included the reduction of rations for the entire camp.

On numerous occasions while the accused was in charge, Japanese camp personnel, particularly a medical officer, stole and used Red Cross packages that had been furnished to the camp for the use and comfort of the prisoners.

For the Defense. The defense introduced testimony of Col. Menjiro Fukumoto, Fukuoke camp commander from July 1944 until September 1945 and Rikitake's immediate superior. He testified that the accused was a very efficient officer and a man of common sense and moderation in all things. The agreement with the civilian-run plant in which the prisoners worked was made by the war minister, and the accused did not have authority to punish civilian supervisors employed there. He also testified that the main camp furnished rations in accordance with army regulations, but the accused had camp gardens planted, installed salt-making machines, and personally drove as far as fifty kilometers to obtain additional food for his camp. POWs were given the same rations of food and clothing as the Japanese guards in the camp. The barracks were adequate and were in fact better and more spacious than those furnished to the guards.

The hospital was large and afforded good facilities. For this reason sick prisoners were sent to the camp of the accused on arrival in Japan. Two categories of Red Cross supplies were sent to the camp: One was material to protect POWs during air raids — which they were not authorized to receive, and the other consisted of items that Colonel Fukumoto himself directed be withheld until Christmas. He testified that he had made several inspections of the camp and observed no mistreatment of prisoners. Guards at the camp were not authorized to beat prisoners, burn them, or require them to stand at attention for long periods of time.

The defense introduced the testimony of the chief secretary of the POW Information Bureau. He stated that he was present at the camp when 100 prisoners arrived in January 1945. A total of 1,620 prisoners of war had started from Manila, but as a result of air raids, exposure, and malnutrition only 550 arrived in Japan. All these prisoners were in bad shape (see Case 154). One hundred of the 550 were sent to Rikitake's camp, but thirty of them died. The remaining prisoners at Camp Number 3 had their health restored and were very grateful to the accused for the good treatment accorded to them.

The accused was the last witness to take the stand, to testify in his own behalf. He stated that he arrived at the camp on March 6, 1944, and immediately called a meeting of camp personnel. He told them that the prisoners had been taken on the battlefield, in honor, and that it was not the individual's fault that he had been captured. The prisoners, as enemies, had to be protected, especially from the civilian population.

He testified regarding the department heads and personnel at the camp. The military guard details were rotated every twenty days, and he had no authority to punish them. He did have the authority to punish the civilian guards employed at the camp. He spoke of all the steps taken to improve conditions in his camp, and of how he had given the POWs all the food, clothing, and Red Cross materials that he had been authorized to give. He stated that he had no knowledge whatsoever of beatings and other atrocities that he was charged with allowing or participating in. He knew of only one instance when a POW was slapped by a civilian at the mill where he was working, and he complained about it to the mill authorities.

His son was in the Japanese army and had not been heard from. Therefore he was deeply sympathetic toward the POWs under his care.

Sentence. Rikitake was found guilty on twenty of the forty-two specifications under charges 1, 2, and 3. He was sentenced to fifteen years imprisonment at hard labor.

Comments by the Court. The record is legally sufficient to sustain the findings and sentence of the commission. The prosecution introduced the testimony, by affidavit, of several American officers who were prisoners in the camp and in a position to know the facts. They agreed that adequate medical care was not furnished, and that POWs were required to work when ill, diseased, and physically unfit. There was ample testimony to sustain the charges of failure to provide adequate clothing and that, while the prisoners were without proper clothes, the Japanese personnel were wearing Red Cross clothing. Testimony showed that there were daily beatings of officers and enlisted men and that the accused participated in some of them and witnessed others: "The deaths of several POWs must be attributed to lack of medicine, clothing, and being required to work when unable to do so. For these the accused may properly be considered responsible."

The testimony of the accused and other defense witnesses strongly contested each allegation made against the accused. The commission resolved this conflict in testimony in favor of guilt and, on all the evidence in the case, it was warranted in doing so. There were no irregularities that injuriously affected any substantial rights of the accused.

Lieutenant General Eichelberger reviewed the case and drafted the following statement:

> In the foregoing case of Yaichi Rikitake, no justifiable basis for clemency appears in the record and Allied papers. Because of the several deaths of prisoners of war directly attributable to the acquiescence of the accused, as Commanding Officer of a prisoner of war camp, in cruel and barbarous atrocities committed by his subordinates, as well as his personal participation in brutalities against prisoners of war, I feel that the evidence warrants a more severe sentence than that imposed. In order that the accused may not escape punishment, the sentence, though inadequate, is approved and will be duly executed. Sugamo Prison, Tokyo, Honshu Japan is designated as the place of confinement.

CASE 25

Masaaki Mabuchi, age thirty-three, completed middle school and four years at Shingu Kogatu, a Shinto seminary. His vocation was that of a Shinto priest. He was drafted into the army in May 1938, commissioned in November 1939, and deactivated in September 1942. He had been in combat service in China from May 1939 until September 1942. He was reactivated in May 1944 as a captain in charge of a raid company.

Jutaro Kikuchi, age twenty-four, was an undergraduate at a higher technical school at the time of his entry into the army in December 1943. He was a probationary officer at the time of the offense with which he was charged. He attained the rank of second lieutenant.

Charges and Specifications. In May 1945 Mabuchi willfully ordered a subordinate to kill 2nd Lt. Darwin Emry, an injured American POW, by decapitation. He failed to discharge his duty as commander to provide adequate and proper medical care for Lieutenant Emry, held captive by his unit, and he failed to control and restrain his men from bayoneting and mutilating Lieutenant Emry's dead body.

In May 1945 Kikuchi, at Hiyoshi, Honshu, Japan, willfully and wantonly committed inhuman atrocities against the dead body of 2nd Lt. Darwin Emry, an American POW, in violation of the laws and customs of war, by bayoneting and mutilating said body.

Prosecution Evidence. A certified copy of a missing air crew report, originally issued by the 398th Bomb Squadron, 504th Bomb Group of the Twenty-First Air Force, was introduced in evidence. This document reported the loss of a B-29 on a mission over Tokyo on May 25, 1945. Along with this report, a deposition by 1st Lt. N. E. Churchill dated April 4, 1946, was introduced, to the effect that, of the personnel listed in the report as missing, five had been recovered and no records existed concerning the fate of the remaining six men. Among the six whose fate remained unknown was one 2nd Lt. Darwin Emry.

Staff Sgt. Francis Tourat, a member of the 361st Quartermaster Grave Registration Company, testified that on November 23, 1945, he was assigned to assist in recovering the bodies of Allied personnel believed to be buried in a Japanese cemetery near Mobara, in Chiba Prefecture. There the suspect grave was opened and six bodies recovered. All were eventually identified by dog tags, laundry marks, and other methods as the missing members of the air crew. On one body a pair of partially decomposed shorts bore the initials DTE. This body was in a moderate state of decomposition, but it could readily be seen that the head had been all but completely severed — only a small piece of skin remained at the throat. In addition ten to twelve stab wounds appeared on the back of the torso.

Capt. Donald Eramwell of the Medical Corps testified that he had examined this body at the Yokohama Cemetery on November 26, 1945, and confirmed the earlier testimony of Sergeant Tourat. Both men testified that the hands were tied behind the back and that there were strands of rope around one ankle.

Witness Minoru Moriyama testified that he was an eye doctor with the First Battalion of the 426th Regiment in the Japanese army. This unit had arrived in Mobara only a few days before May 25. A little after midnight on that date, an American B-29 crashed nearby and he was summoned to the scene by a message from Mabuchi, who was the commander of a raid company in the same outfit. He went to the Choeji Temple, where the raid company was stationed. There he found two injured American fliers. One had a head injury and the other suffered from a broken thigh, the bone protruding through the skin. The witness and one of his enlisted medics cleansed the wounds, set and splinted the fracture, put Mercurochrome on the injuries, and made a general examination, which revealed a rapid but weak pulse, indicating that the injured men were in a state of shock. Both had bled profusely after having crashed, so he injected Vitacamphor as a heart stimulant. It was the only drug available — he had no morphine to ease the pain.

He also testified that he was nervous and scared during the treatment due to the fact that he was an eye doctor and not a general practitioner or surgeon, and that he didn't feel qualified to treat the serious wounds these fliers had. However, since he was the only medical man in the command, he did the best he could. He felt that the injured men were in serious condition, and, since he was not authorized to order the men hospitalized, he wrote a report suggesting that this be done. He expressed the opinion that without further aid the fliers would die. He made his report to the adjutant but received no further orders, nor was he summoned again to attend the injured.

Tadashi Toriyama, a local farmer, testified that on the morning of May 26, he visited the Choeji Temple. There he saw two injured American fliers being treated as earlier described. He remained about fifteen minutes at that time but returned later in the day. When he returned at 10:00 A.M. one of the fliers was dead. The other was alive, his leg in a splint and his mouth very bloody and still bleeding. There were other Americans there, but they were taken away by the Kempeitai. The witness then saw Lieutenant Kikuchi, in the presence of the accused Mabuchi, take a sword and cut the neck of the injured American, so as to all but decapitate the flier.

Witness Genichiro Kawasaki, another farmer, testified that around

2:00 P.M. he saw a Japanese soldier, one of the trainees, stab the corpse twice with his bayonet in the yard of the Choeji Temple. This corpse had already had its head cut off except for a small bit of skin at the throat.

Several former Japanese soldiers in the raid company were called to testify for the prosecution and verified the previous testimonies. They admitted having participated in the bayoneting.

For the Defense. The first witness was Masanori Takahashi, the medic who attended the injured fliers with Medical Officer Moriyama. His account of the treatment was essentially the same. In addition he stated that Moriyama had a conversation with the accused Mabuchi, during which he informed Mabuchi that both fliers were in critical condition and that the one with the head wound would not live until morning. The other flier would probably die due to loss of blood. He testified that Moriyama never asked to be recalled nor did he express any intention of revisiting the injured. He also stated that there had been plenty of morphine in the dispensary when the units arrived a few days previously.

The defense then called the battalion commander, Toiso Kuba. He testified to Mabuchi's good character and his well-known kindness and humaneness. He had received a report of the beheading and regretted it, but felt that it was necessary, proper, and truly a mercy killing.

The accused Mabuchi testified in his own behalf. He confirmed other testimony that he had been informed by Moriyama that death was imminent for both fliers. He said that the Kempeitai ordered him to take appropriate action to hasten the end. He reported that death came quickly to one flier, but the other lingered in anguish, frequently raving and attempting to tear off his bandages and splints. Near noon the man's face began to blacken, and he could stand to see the man suffer no longer. He ordered the decapitation, which is a traditional form of mercy killing approved for use under such circumstances by the Bushido code—a part of the Shinto ethic. As for the bayoneting, he agreed to it only after realizing that his men, who were expecting to meet an American invasion soon in suicidal combat, had the right to, and need for, realistic experience in bayoneting the human body to build their confidence and assurance for their mission of repelling the Americans from their homeland. Although he respected the inviolability of the bodies of the dead, he believed in this instance that a body could serve a worthwhile purpose similar to that of dissecting a body for the benefit of training doctors. He testified that he later gave a fitting burial to the dead and ordered the head priest to offer prayers for the deceased over the grave.

In his own defense Kikuchi testified that he led the party that searched the scene of the crash, put out fires, recovered bodies of the dead, and captured the survivors. He took the survivors to the temple grounds and procured straw and mats to comfort them as much as possible until the doctor arrived. He confirmed the earlier witnesses' testimony, then admitted the decapitation as an act of mercy. Later, while in his quarters, he heard sounds of bayonet practice and, investigating, found several recruits bayoneting the body. He decided to bayonet it himself. He was an instructor but had never been in combat or used a bayonet on human flesh before. Accordingly he stabbed the body twice and returned to his quarters.

Other witnesses included Rev. Goro Hayashi, rector of St. Peter's Episcopal Cathedral, who explained tenets of the Bushido code and the Shinto religion of which it is a part. He testified that a Japanese who ordered such a neck cutting would be motivated by a spirit of compassion and brotherly love. Another expert on the Bushido code testified to the rightness of beheading as showing compassion. A Japanese soldier testified that many Japanese, who were in extreme pain and had no chance of recovery, were beheaded during the Okinawa campaign. This was done to prevent capture as well as to terminate their suffering.

Comments of the Court. A careful study of the conduct of the accused belies the contention that he intended to accomplish euthanasia in ordering the death of his captive. After allowing the American flier to lie on the ground for long hours without competent attention, enduring conscious agony, he ordered the killing at a time when unconsciousness had mercifully rendered the victim insensible to further pain. He permitted the execution to be held before the eyes of more than one hundred local townspeople and soldiers, many of whom applauded the action. Importance was placed on the fact that, in ordering the killing, the accused decreed that the death be accomplished by means of the artful, ceremonial method known as "Kais-Haku," which is quite difficult to perform correctly. This was alleged as further evidence that the accused was not acting in vengeance. However, it may have been selected to give additional practice and experience to the executioner or to display his technique to the crowd.

After the execution—had it been truly a mercy killing under the Bushido code—immediate measures should have been taken for proper disposal of the body. Instead the accused allowed it to be used by his men for bayonet practice. The abuse of the dead is horrifying enough if done in private, but when done publicly, the act is even more revolting. The public display—with laughter, applause, and shouts accompanying it—indicates that this procedure was not intended as bayonet practice alone but was an act of vengeance and a further inciting of national hatred.

The accused ordered the disposal of the body only after it ceased to be of further use to his troops. He ordered it to be buried. Under the Shinto ritual of killing and the usual Japanese customs, the body should have been cremated.

The conduct of both accused after the incident, and after the end of hostilities, casts additional doubt on the sincerity of their claims that they were motivated by honorable ideals. In the official report of the incident, no mention of the decapitation or bayoneting was made. Accused Mabuchi verbally reported the beheading to his superior long after the incident and, even then, made no mention of the bayoneting. After the occupation began, he made no report regarding the location of the grave to the American forces. On learning of the discovery of the bodies, he wrote to prospective witnesses and suggested what their testimony should be. When Kikuchi discovered that an investigation of the incident was being made, he denied that he had been present when the bayoneting occurred. Later he admitted that his statement was knowingly false.

These details reveal a pattern of conduct by both the accused that was scarcely consistent with their professed motives. Their actions are condemned alike by the laws and customs of war, international treaties and covenants, Japanese criminal laws, Shinto ethics, and the Bushido code itself.

Sentence. Mabuchi—Death by hanging; Kikuchi—Confinement at hard labor for twenty-five years.

In the foregoing case of Mabuchi, Lieutenant General Eichelberger wrote these comments in his review: "The sentence is approved. The crimes for which the accused has been convicted are brutal and heinous violations of fundamental principles of human decency, and are so shocking as to preclude extension of clemency. Pursuant to paragraph 5H (regulations governing the trials of accused war criminals), the order directing execution of the sentence is withheld pending the action of the Supreme Commander."

Masaaki Mabuchi went calmly to the gallows at 5:00 A.M. on September 6, 1946.

CASE 78

Toshio Tashiro, age sixty, graduated from grammar school and attended two years of high school. He joined the army on December 1, 1909, but was discharged November 30, 1910, as a superior private. He served as a civilian guard at Tokyo Military Prison from June 12, 1943, until June 1, 1945, when he returned to the army as a captain and became warden of that facility.

Hatsuaki Kambe, age thirty, had eight years of education and was a truck driver before entering the army in March 1939. He was discharged in November 1942 due to wounds received in combat. After recovering, he served as a civilian guard at Tokyo Military Prison until he was reactivated as a corporal on June 1, 1945. He continued to serve at the prison until the end of the war.

Mataishi Okubo, age thirty-three, had nine years of education and was an office clerk until he entered the army in April 1935. He was discharged in March 1937. He served as a civilian guard at Tokyo Military Prison from May 5, 1945, until June 1, when he was recalled as a sergeant major. He remained at the prison until the end of the war.

Keiji Kamimoto, age thirty, had eight years of education and was a clerk for a mining company. He served one month in the army and was discharged. He became a civilian guard at Tokyo Military Prison in September 1944. On June 1, 1945, he was reinstated as a corporal and continued his duties at the prison until the end of the war.

Masao Koshikawa, age fifty-three, had eight years of education before entering the army December 1, 1916. He was discharged on November 30, 1918, as a superior private. He started his career as a civilian guard at Tokyo Military Prison on May 8, 1920, and remained in that capacity until June 1, 1945. On that date he was made a second lieutenant and second in command at the prison, where he remained until September 1945.

The five defendants were tried together in a case that was heard by the court from March 24 until July 8, 1948.

Charges. Tashiro was charged with violations of the laws and customs of war. On May 25 and 26, 1945, he unlawfully ordered subordinates to kill any American POWs who, during an air raid and while their cells were burning, might escape from their cells, thereby causing the deaths of seventeen American POWs. He was also charged with failure to discharge his duty as prison commander in controlling and restraining his subordinates from killing seventeen POWs, and failure to provide for the safety of sixty-two American prisoners.

Kambe was charged with violations of the laws and customs of war and with willfully and unlawfully killing eight Amerian POWs.

Okubo was charged with violations of the laws and customs of war and with the slaying of three American POWs.

Kamimoto was charged with violations of the laws and customs of war and with killing six American POWs.

Koshikawa was charged with violations of the laws and customs of war and with failure to discharge his duty by failing to release, or cause the release of, sixty-two American POWs from their burning cells at Tokyo Military Prison.

On April 1 and May 26, 1945, the accused, with Tashiro as leader, organized and instigated the forming and execution of a common plan or conspiracy designed to fail to release the sixty-two American POWs from their cells at the prison in the event of a fire, air raid, or other disaster.

For the Prosecution. After the incidents of May 25 and 26, the accused, acting with common intent and design, conspired to prevent the government of the United States from obtaining true and accurate information regarding the capture, status, condition of confinement, death, and place of burial of sixty-two American POWs. At different times and places, they also withheld, concealed, and suppressed such information from the Japanese government and fabricated, or caused to be fabricated and transmitted to the Japanese government and the American occupation authorities, false and misleading information regarding these matters.

The prison personnel consisted of one commandant, eight chief jailers, and seventy jailers. At the time of the incendiary bombings, thirteen jailers were away from the prison on vacation, sick leave, or detailed to pick up additional prisoners. Another thirteen jailers were still undergoing training and had not yet been assigned to specific duties.

In October 1945 the accused Toshio Tashiro made a written report to the Japanese army concerning the deaths of the American prisoners. Part of it read:

> As it became impossible to extinguish the fire, the fire fighting activity was stopped; and at the same time a measure to evacuate the prisoners to the outside was taken. However, the enemy's attacks with incendiary bombs was extremely severe, and the violent wind increased the intensity of the fire, and the dangers were acute. Thereupon, the commandant recognized that there was no time to evacuate and ordered the immediate release of prisoners, temporarily stopping the fire fighting activities. It is thought that it was about 0130 hours of the 26th when the commandant ordered the release of the prisoners. As the majority of the prisoners in No. 2 ward were patients or weak persons, the release of these men required some time. Although only ten-odd minutes passed after the release was launched, the wooden structure, which became heated after the stoppage of fire fighting, ignited with unexpected speed. The workshops, located on the windward side, were already engulfed in frightful flames and the premises of the prison were swept by a violent wind, mingled with sparks, and it was impossible to move forward with the eyes open. Two emergency gates were located to the east,

on the windward side, and it was impossible to open them due to the violent blaze from the private houses. Meanwhile, exit was also impossible through the small gate, located to the north, on account of strong burning wind. In the end, only one prison gate remained available for escape.

Under such circumstances, attacks by the Allied planes continued and, due to the close proximity of danger, there was utter confusion in the prison and orders and instructions could not be thoroughly carried out. During this time, jailer Kamimoto, who undertook the opening of No. 4 ward in the face of violent flames, opened four cell blocks located in the central part of the ward, and the jailer Kambe indicated the direction of the gate to the prisoners. At this time, the attacks by the Allied planes became more severe, and the flames were very intense, and the men were about to fall. Just at this time, an incendiary bomb fell on No. 4 ward and its vicinity, making it impossible for them to open the remaining cells. By the time these two jailers tried to escape from the impending danger to their lives, the areas of No. 2 and No. 3 wards were already a sea of flames. Since it was impossible to get out of the prison gate, the jailers resigned themselves to death by burning. However, having remembered the existence of an unfinished cave-type air shelter at the parade ground on the premises, they barely took refuge there.

There were, at that time, 450 Japanese and 62 American prisoners confined at this prison. They were kept totally separated. The Japanese were imprisoned for such offenses as being absent from military duty without official orders, failure to follow orders, and other military related offenses. There were also several political prisoners there. All the American prisoners were airmen, or, as the Japanese referred to them, "fliers."

Tashiro's report continued, describing how the Japanese prisoners were evacuated first, because:

> It was considered that, if the suspected violators of military regulations were released to the outside alone, there was a great chance that they might be injured by the people who lost their parents or children and who were burned out of their homes by the indiscriminate bombing by Allied planes, and who were in an extremely excited state. The necessity of protecting the prisoners was recognized. However, because of the shortage of guards, the Japanese army prisoners were released first. It was planned that these men would act as guards for the other prisoners.

Most of the Americans were buried in a common grave in an air raid shelter between cell blocks 2 and 3. When they were exhumed by occupation forces after the war, many of the bodies examined had broken legs. It could not at that time be determined if the bones had been broken before or after death.

In attempting to identify the sixty-two Americans, Tashiro claimed that all the records had been burned. He made no effort to conceal dog tags, even though he did not tell where they were. American investigators found thirty-two identification tags. Most were found between the kitchen and the wall. Others were located in a pile of rubbish.

From the long list of witnesses the prosecution presented, it became quite clear that, at the time the prison burned to the ground, confusion reigned. Many of the jailers and Japanese prisoners testified. Several things began to emerge from the hearsay, rumors, guesses, observations, and opinions. Several prisoners and jailers had overheard some of the chief jailers bragging that they had "cut some Americans." Several jailers overheard Tashiro give orders that "the Americans are not to be released and, if any break out, cut them down." Numerous prisoners and jailers saw dead Americans in several areas of the prison grounds and some appeared to have been stabbed or bayoneted.

The thirty-sixth witness for the prosecution was Isamu Ishii. He was a civilian guard on duty the night of the fire and was assigned by Chief Jailer Kikuchi to guard the air raid shelter southeast of the detention ward. When the air raid warning sounded, he got keys and, on Kikuchi's orders, opened the doors of the detention ward and escorted the Japanese prisoners to the air raid shelter. He remained in the shelter for about an hour, until ordered by Tashiro to take the prisoners to Yoyogi Parade Ground. He did not know what occurred in the prison during the time he was in the detention ward and the air raid shelter.

The following testimony is an example of the kind presented at the trial:

> On the morning of May 26, about 5:00 or 6:00 A.M., I, with other guards, escorted the prisoners to the inner parade ground, and I saw three dead bodies near the inner gate. One was naked and all were burned. All of the bodies were lying face downward and the brain of one was out, as if his head had been bashed.
>
> I heard at Meguro School and the demobilization center, from Kambe and Kamimoto, that they cut American prisoners with their swords while they were in cell block No. 4.
>
> There were six recruit guards detailed to guard cell block No. 4. They alternated in doing the guarding every thirty minutes.
>
> Two dog tags were found by a group, of which I was a member, after the war in the remains of the watch room, and I heard later that other

dog tags were found there. The watch room was where the identification tags were kept.

In June 1945 Tashiro called a meeting attended by most of the prison personnel, including Koshikawa, and at the meeting Tashiro said that he took all the responsibility for the fire, and for the death of the fliers, and for the personnel to say they knew nothing about it. Another meeting was held at Nikano for the personnel not attending the first meeting, and they were instructed by Koshikawa.

It became known early in the trial that during previous air raids, the Americans had not been evacuated from their cells to a safe place. The Japanese prisoners were always evacuated. The American POWs, brought to Tokyo Military Prison by the Kempeitai, were always treated as criminals, being charged with indiscriminate bombings.

For the Defense. The defense attorneys cross-examined prosecution witnesses and produced many of their own. A complete rehash of all the details leading up to the incendiary bombing, fires, deaths, and plots to alter records was done. However, they did accomplish one very important thing to seriously damage the prosecution's case, as fully described next.

Opinion, Findings, and Recommendations. "We have been impressed by the number of witnesses who claimed that extra-judicial statements were obtained from them by threats of punishment, promises of rewards, yelling, browbeating, threats of, or downright physical violence, or other reprehensible conduct. The fact that several (28) witnesses so complained, plus the fact that there is some corroborative evidence in the record, gives credit to the claims of the witnesses. It would be better that a guilty war criminal go unpunished, than that the review authority should approve or condone such reprehensible conduct by giving evidence, obtained in that manner, fuller credit. We hold that evidence so obtained should be given very little, if any, probative value, unless same is more than colorably corroborated by other credible evidence."

This statement resulted from the actions of a very venomous American captain assigned to the case as an interrogator. He acted, and treated those he questioned, as if they were already convicted criminals, and used Kempeitai tactics to obtain answers. He was reassigned to other duties by the time this trial ended.

Tashiro, the prison commander, was found guilty only on specification 3 — that of contributing to the death of sixty-two American prisoners of war.

Koshikawa, second in command of the Tokyo Military Prison, was found guilty of specification 2 — that of gross negligence in formulating and adopting a plan, jointly with Tashiro, for the release of the American POWs in time of imminent danger, thereby contributing to the deaths of sixty-two American prisoners of war.

Kambe was found guilty of willfully killing eight American prisoners of war.

Kamimoto was found guilty of assault with a sword on an American prisoner of war.

Okubo was found guilty of the killing of two American prisoners of war while they were trying to escape the flames that destroyed the prison where they were being held.

Sentences. All the defendants were sentenced to death by hanging. When the case was reviewed by SCAP, all the sentences were commuted to life imprisonment at hard labor.

CASE 94

The trial began on May 23 and concluded June 2, 1947. The four defendants all served at Fukuaka Prisoner of War Camp Number 18 in Sasebo, Kyushu, Japan.

Sachio Egawa, age thirty-seven, completed two years of commercial school and was a barber before joining the navy on October 10, 1932. He was discharged on November 30, 1934, but was recalled September 12, 1939. He had attained the rank of petty officer by the time of his discharge on August 24, 1945.

Tokuro Fukuda, age forty-five, graduated from higher primary school and was an office worker prior to joining the navy on December 1, 1923. He was discharged on November 30, 1926, but was recalled on December 2, 1941. He rose to the rank of chief petty officer and served until the end of the war.

Denkichi Orito, age forty-eight, graduated from higher primary school and was a farmer. He served in the navy from June 1, 1919, until October 30, 1934. He reentered the navy as a chief warrant officer August 12, 1937, and served until May 30, 1940. On September 5, 1941, he was again recalled, with the rank of lieutenant senior grade. He served as POW camp commander from October 12, 1942, through March 23, 1943, and was discharged on September 1, 1945.

Fukuichi Watanabe, age fifty-eight, graduated from higher primary school and was a farmer. He served in the navy from June 1, 1907, to November of 1923. He was recalled December 10, 1940, and served until February 21, 1944. The highest rank he attained was that of ensign. He replaced Orito as camp commander on March 24, 1943, and served in that capacity until December 5, 1943.

Charges. All four were under the general charge of violations of the laws and customs of war. Egawa was charged with mistreating and abusing prisoners of war by beating them, and with contributing to the deaths of George Bailey and Lester Meyers, American POWs.

Fukuda was charged with mistreating and abusing prisoners of war.

Orito was charged with the failure to discharge his duty as camp CO and restrain members of his command by permitting them to commit atrocities and other offenses against POWs, and with failure to provide adequate food, quarters, and medical care for the POWs under his control.

Watanabe was charged with failure to provide adequate food, shelter, and medical care for the POWs in his care; with unlawfully compelling POWs to perform arduous manual labor while physically unfit to do so; and with failure to discharge his duty as camp CO and restrain members of his command and persons under his supervision, by permitting them to commit atrocities and other offenses against prisoners of war.

For the Prosecution. Evidence was introduced, by means of affidavit and statements, from former prisoners who had been interned in the camp and were in a position to know the facts of the matters at issue.

Prisoner Thompson and others were ordered beaten with clubs. The beatings were so violent that Thompson bled for three days afterward. They were punished for eating extra bread when a Japanese cook made a mistake in issuing it to them.

In August 1943 several POWs were accused of stealing vegetables from farms around the camp. One barracks at a time, the prisoners were lined up in two rows facing each other. Egawa then picked four men and ordered ten of his guards to beat them with clubs. Each man was struck about forty times. When a prisoner fell to the ground unconscious, water was poured over him. When he regained consciousness, the beating was resumed.

Prisoner Bailey was accidentally struck on the head by a hose. While he was resting from the effects of the blow, Egawa came by, placed a gloved hand on his head, and told him that he had no fever and to get back to work. Bailey died two days later.

Prisoner Fredrick E. Dyer secretly kept a diary that was used by the prosecution and is represented here in part:

> April—Three prisoners beaten for eating garbage.

May — Ordered back to work, very weak. Ten men badly beaten for trading.

June — Cook served two rations. All squads clubbed for eating same.

August — Another orgy of beating prisoners. Brutal. Japs enjoy this.

August — Another exhibition of Jap cruelty. All the barracks got beaten.

September — No. 3 squad got a beating for protesting the scarcity of food.

September — Burns and others were beaten by guards with pick handles and fists until Burns became unconscious and had to be helped to his bunk by another prisoner.

February — Thomas was beaten and kicked in the face and stomach until he became unconscious. Because he was old, sick and weak, he was unable to work. The guards told him that he "would die anyway."

April — There were mass beatings of the 250 prisoners.

May — Mass beatings of the 250 prisoners.

August — Again there were mass beatings of the 250.

October — About 200 prisoners were beaten because three of them had made cigarette lighters out of salvaged materials. These beatings were administered despite the fact that three POWs admitted having done the act.

January — Bitter cold wind, freezing hard. One more passed away at 8:15 pm, Mark Franklin, age 46. Prince of a good fellow. His death is a disgrace to Japan. Guards and officers drunk, slapping the dead and making fun of him [Franklin]. Patients all peeved but we can do nothing.

The daughter of the deceased prisoner, Frederick Dyer, testified to her father's handwriting and signature in the diary he kept while a prisoner in the POW camp.

For the Defense. Kiyoteru Nakamura was a civilian attached to the navy as the construction engineer in charge of Sasebo Naval Construction Division. He testified that if a prisoner was sick, he stayed in camp, and no prisoner died on the job. He never heard of any mass beatings or punishment at the camp. He stated that if a prisoner had a complaint, he took it to the CO or his assistant.

Nomura Tomekichi, former rear admiral in the Japanese navy, testified under oath that he knew of no POW who was beaten.

Hiroshi Kodama, a naval guard at the camp, testified under oath that he did not at any time hear or see the camp CO or his assistant beat prisoners. They were liked by both the prisoners and the guards.

Masaru Takahashi testified that he recalled Egawa slapping two prisoners for eating garbage because it would have been "a very bad situation if they got sick from eating garbage." He never observed the CO, the CO's assistant, or anyone else beating anyone. In fact, the leaders of the prison and the guards instructed him to treat the prisoners kindly.

Each of the accused testified in his own defense. They were in complete accord in their statements of lacking knowledge of anyone beating or torturing any prisoner. The CO and his assistant claimed, however, that in a few isolated instances, guards probably slapped some prisoners for rules infractions and, as leaders, they would accept responsibility.

Opinions and Findings. The record was legally sufficient to support the commission's findings.

Orito was found guilty of eleven specifications regarding the failure to restrain members of his command.

Fukuda was found guilty of four specifications involving the mistreatment of prisoners.

Watanabe was found guilty of sixteen specifications involving failure to restrain members of his command.

Egawa was found guilty of all six specifications dealing with mistreatment and abuse, and of the deaths of two prisoners.

Sentences. Chief Petty Officer Egawa was sentenced to death by hanging. Review of the death sentence by SCAP, in this case, failed to reduce the sentence, and Egawa was executed at Sugamo's gallows on August 18, 1948.

Chief Petty Officer Fukuda was sentenced to twenty years' imprisonment at hard labor.

Lieutenant Orita and Ensign Watanabe both received sentences of life imprisonment at hard labor.

CASE 154

Junsaburo Toshino, age forty-five, was a graduate of physical education school and a physical education instructor before joining the army in 1941. He attained the rank of captain before his discharge in 1945.

Shusuke Wada, age forty-three, was a business-school graduate and a civilian employed by the army as an interpreter from 1942 until the end of the war.

Kazutane Aihara, age thirty-six, graduated from middle school and was a teacher and farmer before entering the army in 1941. He served until the end of the war as a leading corporal.

Suketoshi Tanoue, age thirty, completed nine years of school and was a bookkeeper. He served in the army from 1939 through the end of the war and attained the rank of master sergeant.

Jiro Ueda, age thirty-five, had nine years of education and was a railroad worker. He entered the army in 1941 and remained a private until the end of the war.

Sho Hattori, age thirty-eight, served in the army from 1942 until the end of the war. He was a sergeant.

Charges. Toshino, as POW guard commander, willfully and unlawfully mistreated, abused, and caused intense mental and physical suffering, impairment of health, and death to approximately 1,039 American and Allied POWs by neglecting and refusing to provide adequate quarters, food, drinking water, ventilation, sanitary and hygienic facilities, and medical attention; and by refusing to provide a reasonable measure of protection from the hazards of war. He was also charged with causing the deaths of more than thirty American and Allied POWs by neglecting and refusing to restrain military personnel under his control from shooting them, and by ordering subordinates to kill fifteen sick prisoners.

Wada willfully and unlawfully mistreated, abused, and caused intense mental and physical suffering and death to more than 1,039 POWs by refusing to transmit to his superiors requests for adequate quarters, food, drinking water, sanitary and hygienic facilities, medical attention, and reasonable measures of protection. He was also charged with neglecting to restrain military personnel subject to his supervision from beating prisoners of war.

Aihara was charged with mistreating and abusing at least fifty POWs by beating them, killing fifteen POWs by shooting them, and killing eight American POWs by stabbing and decapitating them.

Tanoue was charged with killing fifteen POWs by stabbing and decapitating them.

Ueda was charged with killing fifteen POWs by stabbing and decapitating them.

Hattori willfully and unlawfully mistreated and abused 1,039 POWs by neglecting and refusing to restrain military personnel subject to his control from beating them.

Three other defendants in this case were acquitted.

Summary of Evidence. First Lieutenant Toshino was appointed guard commander in charge of about 1,619 prisoners who were to be transferred from Manila, Philippines, to Moji, Japan. He had direct control of matters pertaining to the prisoners. If at any time he was not satisfied with the accommodations, diet, or water supplied to the prisoners, it was his duty to confer with the shipmaster and obtain changes. If the ship captain refused, he was to negotiate with the liaison officer to obtain necessary supplies. The defendants Wada, his assistant and interpreter; Hattori, second in command; Aihara, third in command; and Ueda were part of the guard troops in his command during the period of December 13, 1944, through January 30, 1945.

The prisoners, 1,590 Americans and 30 British—mainly officers—were loaded aboard the *Oryoku Maru*, a Japanese transport ship, between 1500 and 1800 hours on December 13, 1944. About 550 prisoners were placed in the aft hold, 600 in the forward hold, and 400 in the cargo hold amidships. The ship was also carrying between 1,700 and 2,000 Japanese women, children, and navy personnel from sunken ships.

On December 14 the *Oryoku Maru* was bombed and strafed by Allied planes from 0800 until dark. During the night it was beached near Olongapo Naval Base. At that time the ship was evacuated except for the Japanese guards and POWs. At 0800 on the morning of December 15, the ship was bombed again. At 0830 the prisoners were ordered to abandon ship. There were several other attacks during the evacuation, until the pilots recognized the POWs and stopped the attack. The prisoners were forced to swim or use makeship rafts and, as a result, had to abandon most of their possessions. When they reached the beach, they were marched to an enclosed tennis court, where they could be easily guarded. They were kept there until December 21, when some of them were taken to San Fernando Pampanga. The rest followed the next day. They were quartered in a jail and a theater building until December 25, when they were moved by train to San Fernando La Union. There they were kept, in the open, until they boarded the ships *Enoura Maru* and *Brazil Maru* in the early hours of December 27. About 300 prisoners were loaded aboard the *Brazil Maru* at the last minute. There were no military guards except five Formosans who accompanied them on the ship. Toshino and the other members of his command were aboard the *Enoura Maru* with the remainder of the POWs. They set a course for Formosa, arriving at Takao on January 1, 1945. The two ships remained in the harbor. On January 6 the prisoners aboard the *Brazil Maru* were taken to the *Enoura Maru*. About 60 percent of the prisoners were placed in the lower hold, and the other 40 percent were assigned to the upper hold. The British prisoners left the group on January 8 at Takao. The *Enoura Maru* was bombed on January 9, and many POWs were killed. The survivors were transferred to the

Brazil Maru on January 13, and the ship set sail for Moji, Japan. When they arrived, only 581 prisoners were unloaded.

Surviving prisoners testified to the following facts:

Aihara brutally struck POW Montgomery and several other Americans with his rifle butt and a shovel while they were being loaded onto the *Oryoku Maru*. The prisoners crowded into the holds of the ship needed air and water to survive. In December there were no wind socks or ventilators to supply air. There was only a half-gallon bucket of water for the men in the middle hold, none in the aft hold, and the equivalent of one "GI tablespoon" per man in the forward hold. When complaints were made to Wada about the conditions he replied: "It is no concern of yours."

There was no water or fresh air during the day or night of the fourteenth for the men in the aft and forward holds. The temperature rose to more than 100 degrees in the forward hold. Early on the morning of the fourteenth, the hatch of the forward hold was locked and the temperature rose to 120 degrees. Toshino knew of these conditions and did nothing. The senior POW officer made complaints and requests for air and water through Wada and told him that men were dying of suffocation, but no relief was received. Many men fainted or became delirious and caused disturbances by fighting and slashing other POWs to drink blood. Some crazed men even drank urine. One POW captain was killed by fellow officers because Wada threatened to shoot into the hold if they could not quiet him down. Aihara killed one prisoner who went crazy after the bombings, and about fifty died from suffocation and dehydration.

On the morning of December 15, after the bombing, Aihara fired his rifle into the holds, killing three POWs. While prisoners were being evacuated from the *Oryoku Maru,* Toshino walked around the ship armed with a small saber and a pistol in his right hand. Eight to ten prisoners were standing by the galley eating food they found. They moved away as Toshino approached, but Lieutenant Brewster remained in the galley eating candy. As Lieutenant Brewster left the galley, Toshino apprehended him, spoke to him in Japanese, and motioned with his pistol for him to turn around. As Brewster turned, Lieutenant Toshino cocked the pistol and fired once, striking Brewster in the back of the head. He fell face forward onto the galley floor. The witness testified: "You could hear the thud as he hit the deck, and there was blood on the back of his neck." Other prisoners were in the dining room, picking up cans of Red Cross food prior to leaving the ship, when Toshino entered and shot several of them. He was also seen firing his pistol at POWs who were in the water and coming out of the holds, as was a Japanese lieutenant with a tommy gun.

Aihara shot four POWs trying to leave the forward hold and shot into the water off the starboard side of the ship.

About dark on December 24, while at San Fernando Pampanga, Lieutenant Urabe (not charged), Toshino, Wada, and Tanoue met in Kumura's office. Urabe said something to Toshino like: "Condemn the prisoners of war that would not be able to withstand the journey to capital punishment." Toshino did not oppose the statement, although Tanoue did. Urabe and Wada discussed the death certificates. Toshino then ordered Wada to "round up" fifteen of the sickest POWs by telling the POW medical officers to select the sickest to be sent back to Manila. Toshino ordered Hattori to select a squad to dig a grave and, after the grave was dug, to guard the cemetery. Toshino—with Tanoue, Aihara, and Ueda—brought the fifteen men to the cemetery by truck at 2030 hours. Toshino then ordered Tanoue and Ueda to decapitate the POWs. He also gave the order to bayonet them. Aihara bayoneted three, Ueda one, and the rest were bayoneted by persons other than the accused. Toshino waited until the grave was covered over, then returned to his quarters where he reported to Urabe that the executions were completed. He never reported the executions to anyone else.

The diary of POW Bodine states that on December 27, 1944, 236 POWs boarded the *Brazil Maru* after waiting to board the *Enoura Maru*. Five Formosan guards were assigned to take care of them. There was no food or water on the twenty-seventh, and no food on the ship available to them. There was no water on the twenty-eighth or twenty-ninth. On December 30 each man received half a cup. They arrived at Takao on December 31, and each man received three-quarters of a cup of water. On January 1, 1945, they each got a canteen cup of water, but none the next day. On the third they received two buckets of water for the entire group, eight spoonfuls per man on the fourth, and half a cup each on the fifth. On the sixth the remaining POWs were moved to the *Enoura Maru*. One man died that day.

POW Montgomery testified that there was no food on December 27 or 28. There was a little food on the twenty-ninth, but none on the thirtieth or thirty-first. On January 1, 1945, the group received a sack of hardtack and five rolls per man. After that they received a mess kit of rice for every three men. There was no water on the twenty-seventh or twenty-eighth and only one-quarter cup per man each day after that. Four men died.

POW Threatt testified that on December 27 and 28 they received only leftover food from the guards—not more than two mess kits—for his entire group. After that they got about a quarter of a mess kit of rice per day. They received an average of eight spoonfuls of water each day. Between eight and ten men died.

When POW Beecher asked Wada for water and told him that men would die without it, Wada replied, "If they die it is all right with me." Others asked for food and water and Wada's replies were "No," "Shut up," and "I don't care if you all die," and that he could "see no reason to help enemies of Japan." Several times he slapped prisoners and beat them with ropes and sticks.

The first mate of the *Brazil Maru* testified that there should have been an average of one gallon of water per day for each man during the trip, and that the water was available. He also reported that the Formosan guards contacted Toshino, aboard the *Enoura Maru,* several times daily by semaphore.

POW Speck stated in his diary that he boarded the *Enoura Maru* on December 27 with about eleven hundred other prisoners, and that the hold they were put into had recently been used to transport horses. It had not been cleaned, there were swarms of blowflies, and open buckets for latrines. Many of the men had dysentery, which spread rapidly. There was plenty of room to sit down and stretch their legs at this time. It wasn't nearly as crowded as the *Oryoku Maru.* There was some food—nothing some days and a cup of rice and some soup on others. They ate some raw millet seed left by the horses. On the trip to Takao, they received only a few tablespoons of water daily. The food and water situation did not improve while they were in the harbor at Takao. While there, fifteen to thirty men died daily.

An American plane made a direct bomb hit on the forward hold on December 9, 1945. The affiant had a leg broken during the attack. He had to set it himself with the help of friends. A Japanese medical detail came into the hold on the eleventh and dressed minor wounds but would not go into the forward hold. The affiant was moved onto the *Brazil Maru* on January 13, at which time approximately three hundred POW bodies were taken ashore at Takao to be cremated.

POW Bodine also stated in his diary that the POWs were transferred to the *Enoura Maru* on January 6, and that there were thirteen hundred POWs in one hold. They were given hot food and tea. The hold was seventy by ninety feet, and down inside the ship about fifty feet. There was a fifteen-foot balcony around the hold, about thirty feet high. The hold was extremely crowded. During the night of January 6, feces and urine dripped from the balcony, which was being used as a hospital. Two men fell and killed one of those below. On the morning of the seventh, they received four-fifths of a cup of barley, one-fifth of a cup of cabbage soup, and one-fifth of a cup of tea for every two men. This was repeated in the evening. Thirty-nine prisoners died aboard the *Enoura Maru* during the nights of the sixth and seventh. The flies were terrible, the floor sticky with feces, and there were only six buckets for more than a thousand men to use as latrines. There was some food and tea on the eighth. The men were divided; five hundred were placed in the forward hold and seven hundred in the aft hold. It was very crowded. The middle hold was loaded with bags of sugar as high as the balcony.

It was very cold during the night of the eighth, and there were riots as crazed men tried to steal water and food. Many were killed when the guards broke them up. On the ninth the POWs received one-sixth of a cup of water and barley for breakfast. The ship received a direct hit at about 1000 hours. The hatch-cover planks, men from the balcony, and tubs of water fell into the hold, killing sixteen and seriously injuring about eighty. There was little medicine and no water available. In the forward hold more than 250 were killed outright or were dying. Men started stealing sugar in an effort to stay alive. In the aft hold, the dead were piled up. On the ninth there was one meager cup of barley and some salty pickles for every three men to eat, but there was no water or tea. On the tenth it was very cold in the hold until a new hatch cover was finally installed. By now there were thirty bodies in the hold. On January 11 a five-man medical team and one doctor came into the hold and treated minor wounds. Bodine mentions here that he heard that this medical team would not go into the other hold at all and that about two-thirds of the prisoners there were dead. There were two issues of barley, soup, water, and tea on the eleventh. The liquids amounted to about five-eighths of a cup per man. The cooked barley was bad, almost impossible to eat. By now the smell from the dead bodies was very bad. On the twelfth they got chow early and the dead were removed by a detail of Japanese. More men were getting dysentery. Clothes taken from the dead were used for bandages or, when possible, were worn by the living. Feces and urine from the hospital area covered the area around the latrine and now began running into the sleeping area. Then 9 more died, and 150 men were cremated and buried in a single container. Two hundred men came from the forward hold. "We finally got a good supper—barley, fish, and cabbage salad—about two spoonsful per man." On the thirteenth they were moved to the *Brazil Maru*.

The affidavit of POW Beecher described the food situation aboard the *Enoura Maru* and the pitiful amounts issued to the POWs. The ship's galley was willing to provide much more water, but guards drove the POWs away. Toshino was responsible for this. Affidavits from other prisoners testified to similar facts. Schwartz testified that he saw five cases of Red Cross medical supplies on board. He requested them for the treatment of the wounded, but Wada claimed that no such medical supplies were available. Only after much pleading, and after several days, were Red Cross medical supplies issued. Sulfa drugs, the medicine most needed, had been removed.

POW Montgomery testified that the *Brazil Maru* left Takao on the night of January 13 and arrived at Moji, Japan, on January 29, 1945. More than 1,000 prisoners boarded the ship at Takao, but only 581 debarked at Moji. He then described the terrible conditions of the voyage. The climate grew colder as they drew closer to Japan. The POWs salvaged clothing from the dead, and these were issued to other POWs. The men huddled together for warmth. They stole Japanese mats but were forced to return them after threats.

POW Alsobrook testified that Hattori forbade him to pick up snow and eat it as a source of water, and that he was caught stealing water from a wench by a Formosan guard who beat him and POW Langlois with a rifle barrel three or four times while Hattori watched from forty feet away. The guard let Langlois go but continued to beat the witness for more than an hour, during which time his nose was broken. During the beating, he was clothed only in underwear shorts and a thin blue jacket. It was sleeting and snowing on deck.

POW Threatt also testified that he had no shoes during the voyage, but he acquired a blouse from a dead POW and his group of five men had some rice sacks to help keep them warm. They had stolen them from a pile of about a thousand. "You had to steal them as the guards wouldn't let you have any." This witness lost almost 55 pounds on the journey. Beecher lost about 40 pounds, and POW Mittenthal lost approximately 105 pounds.

For the Defense. This trial was conducted from March 10 to May 9, 1947. Each of the accused testified in his own behalf. All denied having committed any offenses against the prisoners, claimed that they did so only on direct orders, blamed it on someone else, or replied that they did not know anything about specific questions asked of them.

Both Toshino and Wada testified that Wada received the order to select the sickest POWs from Lieutenant Urabe, but that he had not mentioned that they were to be executed.

Toshino testified that he received written orders to command a guard escort from General Kou. Regulations pertaining to his duties were shown to him, and he read a report and the diary of a former guard escort commander and followed them. He wouldn't let the prisoners onto the deck because he feared that the one thousand Japanese sailors from ships sunk by the Allies would hurt them. He thought that the POWs had enough water. He never knew of any of his subordinates mistreating prisoners. He denied making some of his previous statements and said that he was too sick to make a long statement.

Wada testified that he did not have the authority to order POWs or Japanese military personnel to do anything, and that he never refused to transmit requests to Toshino. On one occasion he punished three American POWs for stealing sugar, but Toshino "got on to him" about that.

Aihara testified that he bayoneted three POWs, but that Toshino ordered it. He denied ever firing a shot into the holds where prisoners were located or shooting POWs in the water. He claimed that he never mistreated the prisoners and that 500 witnesses could be called to testify to his good character.

Tanoue testified that he treated sick POWs himself. He tried to change the order about the executions but could not. He was ordered to decapitate seven or eight of them and then told Toshino that he couldn't continue. As medical NCO he did the best he could for the POWs. He said that 350 witnesses could be called to testify to his good character.

Hattori testified about his actions at the executions. He was ordered to have a grave dug and to have his men guard it. He never authorized, permitted, or knew of any mistreatment of prisoners on any of the ships mentioned and had advised Threatt to get a life preserver before leaving the *Oryoku Maru*.

Three POWs testified that Hattori had been a supply sergeant at a POW camp in the Philippines and that he had always given the prisoners the best weight in food that he could, had never been cruel or abusive, and seemed to do the best he possibly could.

Ueda testified that at the cemetery where the executions took place, he was ordered to "thrust" the prisoners. He hesitated, then tried to bayonet a prisoner and missed. He tried again, missed, and Toshino abused him in a low voice. Toshino ordered another soldier to take his place. He then stood by a tombstone and prayed for the POWs.

POW Alsobrook testified that Ueda was liked by all the prisoners in the Philippines POW camp and that he went out of his way to help get extra food, medicine, and smuggled mail into camp. Two other POWs confirmed Alsobrook's testimony. It was stated that 2,000 witnesses could be called to testify to his good character.

Review Opinion and Findings. The special plea of the defense based on an alleged lack of venue in the commission to try the accused was denied.

The objection of the defense to the introduction into evidence of depositions and affidavits, unless the prosecution could show that the witnesses were either dead or too ill to appear, was denied. The request of the defense that the commission refuse to accept copies of prosecution affidavits for independent study by the members thereof was also refused by the court. The defense argued that the action of the prosecution in effect gave the commission a "canned case" for study, while the defense was unable to follow suit. The record shows that the prosecution used ninety-one exhibits and the defense produced thirty-five. The prosecution had eighteen witnesses who appeared before the court; the defense had twenty-one. The reviewer states: "Under the circumstances of the case, the action of the commission can not be said to be in error or to have prejudiced the rights of the accused in any way."

At the opening of the trial, the defense stated that it had not had sufficient time to translate all the affidavits to the defendants, but that the important parts had been discussed by the defense attorneys with the accused concerned. The court's offer to have the affidavits interpreted as they were introduced was waived by the defense, it being stated that the monitors of the accused would give them a running summary of the evidence that would be sufficient as long as the accused were made aware of the evidence against them.

The case was reviewed and an opinion rendered concerning the charges against the accused, along with the reasons and rules relating to findings on each specification. The court findings were then sent to the Eighth Army Judge Advocate General for further review. He summed up Case 154 in a very concise manner: "I concur in general with the statements in the review except as hereafter mentioned. Certain facts are outstanding as follows:

> At the tennis court, where raw rice was given to the prisoners to eat, the guards had cooked rice and fish. When the prisoners first embarked on the Oryoku Maru, they were all well enough to have survived a normal voyage. In the one hold which was not crowded, no death occurred. One hundred tons of water remained on the Brazil Maru upon arrival in Formosa. On the trip from San Fernando La Union to Formosa, aboard the Brazil Maru, only one Japanese died and that was from injuries. On the Brazil Maru there was food left over at its destination and plenty of water. On previous trips, no troops had died because of overcrowding. Passengers could get plenty of water from San Fernando to Takao, Formosa. The ship's captain, Kajiyama, said the use of water was never restricted on the Brazil Maru from San Fernando to Moji, Japan. The holds were filthy and could have been clean.

Wada denied requests for water and other necessities on the spot, so that it was clearly established that he failed to transmit requests for help as charged. Even though Toshino refused some requests for necessities, the pressure to act would have been brought to bear by continued frantic requests. It cannot be said that Toshino might not have eventually succumbed to the pressure, granted additional necessities to the prisoners, and thus have saved lives. The actions of Wada in transmitting requests would therefore not have been futile.

Aihara The action of Aihara shooting into a hold jammed with helpless people justifies his conviction: The two or three prisoners who first mounted the ladder in an effort to reach the deck were shot from the ladder. Additional shots were fired into the crowd below, and several were killed. No question of escape appears, as claimed by the defense, to justify this killing.

Tanoue was a Master Sergeant who knew the order to behead sick prisoners at the cemetery near San Fernando was illegal. He had heard the discussion and participated in it, during which he advocated sending the prisoners to a Manila hospital. However, it was decided that the secret murder should be accomplished. In the Japanese Army, as everywhere, an illegal order is invalid. An experienced Master Sergeant would be expected to have known this. Even if it were a valid order, the penalty for resisting was only ten years in a locale such as this, where they were not in the face of the enemy. Therefore, Tanoue may be said to have made an immoral choice to participate as the active executioner on his own responsibility. Strong mitigation, however, is apparent, from the fact that he urged against the execution. Nevertheless, he chose to participate rather than test the validity of the order.

Ueda was in a different position. He did not participate in the preliminary discussion and was merely a private ordered to bayonet the sick prisoners. This was an illegal act. The defense of superior orders is not valid except in mitigation in war crimes cases. However, mitigation is strong in a strictly "firing squad" type of action. Furthermore, it is not established that his "passes" at the two prisoners involved resulted in their death. He is therefore guilty only of assault against two unidentified prisoners of war. On other occasions he is credited with acts of kindness for which due allowance should be made.

Hattori was recognized as second in command. His most serious offense was voluntarily—on his own responsibility—preventing prisoners from saving their lives by eating snow on the decks. The excuse that the snow might be contaminated is not a defense, because the mere fact that the prisoners were so desperate for water that they tried to eat snow must have told Hattori their need for water was extreme. He had but to step to a water faucet and satisfy that need. His duty required such action. The low sentence received is apparently due to evidence of previous agreeable contacts with prisoners on other occasions.

The facts compellingly established by the evidence in this tragic and shocking tale of human depravity are such as have rarely been set down in history, or indeed, in fiction! The cruelty of Army Captain Toshino, his interpreter and right-hand man Wada, and the cruelty of Formosa-raised Aihara, records a chapter in human relations which attains a new definition of barbarity. Persons against whom such acts are proved would be meted out the most severe punishment available in any land and before any court.

The reviewer of the case, evidence for the prosecution, defense, witnesses, affidavits, depositions, and testimony for both sides demonstrated that the defendant Wada should have received a stiffer sentence.

Sentences. Toshino and Aihara were sentenced to death by hanging. Their convictions were upheld by SCAP's review, and they were executed at Sugamo Prison on August 18, 1948.

Wada was sentenced to life imprisonment at hard labor. Tanoue was to be confined to prison for twenty-five years at hard labor. Ueda received twenty years, and Hattori received ten years, both at hard labor.

Kajiyaama, Yoshida, and Kobayashi were acquitted.

CASE 186

Hisakichi Tokuda, age thirty-one, graduated from Keijo Medical College as a physician. He was a captain in the army, serving from May 1940 until April 1945.

His trial began on September 8, 1947, and ended on January 2, 1948.

Charges. All Class C war criminals brought to trial were charged with violations of the laws and customs of war. Under this charge were eleven specifications:

1. Caused the death of British POW William Holland in July 1945.
2. Caused the death of British POW Thomas Hampson in August 1945.
3. Caused the death of Italian POW Ernesto Saxida in July 1945.
4. Contributed to the death of American POW Herbert McCanst in June 1945.
5. Caused the death of British POW Walter L. Dawson in August 1945.

The other six specifications charged Tokuda with disregarding his duty as commanding officer and medical officer by refusing to furnish medicine and other necessities of survival, refusing the aid of competent, available Allied doctors, and performing medical experiments on Allied prisoners of war, thereby causing the death of at least four POWs and contributing to the death of others.

Tokuda was the senior medical officer and camp commander at Shinagawa, Japan. It was a labor camp until August 1943, when it was designated a hospital camp. It was liberated on August 29, 1945.

During the trial, the question of Tokuda's sanity was raised, and a psychiatric examination was ordered by SCAP. The accused was examined by seven psychiatrists and neuropsychiatrists, both American and Japanese. Most of these medical experts reported that Tokuda was mentally competent to stand trial. Dr. Tsuneo Muramatsu, a Japanese psychiatrist, stated that he had Tokuda under observation in his hospital for twenty days. In the report submitted to the Central Liaison Office, he claimed that "claustrophobia" was not the problem with Tokuda. The problem was a "reaction to confinement." Tokuda informed this doctor that he had attempted to strangle himself twice in Sugamo Prison since his confinement on December 8, 1945.

The commission decided that the accused "is now, and has been, mentally competent since the first day he appeared before this Commission, and this trial will continue."

For the Prosecution. John H. Williamson testified that he entered the British army in 1934. His first two years were spent in India as a line NCO. As a medical orderly he received general and field-ambulance training. He became a Shinagawa POW in November 1942 and remained there until the camp was liberated. He was made acting medical corpsman in charge of Barracks 5, a Japanese special ward supervised by Dr. Tokuda, assisted by Dr. Fujii. He remained at Barracks 5 until the end of the war. At the time of his capture, he was a corporal and was appointed acting head cook. They started manufacturing soybean milk in the camp in April 1945. He described the process: "We drew the soy beans from the kitchen and put them to steep for a period not exceeding twenty-four hours, at which time a medical corpsman, cook, and one of the Japanese civilian supervisors would make the soy bean milk by lifting the beans out of the mizu tub and put them on top of a millstone. There was a hole on the top of the stone. The stone was turned until the beans were crushed and ran out into a container. It was taken from there and put in a small boiler containing water and boiled for about fifteen minutes, taken out and put in a bucket and allowed to cool off before the POW patients received it."

Williamson continued, saying he remembered a British POW named

Holland, who was confined at Barracks 5. Tokuda's diagnosis was originally beriberi. When the patient didn't respond to treatment, Tokuda changed his diagnosis to cirrhosis of the liver and thereafter to stomach cancer. On July 9 the accused told the witness to bring him a cup of soybean milk. He then went with the accused to the operating area, where Tokuda prepared a syringe by drawing twenty cc of soybean milk into it. They then went into the ward and approached Holland. Holland told the accused that he was all right and did not need an injection. Dr. Tokuda stated: "I am a doctor. I know what is best for you." He then gave Holland an intravenous injection of soybean milk that had not been strained or filtered in any way.

When questioned about Holland's reaction, Williamson stated: "He had convulsions, worked his legs, his stomach was working and part of his chest: they were all working, and he was foaming at the mouth, but he did not lose consciousness. He had all this pain, and you could see ... even I could tell he was suffering." The convulsions continued for about six hours, after which he went into a coma. He died at 2:00 A.M. on July 10, 1945.

William Holland's death certificate was signed by Captain Tokuda on July 10. The cause of death was listed as "cirrhosis of the liver."

(Until July 1945 the orthodox method of giving "soy bean solution"—very rich in vitamin B—to the fifty to sixty patients had been by mouth.)

The American and Allied prisoners named in specifications 2 through 5 were all killed in a similar fashion. It required three intravenous injections to kill Ernesto Saxida. Saxida was one of the several Italian naval personnel at the camp who refused to swear allegiance to the Fascist movement toward the end of the war. All these men died extremely violent and painful deaths.

Major Keschner, a POW and a qualified pathologist held at Shinagawa Hospital, stated: "I know of one case of an American soldier named McCanst, a cardiac whose death might have been delayed had Dr. Tokuda called in one of our own physicians to treat this man, as this was one instance where Tokuda had no comprehension of the medical problem, and still did not ask for our aid."

Dr. Dawson-Grove testified that he treated Hampson for bilateral pulmonary tuberculosis. Shortly after Tokuda took over the barracks, Hampson developed a spontaneous pneumothorax (collapse of the lung). About a month later, tubercular pus formed in his chest, and his condition became serious. The accused would not permit the witness to see or treat him. Dr. Dawson-Grove stated: "In the beginning of July, Hampson had five or six sinuses and he slowly went downhill and died. No treatment of any sort. There was no hope for him. He had, the last part of July, an injection of the famous soy bean milk and he died. If all available facilities at the camp had been given to Hampson, he would have lived to be a free man."

Captain Mohnac, former dentist and anesthetist at Shinagawa Hospital, stated that Tokuda insisted on performing operations on prisoners who did not require surgery. He also corroborated testimony of the use of caprylic acid injections for tuberculosis, also vitamin B and sulfur-and-castor-oil injections, and the consequences thereof.

Surgeon Commander Cleave provided an affidavit stating that Tokuda slapped and beat patients and staff members with his fists, and that he once kicked Commander Cecha in the shins for no reason.

Six POWs, seven doctors, a chemist, a dentist, and a surgeon — all of whom had been at the camp — testified for the prosecution.

For the Defense. Several former Japanese army officers — major generals, colonels, majors, and captains from various medical sections testified about the ongoing research involving different solutions being injected into humans, their own past experiences, and the good results obtained. Various exhibits, papers, and articles were introduced into evidence. They dealt with the scientific findings of medical experiments using a variety of acids, vitamins, fatty acids, and soybean oil and the methods of preparation.

Arimi Hamana, president of the Hamashima Pharmaceutical Company, provided a list of drugs his company manufactured and marketed in 1939. It included Capsan, Capsan Emulsion, A-D Capsan, Kapiya, and Fukuyo Capsan. He stated that Germany was the only other country in which caprylic acid crystals were manufactured successfully for medical use.

Other witnesses and exhibits were introduced about Dr. Tokuda's qualifications.

Dr. Kyuhei Nakadate, a teacher of medical jurisprudence at Keio University Medical School, stated that in Japan doctors customarily administered treatments and injected substances that were not officially approved, and that such practices were common, though illegal. Under Japanese law consent of the patient or his family was not required.

Exhibit T was a diploma from the Seoul Medical College, dated March 20, 1940, certifying that Hisakichi Tokuda was a graduate thereof, together with a physician's license, dated May 15, 1940, signed by Japan's minister of health and welfare.

Exhibit U was a report from Colonel Sams, chief of public health and welfare — SCAP, on Japan's public health system. It stated that in the past, a certificate of graduation from a medical college allowed the legal practice of medicine and automatically granted issuance of a medical license. The looseness of medical education standards and the development of many medical schools conducting abbreviated courses, particularly during the war years, had allowed a great number of wholly unqualified persons to practice medicine in Japan. There had never been a medical licensing system in Japan until SCAP instituted one in 1946.

Other witnesses for the defense appear to have done Tokuda's defense more harm than good. Exhibit NN, an affidavit from Henry R. Hudson, claimed that he personally saw five prisoners receive the soybean milk injections and heard many POWs state that they had been injected with the same substance. Hudson, a medical orderly, claimed: "To the best of my knowledge, approximately thirty to forty POWs were given the soy bean milk treatment."

Nathan D. Teters, confined at the hospital during July 1945, stated that Dr. Tokuda injected patients with soybean oil together with other components. He was told about this by the patients who received the injections and by the senior British naval doctor and his assistant. These patients were being treated for beriberi. Six prisoners received the injections followed immediately by suffering beyond description. They lay in the hospital, paralyzed and groaning, for days.

The accused, after being advised of his rights, declined to testify.

Opinion. As to specifications 1, 2, 3, and 5: They charged the accused with causing the death of four Allied prisoners of war. The evidence established that the accused did in fact administer injections of soybean solution, as charged, and that the normal and usual method of giving this soybean milk or solution was orally. It is considered that such injections caused the death of the victims, except in the case of Saxida. The evidence indicated that the injections contributed to rather than caused his death. Reasons for this are:

1. Other victims died after one injection. Saxida received three injections, several days apart, before death occurred.
2. After the third injection, which was given in the jugular vein, a large lump appeared on his neck at the point of injection. This indicated, according to Dr. Dawson-Grove, that some or all of the injected substance had not gone into the vein but into the surrounding tissue.
3. The condition of Saxida's health was such that there was a reasonable doubt that death was caused by the injections alone.

Tokuda should have been put on his guard by the severe reactions that accompanied the first injection, but he continued to give them.

Specification 4 charged Tokuda with contributing to the death of McCanst by refusing available medicine and the assistance of competent Allied doctors, and by engaging in improper medical practices. The accused was found not guilty of improper medical practices but guilty of the rest of the charge.

McCanst suffered from a serious heart condition. Tokuda refused to permit him to have digitalis, which was prescribed for him by Dr. Dawson-Grove. He had previously been administered some and showed marked improvement. The accused did not refuse the digitalis because of a shortage of supplies but rather because he thought it was no good. There was evidence that digitalis was among the Red Cross supplies at the hospital. After the digitalis treatment was stopped, McCanst was given no cardiac medicine of any kind. Dr. Gottlieb, a cardiac specialist, was refused permission to see or treat McCanst. The evidence establishes that McCanst could have lived, at least for a longer period, had he been properly treated. Tokuda was young and inexperienced. His refusal to permit Dr. Gottlieb, a qualified heart specialist, to treat McCanst was arbitrary.

Dr. Tokuda was found guilty on six of the eleven specifications.

Sentences. Dr. Tokuda was sentenced to death by hanging at the Sugamo Prison gallows. The sentence was reviewed by SCAP and commuted to life imprisonment.

CASE 290

This case was tried in Yokohama at the Eighth Army Headquarters Building between March 11 and August 27, 1948, and involved the following Japanese army personnel, medical doctors, and staff members:

Name	Age	Education	Civilian Vocation	Rank/Years in Service
Kajuro Aihara	48	College	Electrician	Capt./1
Hiroshi Akira	54	Army college	Soldier	Col./21
Kyusaku Fukushima	49	Army college	Soldier	Maj. Gen./29
Shinju Goiyama	43	Eight years	Farmer	Capt./3
Shiro Goshima	28	Medical college	Doctor	NA
Goichi Hirako	61	Medical college	Medical Professor	NA
Kenichi Hirao	38	Medical college	Doctor	Capt./3
Masazumi Inada	51	Army college	Soldier	Lt. Gen./35
Shoshin Ito	54	Law college	Lawyer	Maj. Gen/NA
Toshiyuki Kubo	27	Medical college	Doctor	NA

Reiichiro Makino	32	College	Researcher	NA
Yoshio Mori	37	Medical college	Doctor	NA
Kenji Morimoto	37	Medical college	Doctor	1st Lt./7
Nobuyoshi Nogawa	28	Medical college	Graduate student	NA
Miki Ryu	38	Medical college	Doctor	NA
Yoshinao Sato	40	Army college	Soldier	Col./12
Yoshitaka Senba	28	Medical college	Graduate student	NA
Jiro Tashiro	32	Medical college	Doctor	NA
Tomoki Tashiro	29	Medical college	Assistant doctor	1st Lt./6
Taro Torisu	41	Medical college	Doctor	NA/3
Shizuko Tsutsui	31	Medical college	Nurse	NA
Katsuya Yakamura	43	Army college	Soldier	Lt. Col./18
Isamu Yokoyama	57	Army college	Soldier	Lt. Gen./36

An additional seven Japanese were in this trial. They were army officers — a major general, a lieutenant colonel, two captains, and a second lieutenant — who were doctors, and two dentists not in the military forces. All seven were acquitted.

This is the record of the trial of Kajuro Aihara and twenty-two others. This summary describes the events and atrocities and covers all the evidence in support of and in defense of the charges and specifications of which the twenty-three accused were found guilty.

The specifications against the various accused were concerned with one continuous event, or a related series of events, in which military and civilian personnel participated and cooperated with each other. It is suggested that this summary, although arranged to set forth the evidence in support of the various specifications, should be read as if the events were all alleged under one specification.

This trial of Aihara is real, but is presented here as the format for the entire group of accused. The entire group will be recorded in a single table after the specifications are presented.

Summary of Evidence. The following American prisoners of war were members of B-29 crews who were shot down over the island of Kyushu, Japan, in April, May, and June 1945. S. Sgt. Billy J. Brown, 2nd Lt. William R. Fredricks, S. Sgt. Teddy J. Ponczka, 2nd Lt. Dale E. Plambeck, Cpl. John C. Colehower, Cpl. Leon E. Czarnecki, Cpl. Robert B. Williams, Sgt. Jack V. Dengler, Cpl. Irving A. Corliss, Pvt. Merlin R. Calvin, 2nd Lt. Jack M. Berry, and Sgt. Charles Palmer were captured and held at Western Army Headquarters located near the city of Fukuoka. Of these prisoners, eight were sent to Kyushu Imperial University. One had a slight chest wound. All eight were subsequently killed by vivisection.

Specification 1: Kajuro Aihara was in charge of POW affairs. Kormori (allegedly deceased) informed him of the experimental operations performed on POWs and that other prisoners would be released for similar operations.

Eight American POWs were operated on and died after having injections and anesthetic administered to them at the Kyushu University Hospital. Four series of operations were performed, during which the fliers were killed. The first operation occurred on May 17, the second on May 23, the third on May 28, and the fourth on June 2, 1945.

On May 17 Probationary Officer Komori took one airman to Kyushu University. Later, on orders of accused Sato, vehicles were dispatched to take other fliers to the same destination. Sato and Komori advised Ishiyama (deceased) that the accused Yokoyama had given his permission to perform experimental operations on the captured fliers. Komori further stated that he had the "necessary understanding" to operate on the enemy airmen. The accused Goiyama ordered trucks dispatched to transport fliers, on instructions from Sato, although Sato did not have authority to release the fliers for the operations. In his own statement Goiyama admitted that he knew the fliers would not return.

The adjutant section controlled the detention barracks and vehicles at Western Army Headquarters. Goiyama was responsible for the housing and feeding of prisoners of war, but he did not keep records. The accused Sato, Yakamura, Aihara, and Komori were present when the POWs were taken from Western Army Headquarters to Kyushu University and were present in the dissecting room of the hospital when the vivisection of the airmen took place. Aihara told Goiyama to release POWs to Komori for treatment. After the first series of operations, Komori made the statement that at least two of the prisoners died and that he had taken blood from them with which he would made a bedbug poison. Later Komori made arrangements to bring other POWs to Kyushu University for vivisection.

The granting of permission for the removal of a POW from Western Army Headquarters to a civilian hospital was accomplished by a conference between the chief of staff and the chief of the medical section. They would then make arrangements with the appropriate service of the hospital. Orders for the release of POWs for hospitalization came from the chief of staff to the adjutant section. After conferring with the chief of the legal section, the prisoners were escorted from the detention barracks to the hospital.

Komori and Ishiyama frequently came to army headquarters to confer with members of the medical section. Komori was allegedly injured in an air raid on Fukuoka City on the night of June 19, 1945, and died a few days later. Ishiyama definitely died. He was one of the few who succeeded in committing suicide while held in Sugamo Prison.

Yokoyama, as commanding general of Western Army Headquarters, had the responsibility of seeing that all POWs were properly cared for. There were thirty-one POWs on May 1, 1945. Sato stated that at the end of the war, the prisoners were executed without trial. Yokoyama was the only officer at Western Headquarters who could issue such orders.

The accused Akira apparently knew about the release of the fliers and was one of the officers dispatched to transport prisoners to the hospital. Sato informed him of the experimental operations. He said nothing. Sato asked permission of the accused Yokoyama to execute the first prisoners. Yokoyama granted it. Akira also told subordinates, who assisted with transporting prisoners, not to talk about the matter to anyone.

Sato selected the names of the prisoners of war who were released to Kyushu University. He gave the list to Aihara, who, in turn, gave the list to Goiyama. Sato instructed Aihara to keep the list a secret.

Komori, Ishiyama, Makino, Hirao, and Mori were in the dissecting room when the operations were performed. Ishiyama was in charge, with Komori as first assistant. Hirao and Mori passed instruments to Ishiyama. The nurse, Tsutsui, stood by and monitored the patient's condition. Operations were performed on the lungs, liver, brain, stomach, and heart. Parts of the organs and a quantity of blood, drawn from the femoral artery, were removed while the airmen were still alive. After the lung resection, Ishiyama reopened the incision and untied the arteries, causing hemorrhage and death.

Hirao admitted to assisting in some of the operations. At the brain operation he sawed the skull and handled the ligatures.

At different times in May and June, Tsutsui ordered nurses of the First Surgical Clinic, Kyushu University Hospital, to prepare instruments for the experimental operations and to keep the operations a secret.

Hirako, director of the Anatomy Institute and custodian of the dissection room, approved the use of the dissection room for the operations and was present for at least two of them. Afterward he directed subordinates to clean up the room and prepare the bodies for cremation.

Sato, Yakamura, Nogawa, Goshima, Hirako, Kubo, Tomoki Tashiro, Jiro Tashiro, and Ryu were present at the operations. Even though it was extremely improper for a surgeon to continue to participate in an operation that he knew to be experimental, Mori and Hirao removed the stomach of one POW. Morimoto was an observer. Mori performed one heart operation with Makino and Hirao as assistants. Nogawa held the lamp for some of the operations. He and Senba arranged the room prior to the operations.

At the operation in which the femoral artery was cut and the blood drained, Senba injected seawater into the POW's veins. Hirao assisted Komori in this operation.

The first operation was on the lungs. The second series of two operations was on the brain and stomach. The third series of three operations was on the liver, arteries, stomach, and heart. The fourth series of operations was on the lungs and brain.

Specification 2: The accused willfully and unlawfully killed eight American POWs by vivisection.

Specification 3: Hirako directed that certain parts of the bodies of the POWs be removed after their deaths. Makino removed parts of the heart and liver. Goshima removed parts of the wrist and kidneys, while two others removed parts of the intestines, stomach, liver, bladder, suprarenal gland, spinal cord, nerve ganglion, heart, and brain of other POWs. Hirako observed the vivisections and directed his assistants to obtain certain specimens. Tanake (not accused) also removed parts of the bodies under the direction of Goshima. Makino and Ryu assisted with the dissection and removal of body parts. Ryu injected Mueller's solution into the brain before removing it. The head of one POW was removed. Komori took a liver and a quantity of blood to Kaikosha Hospital and stated that he had taken it from one of the POWs.

Morimoto observed others performing an autopsy on one POW while an operation on another was in progress.

Specification 4: The accused willfully and unlawfully maltreated and desecrated the bodies of eight American POWs by mutilating, dissecting, and removing parts of the bodies.

Specification 5: The accused, acting jointly and in pursuance of a common intent and in conjunction with others, willfully and unlawfully prevented the honorable burial of eight deceased American POWs by mutilating, dissecting, removing parts from, and otherwise desecrating the bodies.

Specification 6: This specification is similar to specification 5 but deals with personal and direct involvement of the accused.

Specification 7: On two occasions in May 1945 the accused Goiyama asked for two guards who did not talk too much to guard the prisoners of war that he was taking from the detention barracks. Aihara directed Goiyama to send POWs to Kyushu University and instructed the guards not to mention taking them there.

On one occasion Komori and Aihara went by army truck to Kyushu University, with a prisoner who had a leg injury. On another occasion Aihara, Yakamura, Sato, and Komori were present when POWs were taken from Western Army Headquarters by truck. On other occasions Aihara directed other POWs to be taken to the university. All the POWs taken to the university appeared to be in good health. They did not need medical or surgical treatment and were able to walk into the operating room unaided. The organs that were removed did not appear diseased. Prior to his death Dr. Ishiyama stated that he examined the lung of one POW and found it to be normal.

There were no medical histories, X rays, blood types, or other records for the POWs who were involved.

Specification 8: The accused denied the prisoners POW status and failed to recognize and treat them as such.

Capt. Marvin S. Watkins, pilot of a B-29 that crashed on Kyushu in May 1945, testified before the commission that POWs were taken to Western Army Headquarters, confined in the stockade, placed in a small cell, and kept handcuffed and blindfolded. His testimony was corroborated by other witnesses. Captain Watkins and Sergeant Ponczka, also a POW, had to sleep together in the barracks to keep warm as no bedding was provided to them. In the cell where the POWs were kept, there was only a small box for sanitary purposes, in spite of repeated requests to the guards. No medical attention was given to Sergeant Ponczka, who had been injured by a bamboo spear. Only a rice ball and a few pieces of daikon radish were provided for each meal.

The prisoners were informed that they were not considered POWs. They were captured enemies of the Japanese and would be held in confinement pending trial by a military tribunal. The adjutant section, headed by Goiyama, was responsible for maintenance of the barracks and providing food and clothing. A report was made to headquarters about the name, age, and offenses charged against each prisoner. This report eventually reached the minister of war through the commanding general of Western Army Headquarters. Those who were not to be prosecuted were released from the detention barracks to a detention camp near Fukuoka Army Detention Barracks. It was supervised by Sato and higher ranking officials. During a meeting at which Sato was present, Shoshin Ito, chief of the legal section, reported to the commanding general about the fliers held at the barracks that since the staff section was to take "proper measures," the legal section would not interfere. "Proper measures" was interpreted to mean that the fliers could be executed without trial.

No captured airmen were considered prisoners of war until after the

Kempeitai investigated. The results of their investigation determined whether the airmen were classified as POWs or war criminals. War crimes suspects, under provisions of the "rule for army military tribunals," had no rights under international law. A military tribunal was established at Western Army Headquarters in April 1945 for the trial of airmen suspected of war crimes. However, no American airmen were ever tried before it. In his testimony Sato stated that instructions from Tokyo stated that the fliers "were to be properly disposed of" at Western Army Headquarters. He construed this to mean that they were to be killed. Fukushima announced that the captured fliers would not be called POWs but "enemy fliers." The proposal to kill the fliers without an investigation by the Kempeitai or trial by military tribunal came from Sato and was approved by Yokoyama.

Yokoyama issued orders to dispose of all personal articles. Aihara was responsible for impounding the prisoners and removing their personal effects. Aihara arranged for all personal effects that were not of intelligence value to be thrown into the sea.

The bodies were cremated and the ashes kept at Kyushu University until they were disposed of. No efforts were made to mark or preserve the remains of the POWs. The ashes of some were mixed with those of Japanese dead as part of a plan to conceal the facts.

Specification 9 (and Subspecifications 9A Through 9E): These specifications deal with preventing the POW Information Bureau of the Japanese government and the United States from having accurate identification of the eight POWs; failure to maintain accurate data about the capture, hospitalization, status, and death of the eight POWs; failure to transmit information, transmitting false information, and acting jointly in an effort to falsify records and cover up the atrocities with which they were charged.

During the night of June 19, 1945, there was an air raid on the city of Fukuoka, Japan. Yakamura submitted to the War Ministry a report written by Aihara and approved by Sato, claiming that fifteen enemy fliers had been killed in the air raid. Fukushima, Yokoyama, and Ito knew that the report was false since no POWs were killed that night. After the war Sato went to the Prisoner of War Information Bureau and removed this report.

On August 15, 1945, the detention barracks were torn down and burned in an effort to conceal English writing on the walls. This was ordered by Fukushima, Ito, and Sato after efforts to remove the writing proved futile.

Aihara kept a list of the names of prisoners sent to Kyushu University.

The Trials

After the war this list was burned, as was the report that Sato took from the War Ministry. Ito was informed of the destruction of both.

On August 20, 1945, there was a meeting between Sato, Yakamura, and Fukushima regarding the matter of concealment of the Kyushu incident. There was a decision to report that some of the airmen had been sent to Tokyo and lost in a plane crash at sea, that some of the deaths were caused by a suicide squad, and that some prisoners had been sent to Hiroshima. It was intended that some ashes would be obtained to use in the concealment plan.

In September 1945 Sato informed Aihara of the plan of concealment and that, in the event of an investigation, the Kyushu University incident was to be kept secret. It was to be said that the fliers sent to Hiroshima had died there in the atomic bombing. Aihara would claim to have escorted them there. Inada knew and approved of this plan. Ashes of the fifteen airmen were actually buried in the army cemetery.

A POW investigation committee composed of the accused was formed in November 1945. In January 1946 Fukushima reported that everything had been taken care of. In February 1946 a report was made to the occupation forces about POWs held at Western Army Headquarters that did not include the Kyushu University atrocities. The officer responsible for signing the death certificates did not sign them. Three copies of false reports were sent to Kurume and Fukuoka CIC and the U.S. Military Intelligence Branch of the CIC in December 1945.

Inada knew of the executions and did not want to conceal them. However, he and Sato both wanted to conceal the Kyushu University incident because of the shame and dishonor it would cause Japan. Fukushima stated that it would be better not to report the dispatch of the fliers. He and several others of the accused agreed that if caught, they would place the blame on Komori since he was dead.

Findings. All the suspected war criminals listed were found guilty of violations of the laws and customs of war. Under this general charge were nine specifications, explained earlier in this case. The findings specific to each accused were listed as follows:

Name	Specification								
	1	2	3	4	5	6	7	8	9
Kajuro Aihara	G	NG	G	NG	G	NG	G	G	G
Hiroshi Akira	G	NG	G	NG	G	NG	G	G	G
Kyusaku Fukushima	NG	NG	NG	NG	NG	NG	NG	NG	G
Shinju Goiyama	G	NG	G	NG	G	NG	NG	NG	NG

Name	Specification								
	1	2	3	4	5	6	7	8	9
Shiro Goshima	NG	NG	G	G	G	G	NG	NG	NG
Goichi Hirako	G	G	G	G	G	G	G	G	G
Kenichi Hirao	G	G	G	G	G	G	G	G	G
Masazumi Inada	NG	NG	NG	NG	NG	NG	NG	NG	G
Shoshin Ito	NG	NG	NG	NG	NG	NG	NG	NG	G
Toshiyuki Kubo	G	G	G	G	G	G	NG	NG	NG
Reiichiro Makino	NG	NG	G	G	G	G	NG	NG	NG
Yoshio Mori	G	G	G	G	G	NG	NG	NG	NG
Kenji Morimoto	G	G	G	G	G	G	NG	NG	NG
Nobuyoshi Nogawa	G	G	G	G	G	G	NG	NG	NG
Miki Ryu	NG	NG	G	G	G	G	NG	NG	NG
Yoshinao Sato	G	G	G	G	G	G	G	G	G
Yoshitaka Senba	G	G	G	G	G	G	NG	NG	NG
Jiro Tashiro	G	G	G	G	G	G	G	G	G
Tomoki Tashiro	G	G	G	G	G	G	NG	NG	NG
Taro Torisu	G	G	G	G	G	G	G	G	G
Shizuko Tsutsui	G	G	G	G	G	G	G	G	G
Katsuya Yakamura	G	NG	G	NG	G	NG	NG	G	G
Isamu Yokoyama	G	NG	G	NG	G	NG	G	G	G

Sentences. Akiro Ito, Shinchiro Matake, Tayura Oda, and Hiroonaga Tsurumaru were acquitted. They had been charged with cannibalism but were found not guilty due to lack of evidence. Also acquitted were Kiyoma Horiuchi, Tatsuro Kishi, and Iichiro Jin.

Ryu, Tsutsui, Goshima, Inada, and Makino received sentences of three, five, six, seven, and nine years, respectively, at hard labor. Shizuko Tsutsui was known at Sugamo as "Suzi." She was a civilian nurse and kept Tokyo Rose company in the female prison.

Goiyama and Shoshin Ito both received terms of ten years in confinement at hard labor. Fukushima, Tomoki Tashiro, Kubo, and Jiro Tashiro were sentenced to Sugamo for terms of fifteen years at hard labor. Aihara was sentenced to twenty years, and Hirako and Nogawa both received twenty-five years at hard labor.

Those accused who received life sentences at hard labor were Akira, Morimoto, Senba, and Yakamura.

Five men received sentences of death by hanging. They were Hirao, Mori, Sato, Torisu, and Yokoyama. When these death sentences were reviewed by SCAP, all were commuted to life imprisonment.

This case drew considerable attention from the Japanese press. Many letters were received by the Eighth Army Military Tribunal expressing gratitude for the fairness and legality of the trial. Several are presented here.

Mr. Ogawa and others wrote concerning Nogawa:

> We learned from the newspaper that the above person was tried as one of the accused in the Kyushu University vivisection case, and sentenced to twenty-five years' hard labor by the Far East Military Tribunal. This vivisection incident is a fateful and barbaric conduct which surprised the whole world, and it is beyond conception by civilized individuals. It is only natural for you to deal severely with such war criminals, who are enemies of humanity. We desire that they be dealt with severely. As the saying goes — right prevails in the end. The greater East Asia war, which was instigated by Japanese militarists, has caused the downfall of Japan to the Allied forces who have a high regard for righteousness, freedom and humanity.

Mr. Yoshido stated:

> I beg to say that I deeply regretted to learn that Taro Torisu was sentenced at the Yokohama Tribunal on August 27, 1948, to hang for his role in the Kyushu University vivisection case.
> Before the eyes of the world I feel thoroughly ashamed for this disgraceful conduct of our countrymen. I am very grateful for the generous manner in which your nation has instructed our confused nation in the way of love and humanity, and I firmly believe that your decision was perfectly fair.

Mr. Maeda and other former classmates of one defendant wrote:

> It is only natural that the defendant received capital punishment for his participation in that unsavory incident in which a number of U.S. military men, unfortunately captured during the Pacific war, were vivisected. Such conduct is to be lashed out against as an unexcusable sin against God and man. We, fellow alumnae of the defendant from middle school, can not but help feeling a profound regret for such an incident.

CASE 304

Kurataro Hirano and Yoshitaka Kawane were confined to Sugamo Prison on December 26, 1945, and January 21, 1946, respectively. Their joint trial was conducted from June 7 to June 30, 1948.

This case deals with those who were primarily responsible for the thousands of atrocities committed during the Bataan Death March.

During World War II, American and Filipino troops—first under the command of Gen. Douglas MacArthur, and later under Gen. Jonathan M. Wainwright—made a stand against overwhelming Japanese forces between January 2 and April 9, 1942, on the Bataan Peninsula. After the fall of Bataan, the Japanese commander, Lt. Gen. Masaharu Homma, ordered the prisoners of war to march from Mariveles—at the tip of Bataan—some seventy miles to the San Fernando prisoner-of-war camp in the interior. General Homma estimated that there would be approximately 25,000 Filipino and American prisoners. In actuality there were 76,000 prisoners to be moved. Homma turned the responsibility over to his transportation officer, Maj. Gen. Yoshitaka Kawane.

General Homma was completely occupied with capturing Corregidor, the last fortress before the Philippines fell to the Japanese. It was two months before he learned that more American and Filipino soldiers died on the march than on the battlefields of Bataan.

Along the route hundreds of famished, poorly clothed, and fever-stricken prisoners perished. The Japanese guards committed many atrocities. Along one two-and-a-half mile stretch of road, sixty-two bodies were found. From the 76,000 that began the march, only 54,000 reached Camp O'Donnell. Many escaped, but no one will ever know the exact death toll. Between 7,000 and 10,000—about 2,550 of them Americans—died of malaria, dysentery, starvation, beatings, bayoneting, and executions.

Hirano was commanding officer of the Sixty-First Line of Communications Unit of the Japanese Army in the Philippines from December 22, 1941, and served directly under the accused Kawane. On April 5, 1942, Kawane gave Hirano the responsibility of moving American and Filipino prisoners of war from Balanga to Camp O'Donnell. Hirano was also responsible for the operation of prisoner-of-war camps O'Donnell and Camanatran until December 1942.

Charges. Specification 1 dealt with atrocities committed between April 9 and April 27, 1942, near the Bataan Peninsula, Luzon, Philippines. The accused Hirano was charged with disregarding and failing to discharge his duty by ordering, causing, and permitting the infamous Bataan Death March—actually a series of death marches in which thousands of American and Filipino POWs were forced to march long distances from Bataan to San Fernando and Pampanga even though transportation was available. During the march Hirano unlawfully permitted and condoned the following atrocities:

Specification 1A: The brutal mistreatment and killing by bayonet and shooting, without cause or trial, of Sgt. Joe R. Vaughn, Colonel

McConnel, Pvt. John Osowaki, Pvt. Robert Baldwin, Pvt. Harry La Chance, Capt. David Miller, 2nd Lt. Glen Shaffner, and numerous other helpless and defenseless American and Filipino officers, enlisted men, and unarmed civilians. Many of these POWs were killed outright when, because of illness, disease, or exhaustion, they were unable to continue the march.

Specification 1B: Inhuman treatment of numerous American and Filipino officers and enlisted men by burying them alive.

Specification 1C: Mistreatment and torture of American and Filipino prisoners of war by requiring them to be exposed to the hot sun for prolonged periods without any protection.

Specification 1D: Deliberate failure and refusal to furnish adequate and available food, water, shelter, and medical attention to the POWs; beating, bayoneting, and shooting them when they stopped to secure food by the roadside, depriving them of their shoes, and forcing them to walk barefoot after their feet were cut and bleeding.

Specification 1E: Exposure of the POWs to artillery fire from Corregidor by halting them near Japanese artillery positions, which resulted in the death of many American and Filipino prisoners.

Specification 1F: The systematic stealing, robbing, and looting of personal belongings such as money, jewelry, blankets, cigarettes, cameras, and other articles from the POWs.

Specification 1G: Inhuman confinement of POWs in various camps and compounds along the line of march, particularly at Lubac, where several thousand of them were herded by force into a sheet-metal-roofed warehouse inadequate in size to contain them, thereby causing intense suffering.

Specification 1H: Transporting POWs from San Fernando, Pampanga, to Capas, Tarlac, in sealed boxcars so insufficient in size that many sick and diseased prisoners were forced to stand from early morning until late afternoon with inadequate ventilation, sanitary facilities, food, and water, thereby compounding their illnesses, resulting in the death of many.

Specification 2: Between April 1 and August 1, 1942, while at POW Camp O'Donnell, the accused, charged with the supervision, supply, transportation, welfare, custody, and administration of American POWs, unlawfully failed to discharge his duty by permitting and sanctioning the brutal mistreatment, killing, and deliberate neglect of prisoners of war as specified.

Specification 2A: The failure and refusal to provide adequate food, water, clothing, shelter, hygiene, and available medical supplies, thereby contributing to the sickness, disease, suffering, and death of 1,548 American and 5,000 Filipino POWs.

Specification 2B: Compelling American POWs under his command to perform manual labor while sick, diseased, and physically unable to perform such labor.

Specifications 2C(1) through (10) dealt with the killing of fifteen prisoners of war, mostly American officers, by shooting, and the mistreatment and torture of two American colonels.

The list of specifications against Yoshitaka Kawane read the same as those against Kurataro Hirano, his subordinate.

Summary of Evidence. The prosecution used testimony from witnesses, reports, affidavits, depositions, letters, and other material from the Bataan Death March survivors during the trial. They used testimony of survivors obtained during the trial of General Homma in the Philippines.

On April 9, 1942, the commanding general of the Fourteenth Japanese Army issued orders to the accused to receive all POWs at Balanga, transport them from San Fernando to Camp O'Donnell via the Fourteenth Army Railway, provide medical treatment and food to the Japanese line troops as well as the prisoners, and for all units to work together to facilitate a smooth operation.

The defense reported that the Japanese seriously underestimated the number of prisoners that would be taken, and that the American and Filipino troops had been on reduced rations due to lack of food prior to the surrender of Bataan. They argued that medical supplies were also in short supply and that the men were suffering from vitamin deficiencies.

The defense stated that the reasons prisoners of war were shipped to rear areas were to avoid enemy artillery fire on the POWs, to get them away from the malaria-infected areas of the Bataan Peninsula, and to avoid trouble for POWs from Japanese line troops who had strong hostile feelings about the Americans.

Opinion and Findings. The prosecution introduced evidence by affidavits, statements, excerpts from the record of trial in the case *United States v. Masaharu Homma* and others, photostatic copies and extracts of official records and statements, and other documents. In addition they introduced eight witnesses who testified before the commission. Five of these witnesses identified prosecution exhibits and three were former POWs who had either participated in the death march or had been a prisoner in one of the camps.

At the end of the prosecution's case, the defense made a motion for a finding of not guilty, which was denied. They then introduced seventeen exhibits, four of which were affidavits and were identified by the affiants; one witness who testified directly before the commission; copies of charges and specifications in five other cases; an extract from the record of the Philippines Campaign; two extracts from the Homma trial record; and an extract from the text of General MacArthur's message to Congress.

The decision in this case was based on the doctrine of command responsibility that had been passed upon in numerous other cases tried in Yokohama, Japan, by the reviewing authorities.

Hirano was found guilty on twenty-one of twenty-four specifications. Kawane was found guilty on 26 of 36 specifications.

Sentences. Both Hirano and Kawane were sentenced to be hanged by the neck until dead. They were executed at Sugamo on February 12, 1949.

CASE 329

This case was tried from June 22 to July 6, 1948, and involved the following Japanese navy personnel:

Yutaka Odazawa, age thirty-nine, was a lieutenant junior grade with seventeen years of service.
Kaoru Okuma, age thirty-five, was a lieutenant commander with nine years of service.
Naotada Fujihira, age thirty-seven, was an ensign with twenty-six years of service.
Kiyohisa Noto, age forty-six, was a captain with twenty-five years of service.
Tsunehiko Yamamoto, age twenty-eight, was a lieutenant with two years of service.

Charges. On May 27, 1944, 2nd Lt. Robert Thorpe, an American pilot, was shot down over Kairiru Island, New Guinea. He swam ashore and was captured by the Twenty-Seventh Special Naval Base Force, a Japanese unit stationed there. He was brought to headquarters, interrogated, beaten, used as a target for pistol practice, and beheaded.

For the Prosecution. About noon on May 27, 1944, a messenger arrived at headquarters and announced the capture of the American flier. Noto directed Okuma and an assistant to conduct the interrogation.

Specification 1: Six Japanese naval personnel stationed at the base testified that the American POW was slapped and beaten about the head during the interrogation and that his face was bruised and bleeding. After the interrogation was completed, Okuma turned to the Japanese personnel witnessing it and announced that anyone who wanted to beat the prisoner could do so. Most of the enlisted men rushed in and began beating the prisoner with fists and wooden sticks.

Noto testified that he had given Okuma instructions to interrogate the prisoner but gave no order for him to be beaten. He realized that the beating was wrong and that he should have stopped it.

Fujihira stated that he struck the prisoner several times with his open hand, that Okuma told him that the prisoner was going to die anyway, and that noncommissioned personnel, officers, and civilians could beat the prisoner. These beatings lasted from five to ten minutes and the prisoner's temples were cut and his face was bleeding.

Specification 2: Okuma reported the interrogation to Noto. Noto then told him to "dispose of this prisoner of war." After lunch Okuma and Yamamoto, followed by Odazawa with his sword, returned to headquarters. Sato, the admiral and commanding officer, asked who was going to execute the prisoner, and either Okuma or Yamamoto replied that Odazawa was going to do it.

After more discussion Noto turned to Okuma and said: "Take the prisoner somewhere and do away with him any way that you want." The meaning was clear: He was to be executed. It was a direct order. Nothing was said at the time about whether the prisoner was to be shot or beheaded. Yamamoto and Okuma wanted to shoot the prisoner, and Noto said that would be acceptable. Several minutes later Odazawa arrived at headquarters and was informed that Okuma had left to execute the prisoner, and that he was looking for a volunteer to perform the decapitation. Odazawa said that he wanted to cut him and left immediately.

Okuma returned to the air raid shelter where the prisoner was being held and gave orders to the enlisted men to lead the flier to the area where the execution was to be held. Odazawa, with his sword, accompanied them. When they arrived at the execution area, the grave was already prepared. The prisoner was led near the grave and left standing.

Okuma was the senior officer present and directed the proceedings. He approached Odazawa and asked him to wait a moment before beheading the prisoner as he wanted to practice shooting with his pistol. Odazawa agreed to wait and Okuma fired at the prisoner's left foot. He had intended to hit the ankle but missed. Yamamoto then fired two shots at the prisoner's legs but also missed. Fujihira than said, "You have not done a good job. I'll show you how to do it, as I am an expert." He fired one shot at the ankle and the prisoner staggered. He had been hit in the left leg below the knee. Two other officers fired; one hit the prisoner in the stomach and the other missed. Odazawa said to shoot the prisoner below the hips, because if he was shot above the hips he might die. More shots were fired and the prisoner fell to his knees.

Odazawa then poured water on the prisoner's neck and his sword. He struck one blow to the back of the prisoner's neck. The head was not completely severed, but was hanging by a small bit of flesh. The body fell into the grave and was covered over with dirt.

After the execution Okuma and Yamamoto reported to Sato and Noto at headquarters that they had shot the POW and that Odazawa had beheaded him.

At a conference in October 1945, Sato and Noto ordered all the participants to maintain silence concerning the execution at Kairiru and, if questioned, to state that the prisoner had died of disease.

For the Defense. Captain Noto testified that he told Okuma to interrogate the prisoner and that he made a report to Admiral Sato. Shortly thereafter Sato ordered the execution of the prisoner. Noto stated that he protested the order to Sato, saying that it was not right to execute the prisoner. Noto said that the admiral did not listen to his protests but explained: "I have recently been back in Japan and I have the latest knowledge on the handling of POWs. Those fliers who took part in the air raids on the mainland of Japan have been executed and, under the present circumstances, the Amerians have landed in the western areas — Hollandia and Aitape. The execution of the prisoner cannot be helped." He was a staff officer and would have been sentenced to death if he had not carried out the orders of the commanding officer.

Noto also claimed that he had not heard that the flier had been beaten or shot until he was imprisoned in Sugamo Prison. At the time of this trial, he was serving a twenty-year sentence for his conviction in another war crime case.

Okuma stated that Noto had ordered him to conduct the interrogation. The prisoner's answers were not to the point, so he struck him once with an open hand. When the interrogation was over, someone stepped up and said: "Let me strike him." He did not stop others from beating the prisoner.

All the accused testified in their own behalf. All blamed others, downplayed their own part in the execution, claimed that they did not remember, or blamed their part on direct orders from superior officers.

Admiral Sato was never brought to trial. He committed suicide during the Battle of New Guinea.

Opinions and Findings. The accused were all ably represented by both American and Japanese counsel and had been advised of their rights.

They cooperated fully in their defense. All testified and were given opportunities to present witnesses in their behalf. There was no evidence that any of the accused were insane or otherwise incompetent at the time of the trial or at the time the offenses were committed.

Okuma, Yamamoto, and Fujihira all admitted to beating the prisoner.

The evidence established that Admiral Sato ordered Noto, his chief of staff, to have the prisoner executed. Noto protested but was overruled by Sato. He then transmitted Sato's order to Okuma. Odazawa was designated as executioner. Noto pleaded guilty, hoping his plea of superior orders would be considered by the court.

It was established that Okuma did order, direct, and permit the unlawful killing of the POW. He was the senior officer at the scene of the execution. His plea of superior orders, after pleading guilty to the charge, was entered in the hope of consideration by the commission in mitigation of punishment.

"Okuma, Yamamoto and Fujihira all left for the execution area with the common purpose of participating in the execution. All had their pistols with them. All participated willingly. All aided, abetted and took advantage of an opportunity to torture their victim by using him for pistol practice before he was killed.

"Odazawa consented to the brutal act and informed the shooters to shoot low so as not to make the beheading difficult. The pitiful prisoner might have been spared these last moments of torture had Odazawa seen fit to protest."

All the accused were found guilty.

Sentences. Noto was sentenced to twenty years' confinement at hard labor. Odazawa, Fujihira, and Yamamoto received life imprisonment at hard labor. Okuma was sentenced to death by hanging. He was executed at Sugamo Prison on May 28, 1949.

CASE 339

This case named forty-four individuals. The trial was held at Eighth Army Headquarters in Yokohama, Japan. It began on July 12 and was concluded on December 28, 1948.

Name	Age	Education	Rank/Years in Service
Hisashi Ichioka	56	Naval college	Vice admiral/34
Hisashi Mito	57	Naval academy	Vice admiral/34
Teruhisa Komatsu	60	Naval academy	Vice admiral/39
Tasuku Nakazawa	55	Navy staff college	Rear admiral/34

Noboru Ishizaki	56	Naval academy	Rear admiral/34
Shojiro Iura	47	Naval college	Captain/25
Chojuro Takahashi	49	Naval academy	Captain/23
Yasuo Fujimori	42	Naval academy	Commander/21
Hajime Nakagawa	47	Naval academy	Commander/26
Toshio Kusaka	45	Naval academy	Commander/20
Nobujuki Tadaki	59	Naval academy	Captain/32
Shoichi Kawakami	30	Naval academy	Lieutenant sr grade/8
Sadao Motonaka	27	Naval academy	Lieutenant/3
Masonori Hattori	26	Naval academy	Lieutenant/3
Motohide Yanabe	26	Navy engineering school	Sublt/5
Shozo Anaguchi	35	Navy submarine school	Warrant officer/10

In addition to the above, twenty-eight other navy officers were indicted. They were acquitted.

Charges. All were charged with violations of the laws and customs of war.

Specification 1: The accused, all officers of the Naval Ministry, Naval General Staff, Sixth Fleet submarine squadrons, commanders of submarines, or members of submarine crews of the Imperial Navy stationed at Tokyo; Truk Island; Kwajalein Island; Penang, Malaya; and diverse other places in the southwest Pacific and Indian Ocean areas, acting jointly and in pursuance of a common intent, willfully and unlawfully planned and conspired with each other and with others to beat, rob, torture, and kill all survivors of torpedoed and destroyed Allied vessels including, but not limited to, the United States SS *Jean Nicolet,* SS *Richard Hovey,* SS *John A. Johnson,* and SS *William K. Vanderbilt;* the British SS *Daisy Moller,* SS *British Chivalry,* MV *Sutlej,* SS *Ascot,* SS *Nancy Moller,* and SS *Nellore;* the Dutch SS *Tjisalak;* and the Norwegian MV *Scotia,* and with a common purpose and intent ordered, directed, caused, permitted, and participated in the shooting, mistreatment, and killing of more than eight hundred identified and unidentified prisoners of war and survivors of the torpedoed and destroyed Allied vessels and otherwise particpated in this unlawful plan and conspiracy from and after March 1, 1943.

The accused agreed and conspired with each other to conceal said acts and to prevent the imperial Japanese government and the governments of the Allied nations from obtaining accurate and proper information about the capture, identification, robbing, beating, torture, and killing of more than eight hundred survivors of torpedoed and destroyed Allied vessels and failed to maintain adequate records and withheld, concealed, and suppressed knowledge relative to the above matters and composed fabrications designed to deceive and mislead the said governments relative to these prisoners of war and survivors, and published fabrications to various representatives and agencies of the said governments.

Specification 2: The accused failed to exercise their respective duties to restrain their subordinates from ordering, directing, permitting, and otherwise participating in the beating and torture of said prisoners of war.

Specification 3: The accused, all officers or members of submarine crews of the Imperial Japanese Navy at Penang, Malaya, and other places in the Indian Ocean areas between March 1, 1943, and August 15, 1945, deliberately and feloniously beat and tortured identified and unidentified survivors of torpedoed and destroyed Allied vessels.

Specifications 4–14: Essentially the same as specification 2; however, they deal with specific and individual accused listed in this case.

Summary of Evidence. At the outbreak of the war, Japanese navy regulations provided for compliance with the rules of warfare. On January 3, 1942, Adolf Hitler of Germany, in the presence of Foreign Minister Ribbentrop, met with Japanese Ambassador Oshima, a Class A war criminal. Hitler explained to Oshima that no matter how many ships the Americans had or could build, one of their big problems was providing trained personnel to man them. For this reason American merchant vessels were being sunk without warning in order that all crews possible would perish. Hitler believed that once the word spread that most Allied seamen were being lost to torpedoes, America and its allies would have problems recruiting replacements to man their ships. He stated that because they were fighting for their survival, no humanitarian policies should be practiced. He had given orders that *no* seamen were to be taken prisoner. The submarine crews were to fire on all lifeboats. Oshima had been empowered by his government to discuss the conduct of the war with the Reich foreign minister. He agreed with the views expressed by Hitler and stated that they were forced to follow the methods outlined by him. Oshima and Ribbentrop discussed the German U-boat order that forbade the rescuing of survivors. Oshima conveyed this information to the Japanese naval authorities. The result of the Hitler-Oshima conference was Naval General Staff Directive 107. It abolished Directive 60, which had provided for the protection of prisoners of war.

A top-secret document, the First Submarine Force Order, was issued on March 20, 1943, over the name of the accused Mito as commander of the force. Instructions were given as follows: "Do not stop with the sinking of enemy ships and cargoes. At the same time that you carry out the complete destruction of the crews of the enemy ships, if possible, seize part of the crew and endeavor to secure information about the enemy."

The Trials

The order for the killing of survivors of sunken ships in the Indian Ocean came from the Naval General Staff, through the Sixth Fleet, to the Eighth Submarine Squadron. It was dated March 1, 1943. Takahashi, senior officer of Sixth Fleet Headquarters, said that the order was verbal and was carried to him by Captain Kanaoka, chief of the Eleventh Division, First Section of the Naval General Staff. Komatsu was commander, Ishibashi was staff officer, and Shimamoto was chief of staff of the Sixth Fleet. They all received this order. Shimamoto reprimanded the accused Katsuto, commanding officer of the Fourteenth Submarine Flotilla, for being too lenient to survivors. He told him that the survivors must be killed. Accused Ichioka was instructed by Nakazawa to "completely dispose of survivors."

In March 1943 all submarines were ordered to mount 7-mm light machine guns, on the pretext that they were to be used for antiaircraft purposes. Since these guns were useless for that purpose, they were obviously meant for killing survivors of sunken ships.

The Dutch ship *Tjisalak* was sunk in March 1944 by the Japanese submarine E-8. The commander told his medical officer that the Naval General Staff had ordered that all survivors of sunken ships be slain.

In August 1943 accused Ichioka ordered Otani, commander of submarine E-3, under the command of accused Ishizaki as commander of the Eighth Submarine Squadron, to execute all survivors except high-ranking officers or technicians from whom they could gather information.

Fourteen ships were torpedoed and sunk in the Indian Ocean in 1943 and 1944. The following six examples of ship sinking, personnel abuse, and atrocities are presented here exactly as they were recorded as evidence for the prosecution in this case. They are representative of the sixteen exhibits presented at the trial.

Atrocities to Survivors of the SS Jean Nicolet

Attacking Submarine E-8

In July 1944, the submarine E-8 sank the Nicolet. This sinking was "the same story" as the sinking of the Tjisalak three months earlier. Eighty or ninety survivors were ordered aboard the submarine. They were stripped of all their belongings except for their clothing, were bound and sent forward, under guard, to sit on the submarine deck. After the Master and other prisoners had been taken below, the rest of the survivors were brought one by one and shot to death, bayoneted, or clubbed and slashed with swords. An endeavor was made to execute all of the prisoners except the Master and one Mr. O'Gara. Some of the survivors were forced to run a gauntlet of eight or nine men, and were hit by the butts of guns, heavy instruments, bayonets, etc, and forced into the water with their hands tied. Evidently the members of the submarine crew believed that they had detected enemy aircraft by radar and, though many of the survivors were still sitting on deck with their hands tied behind their backs, the submarine submerged. One seaman managed to untie his hands and another had a pocketknife hidden in the waistband of his pants. They untied and cut the bonds of about fourteen others. The empty lifeboats were machine gunned. Sixteen of the crew were presumed dead, two members determined dead, and eleven were known as survivors, according to an official document from the Navy Department, Bureau of Naval Personnel.

Atrocities to Survivors of the SS Sutlej
Attacking Submarine E-27 or E-37

The Chief Engineer states that after the Sutlej had been torpedoed by a submarine, identified as a Japanese ocean-going type, there was no time for them to get one of the lifeboats away. Several rafts floated off the ship as she sank. The Third Engineer and the affiant swam together to a small raft. One seaman was on it. They picked up several survivors. Ten minutes later, the submarine surfaced. It came near the raft and a line was thrown to them. A submarine officer inquired whether the Master was on the raft. After some questioning, the submarine personnel cut the raft adrift, circled, and returned to ram it. Fortunately, the only damage sustained was a dent in one of the buoyancy drums, as the raft was brushed aside by the bow wave as the submarine steamed past. Previously, sporadic bursts of machine gun fire from the submarine had been directed towards the raft and the survivors in the water. Eventually, there were seven persons on the raft and the affiant could not pick up more because the submarine separated them as she steamed between them. Through hearsay, this affiant learned that the Fourth Engineer, while sitting with a number of other survivors on two rafts tied together, was deliberately rammed by the submarine. Again no serious damage was done to either raft. The submarine remained in the area for about an hour, intermittently firing at them with the machine gun. The Second Engineer underwent the same treatment: his raft was drawn beside the submarine, he was questioned, cut loose and then fired upon with the machine guns; and others on the raft jumped into the water and kept moving the raft around in order to keep it between them and the submarine, which made an effort to ram the raft. It was so small that it merely rode the bow wave. After the submarine had disappeared, these survivors managed to get in touch with two larger rafts carrying the Fourth Engineer, Fitzpatrick, and about

The Trials

ten others. Fitzpatrick told him that the submarine had rammed his rafts and damaged one of them.

Atrocities to Survivors of the SS Ascot
Attacking Submarine E-37

When the SS Ascot was torpedoed on 29 February 1944, the survivors managed to get one raft and two boats safely into the water. The submarine then steamed toward them, and a man on the conning tower, obviously Japanese, hailed them in good English. He asked for the Captain and Chief Officer and was told they were both dead. He asked for the wireless operator and they said he also was missing. These were untruths. The next time the survivors saw the Captain, he was on the submarine carrying his briefcase. He evidently was being forced to identify the Chief Officer, which he did. After the Chief Officer signified that Captain Travers was the Master of the ship, he was allowed to go back to his boat. The submarine then rammed and sank the Captain's lifeboat and the Captain was thrown into the water by one of the Japanese crew. When this affiant saw them transfer a machine gun from the starboard to the portside of the conning tower, he realized their intentions and six or seven of the survivors jumped into the water. The submarine then began machine gunning the men from the Captain's boat in the water, the Chief Officer's boat, and the raft. All of the men who remained on the raft were killed outright or died from their wounds. The survivors remained in the water while the Japanese machine gunned them continuously for two hours. All those who were left, including the Captain, climbed back into the one remaining boat, or onto the raft. The affiant noticed that the Captain was sucking blood from his hands. He was told afterwards that before throwing him into the water, the Japanese had cut his hands. The lifeboat took the raft in tow but after a short time, the rope parted. The affiant saw the submarine again steaming towards the raft and jumped into the water. There was more machine gunning. More men were killed and some seriously wounded. Shortly thereafter, the submarine steamed away. Two days later, the survivors discovered a lifeboat which carried one survivor, a gunner by the name of Hughson. Hughson informed them that after the submarine had ceased firing at the raft, it attacked the lifeboat. All of the occupants with the exception of Hughson had jumped into the water and were never seen again. There were only eight survivors from the Ascot.

Atrocities to Survivors of the SS Nancy Moller
Attacking Submarine RO-110

On 18 March 1944, the Nancy Moller was torpedoed and sunk. The Chief Engineer stated that Chief Gunner Fraser, two Chinese and two

Indians were taken aboard the submarine. He heard the Japanese officer shouting in English to the Chief Gunner, asking him if he was English. He also heard him give the order to shoot the Chinese. Fraser was taken to the conning tower and the affiant did not see him again. The two Chinese were shot and fell into the sea. The submarine then half-submerged and the two Indians were washed into the sea. This affiant saved one of the wounded Chinese and the two Indians. The Chinese man had been shot in the chest and eventually recovered. When the submarine was about two hundred feet away from the raft, it opened fire with a machine gun. The Chief Engineer was the only one wounded — on the thumb of his right hand. The affidavit of Able Seaman Gun Layer Fryers states that twenty minutes after the Nancy Moller had been sunk, he sighted a submarine on the surface about a half mile away. At this time, there were not more than twenty survivors on the three rafts. The submarine was manned by Japanese. Fraser was taken aboard, walked forward to the conning tower and taken into the submarine. The two Chinese and two Indians were taken on top of the submarine. Their raft was allowed to drift away. The last he saw of the two Chinese and two Indians was when they were sitting forward of the conning tower. Soon after Fraser had been taken into the submarine, he heard the sound of machine gun fire. He had noticed two machine guns at each side of the conning tower before being taken down into the submarine. After thirteen days, Fraser was put off at Penang. Three members of the crew of the Nancy Moller provided a list of missing personnel.

Atrocities to Survivors of the Tanker British Chivalry
Attacking Submarine E-37

On 22 February 1944, the British Chivalry was torpedoed and sunk. One of the survivors stated that while he was in a motor lifeboat with twenty-five to thirty persons, the submarine approached to within approximately a half mile and commenced firing machine guns at his lifeboat, and at another which carried the ship's captain. About thirty rounds were fired. When the persons on the submarine were asked what they wanted, one of them shouted, "Captain, captain." The Captain's boat then went alongside the submarine and he was taken aboard. While picking up Third Mate Dahl, who was in the water, the submarine also fired again at the two lifeboats with three or four machine guns. Everyone dived over the side away from the submarine until it passed, continuing its fire as it did so. For the next hour and a half to two hours, the submarine cruised up one side of the lifeboat and back on the other side opening fire with three or four machine guns each time. One of the lifeboats sank after the submarine had fired at it. On one occasion, the submarine came so close it knocked against the lifeboat. Some of the members of the crew were floating away from the boats, as if they were dead, and there were several bodies of members who had been shot, floating on the surface. The water was covered with oil from the ship, and red patches of blood. This affiant believes that twelve to fourteen members of the crew were deliberately killed by the machine guns and five were wounded. A roll call indicated that thirty-eight members of the crew had survived. The Master stated that upon boarding the submarine, he was immediately taken below. He also heard machine gunning which went on intermittently. When he remonstrated with the interpreter about this act, he was informed that he was also to be killed as soon as they finished the interrogation. During the questioning, on two occasions, he was beaten on the head with a heavy ruler for giving wrong information. The first occasion was when they asked him for the ship's call sign. When he gave a false answer, he was immediately beaten because they had an admiralty list of international call signs. On the second occasion, he was asked for the *secret* call sign and gave a false answer. He was beaten again because they knew the secret call sign, having apparently picked it up from an intercepted radio transmission. After two hours of questioning, he was taken out of the salon flanked by the officer in charge and two Japanese sailors with "tommy guns." As he passed through the control room to the foot of the conning tower, the Japanese crew pulled imaginary guns from their pockets and put them to their heads to indicate his fate. He was taken to the deck of the submarine and told to face the conning tower. Two machine guns were trained on him as the officer came forward to secure the blindfold. He awaited his execution, but after some minutes, he heard footsteps approaching. The blindfold was removed and he faced the Commander, who asked the Master if he was married. He answered in the affirmative. He then asked how many children he had and, when the Master answered five, a smile illuminated the Commander's face; and it is to this incident that the Master believes he owes his deliverance. Some ten minutes later, he was taken below and placed in a room close to the engine room. The Commander told him that it was his home. After forty-three days, on the 5th of April 1944, the submarine arrived in Penang.

Atrocities to Survivors of the SS Daisy Moller
Attacking Submarine RO-110

After the Daisy Moller was torpedoed, the Master in a boat with about thirty-five men was fired upon by another Japanese submarine using tracer bullets. The submarine moved ahead of them and, increasing speed, turned in a full circle, to ram them amidships. The boat was cut in half. Immediately thereafter, the submarine made a half-circle to bring machine gun fire upon the men in the water. After firing continuously for three to four minutes, the submarine moved off toward another boat and fired on it. The submarine then approached a third lifeboat, rammed it broadside and machine gunned the men in the water.

In almost every incident of ship sinking, survivor abuse and killings, the respective government of the ship's flag protested to the Japanese government, through the Swiss Legation in Tokyo. The Japanese either denied that such an incident ever happened or they affirmed that all Japanese warships, ships, and boats rigorously observed the laws of war.

The treatment of captured survivors held as prisoners of war was almost as bad as any atrocities mentioned in any of the trials.

Francis O'Gara convinced the submarine captain that he was an American counsul and this saved him from being killed. He was kept in a tiny cell aboard the submarine RO-110 for forty-four days. He was beaten, kicked, and harassed by crew members at all hours of the day and night. The worst beating he received was when the submarine arrived at Penang. He was given a "going-away" present by each crew member. They knocked him down and, after they tired of picking him up only to knock him down again, tied him to a litter to prevent him from falling. He estimated that he received the equivalent of two days' normal rations during the forty-four days he spent aboard the submarine. At Penang he was confined to a small cell from August 15 to September 15, 1944. He received several beatings, witnessed numerous others, and was aware that there were executions of prisoners. There was very little food and no medical attention.

Whenever atrocities were committed on such a scale, there were always survivors, making the job of covering up events, altering data, falsifying records, and concealing information practically impossible for the perpetrators.

As soon as the war ended, the Naval General Staff and the Navy Ministry decided not to answer any questions about the Allied protests involving the actions of their submarines. A conference, chaired by Mito, was held in the Navy Ministry toward the end of September 1945. Katsuta reported that Allied broadcasts revealed that many crew members of the sunken ships had survived. This would make continued concealment impossible. Katsuta was overruled by other naval officers present, who were determined that the facts would remain secret. Carrying out this decision meant that the dates of submarine patrols were falsified and the documents, logs, and records of the submarines involved were destroyed. All this was done on Fujimori's authority.

The accused Yanabe stated that before June 1946, he was ordered to the Investigation Division of the Second Demobilization Ministry and questioned by Fujimori. He was told not to provide any information about his experiences in the Indian Ocean, especially anything pertaining to Submarine E-8. Fujimori believed this to be important because the patrol route of Submarine E-8 was being questioned. Yanabe was informed that, should he divulge certain facts, the submarine officers would have to be tried as war criminals and would receive death sentences. He was told to keep quiet "for the honor of the Japanese Navy." He agreed to Fujimori's proposal because he was frightened. Later he decided to tell the truth.

For the Defense. Isokichi Nishikawa testified for the defense. He was stationed in Penang from April 1943 to February 1945, was employed by the German Embassy, and was assigned to the German submarine base as an interpreter. He reported the locations of German submarine bases, when they were established, and said they were responsible for sinking more Allied ships in the Indian Ocean than the Japanese submarines, and that they brought in "one or two" prisoners of war.

Chikao Yamamoto was assigned to Naval Department Headquarters, Naval General Staff, from January 20, 1943, to January 5, 1945. In his affidavit he stated that the Naval Department consisted of six sections under the command of a chief and vice chief of Naval Department Headquarters. Every order issued to the commander in chief of the combined fleet had to be approved by the emperor. During this assignment, no order to assassinate survivors of sunken enemy ships was ever drafted, and he never received any report from the Eighth Submarine Squadron members indicating that enemy survivors were killed in the Indian Ocean.

Sadatoshi Tomioka testified that from October 1940 until early January 1943, and again from December 1944 until the termination of hostilities, he was assigned to Naval Department Headquarters and to the Naval General Staff. No orders were issued orally to the commander in chief of the combined fleet, and he never received reports from the Eighth Submarine Squadron stating that survivors of sunken ships were killed in the Indian Ocean.

Thirteen other witnesses testified. Some were among the accused, and others were officers and civilians who had been assigned to the Communications Department. All testified to having no knowledge of written or oral orders being received relating to the killing of survivors of sunken ships.

Opinion and Findings. There was a common plan and conspiracy for the destruction of enemy personnel that was initiated at a conference between Adolf Hitler of Germany and Ambassador Oshima of Japan in the presence of Reich Foreign Minister Ribbentrop. Oshima conveyed the decision to annihilate survivors of sunken ships to the Japanese naval attaché. The evidence shows that the Naval General Staff passed the order on to subordinates, orally and secretly, and finally, that it was published by the First Submarine Force as an order on March 20, 1943, according to a Japanese document captured at Kwajalein.

The following chart shows the verdict handed down by the tribunal on each specification charged against the defendants:

Name	Specification			
	1	2	3	4
Hisashi Ichioka	G	NG	NG	G
Hisashi Mito	G	NG	NG	NG
Teruhisa Komatsu	G	NG	NG	NG
Tasuku Nakazawa	G	NG	NG	NG
Noboru Ishizaki	G	NG	NG	NG
Shojiro Iura	G	NG	NG	NG
Chojuro Takahashi	G	NG	NG	NG
Yasuo Fujimori	G	NG	NG	NG
Hajime Nakagawa	NG	G	NG	
Toshio Kusaka	NG	G	NG	
Nobujuki Tadaki	NG	NG	NG	G
Shoichi Kawakami	NG	NG	NG	G
Sadao Motonaka	NG	NG	G	
Masonori Hattori	NG	NG	G	
Motohide Yanabe	NG	NG	G	
Shozo Anaguchi	NG	NG	G	

The record was legally sufficient to sustain the findings of the commission as to each of the accused. There were no errors that injuriously affected any of the accused.

"It is considered that these accused have been found guilty of some of the most heinous, barbaric, sadistic and brutal mistreatments of prisoners in the history of war crimes, which have been tried by the commissions in Yokohama. Willful and wanton murders were committed by some of them under the orders of others of the accused. Helpless prisoners were beaten, clubbed, and thrown in the ocean, with their arms tied behind them, to drown. As a result of the order to annihilate, one submarine commander, now deceased, even went so far as to execute a woman who was a Red Cross worker. Crimes of this type are so foul that it does not require rules of conventions to implant it in the mind that they are wrong."

Sentences. Ichioka—twenty years' hard labor; Mito—eight years' hard labor; Komatsu—fifteen years' hard labor; Nakazawa—ten years' hard labor; Ishizaki—ten years' hard labor; Iura—six years' hard labor; Takahashi—one year hard labor; Fujimori—four years' hard labor; Nakagawa—eight years' hard labor; Kusaka—five years' hard labor; Tadaki—ten years' hard labor; Kawakami—eight years' hard labor; Motonaka—seven years' hard labor; Hattori—five years' hard labor; Yanabe—seven years' hard labor; and Anaguchi—two years' hard labor.

THE SENTENCES

Even today it is impossible to read the judgment of the IMTFE and not be amazed at Japan's spiritual and moral disintegration during the decade prior to the attack on Pearl Harbor. It presents a detailed account of the slow and determined seizure of all branches of the government by the military leaders for the purpose of preparing the minds of the people for military rule and war. The judgment shows how the tentacles of the military, aided by a few civilian leaders, strangled public opinion and the government completely. The statement on page 986 of the findings sums up the overall judgment quite well: "We have come to the conclusion that the charges of conspiracy to wage aggressive wars have been proven and that these charges are criminal in the highest degree."

Class A

The section of the judgment dealing with conventional war crimes — the cruel and inhuman treatment of prisoners of war and civilians — covers more than forty pages. International laws govern the treatment of POWs, and Japan had officially agreed to adhere to the Geneva Convention of 1929. Although the judgment did not specifically charge any of the Class A war criminals with participating in the commission of these crimes, they were unable to escape being implicated in them. The judgment held "that Japan, between 1931 and 1945, had freely practiced torture, murder, rape, and other cruelties of the most inhumane and barbarous character as State policy, to make her aggression so brutal and savage that the will of the people to resist Japan would be broken," and that "during a period of several months the tribunal heard evidence, orally or by affidavit, from witnesses who testified in detail to atrocities committed in all theaters of war on a scale so vast, yet follows so common a pattern in all theaters, that only one conclusion is possible — the atrocities were either secretly ordered or willfully permitted by the Japanese Government or individual members thereof and by leaders of the armed forces."

It did not matter where you were if you were a prisoner of war. In Manchuria, China, Thailand, Indochina, Korea, Japan, Java, New Guinea, or any of the islands in between, you could expect similar treatment; the commanders of the POW camps had all received their training and instructions at the same school. The four main methods of torture were exactly the same wherever they were inflicted. (The school had to have military budgeting and blessing to exist in the first place.)

Each of those sentenced to death was charged either with count 54 — conventional war crimes, atrocities — or count 55 — disregard of duty to prevent breaches of the laws of war. The "Rape of Nanking," the Siam-Burma Railway, and the Bataan Death March are probably the only large-scale Japanese atrocities remembered from World War II. However, the IMTFE records listed the locations and dates of seventy-four large-scale massacres conducted by the Japanese army outside China alone, as evidence that these atrocities resulted from decisions made by the military and were part of Japan's war strategy. Most of these atrocities were ordered by officers who included many high-ranking generals and admirals.

Seven of the twenty-five war criminals were sentenced to death by hanging. In Japanese fashion, Tojo bowed to the judges after receiving his sentence. Itagaki showed disdain for his death sentence with a sneer. Four ex-generals in addition to Tojo and Itagaki received death sentences. They were Doihara, Matsui, Muto, and Kimura. One civilian, ex–Ambassador Koki Hirota, was also sentenced to death. Togo was sentenced to twenty years, and Mamoru Shigemitsu received seven years — the lightest sentence handed down to any of the Class A criminals. The rest of the convicted war criminals received life sentences, to be served at Sugamo Prison.

Of the seven to be executed, only Matsui, former commander in chief in central China, received this sentence because he failed to keep his troops under control during the Rape of Nanking.

MacArthur — designated as reviewing officer of the proceedings — began making preparations for this duty in advance of the tribunal's judgment. As SCAP he was also the agent of the eleven-nation Far East Commission, which was represented in Tokyo by the Allied Council for Japan. Both comprised the same nations represented at the IMTFE. William J. Sebald chaired the Allied Council for Japan and was MacArthur's civilian political adviser.

This council met in MacArthur's office. Each member was asked to review and comment on the sentences and make recommendations. MacArthur's decision would be based on those comments. In his memoirs,

The Sentences 123

With MacArthur in Japan, Sebald described the meeting and recommendations:

> On the day for review, representatives of the other ten FEC nations gathered somberly in a large waiting room in the Dai Ichi building. The usual friendly banter of assembled diplomatic colleagues was missing when I led them into MacArthur's office. The General greeted each diplomat as he entered the room, which was lined with chairs facing the big uncluttered desk. When all were seated, MacArthur returned to his leather chair, gravely looked at us and briefly sketched the purpose of the meeting. He asked each man for comment on the sentences. I was called upon first, presumably on the theory that I would set the pattern by being succinct and unequivocal. Loudly and clearly I said: I have no change to recommend.
>
> These were the other recommendations:
>
> Mr. Patrick Shaw of Australia—No change, but would not oppose reduction in sentences.
> Mr. E. Herbert Norman of Canada—Not opposed to reductions in sentences.
> Gen. Shang Chen of China—No change.
> Lt. Gen. Z. Pechkoff of France—Officially, no change; personal appeal for clemency.
> Mr. B. N. Chakravarty of India—All death sentences to be commuted to life imprisonment.
> Baron Lewe Van Aduard of the Netherlands—Mitigation of sentences: Umezu and Hata, life to 20 years; Shigemitsu, 7 to 2½ years; Togo, 20 to 10 years; Hirota, death to life imprisonment.
> Sir Alvary Gascoigne of New Zealand—No change.
> Dr. Bernabe Africa of the Philippines—No change.
> Lt. Gen. K. N. Derevyanko of U.S.S.R.—No change.
> Sir Alvary Gascoigne for the United Kingdom—No change.

On November 29 and December 2, 1948, defense attorneys filed motions with the United States Supreme Court on behalf of the seven condemned war criminals. As they had done during the trial, the defense based their motions on the hope that MacArthur had exceeded his authority. On December 7 the Supreme Court voted five to four to hear the case. This caused a sensation in Japan. The Japanese expressed admiration of and bafflement over America's legal system. On December 20, after three days of deliberation, the Court voted six to one that "the courts of the United States have no power or authority to review, to affirm, set aside, or annul the judgements and sentences.... The motions for leave to files petitions for writs of habeas corpus are denied."

Sugamo Prison, Tokyo

Sadao Arika. (Courtesy Jack D. Coleman)

Okinori Kaya. (Courtesy John L. Ginn)

Akira Muto. (Courtesy John L. Ginn)

Shunroku Hata. (Courtesy John L. Ginn)

126 Sugamo Prison, Tokyo

Kenji Doihara. (Courtesy John L. Ginn)

Heitaro Kimura. (Courtesy John L. Ginn)

Seishiro Itagaki. (Courtesy John L. Ginn)

Kuniaki Koiso. (Courtesy John L. Ginn)

Iwane Matsui. (Courtesy John L. Ginn)

Takasumi Oka. (Courtesy John L. Ginn)

Jiro Minami. (Courtesy John L. Ginn)

Hiroshi Oshima. (Courtesy John L. Ginn)

Naoki Hoshino. (Courtesy John L. Ginn)

Koki Hirota. (Courtesy John L. Ginn)

Kingoro Hashimoto. (Courtesy John L. Ginn)

Koichi Kido. (Courtesy John L. Ginn)

Mamoru Shigemitsu. (Courtesy John L. Ginn)

Teiichi Suzuki. (Courtesy John L. Ginn)

Shigetaro Shimada. (Courtesy John L. Ginn)

Shigenori Togo. (Courtesy John L. Ginn)

Toshio Shiratori. (Courtesy John L. Ginn)

Toshijiro Umezu. (Courtesy John L. Ginn)

Kenryo Sato. (Courtesy John L. Ginn)

Kiichiro Hiranuma. (Courtesy John L. Ginn)

The day after the Supreme Court decision, December 23, 1948, the executions were scheduled to begin at 12:01 A.M. MacArthur sent a letter to each member of the Allied Council giving the date of the executions and requesting: "Inasmuch as the executions will carry out in pertinent part the judgement of the Allied Powers represented on the tribunal, I request your attendance there as official witnesses for the said powers in order that you may thereafter certify to the execution of that phase of the tribunal's judgement."

Sebald met with MacArthur again and suggested that all photographers be barred from the executions. MacArthur agreed, stating that photographs of the executions "would violate all sense of decency." He then asked Sebald to listen to his review of the sentences, which he proposed to make public the next day. The general upheld all the tribunal's sentences without change and had assembled the reasons for his position on several small pieces of paper. He read these to Sebald in a slow, solemn tone and in a low voice filled with emphasis and intonation. The full text of MacArthur's review is presented in appendix D.

The following table lists the accused by name and shows which of them was found guilty (G) or innocent (NG) on each count. It also shows where there was no finding (NF) and who was not indicted (NI) on a specific count.

IMTFE Judgment

	Count										Sentence
	1	27	29	31	32	33	35	36	54	55	
Araki	G	G	NG	NG	NG	NG	NG	NG	NG	NG	Life
Doihara	G	G	G	G	G	NG	G	G	G	NG	Death
Hashimoto	G	G	NG	NG	NG	NI	NI	NI	NG	NG	Life
Hata	G	G	G	G	G	NI	NG	NG	NG	G	Life
Hiranuma	G	G	G	G	G	NG	NG	G	NG	NG	Life
Hirota	G	G	NG	NG	NG	NG	NG	NI	NG	G	Death
Hoshino	G	G	G	G	G	NG	NG	NI	NG	NG	Life
Itagaki	G	G	G	G	G	NG	G	G	G	NF	Death
Kaya	G	G	G	G	G	NI	NI	NI	NG	NG	Life
Kido	G	G	G	G	G	NG	NG	NG	NG	NG	Life
Kimura	G	G	G	G	G	NI	NI	NI	G	G	Death
Koiso	G	G	G	G	G	NI	NI	NG	NG	G	Life
Matsui	NG	NG	NG	NG	NG	NG	NI	NG	NG	G	Death
Minami	G	G	NG	NG	NG	NI	NI	NI	NG	NG	Life
Muto	G	G	G	G	G	NG	NI	NG	G	G	Death
Oka	G	G	G	G	G	NI	NI	NI	NG	NG	Life

Oshima	G	NG	NG	NG	NG	NI	NI	NI	NG	NG	Life
Sato	G	G	G	G	G	NI	NI	NI	NG	NG	Life
Shigemitsu	NG	G	G	G	G	G	NG	NI	NI	G	7 years
Shimada	G	G	G	G	G	NI	NI	NI	NG	NG	Life
Shiratori	G	NG	NG	NG	NG	NI	NI	NI	NI	NI	Life
Suzuki	G	G	G	G	G	NI	NI	NG	NG	NG	Life
Togo	G	G	G	G	G	NI	NI	NG	NG	NG	20 years
Tojo	G	G	G	G	G	G	NI	NG	G	NF	Death
Umezu	G	G	G	G	G	NI	NI	NG	NG	NG	Life

Count 1—were leaders, organizers, instigators, or accomplices in the formulation or execution of a common plan or conspiracy to wage wars of aggression and wars in violation of international law.
 Count 27—waging unprovoked aggressive war in China.
 Count 29—waging aggressive war against the United States.
 Count 31—waging aggressive war against the British Commonwealth.
 Count 32—waging aggressive war against the Netherlands.
 Count 33—waging aggressive war against French Indo-China.
 Count 35—waging aggressive war against the U.S.S.R. in Siberia.
 Count 36—waging aggressive war against the U.S.S.R. in Mongolia.
 Count 54—Ordered, authorized and permitted inhumane treatment of prisoners of war and others.
 Count 55—Deliberately and recklessly disregarded their duty to take adequate steps to prevent atrocities.

Class C

Reviewing the IMTFE summation of evidence of the treatment of prisoners of war, civilian internees, and inhabitants of countries occupied by the Japanese military during the war is like contemplating hell itself.

The atrocities began in 1937 and continued throughout the war until Japan was defeated in 1945. In China so many civilians were killed that confusion about exact numbers still remains today. There are estimates that between six and ten million were murdered by the Japanese troops. In the "Rape of Nanking" alone, it is estimated that 300,000 Chinese were brutally murdered in less than six weeks. At least 20,000 women and girls were raped by Japanese soldiers. Every province occupied by Japan experienced mass atrocities and massacres. After the Japanese captured a town they would line up their captives on a riverbank and bayonet or machine-gun them into the water. Alternatively they would force them into a building, pour gasoline around it, and set it afire. Anyone trying to escape the flames was shot or bayoneted.

The recorded atrocities and massacres fill page after page of official documents. They show large numbers of entire villages, communities, hospitals, and schools whose occupants were murdered. One witness described the torture and killing of more than 1,000 high school students in Peking (Beijing) in July 1940.

The IMTFE summary also includes the Philippines, where 142,076 American and Filipino civilians and military men died as a result of atrocities. This figure does not include those who survived the indescribable suffering and humiliation, injured or maimed.

The Bataan Death March and the Siam-Burma Railway each claimed over 10,000 POW lives. The Siam-Burma Railway also cost the lives of 30,000 civilian slave laborers.

Fliers and Dutchmen seemed to suffer more and were subjected to worse atrocities than other Caucasians. Airmen were usually murdered quickly, after being subjected to torture. Lack of medical care for those who were injured usually resulted in death. Dutch prisoners were often singled out because their guttural speech made them appear arrogant to their captors.

If any Allied POW escaped and was recaptured, death was immediate. This was usually accomplished by beheading.

As badly as the American and Allied prisoners of war were treated, they generally fared better than natives of the occupied countries.

Class C war criminals were those accused of "crimes against humanity." This language can best be presented as equivalent to the following charges:

1. Violations of laws and customs of war
2. Atrocities committed against prisoners of war
3. Subordinates allowed to commit atrocities
4. Subordinates ordered to commit atrocities
5. Medical treatment or supplies necessary to survival withheld
6. Illegal trials and executions convened
7. Desecration of the dead
8. Medical experiments conducted on prisoners of war
9. Prisoners of war murdered
10. Vivisection performed on prisoners of war
11. Records falsified and/or altered

Some of these charges could be subdivided even further. For example, number 9 includes at least sixteen different strategies ranging from neglect to decapitation. Most of the murdered POWs were tortured before they were killed. Many thousands were tortured and suffered injuries—some permanent — or died as a result. Both of these circumstances meet the requirements of charge number 2.

Some of the Japanese suspects were confined two years or more in Sugamo, awaiting their trials. All those who were sentenced had their sentences reduced by the length of their pretrial confinement.

Researching numerous trials of the Class C war criminals reveals little pattern or uniformity in the sentences handed down by the tribunals. Some received a few years for crimes that appear deserving of the supreme sentence, while others who committed relatively minor crimes were sentenced to forty years at hard labor. The comments by the reviewer in the Judge Advocate's Office state that many of the sentences were "inadequate" or "grossly inadequate." Speaking of Case 339, involving the submariners, he states, "It is considered that, if the commission chose to find these accused guilty, as it did, the punishment meted out should have fit the crime. It is considered that in no case in past cases have sentences been so lenient."

Perhaps boredom or fatigue took over toward the end of the trials.

In part due to the outcry over the Class B executions in the Philippines, by 1949 it was practially impossible to execute a war criminal who had been sentenced to death (see Generals Homma and Yamashita under "Reflections"). An excellent example of this follows:

Yoshinao Sato was a career soldier and a graduate of the army college. In 1945 he was a colonel, chief of air intelligence and air defense, and in charge of captured fliers at Western Army Headquarters in Fukuoka, Japan. He was tried, convicted, and sentenced to death by hanging in two separate but related war crimes cases.

In Case 288 he and others were found guilty of deliberately, feloniously, and with premeditation killing eight American prisoners of war on June 20; eight on August 10; and seventeen on August 15, 1945, by bayoneting, cutting, and beheading them.

None of these American airmen had been tried or convicted by any military tribunal. After the executions Sato and others went to great efforts to conceal the identities and cause of death of these airmen.

Case 290 was discussed under the trial section. Sato selected the prisoners held at Western Army Headquarters who were sent to Kyushu University to be used in illegal vivisection operations. He often watched these operations and actively participated in a plot to conceal them from authorities at the end of the war.

Twenty-three suspects were tried for two different crimes during the Yokohama trials. However, though Sato was the only one condemned to death in both cases, he was not executed for either.

The cases of all war criminals receiving death sentences were reviewed by SCAP. Seventy death sentences were subsequently commuted to life at hard labor.

The Japanese war criminals who were actually executed after receiving death sentences are highlighted by an asterisk (*) beside their names on the following chart. Those listed as civilians had usually previously served in the military and were wounded and reassigned as guards at prisoner-of-war camps after they recuperated.

The Sentences

Case	Defendant	Rank	Charges	Specifications	Verdicts	Sentence
1	Tatsuo Tsuchiya	Civilian	1, 2, 5	8	4 guilty	Life HL
2	Kei Yuri*	First lieutenant	1, 2, 3, 9	3	2 guilty	Death
3	Chotaro Furushima	Camp CO	1, 2, 3	10	8 guilty	Life HL
4	Kaichi Hirate*	Captain	1, 2, 3, 5, 11	31	30 guilty	Death
5	Hiroji Honda	Camp CO	1, 2, 3, 5	9	6 guilty	20 years
6	Isao Fukuhara*	Captain	1, 2, 3	34	15 guilty	Death
7	Kitaro Ishida	NCO	1, 2, 5	9	9 guilty	30 years
8	Shigeru Aona	Camp CO	1, 3, 5	5	2 guilty	10 years
9	Yuhichi Sakamoto	Camp CO	1, 2, 3, 5	12	9 guilty	Life
10	Shigemaru Odeishi	Medical orderly	1, 2	10	9 guilty	10 years' HL
11	Miyoroku Okada	Camp CO	1, 2, 3	14	10 guilty	50 years' HL
12	Nubuo Kanayama	Corporal	1, 2, 3, 5	16	9 guilty	20 years' HL
	Kiyoichi Mori	Camp CO	1, 3	8	8 guilty	15 years' HL
	Tsuyoshi Sakai	First lieutenant	1, 2, 3, 5	9	6 guilty	15 years' HL
13	Motoichi Sakagami	Corporal	1, 2	2	2 guilty	2 years' HL
	Naraichi Chigara	Corporal	1, 2	2	2 guilty	6 years' HL
	Teruo Ono	Private	1, 2	1	1 guilty	2 years' HL
	Shunsuke Eato	Private first class	1, 2	1	Acquitted	
14	Ryunosuke Kimura	Civilian	1, 2	1	1 guilty	10 years
	Tsunesuke Tsuda	Civilian	1, 2	1	Acquitted	
	Taikichi Omoi	Civilian	1, 2	1	1 guilty	10 years
	Yoshinari Minemoto	Corporal	1, 2	1	1 guilty	10 years
	Tokuichi Ichiba	Corporal	1, 2	1	1 guilty	10 years
15	Yaichi Rikitake	Camp CO	1, 2, 3	42	20 guilty	15 years' HL
16	Hiroshi Takeuchi	Camp CO	1, 2, 3, 5, 11	24	16 guilty	22 years' HL
	Kazuo Tanaka	Sergeant major	1, 2, 5	5	3 guilty	7 years' HL

HL beside the length of sentence denotes hard labor. An asterisk (*) beside the name denotes that the war criminal was actually executed.

Case	Defendant	Rank	Charges	Specifications	Verdicts	Sentence
	Torao Sato	Civilian	1, 2	5	4 guilty	8 years' HL
	Keizo Suzuki	Medical orderly	1, 2, 5	6	5 guilty	16 years' HL
	Kichihei Ozawa	Medical sergeant	1, 2, 5	6	2 guilty	2 years' HL
	Kazumasa Maekawa	Sergeant	1, 2	8	7 guilty	16 years' HL
	Hiroshi Miyazaki	Civilian	1, 2	10	10 guilty	30 years' HL
	Hidetoshi Emori	Second lieutenant	1, 2, 3, 5	15	8 guilty	5 years' HL
17	Shigeo Akamatsu	Sergeant	1, 2	6	5 guilty	25 years' HL
18	Fusao Toyama	Guard	1, 2	5	5 guilty	30 years' HL
19	Shinichi Motoyashiki	Civilian	1, 2	8	7 guilty	20 years
20	Tsutomi Shiba	Medical sergeant	1, 2, 3	11	8 guilty	5 years
21	Yasutake Sakakibara	Second lieutenant	1, 2	2	Acquitted	
22	Kiyomi Imai	NCO	1, 2	2	2 guilty	5 years' HL
23	Uichi Ikegami*	First lieutenant	1, 2, 3	4	4 guilty	Death
24	Akiyoshi Isujino	Superior private	1, 2, 5	8	8 guilty	30 years
25	Masaaki Mabuchi*	Captain	1, 2, 3, 7, 9	3	3 guilty	Death
	Jutaro Kikuchi	Second lieutenant	1, 2, 7	2	2 guilty	25 years' HL
26	Ryoichi Shimode	Guard	1, 2	5	3 guilty	20 years' HL
27	Michiharu Ishige	First lieutenant	1, 2, 3, 5	12	12 guilty	35 years' HL
	Shooga Kondo	Civilian	1, 2, 5	10	8 guilty	25 years' HL
	Kyogzo Yumita	Civilian	1, 2, 5	8	5 guilty	15 years' HL
28	(Hajime Kukuta was sentenced. However, the review is missing from the microfilm record.)					
29	Kunimitsu Yamauchi	Interpreter	1, 2	6	6 guilty	40 years' HL
30	Yoshiyuki Ikeda	Superior private	1, 2	4	4 guilty	15 years
	Tadashi Takano	Civilian	1, 2	5	2 guilty	15 years
	Yoshika Yagi	Civilian	1, 2	4	4 guilty	15 years
31	Tatsuo Abe	Civilian	1, 2	3	1 guilty	1 year's HL
32	Tomio Yamada	Civilian	1, 2	8	8 guilty	Life HL
33	Unosuke Mantani	Civilian	1, 2	4	4 guilty	Life

The Sentences

#	Name	Role	Charges	Votes	Sentence
34	Shoichiro Aoki	Civilian	1, 2	7	4 guilty	30 years' HL
35	Seizo Nakagura	Corporal	1, 2	10	9 guilty	40 years' HL
37	Iwao Kawasaki	Sergeant	1, 2	5	3 guilty	25 years' HL
39	Yuhei Hosotani	Camp CO	1, 2, 3, 5	35	5 guilty	5 years' HL
	Hiromo Saito	Doctor	1, 2, 5	7	7 guilty	Life HL
	Yasuo Kobayashi	Doctor	1, 2	8	8 guilty	40 years' HL
	Shigeyoshi Hashimoto	Civilian	1, 2	11	9 guilty	10 years' HL
39A	Mokichi Hara	Guard	1, 2	2	2 guilty	1 year's HL
40	Toranoshin Akamatsu	Civilian	1, 2	19	18 guilty	Life HL
41	Yoshio Kameoka	Interpreter	1, 2	4	4 guilty	Life HL
42	Takeo Fukunaga	Medical orderly	1, 2	2	2 guilty	2 years' HL
43	Sadao Watanabe	Civilian	1, 2	18	18 guilty	30 years' HL
	Eiji Asari	Sergeant	1, 2	2	1 guilty	25 years' HL
	Toshio Takeshita	Superior private	1, 2, 5	5	5 guilty	15 years' HL
	Shigeru Nishioka	Superior private	1, 2, 5	5	5 guilty	15 years' HL
	Yoshimi Hirano	Civilian	1, 2	2	1 guilty	5 years' HL
45	Kuniichi Araki	Medical sergeant major	1, 2, 5	4	4 guilty	Death
46	Genji Minemo	Civilian	1, 2	12	10 guilty	20 years' HL
47	Isojiro Okazaki	Superior private	1, 2	3	2 guilty	2 years' HL
49	Naoza Shimodaira	Civilian	1, 2	6	6 guilty	12 years' HL
	Harushige Kawakami	Civilian	1, 2	5	5 guilty	10 years' HL
50	Yasushi Kimura	Civilian	1, 2	10	10 guilty	5 years' HL
52	Mamoru Shizawa	Private first class	1, 2	20	17 guilty	20 years' HL
53	Seitaro Hata	Doctor	1, 2, 3, 4, 5	11	10 guilty	25 years' HL
	Yukio Asano	Interpreter	1, 2, 5	8	7 guilty	15 years' HL
	Takeo Kita	Sergeant major	1, 2, 3	6	5 guilty	15 years' HL
	Hideji Nakamura	NCO	1, 2	11	9 guilty	20 years' HL
55	Takuji Murakami*	Captain	1, 2, 3	31	27 guilty	Death
	Kyosuke Saito	Doctor	1, 5	12	8 guilty	Death
	Kiyoshi Nishiyama	Medical orderly	1, 2, 5	6	4 guilty	40 years' HL

Sugamo Prison, Tokyo

Case	Defendant	Rank	Charges	Specifications	Verdicts	Sentence
	Shunichi Tanimoto	Guard	1, 2	9	8 guilty	35 years' HL
	Haruo Okada	Guard	1, 2	12	7 guilty	20 years' HL
	Tanimori Yamamoto	Civilian	1, 2	4	4 guilty	15 years' HL
	Satoji Suzuki	Civilian	1, 2	7	6 guilty	15 years' HL
	Kiichi Shirasaya	Guard	1, 2	2	2 guilty	6 years' HL
	Takeshi Beppu	Civilian	1, 2	4	4 guilty	5 years' HL
	Shimekichi Kawabata	Civilian	1, 2	4	3 guilty	5 years' HL
	Jiro Kondo	Civilian	1, 2	2	2 guilty	5 years' HL
	Masahiro Oka	Guard	1, 2	2	2 guilty	3 years' HL
	Kenshi Hirai	Guard	1, 2	1	1 guilty	1 year's HL
56	Shinnosuki Sato	Civilian	1, 2	8	7 guilty	15 years' HL
	Sukeo Tagusari	Civilian	1, 2	14	12 guilty	22 years' HL
57	Seijiro Yamamoto	Civilian	1, 5	2	Acquitted	
	Katsuyoshi Yasuda	Guard	1, 5	3	3 guilty	1 year's HL
	Jiro Tendo	Camp CO	1, 2, 3, 5, 11	16	14 guilty	2 years' HL
58	Masato Hada	Medical private	1, 2, 5	13	13 guilty	Life HL
59	Toshitsugo Yamanaka	Civilian	1, 2	1	1 guilty	4 years' HL
	Teruo Shibata	Civilian	1, 2	1	1 guilty	5 years' HL
	Kensako Baba	Civilian	1, 2	1	1 guilty	4½ years' HL
61	Kenichi Kondo	Medical orderly	1, 2, 5	11	9 guilty	12 years' HL
63	Yoichi Saito	Captain	1, 2, 3, 4, 5	45	31 guilty	25 years' HL
	Kiyofusa Sakaguchi	Superior private	1, 2	6	3 guilty	2 years' HL
	Morio Inouye	Corporal	1, 2	15	12 guilty	15 years
65	Koju Tsuda	Civilian	1, 2	12	12 guilty	Life HL
66	Momoichi Moriyama	Civilian	1, 2	7	5 guilty	12 years' HL
68	Masanobu Narikawa	Civilian	1, 2	10	8 guilty	40 years' HL
69	Takeo Takahashi	Medical corporal	1, 2, 5	8	3 guilty	15 years' HL

(Masato Yoshida – trial stopped due to insanity)

The Sentences

	Name	Rank	Charges	Guilty	Sentence
	Katsuyasu Sato	Civilian	1, 2	48	33 guilty	40 years' HL
	Hyoichi Okuda	Civilian	1, 2	24	20 guilty	33 years' HL
70	Yoshio Ogimoto	Civilian	1, 2	2	1 guilty	5 years' HL
71	Hidemaro Nakajima	First lieutenant	1, 2, 3, 5	28	10 guilty	2 years' HL
72	Masafumi Sugi	Civilian	1, 2	17	14 guilty	40 years' HL
73	Takio Kaneko	Captain	1, 2, 3, 4	27	19 guilty	28 years' HL
	Techiharo Uchida	Sergeant	1, 2, 3, 5	12	8 guilty	15 years' HL
74	Kingoro Fukuda	Guard	1, 2, 4	16	12 guilty	Death
	Masao Shimizu	Guard	1, 2, 4	11	6 guilty	Death
	Chitoku Ise	Camp CO	1, 2, 3, 4, 5	42	14 guilty	Death
	Matatoshi Kono	Camp CO	1, 3, 4, 5	6	6 guilty	Life HL
	Eishi Motoi	Guard	1, 5	6	Acquitted	
	Saburo Shibata	Guard	1, 5	6	Acquitted	
	Taichero Miura	Guard	1, 3, 5	9	2 guilty	20 years' HL
	Kinzo Goto	Guard	1, 3, 5	10	3 guilty	20 years' HL
75	Takanosuke Gunji	Sergeant	1, 2	2	2 guilty	3 years' HL
77	Masashi Sato	Captain	1, 3, 5	15	8 guilty	5 years' HL
	Kyusho Masaki	Interpreter	1, 2	17	12 guilty	20 years' HL
	Matsusaburo Shirakawa	Corporal	1, 2	4	3 guilty	10 years' HL
78	Toshio Tashiro	Captain	1, 3, 4, 9	3	3 guilty	Death
	Hatsuaki Kambe	Corporal	1, 2, 9	1	1 guilty	Death
	Mataishi Okubo	Sergeant major	1, 2, 9	1	1 guilty	Death
	Keiji Kamimoto	Corporal	1, 2, 9	1	1 guilty	Death
	Masao Koshikawa	Second lieutenant	1, 2, 9, 11	3	3 guilty	Death
80	Fukusaburo Adachi	Civilian	1, 2	14	12 guilty	20 years' HL
81	Kinzaburo Niizuma	Captain	1, 3, 5	10	7 guilty	8 years' HL
	Kenichi Kikuchi	Civilian	1, 2	4	3 guilty	8 years' HL
	Umesaku Nakao	Medical corpsman	1, 2, 5	3	3 guilty	5 years' HL
	Nobumasa Takeda	Lance corporal	1, 2	4	1 guilty	5 years' HL
82	Masauki Kiryu	Interpreter	1, 2	3	1 guilty	2 years' HL

Case	Defendant	Rank	Charges	Specifications	Verdicts	Sentence
	Takeo Shuraki	Corporal	1, 2	4	4 guilty	25 years' HL
	Minoru Kobayashi	Corporal	1, 2	2	2 guilty	15 years' HL
83	Hirozo Goto	Civilian	1, 2	3	2 guilty	30 months' HL
	Noboru Kodama	Civilian	1, 2	2	2 guilty	30 months' HL
	Tetsuya Murakami	Civilian	1, 2	3	2 guilty	18 months' HL
	Takeki Nishimura	Civilian	1, 2	3	1 guilty	2 years' HL
	Motomu Okamoto	Civilian	1, 2	3	2 guilty	2 years' HL
	Ko Osako	Captain	1, 2, 3, 5	4	4 guilty	2 years' HL
84	Tetsotoshi Yasaru	Lieutenant	1, 2, 3, 5	26	16 guilty	15 years' HL
85	Hajime Honda*	Civilian	1, 2	6	6 guilty	Death
86	Makoto Kimura	Civilian	1, 2	3	1 guilty	1 year's HL
88	Juso Yamamoto	Civilian	1, 2	6	4 guilty	20 years' HL
90	Sannojo Fujii	Civilian	1, 2	2	1 guilty	5 years' HL
91	Hasanoru Takahashi	Civilian	1, 2	3	2 guilty	5 years' HL
	Shoshaburo Fujita	Civilian	1, 2, 5	3	3 guilty	10 years' HL
	Kiyoshi Yui	Civilian	1, 2	4	4 guilty	30 years' HL
	Hikari Suzuki	Civilian	1, 2	14	13 guilty	30 years' HL
	Saburo Nizukoshi	Captain	1, 2, 3, 5	8	7 guilty	30 years' HL
	Sadaharu Kobayashi	Sergeant	1, 2	12	11 guilty	30 years' HL
	Chuta Sasazawa	Captain	1, 2, 3, 5	29	27 guilty	Death
	Yoshio Nishikawa	Civilian	1, 2	4	4 guilty	15 years' HL
92	Tetsuo Mizuno	Sergeant major	1, 2, 3, 5	10	3 guilty	5 years' HL
	Eisuke Watanabe	Medical lance corporal	1, 2, 5	11	8 guilty	40 years' HL
	Kunzio Kasuya	Civilian	1, 2, 5	10	9 guilty	20 years' HL
	Yoshiro Kotani	Civilian	1, 2, 5	7	6 guilty	10 years' HL
	Mitsuo Saito	Civilian	1, 2, 5	9	9 guilty	30 years' HL
	Seitaro Washimi	Lieutenant	1, 2, 3, 5	19	16 guilty	40 years' HL
	Kaoru Otsuki	Interpreter	1, 2	4	2 guilty	3 years' HL

The Sentences

#	Name	Rank	Charges	Guilty	Sentence
	Yoshio Myazaki	Lieutenant	1, 3, 5	12	12 guilty	40 years' HL
94	Sachio Egawa*	Chief petty officer	1, 2	6	6 guilty	Death
	Tokuro Fukuda	Chief petty officer	1, 2	4	4 guilty	20 years' HL
	Denkichi Orita	Lieutenant senior grade	1, 3	19	11 guilty	Life HL
	Fukuichi Watanabe	Ensign	1, 2, 3	21	15 guilty	Life HL
97	Kazuo Fukami	Superior private	1, 2	10	4 guilty	10 years' HL
99	Sokochi Sano	Lieutenant	1, 2, 3	50	6 guilty	2 years' HL
	Shoji Onodera	Sergeant	1, 2	7	4 guilty	5 years' HL
100	Morizo Shinjo	Civilian	1, 2	8	8 guilty	28 years' HL
102	Yoshiyuki Inoue	Civilian		6	6 guilty	8 years' HL
	Takaji Okada	Camp CO	1, 2, 3, 5	23	18 guilty	4 years' HL
104	Seichi Naganuma	First lieutenant	1, 2, 3, 5	21	11 guilty	25 years' HL
	Nubua Homma	NCO	1, 2, 5	5	5 guilty	15 years' HL
	Kiyomi Iwabuchi	NCO		2	1 guilty	5 years' HL
	Isamu Sasaki	Civilian	1, 2	4	4 guilty	12 years' HL
	Isami Kintaichi	Civilian	1, 2	4	4 guilty	12 years' HL
106	Tomoki Nakamura	Lieutenant	1, 2, 3, 5	16	14 guilty	12 years' HL
107	Bunhachi Bando	Guard	1, 2	7	7 guilty	6 years' HL
111	Hiroshi Fujii	Second lieutenant	1, 2, 3, 5	28	13 guilty	12 years' HL
115	Kanechi Kondo	Three-star private	1, 2	4	4 guilty	1 year's HL
117	Kanemasu Uchida	Sergeant major	1, 2	45	23 guilty	20 years' HL
118	Ryoichi Higashiguchi	Interpreter	1, 2	9	8 guilty	25 years' HL
119	Tetsuo Kobayashi	Medical corpsman		6	5 guilty	20 years' HL
120	Toshinori Asaka	First lieutenant	1, 2, 5	82	30 guilty	12 years' HL
	Koichi Takahashi	Sergeant major	1, 2, 3, 5	6	2 guilty	1 year's HL
	Tetsuri Yoshio	Corporal medical corps	1, 2	10	8 guilty	15 years' HL
	Tokuji Yonemura	Civilian	1, 2, 5	5	5 guilty	10 years' HL
	(Yutaka Sagae — Severed from case)		1, 2			
121	Kiyoshi Ogasawara	Civilian	1, 2	4	3 guilty	3 years' HL
	Seisaku Toma	Civilian	1, 2	3	1 guilty	1 year's HL

Case	Defendant	Rank	Charges	Specifications	Verdicts	Sentence
122	Shohei Okeda	Civilian	1, 2	17	7 guilty	15 years' HL
123	Eitaro Uchiyama	Lieutenant general	1, 6	4	2 guilty	30 years' HL
	Kiyotomi Otahara	Major general	1, 6	4	3 guilty	Death
	Norio Yamanaka	Major	1, 6	3	3 guilty	25 years' HL
	Buichi Ono	Captain	1, 6	3	3 guilty	30 years' HL
	Hideo Matsumori	First lieutenant	1, 6	3	2 guilty	10 years' HL
	Yorio Ogiya	Captain	1, 6	4	3 guilty	3 years' HL
	Kanji Nakamichi	Captain	1, 6	1	1 guilty	3 years' HL
	Michio Kunitake	Lieutenant general	1, 6	4	1 guilty	3 years' HL
124	Masayoshi Kato	Civilian	1, 2	7	5 guilty	25 years' HL
126	Toshio Goto	Civilian	1, 2, 5	5	5 guilty	40 years' HL
	Shuichi Takata	Camp CO	1, 2, 3, 5	18	18 guilty	40 years' HL
	Shigeki Eto	Civilian	1, 2	3	3 guilty	30 years' HL
	Benji Ito	Civilian	1, 2	6	6 guilty	20 years' HL
	Tsuzuo Ota	Civilian	1, 2	5	5 guilty	30 years' HL
127	Ryuma Hirano	Second lieutenant	1, 2	2	2 guilty	7 years' HL
	Sadeo Sakano	Civilian	1, 2	2	2 guilty	7 years' HL
128	Sukeo Nakajima*	Captain	1, 2, 3, 5, 9	13	10 guilty	Death
	Sadaharu Hiramatsu*	Civilian	1, 2, 9	4	4 guilty	Death
	Harumi Kawate*	Civilian	1, 2, 9	5	5 guilty	Death
	Tomotsu Kimura*	Civilian	1, 2, 5, 9	5	5 guilty	Death
	Takeo Kirishita	Civilian	1, 2, 5, 9	4	3 guilty	Life HL
	Rikio Shioiri	Private first class	1, 2, 5, 9	4	3 guilty	Life HL
	Kunio Yoshizawa*	Interpreter	1, 2, 5, 9	5	4 guilty	Death
129	Narumi Oota	Camp CO	1, 2, 3, 5	25	22 guilty	Life HL
	Yuji Aoki*	Medical sergeant	1, 2, 5	17	15 guilty	Death
	Tadao Shibano*	Sergeant	1, 2	7	6 guilty	Death
	Michio Kuriyama	Interpreter	1, 2	12	9 guilty	Life HL

The Sentences

No.	Name	Rank	Charges		Verdict	Sentence
	Kengo Katayama	Interpreter	1, 2	5	3 guilty	20 years' HL
	Yoshio Taguchi	Medical orderly	1, 2	8	7 guilty	Life HL
130	Hiroaki Kono	Guard	1, 2	13	11 guilty	Life HL
	Matsukichi Muta*	Civilian	1, 2	30	30 guilty	Death
	Sadamu Takeda*	Civilian	1, 2	10	10 guilty	Death
131	Katsuo Ishizawa	Lieutenant	1, 2, 3, 5	112	108 guilty	25 years' HL
	Koichi Ota	Sergeant	1, 2, 5	4	2 guilty	1 year's HL
	Yasushi Takasago	Civilian	1, 2	16	16 guilty	12 years' HL
	Zenkichi Koiwa	Lance corporal	1, 2, 5	18	16 guilty	13 years' HL
	Heikichi Sato	Civilian	1, 2	16	16 guilty	12 years' HL
	Kishio Sasaki	Civilian	1, 2	10	10 guilty	12 years' HL
	Nisa Tanifuji	Civilian	1, 2	9	9 guilty	8 years' HL
132	Nagayasu Kawabe	First lieutenant	1, 2, 3, 5	12	6 guilty	5 years' HL
133	Masao Uwamori	Camp CO	1, 2, 3	101	67 guilty	3 years' HL
134	Hiroyuki Morita	Guard	1, 2	9	5 guilty	15 years' HL
135	Yagoheiji Iwata	Guard	1, 2	5	4 guilty	12 years' HL
136	Masatoshi Sawamura	Corporal	1, 2, 4, 5	27	22 guilty	30 years' HL
137	Yoshio Suda	Camp CO	1, 3	11	5 guilty	7 years' HL
138	Eiichi Ito	Medical orderly	1, 2	11	6 guilty	8 years' HL
139	Chogo Hashimoto	Superior private	1, 2	8	8 guilty	15 years' HL
140	Akira Nomoto	Captain	1, 2, 3	28	9 guilty	2 years' HL
	Genichi Munehiro	Civilian	1, 2	16	9 guilty	3 years' HL
142	Katsunosuke Watanabe	Civilian	1, 2, 3, 5	11	5 guilty	12 years' HL
143	Kosaku Hazama	Camp CO	1, 2, 3, 5	96	73 guilty	15 years' HL
144	Saburo Matsumuro	First lieutenant	1, 2, 3, 5	11	9 guilty	22 years' HL
145	Ryohei Tanaka	First lieutenant	1, 2, 3, 5	39	37 guilty	25 years' HL
146	Toshitaro Habe	First lieutenant	1, 2, 3, 5	77	42 guilty	8 years' HL
	Yoshitaro Matsumoto	Civilian	1, 2	14	13 guilty	14 years' HL
	Yoichiro Terashita	Superior private	1, 2, 5	6	5 guilty	6½ years' HL
	Tadao Tenabe	Medical sergeant	1, 2	7	5 guilty	2½ years' HL

Case	Defendant	Rank	Charges	Specifications	Verdicts	Sentence
147	Miki Tarodachi	Guard	1, 2	4	3 guilty	1 year's HL
	Tarekichi Nakayama	Guard	1, 2, 5	10	9 guilty	4 years' HL
149	Moota Namba	Camp CO	1, 2, 3, 5	23	16 guilty	25 years' HL
149A	Moota Namba (retrial)	Camp CO	1, 2, 3, 5	19	10 guilty	10 years' HL
150	Tsunesuke Tsuda	Civilian	1, 2	15	14 guilty	40 years' HL
151	Makoto Inaki	First lieutenant	1, 2, 3, 5	66	59 guilty	7 years' HL
	Masaru Mikawa	Sergeant	1, 2	7	7 guilty	5 years' HL
152	Hajime Tamura	Captain/doctor	1, 5	1	1 guilty	25 years' HL
	Hajime Tsutsui	Captain/surgeon	1, 5	2	1 guilty	5 years' HL
	Takeo Yamamoto	Captain/doctor	1, 5	2	2 guilty	Life HL
	Shunishiro Takami	Second lieutenant/doctor	1, 5	1	1 guilty	20 years' HL
153	Yoneo Murakami	Civilian	1, 2	6	5 guilty	5 years' HL
154	Junsaburo Toshino*	Captain	1, 2, 3, 4, 5, 9	18	9 guilty	Death
	Shusuke Wada	Interpreter	1, 2, 3, 4, 5	16	8 guilty	Life HL
	Kazutane Aihara*	Corporal	1, 2, 9	5	4 guilty	Death
	Shin Kajiyama	Guard	1, 2, 5	2	Acquitted	
	Suketoshi Tanoue	Master sergeant	1, 9	1	1 guilty	25 years' HL
	Jiro Ueda	Private	1, 9	1	1 guilty	20 years' HL
	Hisao Yoshida	Guard	1, 9	1	Acquitted	
	Risaku Kobayashi	Guard	1, 9	1	Acquitted	
	Sho Hattori	Sergeant	1, 2, 3, 4, 9	4	1 guilty	10 years' HL
155	Sotaro Murata	Colonel	1, 2, 3, 4, 5	29	20 guilty	Life HL
	Yasuji Morimoto	Captain	1, 2, 3, 5	30	20 guilty	Life HL
	(Masaichi Toyama—Severed from case)					
156	Tsugio Nishida	First lieutenant	1, 2, 3	6	4 guilty	9 years' HL
157	Tetsuo Ando	Civilian	1, 2	3	2 guilty	5 years' HL
158	Hichiro Tsuchiya	Private first class	1, 2	9	8 guilty	15 years' HL
159	Yokinaga Kimura	Civilian	1, 2	10	5 guilty	7 years' HL

The Sentences

	Name	Role	Counts		Verdict	Sentence
160	Masaaki Murai	Civilian		6	4 guilty	8 years' HL
162	Kunio Miyatake	Doctor	1, 2, 5	14	13 guilty	20 years' HL
163	Sotoumon Hosoi	Civilian	1, 2, 5	13	9 guilty	15 years' HL
	Shuichi Shimizu	Medical corps	1, 2, 5	9	3 guilty	4 years' HL
	Masaichi Morita	Civilian	1, 2	12	8 guilty	10 years' HL
164	Ryugo Kanetsuna	Camp CO	1, 2, 3	17	6 guilty	9 years' HL
	Junji Mano	Camp administrator		4	3 guilty	6 years' HL
165	Matsuzo Miumi	Civilian	1, 2	7	4 guilty	6 years' HL
166	Minoru Fujimoto	Civilian	1, 2	12	7 guilty	15 years' HL
	Masatomo Kikuchi	Civilian	1, 2	7	6 guilty	12 years' HL
	Saburo Kozawa	Civilian	1, 2	23	13 guilty	23 years' HL
	Toshio Mizuno	Corporal	1, 2	9	7 guilty	17 years' HL
	Syokei Matsuo	Camp CO	1, 2, 3, 5	37	19 guilty	17 years' HL
	Ryoichi Nemoto	Camp CO	1, 2, 3, 5	16	6 guilty	3 years' HL
167	Tadashi Sato	First lieutenant	1, 2, 3, 5	7	5 guilty	7 years' HL
168	Takeshi Hashimoto	Sergeant	1, 2, 3, 5	34	26 guilty	8 years' HL
169	Masao Hachiya	Recruit	1, 7	1	1 guilty	15 months' HL
	Kensi Ito	Recruit	1, 7	1	Acquitted	
	Mitsuo Takagano	Recruit	1, 7	1	1 guilty	15 months' HL
	Hideo Yoshida	Recruit	1, 7	1	1 guilty	15 months' HL
	Hatsuo Ishimori	Recruit	1, 7	1	1 guilty	2 years' HL
	Masakiyo Shinoharo	Recruit	1, 7	1	1 guilty	15 months' HL
	Kiyoshi Yasue	Recruit	1, 7	1	1 guilty	15 months' HL
171	Kiichi Yamazaki	Civilian	1, 2	6	5 guilty	6 years' HL
	Shuichi Shinoda	Civilian	1, 2	3	3 guilty	2 years' HL
	Masajiro Hirabayashi	Civilian	1, 2	2	2 guilty	4 years' HL
172	Hideo Yasutake	Civilian	1, 2	13	6 guilty	12 years' HL
173	Kiyoshi Obayashi	Civilian	1, 2	3	3 guilty	25 years' HL
173A	Masao Nakanishi	Civilian	1, 2	1	1 guilty	1 year's HL
174	Nobuhiro Miyakawa	Civilian	1, 2	10	8 guilty	22 years' HL

Sugamo Prison, Tokyo

Case	Defendant	Rank	Charges	Specifications	Verdicts	Sentence
175	Mitsuzo Inagaki	Warrant officer	1, 2, 3	14	14 guilty	30 years' HL
176	Tatsuro Fujita	Civilian	1, 2	1	1 guilty	5 years' HL
	Eiichi Hozumi	Civilian	1, 2	1	1 guilty	5 years' HL
	Kanemasu Uchida	Civilian	1, 2	1	1 guilty	5 years' HL
	Kumaichi Maeda	Civilian	1, 2	1	1 guilty	2 years' HL
	Kanzaburo Yokoyama	Civilian	1, 2	1	1 guilty	5 years' HL
177	Fukujiro Akiyama	Civilian	1, 2	2	1 guilty	2 years' HL
178	Hiroichi Uno	Civilian	1, 2	19	13 guilty	10 years' HL
179	Yoshio Nakanishi	Second lieutenant	1, 2, 3, 5	32	16 guilty	15 years' HL
180	Gisaburo Mariyama	Guard	1, 2, 3	25	16 guilty	15 years' HL
181	Yuzuru Noguchi	Colonel	1, 2, 3, 5	62	45 guilty	22 years' HL
	Takeo Terada	Captain	1, 2, 4, 5	7	7 guilty	37 years' HL
	Masatara Takuma	Sergeant	1, 2	6	6 guilty	31 years' HL
	Tokio Watanabe	Doctor	1, 2, 5	3	2 guilty	12 years' HL
	Yohachi Kurokawa	First lieutenant	1, 2	2	1 guilty	2 years' HL
	Kojuro Okazaki	Lieutenant colonel	1, 3, 5	17	16 guilty	20 years' HL
	Shigeru Ariizumi	Captain	1, 3	3	2 guilty	1 year's HL
	Tatsumi Ushihara	Interpreter	1, 2, 5	4	3 guilty	10 years' HL
	Goro Uchida	Captain/doctor	1, 3, 5	14	4 guilty	17 years' HL
	Isamu Goto	Captain	1, 3, 5	25	Acquitted	
	Yasutosi Mizuguchi*	Second lieutenant/doctor	1, 2, 5	14	14 guilty	Death
	Rinsaburo Shita	Lance corporal	1, 2	10	8 guilty	33 years' HL
182	Hiroshi Tanaka	Second lieutenant	1, 2	40	26 guilty	16 years' HL
	Todao Asakura	Lance corporal	1, 2	5	Acquitted	
	Yukio Hitosugi	Sergeant	1, 2	13	7 guilty	10 years' HL
	Nakazo Ieda	Sergeant	1, 2	6	4 guilty	4 years' HL
	Jirokichi Kameda	Civilian	1, 2	5	4 guilty	5 years' HL
	Shoji Kawai	Civilian	1, 2	19	10 guilty	18 years' HL

The Sentences

	Name	Rank	Charges	Verdict	Sentence
	Kameki Kawamura	Civilian	1, 2	13	9 guilty	18 years' HL
	Tomohisa Kawamura	Master sergeant	1, 2	3	2 guilty	1 year's HL
	Nobuo Kokubo	Civilian	1, 2	7	3 guilty	4 years' HL
	Kinpichi Kondo	Civilian	1, 2	6	1 guilty	1 year's HL
	Minoru Mayeda	Leading private	1, 2	1	Acquitted	
	Tatsuo Mizuno	Sergeant	1, 2	8	4 guilty	8 years' HL
	Akihisa Murase	Civilian	1, 2	4	1 guilty	1 year's HL
	Tatsuo Nakagawa	Civilian	1, 2	5	3 guilty	6 years' HL
	Hideo Sakai	Civilian	1, 2	4	2 guilty	4 years' HL
	Yoshikazu Sawano	Civilian	1, 2	9	4 guilty	4 years' HL
	Tokuichi Tanaka	Civilian	1, 2	37	25 guilty	30 years' HL
	Isao Yadoiwa	Civilian	1, 2	15	13 guilty	15 years' HL
	Masakazu Yamagishi	Civilian	1, 2	4	2 guilty	3 years' HL
	Isamu Hara	Civilian	1, 2	4	2 guilty	3 years' HL
	Genzo Kato	Sergeant	1, 2	3	2 guilty	2 years' HL
	Masao Hayashi	Civilian	1, 2	3	2 guilty	18 months' HL
183	Taizo Mimura	Civilian	1, 5	5	3 guilty	5 years' HL
184	Masami Kanno	Civilian	1, 2	9	6 guilty	7 years' HL
	Takeo Watanabe	Civilian	1, 2	6	4 guilty	10 years' HL
185	Takaji Ryu	Civilian	1, 2	3	3 guilty	7 years' HL
	Kazuo Tanaka	Sergeant	1, 2	3	3 guilty	2 years' HL
186	Hisakichi Tokuda	Captain/doctor	1, 2, 3, 5, 8	11	6 guilty	Death
187	Kunizo Katsuki	Civilian	1, 2	2	1 guilty	5 years' HL
188	Shigeru Numajiri	Lieutenant	1, 2, 3, 4, 5	8	6 guilty	18 years' HL
	Shigeo Eizumi	Civilian	1, 2, 5	4	2 guilty	5 years' HL
	Imajiro Kira	Civilian	1, 2	4	2 guilty	15 years' HL
	Takashi Neishi	Civilian	1, 2	3	3 guilty	5 years' HL
	Takayoshi Shinkae	Civilian	1, 2	2	1 guilty	3 years' HL
	Sanzo Tanno	Medical orderly	1, 2, 5	2	Acquitted	
	Shozo Takahashi	Medical orderly	1, 2, 5	4	Acquitted	

Case	Defendant	Rank	Charges	Specifications	Verdicts	Sentence
	Minoru Kurakawa	Civilian	1, 2	3	Acquitted	
189	Yasuhiko Kuroiwa	Sergeant	1, 2	5	5 guilty	10 years' HL
190	Aiijaku Suyenaga	First lieutenant/doctor	1, 2, 3, 5	5	2 guilty	4 years' HL
	Seiichiro Yoshitsuga	Captain	1, 2, 3, 5	20	18 guilty	8 years' HL
191	Wataru Hasegawa	Civilian	1, 2	18	16 guilty	14 years' HL
193	Ryutatsu Kamiyasumiba	Civilian	1, 2	4	4 guilty	20 years' HL
	Tokizo Tanaka	Civilian	1, 2	2	Acquitted	
	Hashiyuki Yamazaki	Sergeant	1, 2, 3	7	6 guilty	30 years' HL
	Yoshio Hori	Civilian	1, 2	7	5 guilty	25 years' HL
	Shigeji Shimizu	Civilian	1, 2	4	4 guilty	25 years' HL
194	Yoshio Kurihara	Sergeant	1, 2	3	3 guilty	10 years' HL
195	Matasuke Ishimatsu	Captain	1, 2, 3, 4, 5	13	7 guilty	12 years' HL
	Koseki Yamaji	Sergeant major	1, 2, 5	12	8 guilty	15 years' HL
197	Shinobu Hichino	Medical sergeant	1, 2, 3, 5	5	3 guilty	25 years' HL
	Masanobu Michishita*	Sergeant major	1, 2, 3, 4, 5	6	4 guilty	Death
	Mineo Nojima	Civilian	1, 2, 5	1	1 guilty	Life HL
198	Hiroshi Azuma	Second lieutenant	1, 2, 3	21	15 guilty	Life HL
	Hisao Kaneyama	Civilian	1, 2	7	5 guilty	14 years' HL
	Noburo Ichiyanagi	Quartermaster corpsman	1, 2	2	2 guilty	5 years' HL
	Kiyoji Ishibe	Civilian	1, 2	2	1 guilty	2 years' HL
	Keitaro Fukijima	Superior private	1, 2	5	4 guilty	7 years' HL
	Tokio Minagawa	Civilian	1, 2	1	1 guilty	18 months' HL
	Hiromitzu Saito	Superior private	1, 2	1	1 guilty	5 years' HL
199	Sakujiro Aramaki	Civilian	1, 2	2	2 guilty	20 years' HL
	Akiyoshi Koga	Civilian	1, 2	5	5 guilty	25 years' HL
	Nobuyasu Sugiyama	Civilian	1, 2	7	7 guilty	20 years' HL
	Fukuma Yamaguchi	Civilian	1, 2	6	5 guilty	25 years' HL
	Takenosuke Fujisaki	Civilian	1, 2	5	3 guilty	20 years' HL

The Sentences

	Name	Rank	Charges	Count	Verdict	Sentence
	Tomoe Nishimura	Civilian	1, 2	4	3 guilty	15 years' HL
	Toraichi Takashita	Civilian	1, 2	4	4 guilty	15 years' HL
200	Fumio Ueda	Civilian	1, 2	3	3 guilty	15 years' HL
	Shoichi Fugii	Guard	1, 2	3	3 guilty	15 years' HL
	Hiroshi Yamamoto	Guard	1, 2	4	4 guilty	15 years' HL
	Tatsumi Date	Guard	1, 2	3	2 guilty	10 years' HL
202	Toshihisa Yamamoto	Civilian	1, 2	3	3 guilty	3 years' HL
203	Toshio Hatakayama	Colonel	1, 2, 3, 5	29	25 guilty	12 years' HL
204	Shigekazu Kiya	Medical sergeant	1, 2, 3	8	4 guilty	2 years' HL
205	Masaji Takaku	Seaman	1, 2	7	7 guilty	10 years' HL
206	Hideo Ishizaki*	Commander	1, 4, 9	2	2 guilty	Death
	Masao Kataoka*	Sergeant major	1, 4, 9	2	2 guilty	Death
	Zentaro Watanabe*	Superior private	1, 9	1	1 guilty	Death
	Takeji Fujino	Superior private	1, 9	1	1 guilty	Death
	Kikuo Tomioka*	Corporal	1, 9	1	1 guilty	Death
	Shoji Ito*	Lieutenant colonel	1, 9	1	1 guilty	Death
208	Kaneichi Koike	Captain/lawyer	1, 6	10	10 guilty	4 years' HL
210	Tomikuni Watanabe	Seaman	1, 2	4	3 guilty	5 years' HL
211	Shinichi Tanaka	Medical orderly	1, 2, 5	4	1 guilty	18 months' HL
212	Tokio Tobita	Sergeant	1, 2	5	4 guilty	30 years' HL
214	Junsho Hayashi	Camp CO	1, 2, 3, 5	28	12 guilty	3 years' HL
216	Katsuo Kohara	Petty officer first class	1, 2	5	2 guilty	5 years' HL
217	Noboru Seki	Warrant officer	1, 2, 3	8	8 guilty	20 years' HL
218	Nakakichi Asoma	Seaman	1, 2	7	4 guilty	12 years' HL
	Masamori Nishi	Seaman	1, 2	9	9 guilty	15 years' HL
	Chikayoshi Sugeta	Seaman	1, 2	7	5 guilty	10 years' HL
	Toshihiro Obara	Seaman	1, 2	7	4 guilty	5 years' HL
	James K. Sasaki	Interpreter	1, 2, 3, 4	3	2 guilty	18 years' HL
	Bunichi Mori	Seaman	1, 2	6	4 guilty	8 years' HL
	Sashizo Yokura	Commander	1, 3, 4, 5	3	2 guilty	25 years' HL

Case	Defendant	Rank	Charges	Specifications	Verdicts	Sentence
219	Terukichi Saito	Civilian	1, 2	8	8 guilty	10 years' HL
	Shooichi Sasaki	Civilian	1, 2	3	2 guilty	5 years' HL
	Kiyamatsu Suda	Civilian	1, 2	6	5 guilty	7 years' HL
	Seiichi Yutani	Civilian	1, 2	4	3 guilty	10 years' HL
220	Yoshio Mitsuhashi	Sergeant major	1, 2, 3	18	11 guilty	5 years' HL
	Masatake Natao	Acting camp CO	1, 2, 3, 4	37	Acquitted	
	Ko Nemoto	Acting camp CO	1, 2, 3, 5	25	12 guilty	5 years' HL
221	Hiroshi Ushioda	Medical sergeant	1, 2, 5	8	8 guilty	10 years' HL
222	Takanori Yamanaka	Medical sergeant	1, 2, 5	30	10 guilty	4 years' HL
223	Toshi Akutsu	Captain	1, 2, 3, 5	8	2 guilty	5 years' HL
224	Iju Sugasawa*	Colonel	1, 4, 9	1	1 guilty	Death
	Kazumoto Suematsu*	First lieutenant	1, 4, 9	1	1 guilty	Death
	Tsuguo Iwanuma	Warrant officer	1, 2, 5, 9	3	3 guilty	Death
	Masakatsu Hozumi*	Sergeant	1, 2, 9	2	1 guilty	Death
225	Masaharu Ozawa	Sergeant	1, 2, 5	8	2 guilty	4 years' HL
	Yutaka Ninomiya	Camp CO	1, 2, 3, 5	30	14 guilty	5 years' HL
	Manzo Wakamatsu	Major	1, 2, 5	20	16 guilty	18 years' HL
226	Tsurugi Komatsu	Civilian	1, 2	33	33 guilty	25 years' HL
	Masao Suzuki	Civilian	1, 2	7	7 guilty	13 years' HL
	Ken Suzuki	Civilian	1, 2	3	3 guilty	4 years' HL
227	Masataro Nakatani	Civilian	1, 2	6	4 guilty	5 years' HL
228	Masaji Ino	Sergeant	1, 2, 3, 5	22	14 guilty	Life HL
	Chosuke Onodera	Civilian	1, 2	11	8 guilty	Life HL
229	Takaji Wachi	Lieutenant general	1 Use of Red	5	2 guilty	6 years' HL
	Saburo Watanabe	Major general	1 Cross symbol	5	Acquitted	
	Masakiyo Yasukawa	Major	1 to transport	2	1 guilty	18 months' HL
	Kishiro Yasuda	Ship captain	1 munitions	5	Acquitted	
	Yasumori Mori	Lieutenant colonel	1 and troops	2	Acquitted	

The Sentences

	Name	Rank	Charges		Verdict	Sentence
	Shigeru Omori	Major/doctor	1 aboard a	2	Acquitted	
	Fusataro Teshima	General	1 Japanese	2	1 guilty	3 years' HL
	Takazo Numata	Chief of staff	1 hospital ship	11	2 guilty	7 years' HL
230	Yoshio Tsuneyoshi	Captain	1, 2, 3, 5	18	12 guilty	Life HL
231	Yoshiaki Kariya	Civilian	1, 2	22	22 guilty	11 years' HL
232	Kazuo Maeda	Major	1, 3, 4, 5	36	32 guilty	30 years' HL
233	Iku Takasaki	Major	1, 2, 3, 5	32	22 guilty	25 years' HL
234	Mutsuo Okubo	Sergeant major	1, 2	4	3 guilty	2 years' HL
235	Eiichi Noda	Corporal	1, 2	10	10 guilty	20 years' HL
236	Mitsuyoshi Fujita	Interpreter	1, 2	4	2 guilty	6 months' HL
237	Kenji Iwataka	Captain	1, 2, 3, 5	40	40 guilty	30 years' HL
	Hideo Suzuki	Lieutenant commander	1, 2, 3, 5	54	53 guilty	15 years' HL
	Inokichi Matsumoto	Rear admiral	1, 2, 3, 5	35	31 guilty	25 years' HL
	Satoru Nakazawa	Lieutenant/surgeon	1, 5	8	8 guilty	10 years' HL
238	Masayoshi Murata	Petty officer	1, 2	5	2 guilty	4 years' HL
239	Takeyasu Nishi	Civilian	1, 2	10	8 guilty	8 years' HL
240	Shigeji Mori	Lieutenant colonel	1, 2, 3, 4, 5	9	5 guilty	Life HL
241	Keiji Nagahara	Captain	1, 2, 3, 5	44	1 guilty	1 year
242	Kazuo Takenaka	Second lieutenant	1, 2, 3, 5	30	23 guilty	4 years' HL
243	Shigetsuchi Asada	Civilian	1, 2	3	3 guilty	3 years' HL
	Ietoshi Noda	Civilian	1, 2	6	3 guilty	3 years' HL
244	Michizo Shiina	Prison governor	1, 3, 5	20	13 guilty	12 years' HL
	Sheijiro Shimano	Jailer	1, 2	3	3 guilty	4 years' HL
	Kunihiko Osada	Jailer	1, 2	9	6 guilty	15 years' HL
	Takeo Kodama	Jailer	1, 2	2	1 guilty	2 years' HL
	Otokichi Yokoyama	Jailer	1, 2	3	1 guilty	2 years' HL
248	Mitsujiro Saramoto	Warrant officer	1, 2	10	2 guilty	3 years' HL
	Tatsumi Hato	Civilian	1, 2, 3, 5	4	2 guilty	20 years' HL
249	Ichiji Kinari	Camp CO	1, 3, 5	34	12 guilty	2 years' HL
250	Yukio Okabuchi	Civilian	1, 2	4	3 guilty	20 months' HL

Case	Defendant	Rank	Charges	Specifications	Verdicts	Sentence
	Nobuo Ikadazu	Civilian	1, 2	2	Acquitted	
	Asao Ijitsu	Civilian	1, 2	2	2 guilty	1 year's HL
	Fusao Shinya	Civilian	1, 2	18	7 guilty	8 years' HL
251	Nobuo Ito	Major	1, 6	4	4 guilty	Death
	Kaiji Matsuo	Major	1, 6	3	3 guilty	20 years' HL
	Toshiatsu Kataura	Lieutenant	1, 6	4	3 guilty	15 years' HL
	Hirokichi Santo	Lieutenant	1, 6	3	3 guilty	20 years' HL
252	Shintaro Ouchii	Ensign	1, 2, 3, 5	15	9 guilty	4 years' HL
253	Sueharu Kitamura	Chief mate	1, 2, 5	15	9 guilty	Death
254	Hisao Moro	First lieutenant	1, 2, 3	17	10 guilty	7 years' HL
255	Akira Yanagizawa*	Civilian	1, 2, 9	14	14 guilty	Death
	Masaji Sekihara*	Civilian	1, 2, 9	16	16 guilty	Death
	Yoshihiro Susuki*	Civilian	1, 2, 9	9	9 guilty	Death
	Hiroshi Obinata*	Civilian	1, 2, 9	13	11 guilty	Death
	Eiichi Ujishiki*	Civilian	1, 2, 9	13	13 guilty	Death
	Yonesaku Akiyama*	Civilian	1, 2, 9	5	5 guilty	Death
	Norimasa Oshima	Civilian	1, 2, 9	6	6 guilty	46 years' HL
256	Kazuo Arakawa	Guard	1, 2	4	4 guilty	6 years' HL
258	Hanji Akatsuka	Seaman	1, 2, 7, 9	1	1 guilty	Death
	Muneo Enomoto*	First lieutenant	1, 2, 3, 7, 9	2	2 guilty	Death
	Matsuo Fujinaka*	Petty officer	1, 2, 7, 9	1	1 guilty	Death
	Norio Fukumoto	Seaman	1, 2, 7, 9	1	1 guilty	5 years' HL
	Masaji Furuno	Seaman second class	1, 2, 7, 9	3	3 guilty	Death
	Toshio Goto	Lead seaman	1, 2, 7, 9	1	1 guilty	Death
	Morimitsu Hagido	Seaman	1, 2, 7, 9	1	1 guilty	Death
	Shigeichi Ikehara	Seaman	1, 2, 7, 9	1	1 guilty	Death
	Morikaji Ikemiyagi	Seaman	1, 2, 7, 9	1	Acquitted	
	Yoshiaki Inami	Seaman	1, 2, 7, 9	1	1 guilty	Death

The Sentences

Name	Rank	Charges	Count	Verdict	Sentence
Katsutaro Inoue*	Executive officer	1, 2, 3, 4, 7, 9	13	13 guilty	Death
Otohiko Inoue*	Lieutenant	1, 2, 3, 4, 7, 9	14	14 guilty	Death
Taneyoshi Kamishinbara	Seaman	1, 2, 7, 9	1	1 guilty	Death
Kenji Kawahira	Seaman	1, 2, 7, 9	1	Acquitted	
Kazuo Kimoto	Seaman	1, 2, 7, 9	1	1 guilty	Death
Mitsuno Kitada	Seaman	1, 2, 7, 9	1	1 guilty	Death
Seisho Kohama	Seaman	1, 2, 7, 9	1	1 guilty	Death
Hisayoshi Kubo	Seaman	1, 2, 7, 9	2	2 guilty	Death
Ryoyo Kuwae	Lieutenant	1, 2, 3, 4, 7, 9	1	1 guilty	Death
Sahachi Kuwano	Seaman	1, 2, 7, 9	1	1 guilty	Death
Yuichi Maejima	Lieutenant	1, 2, 3, 4, 7, 9	2	2 guilty	Death
Takeshi Maeuchihara	Seaman	1, 2, 7, 9	1	1 guilty	Death
Minoru Makuda*	Lieutenant	1, 2, 3, 9	2	2 guilty	Death
Kakutaro Matake	Seaman	1, 2, 7, 9	1	1 guilty	Death
Fusao Miyahara	Seaman	1, 2, 7, 9	1	1 guilty	Death
Yoshiyuki Morooka	Lieutenant	1, 7, 9	1	1 guilty	20 years' HL
Shimpei Mukumoto	Lieutenant	1, 4, 7, 9	2	2 guilty	Death
Iwayoshi Nadahara	Ensign	1, 2, 7, 9	1	1 guilty	Death
Hirotoshi Nakazono	Superior seaman	1, 2, 7, 9	1	1 guilty	Death
Tadakuni Narisako*	Seaman	1, 2, 7, 9	1	1 guilty	Death
Eikichi Oshiro	Seaman second class	1, 2, 7, 9	1	1 guilty	Death
(Shigeru Sasaki—Severed from case)					
Tadayuki Seyama	Petty officer	1, 2, 4, 7, 9	1	1 guilty	Death
Yoshio Shirakata	Seaman first class	1, 2, 7, 9	1	1 guilty	Death
Masonori Someya	Seaman	1, 2, 7, 9	1	1 guilty	Death
Shizuo Sumitoko	Chief	1, 2, 7, 9	1	1 guilty	Death
Yasumasa Taguchi*	Ensign	1, 2, 7, 9	2	2 guilty	Death
Nobuyuki Taike	Petty officer	1, 2, 7, 9	1	1 guilty	Death
Naoichi Takamura	Superior seaman	1, 2, 7, 9	1	1 guilty	Death
Yoshio Tauchi	Seaman first class	1, 2, 7, 9	1	1 guilty	Death

Case	Defendant	Rank	Charges	Specifications	Verdicts	Sentence
	Seichi Terashima	Seaman	1, 2, 7, 9	1	1 guilty	Death
	Takashi Tezuka	Superior seaman	1, 2, 7, 9	1	1 guilty	Death
	Masonori Uchikura	Seaman first class	1, 2, 7, 9	1	1 guilty	Death
	Tameichi Urayama	Seaman	1, 2, 7, 9	1	1 guilty	Death
	Yoji Yamakawa	Seaman	1, 2, 7, 9	1	1 guilty	Death
	Tsuyoshi Yoshihara	Petty officer	1, 2, 7, 9	2	2 guilty	Death
259	Hitoshi Okamoto	First lieutenant	1, 2, 3	17	4 guilty	25 years' HL
	Shishitaro Yoshinaga	Lance corporal	1, 2, 3	18	16 guilty	12 years' HL
	Kazuo Kinugasa	Lance corporal	1, 2	2	1 guilty	18 months' HL
	Rai O Ran	Guard commander	1, 2, 3	4	3 guilty	2½ years' HL
	Ei Hatsu Rin	Chief guard	1, 2, 3	6	4 guilty	4 years' HL
	Mo Ei Chin	Guard commander	1, 2, 3	14	6 guilty	6 years' HL
	Tateo Yamasaki	First lieutenant	1, 2, 3	16	Acquitted	
	Sotojiro Tamura	Warrant officer	1, 2, 3	13	Acquitted	
	Noboru Nagai	First sergeant	1, 2, 3	39	Acquitted	
	Hatsuo Muta	Corporal	1, 2	18	Acquitted	
260	Usaji Hida	Guard commander	1, 4	1	Acquitted	
	Yasuo Kohara	Guard	1, 2, 9	1	1 guilty	Life HL
	Tokuichi Takamura	Guard	1, 2, 9	1	1 guilty	Life HL
	Asaichi Yoshimura	Guard	1, 2, 9	1	1 guilty	Life HL
	Tamotsu Takezoe	Guard	1, 2, 9	1	1 guilty	Life HL
262	Shigeru Fukuda	Corporal	1, 2	6	5 guilty	2 years' HL
263	Takahisa Arai	Civilian	1, 2	7	2 guilty	3 years' HL
264	Tsutafu Kimura	Civilian	1, 2	6	6 guilty	18 months' HL
265	Kimiya Ichinoe	Lieutenant colonel	1, 3	7	7 guilty	Death
	Sadamu Motokawa*	Second lieutenant	1, 2, 9	1	1 guilty	Death
	Kenichi Yanagizawa	Warrant officer	1, 2, 9	1	Acquitted	
	Masao Kuwabara	Guard	1, 2, 9	1	1 guilty	Life HL

The Sentences

	Name	Rank	Charges	Count	Verdict	Sentence
	Goro Yamanaka	Guard	1, 2, 9	1	Acquitted	
	Shoichiro Matsumoto	Master sergeant	1, 2, 9	1	Acquitted	
266	Rokuro Sunobe	First lieutenant/doctor	1, 5	1	1 guilty	2 years' HL
267	Iichiro Morimoto	Major general	1, 3, 5	119	80 guilty	20 years' HL
	Chomatsu Tamura	Medical lance corporal	1, 2, 5	5	Acquitted	
	Toshio Toda	Second lieutenant	1, 2, 3, 5	15	5 guilty	8 years' HL
268	Yasumasa Yamamoto	Second lieutenant	1, 2, 3, 5	33	7 guilty	3 years' HL
	Soichi Miura	Sergeant	1, 2	19	6 guilty	3 years' HL
	Tezio Takashima	Civilian	1, 2	7	4 guilty	3 years' HL
	Shuji Kamada	NCO	1, 2	13	8 guilty	4 years' HL
	Iseo Hatakeyama	Camp CO	1, 2, 3, 5	47	10 guilty	3 years' HL
	Masonosuke Kurata	Medical corpsman	1, 2, 5	10	2 guilty	3 years' HL
	Shigeru Osanai	Civilian	1, 2, 5	8	5 guilty	3 years' HL
270	Takayoshi Sakaino	Sergeant major	1, 9	1	1 guilty	Life HL
271	Makoto Umeda	Civilian	1, 2	8	1 guilty	18 months' HL
272	Kap Chin Song	Korean police	1, 2, 5	3	3 guilty	10 years' HL
273	Kenichi Ogihara	Private first class	1, 2	16	9 guilty	4 years' HL
274	Kunio Saruwatori	Civilian	1, 2	8	8 guilty	20 years' HL
276	Seiji Nozaki	Lieutenant general	1, 3, 7	8	Acquitted	
	Chiyoshi Shimoda	Colonel	1, 3, 7	8	4 guilty	40 years' HL
	Yoshio Shingo	Major	1, 2, 7	8	4 guilty	5 years' HL
	Hyoma Kasai	Major	1, 2, 7	8	Acquitted	
	Toichi Taka	First lieutenant	1, 2, 7	8	4 guilty	5 years' HL
	Yosa Sakai	Lieutenant	1, 2, 7	8	Acquitted	
	Unosuke Motomiya	Civilian	1, 2, 7	8	4 guilty	5 years' HL
	Tojiro Yanagizawa	Civilian	1, 2, 7	8	4 guilty	1 year's HL
	Isaburo Ishii	Civilian	1, 2, 7	8	4 guilty	1 year's HL
	Tazuko Ishihara	Civilian	1, 2, 7	8	Acquitted	
	Wakako Hagihara	Civilian	1, 2, 7	8	Acquitted	

(Seitaro Fujisaki — Severed from case)

Sugamo Prison, Tokyo

Case	Defendant	Rank	Charges	Specifications	Verdicts	Sentence
	(Naozo Ishida—Severed from case)					
	Kazuya Sakakibara	Civilian	1, 2, 7	8	4 guilty	1 year's HL
	(Kanji Nemoto—Severed from case)					
	Jimbei Aoyagi	Civilian	1, 2, 7	8	Acquitted	
	Shotaro Sugo	Civilian	1, 2, 7	8	Acquitted	
	Tomoichi Suzuki	Civilian	1, 2, 7	8	4 guilty	1 year's HL
277	Tadashigo Shiomi	Warrant officer	1, 2	3	1 guilty	2 years' HL
278	Sai Yamashita	Lieutenant	1, 2	7	7 guilty	18 years' HL
	Masayuki Naka	Civilian	1, 2	4	4 guilty	10 years' HL
279	Zenichiro Yasuda	Guard	1, 2	7	6 guilty	5 years' HL
	Hajime Makao	Civilian	1, 2	3	3 guilty	2 years' HL
	Masakatsu Oyama	Civilian	1, 2	3	3 guilty	2 years' HL
281	Tamae Kondo	Colonel	1, 3, 5	10	5 guilty	5 years' HL
282	Yuzuru Sanematsu	Captain	1, 3, 4	2	2 guilty	40 years' HL
	Kanenobu Itagaki	Captain	1, 3	8	1 guilty	4 years' HL
283	Michiji Otake	Camp CO	1, 3	7	4 guilty	3 years' HL
286	Koji Suzuki	Civilian	1, 2	6	4 guilty	2 years' HL
	Misao Sukegawa	Civilian	1, 2, 5	8	6 guilty	9 years' HL
287	Fumio Fujiki	Sergeant	1, 2, 5	7	7 guilty	6 years' HL
288	Kajuro Aihara	Captain	1, 9	3	1 guilty	5 years' HL
	Hiroshi Akira	Colonel	1, 3, 4, 9	4	Acquitted	
	Kyusaku Fukushima	Major general	1, 3, 4, 9, 11	4	4 guilty	Death
	Masazumi Inada	Lieutenant general	1, 3, 4, 9	5	Acquitted	
	Tokuji Enatsu	Staff officer	1, 9	3	Acquitted	
	Shoshin Ito	Major general	1, 3, 4, 9, 11	4	4 guilty	Death
	Iichiro Jin	Adjutant chief	1, 9	3	Acquitted	
	Yoshinao Sato	Colonel	1, 9, 11	3	3 guilty	Death
	Katsuya Yakumaru	Lieutenant colonel	1, 9	3	2 guilty	Life HL

The Sentences

Name	Rank	Charges	Verdict	Sentence
Minoru Nakamura	Staff officer	1, 9	Acquitted	
Takanobu Kaku	Staff officer	1, 9	1 guilty	25 years' HL
Isamu Yokayama	Lieutenant general	1, 3, 4, 9, 11	3 guilty	Death
Hideto Kobuyama	Staff officer	1, 9	2 guilty	20 years' HL
(Mitsushige Inoue — Severed from case)				
Yusei Wako	First lieutenant	1, 9	2 guilty	Death
Koshi Yukino	Staff officer	1, 9	Acquitted	
Kaneyoshi Ikeda	Staff officer	1, 9	1 guilty	20 years' HL
Tatsuo Itezona	Staff officer	1, 9	1 guilty	Life HL
Tomenosuke Kusumoto	Staff officer	1, 9	1 guilty	40 years' HL
Sodayoshi Murata	Judicial staff	1, 9	Acquitted	
Hiroji Nakayama	Staff officer	1, 9	1 guilty	Death
Masahiko Narazaki	Staff officer	1, 9	1 guilty	Death
Hidehiko Noda	Staff officer	1, 9	1 guilty	25 years' HL
Minehiro Ohno	Judicial staff	1, 9	1 guilty	30 years' HL
Tamotsu Onishi	Judicial staff	1, 9	1 guilty	20 years' HL
Takahashi Otsuki	Staff officer	1, 9	1 guilty	30 years' HL
Kentaro Toji	Intelligence officer	1, 9	1 guilty	Death
Kiyoharu Tomomori	Lieutenant general	1, 3, 4, 9	2 guilty	Death
Hitoshi Yamauye	Staff officer	1, 9	1 guilty	25 years' HL
Fukuichi Yamamoto	Staff officer	1, 9	1 guilty	30 years' HL
Kanji Yoshida	First lieutenant	1, 9	2 guilty	30 years' HL
Tokuzo Tsuchiyama	Staff officer	1, 9	1 guilty	20 years' HL
Ichiro Maida	First lieutenant	1, 9	1 guilty	Life HL
Tasuku Okada*	Lieutenant general	1, 4, 6, 9	5 guilty	Death
Hajime Onishi	Colonel	1, 4, 9	4 guilty	Life HL
Naofumi Yasuda	Major	1, 4, 9	1 guilty	15 years' HL
Seiichi Adachi	Lieutenant colonel	1, 4, 9	2 guilty	17 years' HL
Masakuma Yonemaru	Colonel	1, 4, 9	3 guilty	25 years' HL
Rikio Yamata	Captain	1, 4, 9	1 guilty	20 years' HL

289

164 Sugamo Prison, Tokyo

Case	Defendant	Rank	Charges	Specifications	Verdicts	Sentence
	Takayashi Fujita	Sergeant	1, 9	1	1 guilty	10 years' HL
	Mataichi Furuyama	Corporal	1, 9	1	1 guilty	10 years' HL
	Shigeaki Hayashi	Private first class	1, 9	1	1 guilty	10 years' HL
	Keishi Tsuchiyama	Corporal	1, 9	1	1 guilty	10 years' HL
	Eijiro Yamamoto	Sergeant	1, 9	1	1 guilty	10 years' HL
	Kiyoshi Kondo	Sergeant	1, 9	2	2 guilty	10 years' HL
	Suetaka Kawakami	Sergeant	1, 9	2	2 guilty	10 years' HL
	Haruo Kuwada	Sergeant	1, 9	1	1 guilty	10 years' HL
	Yoshitaka Tsuruda	Sergeant major	1, 9	3	3 guilty	10 years' HL
	Hideshi Nobuta	Sergeant	1, 9	1	1 guilty	10 years' HL
	Yasui Sugai	Second lieutenant	1, 9	1	1 guilty	10 years' HL
	Mitsuo Tanabe	Probation officer	1, 9	1	1 guilty	10 years' HL
	Kiyoshi Yatagai	Probation officer	1, 9	1	1 guilty	10 years' HL
	Kikumoto Narita	First lieutenant	1, 4, 9	6	6 guilty	30 years' HL
290	Kajuro Aijara	Captain	1, 3, 7, 10, 11	16	13 guilty	20 years' HL
	Hiroshi Akira	Colonel	1, 3, 7, 10, 11	15	12 guilty	Life HL
	Kyusaku Fukushima	Major general	1, 3, 7, 10, 11	15	6 guilty	15 years' HL
	Shinju Goiyama	Captain	1, 3, 7, 10, 11	15	3 guilty	10 years' HL
	Shiro Goshima	Doctor	1, 7, 11	7	4 guilty	6 years' HL
	Goichi Hirako	Doctor	1, 3, 7, 10, 11	18	16 guilty	25 years' HL
	Kenichi Hirao	Doctor	1, 7, 10, 11	7	7 guilty	Death
	Kiyoma Horiuchi	Major general/doctor	1, 3, 7, 10, 11	15	Acquitted	
	Masazumi Inada	Lieutenant general	1, 3, 7, 10, 11	15	1 guilty	7 years' HL
	Akiro Ito	Dentist	1 (cannibalism)	1	Acquitted	
	Shoshin Ito	Major general	1, 3, 7, 10, 11	15	4 guilty	10 years' HL
	Iichiro Jin	Lieutenant colonel	1, 3, 7, 10, 11	15	Acquitted	
	Tatsuro Kishi	Second lieutenant	1, 7	3	Acquitted	
	Reiichiro Makino	Doctor	1, 7, 10, 11	7	4 guilty	9 years' HL

The Sentences

	Name	Rank	Charges		Verdict	Sentence
	Shinchiro Matake	Captain	1 (cannibalism)	1	Acquitted	
	Yoshio Mori	Doctor	1, 7, 10, 11	7	6 guilty	Death
	Kenji Morimoto	First lieutenant/doctor	1, 7, 10, 11	7	6 guilty	Life HL
	Nobuyoshi Nogawa	Medical student	1, 7, 10, 11	7	6 guilty	25 years' HL
	Tayura Oda	Lab worker	1 (cannibalism)	1	Acquitted	
	Miki Ryu	Doctor	1, 7, 10, 11	7	4 guilty	3 years' HL
	Yoshinao Sato	Colonel	1, 3, 7, 10, 11	15	15 guilty	Death
	Yoshitaka Senba	Medical student	1, 7, 10, 11	7	6 guilty	Life HL
	Tomoki Tashiro	Doctor	1, 7, 10, 11	7	6 guilty	15 years' HL
	Taro Torisu	Doctor	1, 3, 7, 10, 11	7	7 guilty	Death
	Hironaga Tsurumaru	Captain/doctor	1 (cannibalism)	1	Acquitted	
	Shizuko Tsutsui	Nurse	1, 7, 10, 11	7	6 guilty	5 years' HL
	Katsuya Yakamura	Lieutenant colonel	1, 3, 7, 10, 11	15	8 guilty	Life HL
	Isamu Yokoyama	Lieutenant general	1, 3, 7, 10, 11	15	11 guilty	Death
	Toshiyuki Kubo	Doctor	1, 7, 10, 11	7	6 guilty	15 years' HL
	Jiro Tashiro	First lieutenant/doctor	1, 7, 10, 11	7	6 guilty	15 years' HL
291	Kakuzo Iida	Ensign	1, 2, 3, 4, 5	21	18 guilty	Death
	Niro Akita	Captain/surgeon	1, 5	1	1 guilty	Death
	Saburo Higurashi	Lieutenant commander	1, 3	1	1 guilty	32 years' HL
	Mitsunari Yamaguchi	Lieutenant commander	1, 3	1	1 guilty	Life HL
	Toru Mizuno	Lieutenant	1, 3	1	1 guilty	15 years' HL
	Hidechika Sakuma	Captain	1, 3	1	1 guilty	22 years' HL
	Yukio Takahashi	Senior lieutenant/doctor	1, 3, 5	1	1 guilty	27 years' HL
	Tsutomu Takamoto	Lieutenant/doctor	1, 5	1	1 guilty	3 years' HL
292	Keiji Nagahara	Camp CO	1, 2, 3	5	2 guilty	2 years' HL
294	Toyokazu Hikita	NCO	1, 2	8	6 guilty	4 years' HL
	Kiyoshi Tanabe	NCO	1, 2	3	3 guilty	2½ years' HL
295	Kenji Hirano	First lieutenant	1, 5, 9	3	2 guilty	Life HL
296	Ippei Tamura	Second lieutenant	1, 3, 4, 9	3	1 guilty	12 years' HL
	Mitsumasa Oku	Superior private	1, 9	1	Acquitted	

Case	Defendant	Rank	Charges	Specifications	Verdicts	Sentence
	Tahichi Minamide	Superior private	1, 9	1	Acquitted	
297	Kiyozo Fukunaga	First lieutenant	1, 3	1	1 guilty	Life HL
298	Iwao Inanaga	Superior private	1, 2	5	4 guilty	5 years' HL
299	Kazuo Sato	Civilian	1, 2	11	9 guilty	7 years' HL
	Kaoru Funaki	Civilian	1, 2	13	13 guilty	10 years' HL
300	Tsuneo Ishikawa	Camp CO	1, 3	37	37 guilty	4 years' HL
301	Umetaro Makino	Civilian	1, 2	3	3 guilty	2 years' HL
304	Kurataro Hirano*	Unit commander	1, 2, 4, 5, 7, 9	22	20 guilty	Death
	Yoshitaka Kawane*	Unit commander	1, 2, 4, 5, 7, 9	31	23 guilty	Death
305	Kaname Sakaba	Colonel	1, 2, 3, 5	207	119 guilty	Life HL
	Kunji Suzuki	Colonel	1, 3, 5	127	84 guilty	Life HL
306	Etsuji Noguchi	Sergeant major	1, 9	1	1 guilty	12 years' HL
307	Tamotsu Furukawa	Rear admiral	1, 4, 9	2	2 guilty	20 years' HL
	Gosuke Taniguchi	Captain	1, 3, 9	2	Acquitted	
	Takao Sanokawa	Captain	1, 3, 9	2	Acquitted	
	Sazae Chiuma	Ensign	1, 3, 9	1	Acquitted	
	Yoshiyotsu Moritama	Captain	1, 3, 9	1	1 guilty	10 years' HL
	Toshisuke Tanabe	Lieutenant senior grade	1, 3, 9	1	1 guilty	10 years' HL
	Keiichi Nozaka	Lieutenant senior grade	1, 3, 9	1	1 guilty	10 years' HL
	Yoshio Nakata	Ensign	1, 9	1	1 guilty	10 years' HL
	Toshioka Maeda	Lieutenant junior grade	1, 9	1	1 guilty	10 years' HL
	Katsuto Imai	Ensign	1, 9	1	Acquitted	
308	Tahei Tsuda	Interpreter	1, 2	1	1 guilty	6 months' HL
310	Shoji Kono	Major general	1, 5	2	Acquitted	
	Toshio Toyama	Captain	1, 2, 4, 5	79	44 guilty	Life HL
	Nobushige Wachi	Second lieutenant	1, 2, 3, 5	31	15 guilty	8 years' HL
	Ranjo Fujino	Lieutenant colonel	1, 2, 3, 5	18	3 guilty	5 years' HL
	Tsune Nemoto	First lieutenant	1, 2, 3, 5	5	2 guilty	3½ years' HL

The Sentences

311	Eiichi Murakami	Mine guard	1, 2	10	8 guilty	5 years' HL
	Fukujiro Kakinoki	Mine guard	1, 2	12	5 guilty	3 years' HL
312	Goro Kimura	Civilian	1, 2	9	8 guilty	8 years' HL
	Kumataro Tanaka	Civilian	1, 2	10	9 guilty	9 years' HL
	Tomezo Matsuoka	Civilian	1, 2	11	9 guilty	9 years' HL
313	Hirokazu Tanaka	Sergeant major	1, 2	8	5 guilty	8 years' HL
314	Yosoichiro Ebi	Civilian	1, 2	1	1 guilty	30 years' HL
	Morikado Kobayashi	Civilian	1, 2	1	1 guilty	40 years' HL
	Keiji Higuchi	Civilian	1, 2	1	Acquitted	
	Yoshio Hosano	Civilian	1, 2	1	Acquitted	
	Itchisaku Kojime	Civilian	1, 2	1	1 guilty	25 years' HL
	Keichi Sakai	Civilian	1, 2	1	1 guilty	10 years' HL
	Kenichi Nozaki	Civilian	1, 2	1	1 guilty	35 years' HL
315	Jukichi Sasaki	Mine guard	1, 2	14	4 guilty	5 years' HL
	Kakuji Ishigaki	Mine guard	1, 2	10	Acquitted	
316	Ko Nishikawa	Quartermaster	1, 2	5	4 guilty	8 years' HL
317	Munehiko Oshiwa	Lieutenant	1, 9	1	1 guilty	7 years' HL
	Isamu Sato	Lieutenant commander	1, 4, 9	1	1 guilty	20 years' HL
318	Tetsuo Taniguchi	Ensign	1, 9	1	1 guilty	Death
	Isamu Sato*	Commander	1, 4, 9	2	1 guilty	Death
	Satohiko Kida	Captain	1, 4, 9	1	1 guilty	40 years' HL
	Masayoshi Yoshida	Lieutenant	1, 4, 9	1	1 guilty	40 years' HL
319	Masutaro Iwasaki	Major	1, 4, 9	2	2 guilty	15 years' HL
320	Kohei Akaike	Superior seaman	1, 2	3	3 guilty	7 years' HL
	Yoshie Komine	Petty officer	1, 2	17	17 guilty	40 years' HL
321	Riichi Kitashima	Lieutenant colonel	1, 3, 5	5	4 guilty	5 years' HL
325	Kenzo Yamada	First lieutenant	1, 2, 5	9	9 guilty	18 years' HL
	Yoshiaki Irie	Sergeant	1, 2, 5	12	12 guilty	16 years' HL
326	Seitaro Fujita	Sergeant	1, 9	1	1 guilty	30 years' HL
	Shigeru Kimura	First lieutenant	1, 3, 9	1	1 guilty	2 years' HL

Case	Defendant	Rank	Charges	Specifications	Verdicts	Sentence
	Itsuo Mikota	Major	1, 4, 9	1	1 guilty	Life HL
	Minoru Nakagawa	Second lieutenant	1, 4, 9	2	1 guilty	30 years' HL
	Shuzo Uda	Warrant officer	1, 3, 9	1	1 guilty	6 months' HL
327	Katsuma Fukuda	Sergeant	1, 2	4	4 guilty	12 years' HL
328	Hiroshi Anjo	Lieutenant colonel	1, 2, 3, 5	20	5 guilty	4 years' HL
	Hideo Fujioka	Lieutenant colonel	1, 2, 4, 5, 9	18	11 guilty	Life HL
	Tomekichi Hamada	Sergeant major	1, 9	7	1 guilty	2 years' HL
	Otogoro Ishida	Lieutenant general	1, 3	7	1 guilty	1 year's HL
	Hideichi Kobayashi	Warrant officer	1, 9	1	Acquitted	
	Shinpachi Konishi	Lance corporal	1, 9	1	Acquitted	
	Michio Kunitake	Lieutenant general	1, 3, 4, 5, 9	20	12 guilty	Life HL
	Sadaya Matsuda	Seaman	1, 9	2	1 guilty	2 years' HL
	Takao Mori	Military policeman	1, 9	3	Acquitted	
	Shigemi Morimoto	Military policeman	1, 9	3	Acquitted	
	Tsugio Nagatoma	Major general	1, 4, 5	19	13 guilty	Life HL
	Masamoto Nakano	Interpreter	1, 2	1	1 guilty	2 years' HL
	Kojiro Oba	Colonel	1, 3	7	4 guilty	10 years' HL
	Takekazu Oikada	Military policeman	1, 9	2	Acquitted	
	Sanji Okida	Lieutenant general	1, 3, 4	7	6 guilty	Life HL
	Buichi Ono	Captain	1, 3	7	Acquitted	
	Ikoma Shiuchi	Second lieutenant	1, 3, 4, 5, 9	15	9 guilty	Life HL
	Ryuzaburo Sugiura	Warrant officer	1, 4, 9	2	Acquitted	
	Izou Takahashi	Military policeman	1, 9	3	Acquitted	
	Hiroaki Takayama	Military policeman	1, 9	1	Acquitted	
	Chikara Takeda	Sergeant major	1, 9	4	Acquitted	
	Ryoichi Tateno	Military policeman	1, 9	2	Acquitted	
	Kazuyoshi Tsuno	Military policeman	1, 9	1	Acquitted	
	Eitaro Uchiyama	Lieutenant general	1, 3, 4, 5	20	12 guilty	40 years' HL

The Sentences

	Yasuo Wada	Warrant officer	1, 3, 9	5	5 guilty	5 years' HL
	Yoshio Yamamura	Colonel	1, 3	7	Acquitted	
	Norio Yamanaka	Major	1, 3, 4	7	5 guilty	8 years' HL
329	Yutaka Odazawa	Lieutenant junior grade	1, 9	1	1 guilty	Life HL
	Kaoru Okuma*	Lieutenant commander	1, 2, 4, 9	5	4 guilty	Death
	Naotada Fujihira	Ensign	1, 2, 9	2	2 guilty	Life HL
	Kiyohisa Noto	Captain	1, 9	1	1 guilty	20 years' HL
	Tsunehiko Yamamoto	Lieutenant	1, 2, 9	2	2 guilty	Life HL
330	Taichi Sato	Captain	1, 2, 4, 5	7	7 guilty	8 years' HL
331	Fukuji Takahashi	Labor foreman	1, 2	18	8 guilty	4 years' HL
334	Tsunee Abe	Civilian	1, 2	2	2 guilty	5 years' HL
	Seiji Sakai	Civilian	1, 2	2	2 guilty	5 years' HL
335	Okuji Tonomura	First lieutenant	1, 4, 9	2	2 guilty	9 years' HL
	Kozo Hatano	Corporal	1, 9	1	1 guilty	3 years' HL
	Fujio Mutsuro	Lieutenant colonel	1, 4, 9	3	2 guilty	35 years' HL
	Jiro Takeuchi	Sergeant major	1, 9	1	1 guilty	3 years' HL
336	Sazae Chiuma	Ensign	1, 9	2	2 guilty	10 years' HL
337	Seiichi Terada	Lieutenant general	1, 3, 4	13	7 guilty	Life HL
	Shojiro Kawamorita	Lieutenant colonel	1, 3	13	3 guilty	5 years' HL
	Kizo Mikami	Lieutenant general	1, 3	13	3 guilty	12 years' HL
	Shiro Nonogaki	Lieutenant colonel	1, 3, 4	13	Acquitted	
	Atsutaka Saruwatari	Colonel	1, 4	13	3 guilty	4 years' HL
	Masanari Shibuya	Lieutenant colonel	1, 4	13	Acquitted	
	Masayuki Uchida	Major	1, 4	13	Acquitted	
	Mamoru Fushimi	Colonel	1, 4	13	3 guilty	10 years' HL
	Miso Matsumae	Colonel	1, 3	13	Acquitted	
	Zenichi Muto	Major	1, 4	13	Acquitted	
	Tokio Oga	Colonel	1, 4	13	2 guilty	4 years' HL
	Tomisaburo Sawa	Superior private	1, 2, 9	2	2 guilty	5 years' HL
	Hideo Tsuji	Major	1, 4	13	Acquitted	

Case	Defendant	Rank	Charges	Specifications	Verdicts	Sentence
	Toru Ogawa	Second lieutenant	1, 4	13	1 guilty	2 years' HL
	Taichi Deguchi	Master sergeant	1, 2, 4, 9	7	6 guilty	Death
	(Manichi Nishitani—Severed from case)					
338	Saburo Matsuura	Sergeant	1, 2	5	5 guilty	3 years' HL
	Yuetsu Fukumura	Private first class	1, 2	9	9 guilty	2 years' HL
339	Hisashi Ichioka	Vice admiral	1, 3, 9, 11	4	2 guilty	20 years' HL
	Hisashi Mito	Vice admiral	1, 3, 9, 11	4	1 guilty	8 years' HL
	Teruhisa Komatsu	Vice admiral	1, 3, 9, 11	4	1 guilty	15 years' HL
	(Kyugoro Shimamoto—Case continued)					
	Tasuku Nakazawa	Rear admiral	1, 3, 9, 11	4	1 guilty	10 years' HL
	Noboru Ishizaki	Rear admiral	1, 3, 9, 11	4	1 guilty	10 years' HL
	Haruo Katsuta	Rear admiral	1, 3, 9, 11	4	Acquitted	
	Masao Teraoka	Captain	1, 3, 9, 11	4	Acquitted	
	Shojiro Iura	Captain	1, 9, 11	3	1 guilty	6 years' HL
	Chojuro Takahashi	Captain	1, 3, 9, 11	4	1 guilty	1 year's HL
	Yasuo Fujimori	Commander	1, 3, 9, 11	4	1 guilty	4 years' HL
	Kiyonori Otani	Commander	1, 9, 11	3	Acquitted	
	Hajime Nakagawa	Commander	1, 9, 11	3	1 guilty	8 years' HL
	Kinzo Tonozuka	Commander	1, 9, 11	3	Acquitted	
	Toshio Kusaka	Commander	1, 9, 11	3	1 guilty	5 years' HL
	Tsuruzo Shimizu	Commander	1, 9, 11	3	Acquitted	
	Masao Ishibashi	Lieutenant commander	1, 9, 11	3	Acquitted	
	Nobuyuki Tadaki	Captain	1, 3, 9, 11	6	2 guilty	10 years' HL
	Shoichi Kawakami	Lieutenant senior grade	1, 4, 9, 11	6	1 guilty	8 years' HL
	Toranosuke Iiyama	Lieutenant junior grade	1, 4, 9, 11	5	Acquitted	
	Shigenori Osawa	Lieutenant commander	1, 9, 11	3	Acquitted	
	Tomoya Nawa	Lieutenant	1, 9, 11	3	Acquitted	
	Sadao Motonaka	Lieutenant	1, 9, 11	3	1 guilty	7 years' HL

The Sentences

Masonori Hattori	Lieutenant	1, 9, 11	3	1 guilty	5 years' HL
(Goichi Katayama—Severed from case)					
Masao Motohashi	Surgeon general	1, 9, 11	3	Acquitted	
Motohide Yanabe	Sub lieutenant	1, 9, 11	3	1 guilty	7 years' HL
Toyosuke Izumi	Sub lieutenant	1, 9, 11	3	Acquitted	
Shozo Anaguchi	Warrant officer	1, 9, 11	3	1 guilty	2 years' HL
Kampei Munenaga	Warrant officer	1, 9, 11	3	Acquitted	
Mitoku Kobuke	Warrant officer	1, 9, 11	3	Acquitted	
Sakuichi Okuda	Warrant officer	1, 9, 11	3	Acquitted	
Masaru Gonda	Superior petty officer	1, 9, 11	3	Acquitted	
Hitoshi Hashimoto	Superior petty officer	1, 9, 11	3	Acquitted	
Masao Umehira	Petty officer	1, 9, 11	3	Acquitted	
Asao Yamada	Petty officer	1, 9, 11	3	Acquitted	
Tsuneji Wada	Lieutenant	1, 9, 11	3	Acquitted	
Shingo Takahashi	Lieutenant	1, 9, 11	3	Acquitted	
Keizo Noguchi	Lieutenant	1, 9, 11	3	Acquitted	
Tadayuki Chuba	Sub lieutenant	1, 9, 11	3	Acquitted	
Kenji Iwanaga	Lieutenant commander	1, 9, 11	3	Acquitted	
Yoshio Mitsuoka	Warrant officer	1, 9, 11	3	Acquitted	
Kinji Kamae	Warrant officer	1, 9, 11	3	Acquitted	
Morimasa Kumatani	Chief petty officer	1, 9, 11	3	Acquitted	
Kaname Haraguchi	Lieutenant senior grade	1, 7, 9	2	1 guilty	8 years' HL
Munehei Takeyoshi	Lieutenant senior grade	1, 7, 9	2	1 guilty	8 years' HL
Tenjiro Murase	Petty officer	1, 7, 9	2	1 guilty	5 years' HL
Kuramatsu Yamakawa	Ensign	1, 4, 5, 7, 9	3	2 guilty	15 years' HL
Genzo Akiba	Seaman	1, 7, 9	1	Acquitted	
Teruo Akita	Petty officer	1, 7, 9	1	1 guilty	3 years' HL
Shusaku Takano	Petty officer	1, 7, 9	1	1 guilty	5 years' HL
Eiichi Kasatani	Petty officer	1, 7, 9	1	1 guilty	5 years' HL
Daisaku Mori	Petty officer	1, 7, 9	1	1 guilty	5 years' HL

340

Case	Defendant	Rank	Charges	Specifications	Verdicts	Sentence
	Jiro Nishino	Petty officer	1, 7, 9	1	1 guilty	3 years' HL
	Sakae Okura	Seaman	1, 7, 9	1	1 guilty	5 years' HL
	Toshio Shiro	Seaman first class	1, 7, 9	1	1 guilty	3 years' HL
	Takeji Shiroshita	Superior seaman	1, 7, 9	1	Acquitted	
	Isaburo Tajima	Petty officer	1, 7, 9	1	1 guilty	4 years' HL
	Shinryu Yasukawa	Petty officer	1, 7, 9	1	Acquitted	
	Koichiro Yamanaka	Petty officer	1, 2, 7, 9	2	1 guilty	4 years' HL
342	Kiichi Yoshida	Captain	1, 3, 5	5	4 guilty	6 years' HL
344	Taichi Ito	Major	1, 4	1	1 guilty	1 year's HL
346	Rimpei Kato	Lieutenant general	1, 3, 4	2	2 guilty	18 years' HL
	Okikatsu Arao	Colonel	1, 3, 4	2	2 guilty	6 years' HL
	Goro Isoya	Lieutenant general	1, 3, 4	2	2 guilty	1 year's HL
	Cholo Mononobe	Lieutenant general	1, 3, 4	2	2 guilty	1 year's HL
	Hiroshi Nukata	Lieutenant general	1, 3, 4	2	2 guilty	6 years' HL
	Bunro Saheki	Lieutenant general	1, 3, 4	2	2 guilty	24 years' HL
	(Mitsuo Tomita—Severed from case)					
	(Yehei Toyama—Severed from case)					
	Tadakazu Wakamatsu	Lieutenant general	1, 3, 4	2	2 guilty	2 years' HL
347	Yoshinari Tanaka*	Lieutenant colonel	1, 3, 4, 9	2	2 guilty	Death
348	Minoru Nomi	Captain	1, 4, 9	1	1 guilty	Life HL
	Yutaka Yokoyama	Lieutenant junior grade	1, 9	1	1 guilty	8 years' HL
	Akira Suzuki	Lieutenant junior grade	1, 9	1	1 guilty	8 years' HL
	Hisayoshi Shiinoki	Military policeman	1, 9	1	1 guilty	8 years' HL
349	Hiroichi Konishi	Civilian policeman	1, 2, 4	9	4 guilty	8 years' HL
	Tokiichi Koizumi	Civilian	1, 2, 3	13	10 guilty	2 years' HL
	Minoru Takeuchi	Civilian	1, 2, 5	11	10 guilty	12 years' HL
	Masaichi Horie	Civilian	1, 2	1	1 guilty	3 months' HL
351	Eisaku Funaki	Factory guard	1, 2	1	Acquitted	

The Sentences

Kyui Hada	Factory guard	1, 2	Acquitted	
Kichiji Harada	Factory guard	1, 2	Acquitted	
Sakuzo Hori	Factory guard	1, 2	Acquitted	
Jammatsu Ishiyama	Factory guard	1, 2	Acquitted	
Shiroji Ito	Sergeant/executive officer	1, 2, 3	3 guilty	15 years' HL
Yosichi Ito	Factory guard	1, 2	1 guilty	1 year's HL
Shamatsu Iwanami	Factory guard	1, 2	1 guilty	3 years' HL
Yuzo Karube	Factory guard	1, 2	1 guilty	2 years' HL
Shinnosuke Kawaguchi	Factory guard	1, 2	1 guilty	7 years' HL
Koei Kobayashi	Factory guard	1, 2	1 guilty	3 years' HL
Ryoji Kobayashi	Factory guard	1, 2	1 guilty	2 years' HL
Eihachi Kunikane	Factory guard	1, 2	Acquitted	
Kuraichi Kurada	Factory guard	1, 2	1 guilty	1 year's HL
Kyujiro Matsuo	Factory guard	1, 2	1 guilty	1 year's HL
Tetsu Mimura	Factory guard	1, 2	Acquitted	
Yoshisuke Minami	Factory guard	1, 2	Acquitted	
Zenji Morimoto	Factory guard	1, 2	Acquitted	
Rokushi Nakamura	Factory guard	1, 2	Acquitted	
Minoo Nakayama	Factory guard	1, 2	Acquitted	
Yoshizo Nasuno	Factory guard	1, 2	1 guilty	1 year's HL
Gontoro Nishina	Factory guard	1, 2	Acquitted	
Zensaku Ogawa	Factory guard	1, 2	Acquitted	
Soji Onishi	Factory guard	1, 2	Acquitted	
Iwazo Ono	Factory guard	1, 2	1 guilty	2 years' HL
Takematsu Ono	Factory guard	1, 2	1 guilty	18 months' HL
Toshihiko Ono	Factory guard	1, 2	Acquitted	
Isao Sato	Factory guard	1, 2	1 guilty	2 years' HL
Kushiro Sato	Factory guard	1, 2	1 guilty	15 years' HL
Shinichiro Sato	Factory guard	1, 2	1 guilty	1 year's HL
Kiyoshi Seino	Factory guard	1, 2	1 guilty	18 months' HL

Case	Defendant	Rank	Charges	Specifications	Verdicts	Sentence
	Niichiro Shimabara	Factory guard	1, 2	1	Acquitted	
	Ryoei Shirai	Factory guard	1, 2	2	Acquitted	
	Takesi Suda	Factory guard	1, 2	1	1 guilty	15 years' HL
	Kiyotaka Sugazawa	Medical sergeant major	1, 2	3	1 guilty	1 year's HL
	Masaji Takizawa	Factory guard	1, 2	1	Acquitted	
	Shohei Watanabe	Factory guard	1, 2	1	Acquitted	
352	Kichiji Yamamoto	Factory guard	1, 2	1	1 guilty	15 years' HL
	Tatsuhiko Furuya	Sergeant major	1, 2	7	7 guilty	20 years' HL
	Tomizo Hanamori	Civilian	1, 2	5	5 guilty	12 years' HL
	Akira Otaki	Civilian	1, 2	7	4 guilty	5 years' HL
	Takeo Kanamaru	Civilian	1, 2	6	4 guilty	7 years' HL
	Masaji Yamamoto	Civilian	1, 2	2	2 guilty	4 years' HL
	Shuji Yoritsune	Civilian	1, 2	3	1 guilty	2½ years' HL
353	Masaichi Toyama	Medical orderly	1, 2, 9	2	1 guilty	4 years' HL
354	Manichi Nishitani	Guard	1, 2	4	4 guilty	5 years' HL
356	Shintaro Nakagawa	The accused in this case were civilian police not engaged in the war effort. The "victims" of the mistreatment and abuse were Chinese nationals, living in Japan, who had been arrested and convicted under Japanese laws in effect at the time. Therefore the IMTFE had no jurisdiction in this case.				
	Junichi Okamoto					
	Tsunetaro Takeuchi					
	Hideo Oya					
	Toshihara Waki					
	Yoshiichi Kimura					
	Masao Suzuki					
	Yoshinori Enoki					
	Kazuo Kihara					
	Kenpei Ishikawa					
	Genosuke Kumazono					
	Kenshiro Matsumoto					
	Nishio Yamaguchi					

The Sentences

	Yasuo Gomi					
	Heikichi Nakajima					
	Jiro Kageshita					
	Ichitaro Nakano					
	Norio Ohno					
	Yoshiatsu Miwa					
	Masayoshi Takagi					
	Jutaro Kubota					
357	Seizo Taika	Second lieutenant	1, 9	1	1 guilty	1 year's HL
358	Eiichi Sugihara	Lieutenant colonel	1, 3, 4, 5	4	2 guilty	5 years' HL
361	Tetsutaro Kato	First lieutenant	1, 2, 4, 9	5	5 guilty	Life HL
362	Teruo Akamine	First lieutenant	1, 9	1	1 guilty	Life HL
	Mitsushige Inoue	Sergeant major	1, 9	1	1 guilty	10 years' HL
363	Hajime Umino	Lieutenant	1, 9	1	1 guilty	7 years' HL
364	Jiro Hamamoto	Warrant officer	1, 4, 9	4	4 guilty	15 years' HL
365	Noboru Hashiyama	First lieutenant	1, 9	1	1 guilty	Life HL
366	Suekatsu Matsuki	Sergeant major	1, 9	1	1 guilty	20 years' HL
368	Masaji Nagaoka	Corporal	1, 9	1	1 guilty	10 years' HL
369	Keijiro Otani	Colonel	1, 3, 4, 5	16	12 guilty	10 years' HL
370	Norifumi Otosu	First lieutenant	1, 9	1	1 guilty	30 years' HL
371	Torao Yuasa	Lieutenant senior grade	1, 4, 9	2	1 guilty	8 years' HL

Note: Fifty-nine cases are not included in this table. Eight were duplications of listed cases. The other fifty-one were not included in the microfilm records since the defendants in each case were acquitted.

THE EXECUTIONS

The IMTFE rendered its verdicts on the Class A war criminals on November 12, 1948. The condemned prisoners were scheduled for execution on December 1. On November 29 and December 2, the defense filed motions with the United States Supreme Court for leave to file petitions for writs of habeas corpus. The three filed on November 29 were on behalf of Tojo, Doihara, and Hirota. Those filed on December 2 were for Kido, Oka, Sato, and Shimada. MacArthur postponed all the executions until the Court could make a ruling on the petitions. On December 20 the petitions were denied, and a new time and date of 12:01 A.M., December 23, 1948, were set for the executions to begin.

Though the condemned men were not aware of it at the time, they had but six weeks to prepare themselves for death. The security at Sugamo became so strict that it bordered on paranoia. The condemned war criminals could not go anywhere unless handcuffed to a guard. An officer or NCO also walked closely behind the handcuffed pair. A guard was beside the cell door twenty-four hours a day. The cells were lit around the clock, and there was no privacy at any time. When they slept, the prisoners had to have their faces and hands uncovered and in view at all times.

After they had been sentenced, they were not allowed a pencil, sheet of paper, or books of any kind. Tojo, acting as spokesman for the seven condemned men, finally sent word to the commanding officer that, under the Geneva Convention and the Potsdam Declaration, they were allowed to have religious books. The commanding officer agreed. When they were finally allowed pencil and paper, the pencils were so short that they were difficult to use, and the paper was so small that it was practically impossible to write even a short letter.

The prison's Buddhist priest, Dr. Shinsho Hanayama, had been at Sugamo since February 28, 1946, and had already attended and comforted many Class C prisoners who were executed. He conducted weekly services in the prison chapel and spent considerable time with the relatives and families of all the prisoners confined at Sugamo. He also gave weekly lectures at Tokyo University. After the IMTFE judgments were rendered, he spent most of his time at Sugamo with the seven condemned Class A prisoners.

Doihara used Hanayama to assist him in convincing his wife and two sons to forsake Shintoism and embrace Buddhism.

The two men met five times between November 19 and the night of the execution. In their first meeting Doihara informed the priest that at the moment the sentences were pronounced, all his worries had left him. Almost at once he had begun to feel brighter. By this time religious books were permitted in the prison, and Hanayama lent him several books on Buddhism.

Doihara and the priest had several long discussions about the various sects of Buddhism, and the prisoner confessed that he had been of the Zen sect of Buddhism since becoming an officer in the army. He repeatedly requested Hanayama to relay his beliefs about Buddhism to his family.

In the Japanese tradition, near the end he gave the priest hair and nail clippings to pass on to his family. Another custom was honored when Hanayama asked the condemned man for a tanka — a classical poem. Doihara wrote:

>Farewell to thee
>moon in the window.
>My life is but for the eve
>and I am loath to leave thee.
>>My past is a dream
>>of sixty winters
>>and how peaceful and serene I be,
>>a soul to be saved.
>Blessed with the happiness
>of the faithful, though I be
>told my time is come,
>my heart does give a sudden beat.
>>How sad the voice
>>of the train through the night.
>>It sounds
>>of life transient.

Hirota was seventy-one years old, the father of two sons and two daughters. Until the end he wrote letters to his family addressed to his wife, who had died years earlier.

Hanayama met with him four times between sentencing and execution but, after sentencing, Hirota became even quieter and more remorseful than he had been during the trial. Hanayama had difficulty communicating with him. When asked for some nail and hair clippings, he told the priest that he did not think it was important to his family. He also informed Hanayama that he had never interfered with his children's religious beliefs or training. He was unable or refused to discuss his own religious beliefs with the priest. When asked for a poem, tanka, or memories to relay to his family, he replied: "My achievements speak for themselves for everything that has been done since I entered the service of the public. I have told you all that I would. I have come along in the feeling that everything finally ends in blankness, and that I have said what there was to be said, done what there was to be done, and that there is really nothing else to talk about. We can but live as nature wills it, and die as she wills it."

Hirota seemed to draw within himself and was unusually quiet and pathetic. Other condemned prisoners tried but failed to communicate with him. He told Hanayama that he already had a posthumous name, which had been selected after his wife's death by three temples in Fukuoka, and he would be satisfied with that. However, when asked what it was, he did not seem to remember. He was unable to talk about his wife. Hanayama promised to meet with his children and assist them in any way possible.

Itagaki was sixty-four years old. His family consisted of a wife, three sons, and two daughters. One of his sons was a captive of the Russians in Siberia.

At his first meeting with Hanayama, he informed the priest that he was very pleased to have received the death sentence and did not want his family to have a funeral ceremony for him. Only his picture and nail and hair clippings were to be given to his family. He complained that Sugamo officials had taken his false teeth and glasses away, but he was making out all right, since American food was soft and he could still see well enough to read.

At their second meeting, he discussed his feelings and wrote a letter he wanted his family to receive. He stated:

> Even though I die, my children will carry life on. Although my physical self shall perish, it will unite with nature in her grandness and will become one with nature that is God, that is Buddha. History always repeats itself in that life knows no death. Looking back over my life, I feel so overwhelmed with remorse that I do not know what to do with

myself. I cannot but feel that the labor of our whole lives has been in vain. Therefore I am feeling that by becoming a spiritual guardian saint of the nation, I can strive to obtain in death what I was unable to while alive.

Hanayama met with Itagaki five times before he was executed. He asked the priest to hold Buddhist services for him at two separate temples after his death, one for his family and one for the imperial household, and he gave the priest the following tanka:

> I have found, at last
> that in this world of deceit
> the way of Buddha
> is the one truth.
>   I am going,
>   following those saints
>   who look over our people
>   ever eternal.

Kimura was sixty-one years old. His wife was fifty-one, their oldest son eighteen and their oldest daughter twenty at the time of his execution. Some of his family were Christian, while others followed the Buddhist faith. He had some Christian faith but was reluctant to be baptized. At his family's request a Catholic priest came to Sugamo, but he again refused to be baptized.

After sentencing, his first meeting with Hanayama was held in a recess room adjoining the prison chapel, with his family. As a lecturer at Tokyo University, Hanayama had met many young students and was immensely impressed with Kimura's eldest son, Taro. When he commented that he envied him for fathering such a son, Kimura replied: "Whatever my children have that wins the praise of others, they owe it all to my wife, she is a splendid woman."

During a meeting between the two men on November 29, Kimura was handcuffed to an officer by the right hand. On this date the priest met with several of the condemned men and each was handcuffed to an officer. At earlier meetings they had been handcuffed to noncommissioned officers or enlisted men.

Hanayama delivered several tankas from Kimura's wife and one from his daughter. After reading them Kimura appeared deeply impressed. He then read a very long letter from his son Taro and wept. Later he confided to Hanayama that he was struck with admiration that a youth of that age could write so splendidly and have so noble a spirit.

Shortly after this meeting prison officials told Hanayama that he could go home. He said, "It finally dawned on me that things had taken a sudden change." He was under the impression that the executions were to take place either that night or the next. He did not realize they had been delayed while the Supreme Court made its decision.

On December 1 Hanayama spent all day visiting members of the condemned men's families. When he went home in the evening, Mrs. Kimura and two of her children arrived and visited with him until almost midnight. It was a very long day for an old man. The daughter, Yuriko, told the priest, "I am a Christian and father may, because he is dying a Buddhist, feel constrained and not leave any words for us. I am worried about that and want him to feel free to leave us something. Will you please tell him about how we feel?" This was done at the next meeting, and Kimura agreed, telling Hanayama that he understood and respected his family's feelings. He then wrote:

> How bitter to know
> the fall of the cherry,
> when once in the spring
> it bloomed to charm the eyes of men.
>   Ne'er may I forget
>   the lessons and the teachings
>   for my living children
>   that they may live, both strong and true.
> The foundation of the nation
> ever sure and secure they be
> and would that you, my beloved
> watch them over.
>   My physical self be sacrifice
>   to a lasting peace is offered
>   and may it be that I, seven times
>   receive a new life, to serve the nation.

Matsui was seventy-one years of age; his wife Fumiko was fifty-six. They had no children of their own but had adopted a daughter. Matsui had once been a follower of Shintoism but had changed to Buddhism and wanted his wife and daughter to change also.

When he returned from China, he brought soil containing the remains of war dead, both Japanese and Chinese, and had a Buddhist altar built behind his home. For the unveiling he enlisted both a Catholic and a Buddhist priest to perform mass for the dead.

In his meetings with Hanayama, he seemed resigned to his death but concerned about the health and mental state of his wife. He was afraid that she might commit suicide on his execution. Hanayama calmed him by assuring him that he would spend time with Fumiko and explain everything to her.

Matsui became very worried when he found that the execution order had been postponed. He was afraid that the Court might reduce his sentence to life imprisonment. He told Hanayama: "I am in the belief that it's the mercy of Kwannon, Buddha, that I am to be executed. If I should be given life imprisonment by the Supreme Court, it will make it really quite difficult for me."

Regarding the Nanking incident, as he referred to what the court called the "Rape of Nanking," he told Hanayama:

> The Nanking incident was a terrible disgrace. Shortly after entering Nanking, when memorial services were being held for the dead, I mentioned that services should be performed for the Chinese dead also, only the others, including my Chief of Staff, said that they would not understand and that it would affect the morale of the Japanese troops, and then even the Divisional Commanders became engaged in the thing. Immediately after the memorial services, I had them assembled and wept tears of anger at them, as Commander in Chief. Both Asaka and Lt. General Yamagawa, Area Commanders, were there but I told them all that after all that effort to emblazon Imperial prestige, everything had been lost in one moment through the brutalities of the soldiers. And can you imagine it, after that, they laughed at me. For one extreme example, one of the Divisional Commanders even came up asking "What's wrong about it?" I am really, therefore, quite happy that I at least should have ended up this way, in the sense that it may serve to urge self-reflection on that many more of the military of that time. After things turning out this way, I am really wanting to die at any time.

Muto was fifty-seven years old. His wife, oldest daughter, and mother-in-law all lived in an old shack on a burned-out property they owned near Tokyo. Muto and his family embraced the Honganju school of the Shinshu sect of Buddhism. He claimed to have studied several sects of Buddhism and Christianity while he was a lieutenant and captain in the army, but was unable to find himself in Christianity.

In their first meeting, Hanayama discussed the various books he had been distributing to the condemned men and then talked about Hirota's mental state. He stated: "Of the seven of you, Hirota alone appears to be so lonely and sad." Muto replied: "Hirota is a man of great moral strength and I believe that he will be perfectly all right. If there should be anything ignoble or unsightly in what we do, please straighten us up."

During the third meeting, held on November 29, Tojo was brought into the meeting room. Muto seemed comparatively restrained in his manner toward Tojo. The priest read letters to him from both his daughters, Hatsuko and Chiyoko. Both letters were bright and full of love and understanding.

At the fourth meeting, Muto told the priest that he had written some tanka poems and songs. He informed Hanayama that his religious beliefs had deepened and strengthened since the verdict was read, and said: "I have written what I feel every day, without embellishment and without playing heroic or gallant, and although none of them are very good, they are just what popped into my mind."

> No greater glory can there be
> that with only one self
> to offer, I be
> a sacrifice to peace.
>> Fated as I was to die
>> on that southern Isle
>> what can I have to regret,
>> this life of mine.
> The scent of the chrysanthemum
> 'tis gone, and Buddha
> is looking down on me, from above.
>> The lone chrysanthemum
>> how brilliant 'tis
>> in the candlelight.

Tojo was sixty-five years old and his wife, Katsuko, sixty. They had four daughters and three sons. The family religion was Shintoism, but Tojo had earlier changed to Buddhism.

At his first meeting with Hanayama, Tojo was handcuffed to two enlisted men and also had an officer guarding him. The priest read him a will, prepared by Satoshi Oie, and then spoke to him about the faith of Shibano Tadao, who had been executed earlier. Tojo then read from some notes and gave Hanayama messages to transmit. The notes were in two parts—public and private. The four points in the public message were as follows:

1. The trial is over, and having fulfilled my duties, to some extent, I am filled with relief. The sentence so far as I am concerned, is as

deserved. I am sorry though, that I was not able to assume the responsibility by myself and that I brought my colleagues trouble. I sincerely regret it. At least, through the trial, nothing was carried up to the Emperor and on that point I am being comforted. Only for those of my countrymen who suffered from the war, my death sentence does not in the least absolve me from my responsibilities. I am sincerely sorry for that.

2. Concerning the verdict, I wish to avoid saying anything about it, at this time. Matters of humanity, of the atrocities committed against prisoners, I fully regret and believe quite deplorable. It is fully my own responsibility that I was unable to drive home, in the army and elsewhere, the traditional benevolence of the Japanese people and the humanity of the Emperor. I only want the peoples of the world not to misunderstand this; that this was brought about by the indiscretions of a small part of the military, and that the entire Japanese are not so, neither is the army as a whole. I only hope the people of the world do not misunderstand the score. In other words, I want them to realize that it was the misconduct of a part of the military.

3. Only three years have passed since World War II was ended, and dark troubles and disturbances still envelop the whole world. Taking the dark clouds covering the Far East into special notice, I cannot but be afraid for the future awaiting Japan. Yet I am in the firm conviction that the spirit of Japan that has been cultivated and nurtured for on to thirty hundred years will not be lost in a day. I want to go my way, firmly convinced that in the final reckoning, the efforts of the Japanese people with world-wide sympathies and love will rebuild again. I believe that in the light of the true understandings and sympathies attained in the last war, the future of the people of East Asia, living here for ages, will be blessed with prosperity.

4. For the war-dead, the dead who died of wounds, who suffered from the war and for their people, I request further sympathies, not only from the government, but also from the Allied Powers as well. These people have simply died and worked in all sincerity and devotion for their country and, if there is any crime committed for their war, it is the crime of men like me, the leaders. With my execution, judgement will have been passed. The men in Sugamo are carrying out their sentences. I beg sympathetic consideration for the families of the war criminals. I also beg that the people kept in Soviet Russia be repatriated to Japan proper at the earliest possibility.

The above matters are things that have me worried, even though I may be, shortly, executed.

The private notes were to be given to his family. Tojo wanted them to know that he was healthy and feeling very well. He wished that the execution would be carried out as early as possible and, morning and night, Buddha was with him. He had petitioned for his wife and daughters to be his visitors, and he let them know that arrangements had been made so that there would be no confiscation of the property they lived on. He also expressed his gratitude.

Tojo requested that a book on the interpretation of the Holy Scriptures be brought to him. Hanayama had given each of the Class A prisoners a copy of this book before the sentences were read, and Tojo had taken special pains and care in reading it, writing tankas and various explanations in it. On the morning of sentencing, he told Hanayama, "This is of great importance to me and I do not want them to take it away from me when I am executed." He handed it over to his wife and requested another one as soon as possible, but Sugamo officials would not let him have it since they feared that he might somehow kill himself with it. Only after he complained to the prison commander about prisoners' rights under international law was he able to obtain it. This made Hanayama very happy, as he was able to bring in books for the other condemned men as well.

At the next meeting Hanayama read Tojo the letters sent by his family and they prayed and discussed religion. Tojo usually carried beads, which he used in his prayers, in one of his handcuffed hands. He told Hanayama that he did not personally think that a funeral ceremony was necessary, but if his family wanted to have one, he would greatly appreciate having Hanayama perform it. They then discussed posthumous names for himself and his wife.

During the third meeting, arrangements were made for Tojo's hair and nail clippings, false teeth, glasses, and prayer beads to be given to his family. Hanayama asked him to explain his attempted suicide in order for him to dispel rumors about it. Tojo said: "It boils down to this. I had been teaching my subordinates, through the code of the battlefield, never to be captured—to choose death if such an occasion should arise—and I only tried to practice what I had preached. The others had all received notice the day before, whereas in my case, the military police came unexpectedly. So I shot myself at once. Yes, and I want my family to be told that I used the army pistol that Hidemasa [the husband of Tojo's second daughter] used to kill himself with, because I feel that no one knows that. Only in my case, they took first-aid measures immediately."

At their last meeting, he admitted that he did not consider Shintoism a religion and spent a lot of their time together preaching to the priest. This seemed both to amuse and please Hanayama. Tojo not only had an intelligent grasp of religion but enjoyed putting it into words. Before they parted he presented Hanayama with the following tanka to relay to his family:

> Nothing is there
> that beclouds my soul
> as I, in the fullness of my heart
> prepare to journey west.
>   Tarry not, my young, my dears
>   to board the ship of glory
>   for under one great canopy
>   we reach the distant shore.

One war criminal was executed by firing squad: Satoshi Oie had been a colonel and former commanding officer of Negro Island Garrison in the Philippines. He was tried in Manila and sentenced to be executed by firing squad. He was transferred from the Philippines to Sugamo Prison in September 1948 to serve as a witness at several Class B and C trials being conducted in Yokohama. The order for his execution was received on October 22, 1948.

Dr. Hanayama was lecturing at Tokyo University when the summons from Sugamo reached him. He rushed to the prison and spent the entire day with Oie. Both of them were of the same Jodo Shu sect of the Buddhist religion and got along well. At midnight he gave Oie the last rites. They drank some ceremonial wine, ate cakes, and exchanged farewells. Oie also thanked Chaplain Major Walsh and his American guards at Sugamo.

He was then taken outside and placed in a U.S. Army Red Cross bus, along with Major Walsh, Dr. Hanayama, and six guards armed with rifles. There were at least ten Jeeps with officers and other officials in front and in back of the bus as they proceeded, in convoy formation, along the seven miles to the Camp Drake firing range. Camp Drake, the former Azabu Regiment Headquarters, was home to the First Cavalry Division.

To the amazement of everyone on the bus Colonel Oie fell asleep about halfway between Sugamo and Camp Drake and began to snore rather loudly. Upon arrival at the rifle range, he was awakened. Hanayama again bade him farewell and walked away. The guard tied Oie to a post to keep him from falling when he was shot. He thanked everyone, including the guards who were to be the firing squad. At 1:30 A.M., October 23, 1948, Satoshi Oie's sentence was carried out. Hanayama returned to the body and read the Sutra. A doctor pronounced him dead and the body was untied and carefully placed in a casket.

After the detail arrived back at Sugamo, Hanayama and the officers proceeded to the Officers Club, where all of them shook Hanayama's hand and congratulated him on the final attitude presented by Colonel Oie. They were still marveling at his calm ability to sleep when he knew he was about to be executed.

When he returned to his home later that night, the priest read the poems given to him by Oie for delivery to his family:

> Oh, how sad and lonesome a stranger in a strange land one is!
> With whom shall I speak about my daily life?
> To whom shall I tell my merits on the battle field?
> The vicissitude of life is just like floating cloud!
>
> Nampachi was a man and died for the cause of righteousness,
> Teiba showed us the love's extremity of loving even enemy.
> There is one road of Truth infallible for all ages and in all countries.
> How beautiful the faithfulness is! How eternal the faithfulness is!
> I'll sing the melody of truth. I'll march on the road of truth.
>
> Praying to Buddha, I know the light of his benevolence is everywhere.
> Everything in nature is vain, and there exists no "I" and no "Mine."
> There is no one who hurts and no one who is hurt.
> Everything is being covered by his light and is as good as nothing.
>
> My heart is always loitering outside this world.
> The limitless glory is soaring before my eyes.
> Meditating and praying with my whole soul, I believe in only this truth.
> There is no one to hurt me above and under the sky.
> I'll sing the melody of truth, I'll march on the road of truth.
>
> When you yearn for me, come on the road of faithfulness
> For I am always living in faithfulness.
> I have done nothing to be told from father to children,
> But now I start on the road of truth.

> May our children bloom out forever,
> Being praised as cherry blossoms or plum flowers.

All prisoners at Sugamo attended services in the chapel, which had been provided with a Buddhist shrine by the American officials. Altars could be changed from Buddhist to Christian within minutes and both services were held weekly for the prisoners, who attended on a voluntary basis. Quite a few prisoners attended Christian services, but most were of the Buddhist faith. Special arrangements were made for the condemned men. The Buddhist or Christian priest attended these war criminals as often as they requested.

The condemned men were notified of the exact time they were to be executed. Since the U.S. Eighth Army, under the command of Lieutenant General Eichelberger, was to conduct the executions, the army's *Restricted Manual on Procedure of Executions* applied: "The person will be notified of the time of execution no less than twenty-four hours prior to his execution."

At 9:00 P.M. on December 21, 1948, Col. Morris Handwerk, the commanding officer at Sugamo; Capt. Paul McNeish, the adjutant; interpreter Sugino; Chap. Maj. Patrick Walsh, and Dr. Hanayama met in the chaplain's office to make the official pronouncements.

Under the direction of Capt. Charles Broom, Jr., five other officers brought the seven men, one at a time, in alphabetical order, into the chaplain's office. The prison commander announced to each man: "The execution will take place at 00:01 hours on December 23, 1948, at Sugamo Prison." Most of the prisoners were composed and showed relief at knowing the exact time of their execution, because they were prepared for it. The only one showing any sign of stress was Hirota. Tojo was very pleased, since he had been under the impression that they might be executed in some other country. After the announcement each man was asked if he had any last requests, and they were informed that Hanayama would be in attendance from 5:00 P.M. the next day until the time of execution.

All of them had requests concerning delivery of last letters, pictures, poems, wills, prayer beads, and other personal belongings to their families, and most of them requested further meetings with Hanayama. Tojo, the last man and spokesman for the seven, listened to the announcement, said, "very well," and bowed to the commander. When asked if he had any requests, he said:

> Several weeks ago I sent a petition to the Colonel. Almost everything
> I requested has been granted and I wish to tender to you my thanks and

The Executions

appreciation. However, your precautionary measures are too strict. We will never try to kill ourselves. We will show you that we can die noble deaths. For example, you guard us at all times, even when we use the toilet, and this to the Japanese is an unbearable thing. I am sure that if this were done to you, you would understand.

Another thing is so trivial a thing, but we would like to have at least one Japanese meal. Because we are Japanese after all. Anything, even sushi, will do, and we would like at least one drink. Most of the families of my colleagues in here are in wretched condition. Unlike the American Army, they are economically poor and I would like some measures taken so they can manage to live. To put it in concrete form, turn over the wages of their work, done here every day, to their families.

To this last request, Colonel Handwerk answered, "That is out of my power. I am only following orders of my superiors." Tojo bowed to the colonel and was weighed and taken back to his cell.

The weighing of each man was important. The procedure used by the U.S. army for hanging was a proven English one. To determine how far a man must drop in order for his neck to be broken, his exact weight and height, health, physical condition, and age had to be taken into consideration. Tojo weighed 130 pounds and, using this formula, would be dropped exactly seven feet, six inches.

On the morning of December 22, the Allied Council held a regular meeting. That afternoon Sebald, chairman of the council, made appointments to see each member between five and six that evening. When he called on these members at their residences, he presented each one with a letter from General MacArthur instructing them to bear witness to the executions. Patrick Shaw, the representative from Australia, turned bright red and said: "Let's have a drink." General Derevyanko said: "Yes, I will come." General Chen turned pale and stated: "Of course I will come. What shall I wear?" Sebald suggested that he wear his uniform.

MacArthur's own 720th MP Battalion provided two sedans and a Jeep full of armed MPs to escort the witnesses and provide protection if it was needed. They all met at Sebald's residence, had drinks to ease the mounting tension, and then drove to Sugamo Prison in convoy fashion.

Meanwhile the condemned men spent their last day writing farewell letters and poems to their families. They also received a meal of rice, miso soup, broiled fish, bread, jam, and coffee.

At 11:30 P.M., in the Buddhist chapel, Hanayama met the first group to be executed. They entered the room in the same order that would be followed when they entered the gallows. Doihara came first, followed by

Matsui, Tojo, and Muto. Each man had a guard on each side, and both his hands were cuffed to a strong band similar to a loincloth. It went around the body as a belt but had an extra piece that went from front to back between the prisoner's legs. It was slightly uncomfortable and rendered the men practically helpless.

After being informed that he had only fifteen minutes, Hanayama lit incense sticks and had the four men place them in an incense burner — which he had to lower since the prisoners could not raise their arms. He had them sign their names on pieces of paper, folded them, and placed them beside the altar. The priest then held a cup of ceremonial wine to each man's lips while he drank. He read the first three and the last eulogies of the Sutra of the Three Promises while the men had their heads bowed and their eyes closed. When the priest finished, they all thanked him and shook hands with him, Chaplain Walsh, and several other officers who were present.

They then left the chapel, crossed the courtyard, and, during this three- to four-minute walk, chanted Namu-Amida-Butsu, a Buddhist prayer. At the entrance to the gallows, Tojo asked Matsui if he, as the group's elder, would lead them in their *Banzais*. All four men turned to face toward the Imperial Palace and shouted *"banzai"* three times. The word *banzai* can mean many things to the Japanese, but on this night and in front of the gallows, it had only one meaning — "Long live the Emperor."

When Sebald and his Allied Council arrived at Sugamo Prison they were met by Colonel Handwerk. At 11:50 P.M. they left the main prison office and walked to the gallows. As they entered the brightly lit gallows building, they were directed to a low, narrow platform from which they were to witness the executions. They faced a large, elevated platform over which hung five stiff ropes, each ending in a noose. The ropes were made of four-ply manila as required by army regulations. The execution platform was reached by an open stairway with thirteen steps. Quite a number of American officers were in the room, most of them doctors.

Only seconds after midnight, the four war criminals entered the gallows, assisted by their guards and accompanied by the prison chaplain, who was praying in a low voice. Each man was identified as he passed before the witnesses. They wore ill-fitting U.S. Army-issue clothing that made them look even older than they were. They mounted the platform and walked to each of the first four trapdoors. Another identification was made, black hoods were placed over their heads, and the ropes and nooses were adjusted and aligned with the noose coil located slightly to the rear and on the left side of each prisoner's head. The chief executioner reported to the officer in charge that the war criminals were prepared for execution. The single order could be heard throughout the room. "Proceed!" Instantly four trapdoors sprung open simultaneously with a sound similar to a rifle shot.

One doctor immediately went to each body and, with a stethoscope, listened to the prisoner's heart. A senior doctor was then called to each of the bodies and, in turn, reported: "I declare this man dead" — Doihara at 12:07, Tojo at 12:10, Muto at 12:11, and Matsui at 12:13. The bodies were removed and placed in wooden caskets, each carried out by two men.

The next group of three men was assisted to the gallows in the same manner as the first. Itagaki led the way, followed by Hirota and Kimura. Sebald later stated: "Hirota turned his head and looked straight into my eyes. It was an exchange of glances in which he seemed to appeal to me for sympathy and understanding." With military precision the traps were sprung, and the senior doctor stated: "I pronounce this man dead" — Itagaki at 12:32, Hirota at 12:34, and Kimura at 12:35.

Sebald and his subdued group walked quickly and quietly back through the main building to the Officers Club, where each ordered a drink of straight whiskey. Shaw was in a hurry to get home, so the group soon left Sugamo. Sebald took Derevyanko in his car since the Russian and Chinese representatives were not on speaking terms. Sebald later stated in his memoirs: "I derived some satisfaction from surviving this unwanted ordeal in better shape than my colleagues, judging by their reactions and appearance."

Shortly after the executions, Hanayama was allowed into the gallows building, where the seven caskets had been placed. He conducted the final Buddhist rites, while Chaplain Walsh stood beside him with a flashlight to illuminate the pages of his Scripture book. When his duties were complete Hanayama went to the Officers Club. There he was congratulated by all the officers. Colonel Handwerk told him: "Everything went off so splendidly, and we all feel that it was greatly your work that made it possible. We wish to thank you. Everyone here greatly appreciates all that you have done."

The bodies of the deceased men were taken to a crematorium. The ashes were collected by Eighth Army officials, and later taken by plane to be scattered over the ocean off Japan.

Shortly after the executions, Hanayama himself said:

> The seven men to whom I had spoken and laughed with, just a short while ago, now lay there in peace and quiet, without life. I doubt if there are many cases where the dividing line between life and death comes

to be as thin as this one. For me the deaths of the seven men, who have gone to their deaths with not a sign of grief or agitation, in their customary composure and calm, will engrave an impression that I will not forget for the rest of my life.

The next day the priest held a prearranged press conference at Tokyo University and announced the religious state in which the men died. Although one obnoxious and persistent American reporter kept asking personal questions about body and facial details and appearances, never believe that a very kind Buddhist priest cannot, at least once in his life, chomp down on a man as well as any drill sergeant in the U.S. Army!

The Class C executions were carried out in exactly the same manner as the Class A executions, except for the number of witnesses. Two witnesses were required under U.S. Army regulations and procedures. On some occasions there were more than two.

There were never any mishaps or mistakes associated with the executions. However, one Class C criminal spent considerable time exercising his neck muscles by "bridging" on his head. He developed muscles in his neck to the point that it was twice the normal size. He was hanged for almost half an hour before he died — three times longer than normal.

Dr. Hanayama and Chaplain Walsh spent extra time with all the men scheduled for execution. By a large majority the condemned war criminals died as most men would prefer to die — calm, strong willed, and believing that there is a better place on the other side. All the executions were conducted at night, usually after midnight. Many of the prisoners apologized for the trouble, late hours, and inconvenience they caused their American guards.

There follows a record of all the Class C executions conducted at Sugamo Prison.

Headquarters, Sugamo Prison

Executions

Name	*Date*
Kei Yuri	April 26, 1946
Isao Fukuhara	August 9, 1946
Kaichi Hirate	August 23, 1946
Masaaki Mabuchi	September 6, 1946
Uichi Ikegami	February 14, 1947
Hajime Honda	July 1, 1948
Sadamu Motokawa	July 1, 1948

The Executions

Matsukkichi Muta	July 1, 1948
Sadamu Takeda	July 1, 1948
Yoshichi Takagi	July 1, 1948
Iju Sugasawa	July 1, 1948
Kazumoto Suematsu	July 1, 1948
Masakatsu Hozumi	July 1, 1948
Sachio Egawa	August 18, 1948
Junsaburo Toshino	August 18, 1948
Kazutane Aihara	August 18, 1948
Sukeo Nakajima	August 18, 1948
Sadahara Hiramatsu	August 18, 1948
Harumi Kawate	August 18, 1948
Tonatsu Kimura	August 18, 1948
Kunio Yoshizawa	August 18, 1948
Masonobu Michishita	August 18, 1948
Takuji Murakami	August 18, 1948
Satoshi Oie	October 23, 1948
Masao Nichizawa	November 6, 1948
Tadao Shibano	November 6, 1948
Yasutosi Mizuguchi	February 12, 1949
Kuratano Hirano	February 12, 1949
Yoshitako Kawane	February 12, 1949
Hideo Ishizaki	February 12, 1949
Kikuo Tomioka	February 12, 1949
Zentaro Watanabe	February 12, 1949
Masao Kataoka	February 12, 1949
Shoji Ito	February 12, 1949
Yoshinari Tanaka	April 9, 1949
Sadaaki Konishi	April 30, 1949
Kaoru Okuma	May 28, 1949
Isamu Sato	July 9, 1949
Akiyama Yonesaku	August 20, 1949
Masaji Sekihara	August 20, 1949
Akira Yanagezawa	August 20, 1949
Hiroshi Obinata	August 20, 1949
Yoshihiro Susuki	September 3, 1949
Eiichi Uchiki	September 3, 1949
Tasuku Okada	September 17, 1949
Yuji Aoki	November 11, 1949
Muneo Enomoto	April 7, 1950
Otohiko Inoue	April 7, 1950
Katsutaro Inoue	April 7, 1950
Yasumasa Taguchi	April 7, 1950
Tadakuni Narisako	April 7, 1950
Matsuo Fujinaka	April 7, 1950
Minoru Makuda	April 7, 1950

THE AMERICANS

In March 1948 I enlisted in the U.S. Army. After completing basic training and leadership school at Fort Jackson, South Carolina, I was assigned to Sugamo Prison in Ikebukuro, Japan. I served as a main gate guard until November 1948, when I alternately rode shotgun on nighttime Jeep patrol around the prison and worked at the main gate.

On December 23, 1948, I was assigned to duty as a tower guard over the prison armory. That was the night the seven condemned Class A war criminals were executed. Security was extremely tight, and a sense of quiet solemnity prevailed throughout the prison. It was the only time I served as a tower guard. I recall boasting to some of my friends that I must have earned some trust to get assigned to the armory tower at such a crucial time. One of them replied: "Sure, and if anything had happened, you would still be on your way to Mars. There's about ten tons of munitions in the armory directly under that tower!"

There could have been no place in occupied Japan where an American GI would have preferred to serve. The food was excellent. The place was clean and well landscaped. In one sense a GI had a good feeling because he had been selected to serve at Sugamo. There was a strong sense of duty, from prison commander down through the ranks. There was discipline. Exact and prompt performance was expected, and the feeling that existed among the Americans was: "I'm doing a good job, and I'm enjoying it."

Most of the enlisted men stationed at Sugamo were in their late teens or early twenties and typical Americans. They were interested in everything, including the new and different country and the people surrounding them as well as their jobs, sports, recreation, and Japanese girls. Time they had for recreation was considerably more than the time spent on duty. Many were involved in sports activities. Sugamo had excellent baseball and football teams, Ping-Pong tournaments, and the first bowling alley in Japan. There was a post theater, enlisted men's and officers' clubs, and a service club where dances were held. Tokyo was a short bus or commuter train trip away, and one could see the latest movies at the

Ernie Pyle theater, visit many beautiful parks, or stroll through the Ginza district.

At Sugamo's service club I met an American girl, dated her, and was married in the prison chapel in the spring of 1949. We rented part of a beautiful Japanese home in Shinjuku and spent a lot of time with the family we rented from, learning the language and Japanese customs. We bought a Jeep from a soldier who was returning to the States, and, when we could get enough time together, we went skiing in the Japanese Alps and visited other places in Japan — especially the seaside towns.

There was a small Japanese archery range near Sugamo where I learned Japanese archery, which is uniquely different from American-style archery.

The soldiers at Sugamo were, in general, excellent representatives of America and democracy. Some spent considerble amounts of their free time teaching American sports to Japanese schoolchildren, teaching the English language to all who would listen, and some went to GI schools or took correspondence courses to advance their own educations.

Many of the young single men made more honest women out of prostitutes. Early in the occupation, thousands of Japanese women were homeless, hungry, and destitute. Their only recourse was to turn to prostitution for survival. Many set up housekeeping with American soldiers. Many lonely soldiers found that by sharing their income with these women, both lives improved. Some enduring love affairs and marriages resulted.

Other American soldiers fell in love with Japanese girls and found that they were required to meet standards set by the girl's father and family. They had to prove that they were gentlemen and possessed honorable intentions for an extended period of time before marriage was permitted.

Many Japanese nationals worked at Sugamo as carpenters, plumbers, painters, houseboys, landscapers, sanitation crews, clerks, typists, and secretaries. Most of them were consistently pleasant, efficient, intelligent, and curious. We learned from them, and they from us.

Shortly before the Korean War began, I was transferred to the sanitation section. Duties there included the supervision of Japanese employees in maintaining a program to keep the population of flies, mosquitoes and other bugs and rodents about the prison as low as possible. In less than two months, the North Koreans overran South Korea. By then I had become very fond of the Japanese workmen in my section. When they learned I was leaving for Korea, they asked if I would come by one of their homes after work. I asked for directions and stopped by one employee's house. It was small but tidy, and all the employees in the sanitation section were there. The owner was the oldest employee and therefore spokesman for the group. They presented me with a large bottle of sake and two Japanese scrolls as a going-away gift. I said I would be honored to share the sake with them, and they all smiled broadly.

On my arrival in Japan, I had noticed that the Japanese had a different smell about them. I became accustomed to this difference and discussed it with fellow GIs. We thought it was caused by differences in diet. While we were enjoying each other's company at the sanitation section party, the elder Japanese asked me if he could ask a personal question. I said, "Yes, sure." He asked me if I was positive I wouldn't get angry, because they were curious about something they had never before asked an American, and they felt unsure of themselves. I told him I was sure that I would not be offended. Then he said, "Ginnson [Mr. Ginn], why do the Americans smell so bad?" I laughed and told him that it was the effect of our diet—the food we ate. Driving home later that evening, I thought about this event and was amazed to learn this difference applied to me even more than to them. I never thought that they smelled *bad*, however, only different.

The American men at Sugamo were at a distinct disadvantage when the Korean War started. We were near the battle zone but we had not practiced being soldiers during the time we had been at Sugamo. Life was good, and soft. About 325 men of the 450 Sugamo soldiers were transferred to different outfits to help build up division strength. Most of us were sent to the Twenty-Fourth Infantry Division, or the First Cavalry Division, where we all discovered the true meaning of "cannon fodder." Many died and many more were wounded. The few who survived the Korean War without physical or mental wounds were lucky indeed. If the U.S. Army didn't learn anything from this, it should have.

In March 1989 there was an article in the Spokane, Washington, *Spokesman Review,* about William Mahoney, an attorney who had been an assistant prosecutor at the Japanese war crimes trials. A former state representative, he went to Japan in 1946 to assist Chief Prosecutor Joseph Keenan, a personal friend. Keenan became ill during the trial, and Mahoney was appointed acting chief prosecutor. After the trial Mahoney sent one set of trial records to the National Archives and brought another set home with him to Portland, Oregon. He later gave the second set of records to his son, Daniel, with instructions that they were to be donated to Gonzaga University, where both had earned degrees in law.

When I read the article, I knew that I must write this book. I had a copy of a manuscript written by Sugamo's Buddhist priest, Hanayama, and many photographs and newspaper clippings about various war criminals, Tokyo Rose, our war with Japan, and related articles dating from 1947. Hanayama's manuscript was eventually translated into a book titled *My Three Years with the Condemned War Criminals.*

My copy of the original Hanayama manuscript was in need of professional preservative care. Shortly after the Mahoney article appeared in the Spokane newspaper, I called Robert L. Burr, the Crosby Library director, and made arrangements to research the Japanese war criminal trial records and make copies of those I needed. I spent an intense week selecting papers and copying them. I also made a copy of Hanayama's manuscript and presented my original copy to Mr. Burr in appreciation of his extremely helpful assistance.

In the January 1990 issue of the *Disabled American Veteran (DAV)* monthly magazine, I placed a small personal ad, requesting assistance from anyone who had served at Sugamo Prison. I needed letters and photographs from survivors, listing their assignments, dates served, and personal experiences.

When I left Sugamo to go to Korea in 1950, I was assigned to the First Cavalry Division, Fifth Battalion, L Company, and found, for the first time in my life, the real meaning of loneliness. I knew no one, and it seemed that everyone in the world was shooting at me. Also, I realized that I had surely left my big family—the men of Sugamo. For forty years I never saw or heard from anyone who had been with me at Sugamo. When I placed that request for information in *DAV* magazine, the correspondence began with a trickle and shortly became a small flood. Since I have been corresponding with the Sugamo men, several have died and several more have become ill. The majority have provided me with some outstanding and extremely useful information.

Practically everyone responding to my request for information on Sugamo emphatically stated that it was the best duty they experienced while in the army. Most soldiers assigned to Sugamo were given an orientation about the prison's operations and purpose. Most of the men assigned to duties relating to executions were required to sign a document swearing never to discuss or write about them. Others were not required to sign those documents. The prison management apparently assumed that any soldier would be proud to assist in executing condemned war criminals. This was not always true.

A few men assigned to assist in the executions, or to attend as witnesses, experienced extreme difficulty in adjusting their lives. Even though

The Americans

they claim that at the time (1948-50) they didn't mind and didn't complain to their superiors, they have since experienced painful memories of the executions. Several have never told their wives or families about the executions and would much prefer to have the memories erased.

From the small ad placed in the *DAV* magazine, I have obtained a list of thirty-five men who were stationed at Sugamo. In May 1991 we held our first reunion in Nashville, Tennessee. Eighteen men were able to attend. We now have a roster of more than one hundred men and expected at least sixty to attend the reunion planned for May 1992.

Appendix E is an official Prison Roster of American soldiers stationed at Sugamo. In December-January 1948-1949 four hundred forty-three officers and enlisted men were stationed there, plus thirty Eleventh Airborne troops from the 188th Parachute Infantry Division assigned to the prison on temporary duty in 1948 for special guard duty before the executions of the condemned Class A war criminals.

Since the normal tour of duty at Sugamo was about two years, it can be assumed that from October 1945, when the Eighth Army assumed responsibility for Sugamo Prison functions, until May 1952, when it was turned over to the Japanese penal system, approximately sixteen hundred American soldiers had been stationed there.

The following are some excerpts and information provided by some of the Sugamo men with whom I have been corresponding.

The first man I saw was Robert N. Shively from California. He and his family stopped by my home in Walla Walla on their way to visit northern Idaho. We looked at each other with the sudden realization of what forty-plus years can do to you. As we were talking it dawned on me that he had beaten the socks off me in Ping-Pong at the Service Club on several occasions.

I decided early on that correspondence should be accompanied by photographs, since anyone having served at Sugamo would need assistance in activating such old memories. I was correct in this matter.

In one of Robert Shively's first letters he wrote:

> It was good to hear from you and, indeed, I do remember you from the pictures. I hope that I will be able to assist you in your efforts for this book.
>
> My first duty at Sugamo, in June 1947, was in the Sanitation Section, covering the entire perimeter and buildings with DDT and insect and rodent control. I spent a few months in the guard section (tower and green relief). I played football for several years — during the 1947-48

Robert N. Shively (left), Talmadge Blankenship (right). (Courtesy Robert N. Shively)

seasons. We were league champs in 1947. Some of the enclosed photographs reflect the construction of the football field.

I was later assigned as a jailer for Tojo and the Big 25. What an honor for a seventeen year old kid. I actually joined the army in January 1947 at the young age of sixteen. It was amazing to see Tojo, Shigemitsu and others, who were the leaders of Japan during the war years, pulling K.P. duty. It was during this assignment that I met Tokyo Rose. She was kept in a different section of the prison than the men. Her guards were Japanese women. When she was released from Sugamo to return to the States, I gave her two packs of Kool cigarettes. During the time I was a jailer, I was able to get ole Hideki Tojo to autograph a $100 silver certificate that I had folded away in my wallet. That autograph, plus the fact that is a one and only souvenir makes it quite valuable.

I left that assignment to be transferred to the Labor Department. There we did all the hiring, firing, payroll, and training of the local civilian employees, such as cooks (prisoner's mess), laundry, painters, etc. We were also blessed with the chore of escorting the local garbage truck through their assigned rounds each day.

In some of the photos I am sending you shall see some of the prisoners digging ditches. This labor was assigned and was detailed as green relief (prisoners in green fatigues, working outside gardening, pulling weeds, etc.). The prisoners in these photos have been tried and confined to Sugamo for varying lengths of time at hard labor. The duty of guards was assigned in the following manner:

Prison guards (tower and walking guards) were scheduled as 24 hours on duty and 48 hours off. The next schedule, prior to your next 24 hours, would be 8 hour shifts as green relief. Fatigues were the uniform for this duty. We did use some wooden towers for this, but primarily you would be standing with a carbine and moving from area to area as required to complete whatever tasks were assigned. A lot of the chores were just policing trash and weed pulling. The prisoners were also used to construct the football field.

I just remembered — I was the best ping pong player at the prison. I even played at Japanese parks with their top players at that time. I also taught touch football at a Japanese prep school named Jyu Gauken (Freedom School). I spent quite a bit of my free time teaching them touch football. They had a field day and were proud to be able to play tag football. I received, through headquarters, a nice letter in appreciation of my efforts. This letter was published in The Stars and Stripes.

Robert was discharged in 1953 because of diabetes. He graduated from California Polytechnic University with a bachelor of science degree in agricultural business management. He and his wife, Betty, have three children and seven grandchildren.

Lt. Col. Lonnie B. Adams served at Sugamo Prison from December 1949 until June 1952. He arrived at Sugamo as a first lieutenant and was assigned to a guard company as guard commander for about three months until a replacement arrived. He was then assigned as prison officer under Captain George Reimer. It was in this position that Lonnie was promoted to captain. As prison officer, Lonnie made some dramatic changes that not only improved conditions for the prisoners but gave them the opportunity to obtain trade skills through an education program. He received a commendation ribbon with a metal pendant for these improvements. He was also able to operate the prison with three hundred less men when the Korean War started.

He wrote:

> Many people did not realize the magnitude of the work that was done at Sugamo with the war criminals, and I should say this about them. They were very, very disciplined and, knowing them individually, you could never realize that they committed some of the atrocities that they had been charged [with] and found guilty of committing.

Dear Pvt. Robert Shively

First of all we want to thank you for the splendid result we acheived in the football game at the Athletic Meeting of our school on Sunday the 7th.

In the performance of the Athletic Meeting we, the boys, had to show a cheerful and vivid game, so we chose american football as it seemed to fit our spirit.

But we never played a real football game before, and if we had played it without any advices and coaching, it would have been very miserable. So this result (our game was much admired by the spectators.) is really due to your skillful coaching.

Here we thank you for all your kindness again. And we hope you might be able to come out again, and give us your helpful coaching.

truly yours

The Americans

Lonnie had acquired a large collection of photographs, both inside and outside Sugamo, which he generously shared with me. In his second letter to me he wrote:

> I have enclosed more photographs for your information. This group shows mostly improvements to the prison hospital. You will note in one that there is a prisoner sitting on the floor in the corner of his cell. This man was a medical doctor. He was tried and sentenced to death. Shortly after he received the death sentence, he became completely catatonic. For about a year-and-a-half we fed him through his nose once a day on a liquid diet. Strangely enough, two weeks after his sentence was commuted to life imprisonment he returned to complete sanity and asked for his medical books to be returned.

This convicted war criminal was Hisakichi Tokuda. He was indeed sentenced to death for his war crimes. He was thirty-one years old and a graduate of Keijo Medical College. He served in the Japanese Imperial Army as a captain from May 1940 until April 1945. His case number is 186, and his trial is discussed in the Class C trial section.

Lonnie died on August 17, 1990, of cancer at the age of seventy-three. He and his wife had five children. One son, at the time of Lonnie's death, was a lieutenant colonel serving in Korea. All the children were at their father's funeral, where he received full military honors after a very moving funeral mass at the Military Cemetery in Bushnell, Florida.

Lieutenant Colonel Adams's commendation is shown on page 204.

Harry Anderson of Illinois wrote:

> I saw the blurb in the Voice of the Angels, January Issue. I was an 11th Airborne Trooper. I arrived in Zama, Japan (tent city) in January of 1947, was processed and sent to the parachute maintenance company in Sendai. In March I was assigned to Sugamo Prison as a guard. I was at Sugamo until after the Class A executions, and was then transferred to the 209th MP company in Yokohama.
> Once when I was serving as a permanent C.Q. (24 hours on, 48 hours off), I had been doing a pretty good job and was put in for corporal. I was notified of this when I came off duty and, when I got off, I went to Tokyo to celebrate. I missed bed check that night, sooo the next day I was informed that I wouldn't be making corporal anytime soon.
> I recall that I came close to making the Colonel's orderly a few times

Opposite: Letter published in *The Stars and Stripes* to Robert N. Shively written by players from Jyu Gauken (Freedom School).

HEADQUARTERS

JAPAN LOGISTICAL COMMAND

COMMENDATION RIBBON WITH METAL PENDANT

First Lieutenant LONNIE BOTHWELL ADAMS, JR., O1518265, Military Police Corps, United States Army, distinguished himself by meritorious service from 30 June 1950 to 31 March 1952 while serving as Assistant Operations Officer and Prison Officer of Sugamo Prison, 8066th Army Unit. In this position Lieutenant ADAMS performed his duties in a manner as to preclude any untoward incidents and earned the complete confidence of both his Commander and the inmates. Lieutenant ADAMS instituted prisoner government to a degree unprecedented in Japanese penal institutions. This innovation made possible the successful transition to the use of Japanese penal guards at a time when it was necessary to commit the bulk of the military personnel to Korea. He organized the prison school and entertainment and persuaded Japanese charitable and religious organizations to donate for the prisoners' welfare supplies not procurable through normal channels. The stabilizing influence and the astute leadership of Lieutenant ADAMS materially assisted in the successful completion of a military mission of international importance. The achievements of Lieutenant ADAMS were in keeping with the high traditions of the military service and reflect great credit upon him.

JLC GENERAL ORDERS NO. 68   1952

OFFICIAL
SEAL

Opposite page: **Lieutenant Colonel Adams's commendation.** *Above:* **Harry Anderson (front). Identity of man behind him is unknown. (Courtesy Harry Anderson)**

but the inspections were so strict that we were checked for GI underwear, GI socks, and even if we were carrying GI hankies.

Another time I came back to the Quonset hut pretty well tanked, fell on my bed and was asleep immediately. My fellow soldiers carried me, bed and all, to the latrine, put me under a cold shower and left me. At the time, I felt that with friends like that, who needs enemies? Then there was the time when these same soldiers and I took the springs off a late friend's cot, tied the cross overs with string and listened to him cuss when he went through, instead of to, bed.

I can remember some of the guys going to Tokyo one day with MP armbands in their pockets. They went to a place that was buying cigarettes, watches, and other black market materials. They put on their armbands and raided the place. They then took the confiscated supplies across town to another black market place, resold it, and bought a motor boat to ride around Tokyo Bay.

On the more morbid side — when the hangings occurred, the base was closed and we were on alert. The prisoners sang their national song when they left their cell blocks on the way to the gallows. I suppose Dr. Hanayama told you that a few of them exchanged their Buddha for a cross before they were executed. According to my memory, they were fingerprinted after they were pronounced dead. They were then placed in wooden caskets with handles on the corners. They were placed in the back of 6 x 6s and taken to be cremated. The ashes were scattered somewhere at sea so that the Japanese couldn't enshrine or martyr them. We were told all of this by some of the guys that had to carry them out. I was never a witness and I'm glad. I had been raised in a very strict Baptist environment and my emotions about killing defenseless people were confused.

After Sugamo and my transfer to the 209th MP Company, I extended my enlistment by one year to stay in Japan but, shortly after that, the powers-that-be decided that thirty months in Japan was enough and I was transferred to an MP company in Fort Sill, Oklahoma. I was discharged on June 27, 1950. From the people I've talked to over the years, I'm glad I missed the Korean conflict.

I've kicked around in security and police work most of my adult life and even got called up for the Cuban Crisis. Typically, the government didn't send me anywhere, but I served as an Air Force Air Police Operations Sergeant.

Harry has eleven children and, at last count, twenty grandchildren. He plans to retire soon from the Pinkerton Security Company.

Bill Anthony of California wrote:

I arrived in Japan in May, 1947 and was assigned, through Zama, to F Troop, 8th Cavalry. We were stationed in a bombed out, but partially remade, optical factory in Omiya, Japan. General Chase was the Commanding General. In August of 1947, I was assigned to Sugamo. Upon arrival I was posted as a jailer. I worked in cell block number 4 where some war criminals were still being tried and some had already been sentenced to terms. The condemned prisoners were confined to the north end cell block. Blue Prison housed several female prisoners, among whom was Tokyo Rose.

The day to day operation of the prison was given to Capt. Charles Broome Jr., Operations Officer. His assistant was Lt. Lee P. Vincent. At that time, the Commanding Officer of Sugamo was Col. Dana C. Schmahl. The Operations Sergeant was 1st Sgt. Howard Quick who shared the office with Broome, Vincent, and the NCO of the gate guards. The NCO in charge of the jailers was T/Sgt. Ballard (29th Div.

William Harrigan (left), Max E. Goodrich (right). (Courtesy Max E. Goodrich)

Omaha Beach). Capt. William F. Harrigan was the Det. Cmdr. of the personnel outside the prison walls. He was in charge of feeding, clothing, paying, and discipline. He was highly regarded by everyone I knew at Sugamo. Sgt. Max Goodrich was his First Sergeant.

I was put in charge of the gate section after the death of the then NCO/IC who was killed in a traffic accident involving a trolley car in Tokyo. I had this job from October, 1948 until I came home in June, 1949.

One Class A—Umezu—died of cancer in 1949. I used to take him his mail. All Class A war criminal mail was photographed by a Topographical Engineering Co. and they received the copy only. This was a suicide prevention. The prisoners were a disciplined lot.

Tojo wore a beret when sleeping. Prisoners were required to sleep with their heads toward the cell door and hands and faces were required to be exposed at all times. Tojo would raise holy hell on occasions when his beret fell across his face while sleeping and a jailer would push it away from his face with his night stick. He would always write to the Operations Officer, telling him about these incidents in a formal protest.

Fred Barwise of Florida was the last known enlisted man to see Sugamo before it was demolished. He was assigned to Sugamo in late 1947, after basic training and NCO school. He first served as a guard and then was assigned to the Engineering Section as an electrical assistant until he got shocked about eighteen times and blew most of the fuses out at Sugamo. He then managed to get the position of being in charge of prison supply. In this position Barwise excelled. He got to know more of the men and officers than most Sugamo guards or jailers and he thoroughly enjoyed life at Sugamo. He wrote:

> John, I loved Sugamo. It was an absolute vacation for me. Every Friday afternoon at 4:00, I would lock the door to prison supply, head for the showers, change clothes, and was through the main gate by 5:05. I stayed away all weekend. On Monday morning, at 7:05, I was back, checked my bed, showered, changed clothes, and would have prison supply open by 7:58.
>
> I spent more time at the 720 MP Battalion than Sugamo. One of my best buddies, David Leonard, was the official dog catcher for all the military areas in Tokyo. He used to call me and make arrangements for when I was off duty and could make dog runs with him. One day I helped him round up a dog at the USA House, the residence of Admiral Joy. You will remember him as he was a close friend of MacArthur's and, later, officer-in-charge of the Panmunjon, Korea truce negotiations. Well, ole Dave was supposed to take this dog to the vet at Tokyo Quartermaster Depot in Shinagawa to be put to sleep. Instead, we took him to the bridge by the 720 MPs and tossed him in the water. Dave felt so sorry for the dog and could never face taking one to the vet to be exterminated. He felt that it at least had a chance in the water. When I think back now, it scares me about the things I got away with.
>
> Thinking back, I surely miss the cherry blossoms, my favorite hangouts and, most especially, my youth in the Orient.
>
> It is most ironic, to say the least, that my wife's departure from Japan to the United States hinged on a former Sugamo prisoner. One that I issued cigarettes, bedding and other supplies to. He became Japan's Prime Minister and signed her passport in 1957. He was none other than Nobusuke Kishi.

Fred served in World War II, Korea, and Vietnam. He has also written several poems describing life and events at Sugamo.

William B. Bickwermert of Texas was one of the first to answer my request for information regarding Sugamo personnel. He wrote:

> I read, with interest, your solicitation in the January '90 DAV issue for Sugamo Prison veterans. Count me as one of the few.

Barry Gordon (left), William Bickwermert (right). (Courtesy William Bickwermert)

> I served, as an enlisted man, at Sugamo in various capacities from September, 1947 to June of 1950 and again from October, 1950 to February of 1952. The break in 1950 was due to service in Korea with the 24th Infantry Division. I returned to the U.S. in February, 1952.
>
> I am interested in hearing from you. If my memory, and photos, serve me correctly, I was the non-commissioned officer in charge of the honor guard for your wedding at Sugamo in 1949. I do not remember the young lady, but I do indeed remember you.

In another letter he reported:

> I have just finished reviewing a guard book I have somehow managed to keep through the years. The notes indicate that on August 26, 1948

Sugamo Prison, Tokyo

Tokyo Rose was brought to Sugamo Prison, in a G.H.Q. staff car, and placed in Blue Prison [for women prisoners]. There were five Japanese nationals living on the post, one family. They were to be allowed entrance and exit at any time of the day or night. There is information that one prisoner committed suicide in number 2 cell block on September 8, 1948. Another entry shows that a prisoner from number 2 cell block attempted suicide early in the morning of August 20, 1948. This leads one to believe that things were busy in number 2 cell block.

I met Tokyo Rose while she was a prisoner at Sugamo in 1948. I had the opportunity to talk with her for brief periods while she was being interrogated by the war crimes tribunal, and once while she was being held at her cell.

My wife, children and I made a trip to Chicago in 1954; we went to North Clarke St. where the Japanese had a community of shops, stores, apartments and restaurants. We went into a book store (after visiting a few other shops), the name I do not recall, to browse through some books and papers on Japan. A Japanese woman, apparently a clerk, approached and asked if she could help me. I was shocked! I recognized her as Tokyo Rose. After looking at some photographs in a magazine, I picked up another book and turned unexpectedly to a photo of "Rose" being taken from Sugamo in 1948. I pointed to the picture and told the Japanese lady that I had met the woman in the picture. Her face was blank. I tried to read something of recognition in her eyes, but nothing was there. I asked if she had seen Japan after the war. She replied that she had never been there in her life. I knew that her answer was not true, for I had recognized her, but I dared not call her hand in that tightly knitted neighborhood (at least I thought that). After a few more minutes of browsing, and noting the side glances the female clerk had been cutting in my diretion, we thanked her and departed. Adjacent to the bookstore, and with a common wall, was a restaurant which we entered. Upon giving our order I got into conversation with the waitress. I asked about the woman in the bookstore next door. She declined to answer. I asked my wife to speak with the waitress and ask the same question. She did so. The waitress confirmed my suspicions. She told us that the female clerk in the bookstore was, in fact, Tokyo Rose. I immediately returned to the bookstore to get another glimpse of the woman, which I did, but fleeting, for she came out from the back, caught sight of me and disappeared. That was the end of my second meeting with Tokyo Rose.

Information on me: I arrived in Japan on Christmas Eve, 1946 at Yokohama Port. We were trucked to Zama. Billeting was in field tents. The barracks used by the Japanese Officer Corps Cadets were boarded up because their safety had not been determined. There was a fire that night and tent city disintegrated. We were moved into the "unsafe" billets, there was no place else to go. I stayed there two or three days, and was shipped by truck to the 7th Cavalry in downtown Tokyo. I remained with the Cavalry until September 1947, at which time I was transferred to Sugamo Prison.

When I arrived at Sugamo in September of 1947, I was a private. What to do with privates? was probably the leading question the brass kicked around. "Put them in the cell blocks" I'm certain was the answer. I was assigned to block duty; I don't recall the specific block. I stayed in the blocks for a span of time. I remember an incident while assigned there. As you might recall, bath areas for the prisoners were located in the main corridors at each level [for orientation, the cell blocks intersected the main corridors]. I was assigned, with one other guard, to take a group of prisoners to the open bath for their daily routine. The group size was seven or eight. Schick safety razors were carefully inspected by the guards for blade nicks, breaks in the blade, and secure handle guards before being issued. The guards were required to maintain a strict visual accountability of the razors at all times. This was done to preclude a prisoner from chipping a piece of the blade and swallowing it in an attempt at suicide, or hiding the chip from the guard in a body cavity for the same purpose on returning to his cell. With this particular group, after retrieving the razors, I noticed that one of the blades had a good size chip broken from it. I went directly to the block sergeant and told him of the problem, leaving the prisoners, still in their "bathing suits," with the remaining guard. On our immediate return to the bathing area, a prisoner was required to take a close-knit piece of cotton and hold it tightly over the tub drain as the water was released. This was to catch the chip if it had accidentally been broken and was in the tub. It was not found. Next came a body cavity search by the medics. It was still not found. An officer, who had been summoned to the site, required the prisoners to robe themselves. They were taken to the prison hospital for X-rays. Still no evidence. A prison doctor interviewed the prisoners. It was decided, to the best of my recollection, that none of the prisoners were suicidal. They were returned to their cells without further action.

This incident has nothing to do with the prisoners, it's strictly a tale of a soldier gone bad. The enlisted mess was NCO'd by Sergeant 1st Class. He was an ornery sort and generally difficult to get along with. I did not patronize him, nor did I wish to alienate him. I gave him sufficient berth so that our paths seldom crossed. I was uncomfortable with the man. I will refer to him as "X" or Sgt. "X" in the following narrative.

One evening, while pulling the 6:00 pm to midnight shift with Gordon, I was notified by an authority that enlisted personnel were not permitted to leave the prison after 10:00 pm. I was not given a reason for such an order. A number of young men, knowing beforehand that they could not leave the compound, had telephoned their lady friends to meet them at the main gate. Having met and signed in, they proceeded to the club for a night of enjoyment. When it was time for the ladies to leave, their sponsors would escort them to the gate and sign them out. On occasions, such as this night, if I knew the soldier well, and trusted him, I would allow him to step outside the gate for some late night sayonara and powerful wooing. In a short while his lady friend would depart and the soldier would return with a wave and "Thanks, Bick. See you tomorrow." I saw nothing wrong in allowing this. I retained control of the gate and remained within my instructions.

Near midnight Sgt. "X" stepped up to the gate house. He was drunk, out of uniform, with a distillery smell, and cursing like a sailor. His lady friend was embarrassed over the scene. He pulled from his pocket what his drunkened mind thought was a pass. It was not. He said that he was taking his friend to the train station and continued to walk toward the gate. I advised him of the pass restrictions. He replied, "It doesn't pertain to me." I told him that he wasn't going out and instructed Gordon to escort his lady friend out the pedestrian gate, and to lock it on his return. "X" took objection to this. He cursed me, then staggered up and spat in my face. Before I had a chance to react, his right fist landed on my chin with stunning impact. My helmet spun off my head and I fell against the gate house. I was conscious, but not totally, and saw whole galaxies in my peripheral vision. Before I recovered, he grabbed my necktie and began to sling me around like a shot put. I was still stunned and out of control. I called for Gordon to seize the man, but I didn't know where Gordon was. We both went to the pavement. He retained a tight grip on my tie and was pulling me toward him. I was unable to break his grip. I sensed that he was reaching for my weapon which was secured, for the moment, in my flap-lock holster. He could easily get to it. I called out for Gordon to take the pistol from my holster. He either didn't, or "X" prevented him from doing so. I was making a desperate attempt to gain control of the situation; it evaded me. The man had unbelievable strength. Whiskey was his reinforcement. Gordon couldn't get to the pistol (as was later confirmed). Somehow my body language kept the weapon just out of the drunk's reach. In the tussle he took hold of the lanyard, which was secured to the '45 and my right epaulette, and yanked hard. It was apparently an attempt to break the weapon loose from the holster. His drunkened condition didn't afford him the coordination necessary to take the pistol from me. The lanyard jerked free (I later learned that someone had cut it), probably saving the day for me. "X" flattened to the pavement, but his herculean grip on my tie locked me to him. Somewhere in the down-spiral my tie was cut, freeing me from the man's hold. My physical resistance to his pull catapulted me backwards when the tie snapped. I landed on my right side and elbow. He was up and on me in an instant, but guards, who had arrived from the guard room, preempted his attack. Three were on him, and it took their strength, plus some spectators, to subdue him. He was handcuffed, but when they attempted to place him in the back of the guard jeep, he resisted madly. They wrestled him into the back of the vehicle. It took three of them to hold him secure. He was cursing and kicking as the driver sped off to the guard room.

On arriving at the Administration building, the O.D. had to summon more guards to help get his prisoner from the jeep into the building. As a witness told me afterwards, the guards had to forcibly carry "X," in a horizontal position, into the prison proper, where they placed him in a cell used for such purposes. However, before being placed in the confines he drove his fist through one of the small, reinforced glass panes that filled the gaps between the diamond shaped iron bars of a cell block door. "X" shed some drunken blood because of that blurred punch. They managed him into a cell and slammed the door locked. A guard was stationed at the door to ensure the man did no further harm to himself.

I have no memory that "X" received punishment for his foolishness that night. Considering witnesses to the affair, difficulties that the guards had, damages to the cell where he was committed, and the attempt to take my weapon, I do not see how he possibly could have skirted some degree of punishment. My jacket was ripped, necktie and lanyard cut (due to his madness), my trousers were torn at the knees, and my boots, my beautiful boots, were scarred beyond repair. I was asked later if I wanted to press charges. I declined for I saw no advantage. My only needs were an apology and replacement of my boots and lanyard (the uniform was issue). He met my demands. Physically I came out of the encounter with a severely bruised jaw, scarred knees, skinned hands and a black eye. Also, I had a badly deflated ego. After the attack I was so disheveled that a friend took the remainder of my tour of duty.

You might wonder why I have spent time describing this incident. Sergeant "X"'s day in court was about to arrive.

Following the incident at the gate, Sgt. "X" seemed a changed man. He appeared to become civil and I heard that whiskey was no longer a *daily* diet. However, I was leery of the change.

One evening during a tour of duty, a few months after our encounter, Sgt. "X" approached the gate in a 3/4 ton truck on his way out. The vehicle pulled to the gate and stopped (the vehicular gate was closed at the beginning of the 6:00 to midnight shift). He was in the passenger seat, a Japanese employee was driving. I took the trip ticket which read, "destination: Tokyo." I asked if he had passengers or cargo in the truck since bows and canvas had been installed. He told me that he had a small amount of cargo. I pulled back the canvas from the rear of the truck and was surprised to see so much cargo. I stepped onto the bed of the truck and saw that boxes were filled with canned goods, breads, chilled meats, fresh vegetables, and canned drinks. I went to the passenger side and asked "X" where he was going with such a load of food. He said that officers were having a party at the Gaiji Inn in Tokyo and that he was to deliver the food to the establishment and cook. I had no knowledge of his claim. I did not believe him, however, I returned the trip ticket and waved him on. After a few minutes of self examination, I called the guard room and spoke with the O.D. I described what had just transpired, and asked if he would verify "X"'s claim of a party in Tokyo that night. No! no party was planned. He asked if I knew where "X" was taking the food. I did not, other than what he had told me. He asked that I confidentially notify him when the sergeant returned.

In less than two hours "X" returned. I allowed the vehicle in the gate, stopped it and had a hasty inspection of the cargo area. The food was gone. I waved the vehicle on. I immediately informed the O.D. of "X"'s return. Within a short time the O.D. telephoned and instructed me that if the sergeant arrived at the gate in a vehicle to go out again, I was to give a routine trip ticket check and pass him on. I was not to search the truck. I thought the order strange, but knew to obey. About an hour later a vehicle approached the gate from inside. It was "X." I waved it to a stop, was tempted to search, but stuck to the O.D.'s instruction. Gordon opened the gate and I waved the vehicle on. It had reached the main intersection, turned left towards Ikebukuro, when I saw another vehicle rapidly approaching the gate from the inside. It was the O.D. with two guards. He asked the direction that "X"'s vehicle had taken. I informed him, and they departed. I saw a Japanese police vehicle join them at the main intersection.

Before my shift was over the O.D. returned. He was driving the guard jeep they had departed in, and one guard was in the back with "X." Following close was the 3/4 ton truck with the other guard driving it. The Japanese employee was not present, nor were the Japanese police. Due to the circumstances, I did not check the truck's cargo area on its return.

I later learned that "X" had been under suspicion for some time for black market activities involving food stuffs he had appropriated from the enlisted men's mess. He slipped past the authorities on the first haul that evening, but was followed on the subsequent one. He had been suspected, but had never been caught. His blatant lie regarding an officer's party, the abundance of food stolen during his first trip, and his return to gather more for the black market, are prime examples of his greed and stupidity. His complacency in success is what tripped him up.

"X"'s day in court had arrived. Word filtered to us that he had been court martialed and sent to Leavenworth, Kansas to serve time. If true, a fit ending for an unfit soldier. He had gotten away with too much for too long.

I remained at Sugamo until late June or early July, 1950 when I was sent off to join the 24th Infantry division. I went via Sasebo, in Kyushu. I stayed there one night and was on my way to Korea. I joined the 24th Div., 34th Regt. on line north of Kumchon. On July 29, during an engagement with North Korean tanks and infantry, I was hit with mortar fire. In my haste to vacate the premises, I was shot by a North Korean who had better aim than I had given him credit for. Evacuated through M.A.S.H. channels, the surgeons decided my condition warranted a trip to Japan. My left leg had caught the mortar fragments and rifle fire shattered my left elbow.

I remained in the hospital system in Japan until mid August. I was returned to Korea to the 21st Regt., 24th Div. (the 34th had been relieved of combat duty and returned to Japan. This was done by "paper action," the troops of the 34th stayed in-country and were reassigned to other units of the 24th Div.). I stayed with the 21st until November of 1950, at which time I was dragged out due to combat fatigue. After a short hospitalization in Korea, I was returned to Japan. I remained hospitalized there until late November, at which time I was placed on orders for a return engagement to Korea. I kicked, yelled, cursed and said I wouldn't go, but my objections bounced off deaf ears. Off I went to my demise, I was absolutely certain. At Camp Drake, a Repl-Depl outside of Tokyo, I was unexpectedly taken off orders. No more Korea, during this war!!! I requested a return to Sugamo Prison. My request was approved.

I was reassigned to Sugamo in late November or early December, 1950. I remained there until February of 1952, at which time I was returned to Fort Campbell, Kentucky. I left the Service in June, 1952.

Carl Bustard from Maine has an amazing and phenomenal memory. After over forty years, he still remembers not only most of the Americans who served at Sugamo while he was there but the names of the Japanese, male and female, who worked at the prison and their life histories as well as the war criminals.

Carl entered the army in 1947 and was discharged in June 1950. He was also very lucky: He was put on the last transport ship leaving Japan for the United States before the Korean conflict began.

After basic training at Ford Ord, California, Carl was selected to go through leadership school, as had many of the other men stationed at Sugamo. On graduation from leadership school, Carl discovered the sea

Ziba Berlew (left), Carl Bustard (right). (Courtesy Carl Bustard)

in the same manner I had — the hard way. On the trip to Japan he spent twenty-eight days seasick. When he arrived in Japan, he was selected by the prison commander, Col. Francis W. Crary, for assignment at Sugamo. His first job was as a jailer. He was later promoted to section chief of the special services office supply room. In this position he, like Fred Barwise, excelled and became acquainted with most of the prison personnel.

Carl was a loner and a teetotaler, unusual attributes for a Sugamo man. He writes:

> Sugamo seemed more like home to me than my real home back here in the Maine woods. There was good chow and a comfortable Quonset hut to live in, luxuries which I didn't enjoy much in younger years. My father drove work horses all his life, on farms and in the woods. This was a skill which few possessed but it paid about the lowest salary of any job. I realize that the Army chow and such didn't mean much to some of the guys from the cities but to guys like me it was all a trip to heaven.
>
> Life was good and meaningful for me as a young, ambitious GI at Sugamo. I learned a lot of Japanese history and culture while working with the war criminals. Being a country boy and used to work, I'd work along with the sentenced prisoners in the garden and fields. At first they couldn't understand this and told me that I shouldn't work. I explained to them that I liked to work to get exercise. They accepted and liked me

for this reason. They always asked me if I'd been to Tokyo or Yokohama the night before and inquired about how things were in the two cities. I seriously believe that all Japanese love Japan as much as citizens of other countries can possibly love their countries. I don't think you will ever hear of a Japanese complaining or ridiculing their mother Japan.

One day Captain Conners gave me orders to take some prisoners and go out by the baseball diamond and install three sets of horseshoe stakes. I put them in the exact location he told me to. The prisoners and I thought they were a little too close to the diamond, but orders were orders. The day after the stakes were installed, I met Major Chrietzberg, the baseball coach. He said, "What the hell did you think you were doing putting those stakes so close to the diamond? Do you want some of my players to gut themselves on those stakes? Get them the hell out of here now!" So I told Capt. Conners what had happened and he informed me, in a nice manner, of a different place to install them and keep everybody happy.

In my three years in the Army, I had the good fortune of knowing Sgt. Max Goodrich, Sgt. William Johnson, Sgt. William Maddox, Sgt. Walter Evans, John Kerns, and Bill Anthony. I thought these men were the finest and fairest military men I had ever met. They proved to me that good leaders are born, not made.

A good friend of mine, Tom Ellingwood, has been to see me several times. We took basic training together and were at Sugamo at the same time. He told me that John Kerns was killed before he got off the ship at Pusan Harbor. All the men on that ship had orders to lay flat on the deck and not raise up on account of fire from the Koreans on shore. Ellingwood was close to Kerns and you know Kerns — full of curiosity and just had to know what was going on — he raised up to appraise the situation and was cut in half. Too bad and sad. He was a really likeable fellow.

On the return trip to the States, about two hundred of us from different units throughout Japan were put aboard the ship two days ahead of the rest of the returning troops. We were oriented on guarding fifty military prisoners who screwed up in Japan by committing crimes. They were to be brought to Fort Leavenworth, Kansas. The Commander told us, "If any of you are from Sugamo, don't think you're dealing with the Japanese war criminals here. These men have the same minds you have and know every trick you know, so keep extra alert with them." We had no problems with them.

Before Carl left Japan he was made a buck sergeant and received $129 a month across the board. He saved steadily while at Sugamo. When he returned to Maine in 1950, he paid cash for a home with twenty-five acres of woodland. He married, settled in the home and raised one dozen children, six boys and six girls. He wrote: "The old house is pretty well gone with wear and tear, but I'm sure it will see me through."

Carl worked in the Maine woods and sawmills for over thirty years and recently retired. His fondest memories and dreams are of Sugamo, Japan and the Japanese people.

Jack Coleman of California was stationed at Sugamo from January 1948 until March of 1950. He was in the guard section. He wrote:

> There are so many funny and hilarious incidents that I recall about the guys in the guard section that you could probably write a book just about them. I have many pictures too, but they might prove embarrassing to some of the guys who are now married. At present I am in contact with Don Bowman, Bill Anthony, Harry Anderson, and others from Sugamo.
>
> I met with my old buddy Don Bowman several weeks ago for the first time in thirty-nine years. We must have shaken hands for five minutes and we had a good chat. I wrote you that there were no white or yellow prisons within Sugamo. Bowman reminded me that white was for the administration area (operations, administration, and prison records). Yellow area was the prison work area (prisoners' mess, laundry and shop areas). Red area was the prisoners' lock-up and blue prison was for female prisoners. Don served at Sugamo from 1947 through 1952 and was in both the guard section and a jailer. He has been working for the State of California as a park ranger for a long time.

In his next letter Jack wrote:

> I went to San Jose this past weekend and saw Bill Anthony. I brought your letter and pictures with me for him to see. He was excited and happy to read and look over this material. He was a sergeant in charge of the gate guard section. Bill and I served in the same units in the Korean war, the 57 MP Co. and the 6th Army Escort Det. Bill got out in 1953 and now has his own roofing company.
>
> I had some personal experience with one of the condemned prisoners. His name was Yuji Aoki and he was executed on November 11, 1949. The first time I saw him was about six months prior to his execution. Another guard, the duty officer, and I were dispatched to the 361st Hospital Prison Ward in Tokyo to return Aoki to Sugamo. He had been in there for quite a while undergoing treatment for third stage syphilis which had affected his mind. It was too far along to respond to treatment. He was shackled and handcuffed through a restraining belt. We

Jack Coleman. (Courtesy Jack Coleman)

placed him in the back of a 3/4 ton truck and brought him back to Sugamo. During the trip back, he never looked out the back at the scenery and acted completely oblivious to what was going on. Many times after, I was assigned to watch him during bathing detail or I saw him during routine duties in his cell.

His execution went well, he never kicked or jerked. He hung for about 12-15 minutes before an Army doctor stood on a stool, listened to his heart with a stethoscope and pronounced him dead. During this time one of the witnesses, a Lt. Col., couldn't handle it and threw up. The rope was removed from Aoki and his body was lowered into a wooden casket at the foot of the gallows. There were about fifteen people present at the hanging. These included witnesses, guards, two hangmen, a doctor, and two GIs from Yokohama Graves Registration who took the body to be cremated. One odd thing about the execution was that the noose did not have a hangman's knot. The rope was looped through a cone shaped piece of wood which was placed behind the man's left ear. When the trap was sprung and the rope tightened, the wood block would knock the man unconscious and he would not suffer.

Don Bowman (left), Joseph Gradick (right). (Courtesy Joseph Gradick)

Aoki was a medical sergeant at Naoetsu POW Camp 4-B at Niigata, Japan, between December 7, 1942, and September 20, 1945. On many occasions Aoki, singly and with others, tortured, mistreated, abused, beat, and neglected the prisoners under his control. He frequently forced sick and exhausted prisoners to work and denied them necessary and proper medical care, attention, and supplies, thereby contributing to and accelerating the deaths of sixty Allied prisoners of war.

Jack Coleman retired from the Army as a staff sergeant. He then worked as a civilian in military installations. He worked in the police and security fields for more than thirty years. He currently runs a hardware business in California. He has one daughter and three grandchildren.

Dr. George C. Foster was a naval oral surgeon assigned to Sugamo Prison as chief of dental surgery. In 1947, as a private practical joke, he engraved the words "Remember Pearl Harbor" in Morse code on Tojo's

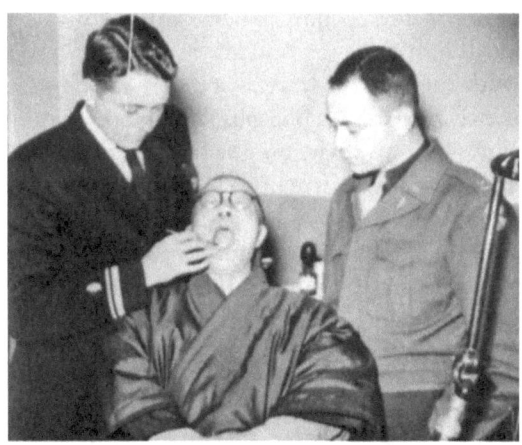

George Foster (left) with Tojo (center) and unidentified dental assistant (right). (Courtesy Max Goodrich)

upper dentures. A friend, who helped concoct the prank, was in a Tokyo bar several nights later and told several of his friends about this little joke. He was overheard by several reporters and a news broadcaster. Naturally the story got out, and Dr. Foster got into a peck of trouble with the navy brass. He was chewed out and was denied a commendation for his work. It is probable that he would have been court-martialed except that what he had done tickled the nation. Letters came from many people who wrote navy and army officials that "the nation needed a good laugh after World War II."

In 1988 Foster wrote: "Needless to say, our sentiments toward the Japanese were not the most favorable so soon after World War II. I figured it was my duty to carry out my assignment. But that didn't mean I couldn't have some fun with it."

Tojo had asked for new teeth so he could speak better at his war crimes trial. Foster was ordered to repair the doctored dental plate, which he did, and Tojo wore them until his execution. Even Tojo found humor in the prank.

Dr. Foster died in December 1989 in Pompano Beach, Florida, at the age of sixty-eight. He had practiced dental surgery at Fort Lauderdale, Florida, until he retired in 1985.

Max Goodrich from Missouri was the top sergeant during my tour of duty at Sugamo. He has provided me with a vast amount of data for this book. Max was assigned to Sugamo from 1946 to 1950. He was assigned first to the prisoner record section as noncommissioned officer in charge (NCO/IC), then as first sergeant, and last as a personnel officer and assistant adjutant with the rank of warrant officer, junior grade.

Max informed me that he had one of the best groups of personnel at the prison, and he gave them the credit they deserved.

He wrote: "One of my instructions to newcomers was to, when writing to folks at home, tell them you are assigned to Sugamo Prison as part of the duty personnel, not as a prison inmate. This did help in preventing answering mothers' letters requesting information about 'What has my good boy done to be locked up in a prison?'"

Before Max entered the army, he worked in security at the Hanford Nuclear Complex in the Tri-City area of Washington state. He stated: "We were told only that they were going to produce an unknown product there, and if it didn't stop the war in 1944 or 1945, it would prevent all future wars." He then added the comment: "Ha."

Chief Warrant Officer, W-3 Max E. Goodrich, Sixty-second Engineer Battalion (Construction), of Ford Leonard Wood, Missouri, retired September 1, 1964, after more than twenty years of service in the U.S. Army. He was appointed warrant officer on October 18, 1949, while stationed at Sugamo. His assignments took him to Japan, Korea, England, Germany, and the following stations in the United States: Camp Wheeler, Georgia; Fort Leavenworth, Kansas; Fort Knox, Kentucky; Fort McClellan, Alabama; and Fort Leonard Wood, Missouri. He has been recognized for his service by the award of the Bronze Star, Purple Heart, Good Conduct Medal with two bronze loops, American Campaign Medal, World War II Victory Medal, Army Occupation Medal, Korean Service Medal with one silver star and one bronze star, United States Presidential Unit Citation, Korean Presidential Unit Citation, Combat Infantry Badge, and several weapons medals.

Max has been married twice. The first marriage produced two children, Carl and Sharon, seven grandchildren, and one great-granddaughter. This marriage ended in divorce. Carl and his wife were killed in an explosion in 1965, leaving four small children.

In 1953 Max married Hazel. After retirement they traveled to Canada twice and from the East to the West Coast of the United States. Most of their time has been spent helping family and friends and raising grandchildren. In 1970, with thirteen people in the family, they outgrew their house in town, bought twenty acres, and designed and built a twenty-one-room home where they still reside. Their hobbies are gardening, landscaping, cooking, sewing, and advising friends and family on carpentry, electrical, plumbing, and mechanical subjects.

Robert Hartley. (Courtesy R. Hartley)

In his last letter, Max wrote, "Thank you for getting the lid off the can that has been kept in the dark for the past forty plus years. It's been a long time, but that assignment to Sugamo has remained at the top of assignments in my mind."

Robert E. Hartley of North Carolina spent five years and ten months in the army and worked for Southern Railway until he retired in 1988. He is married and has four children and six grandchildren.

He wrote:

> I enjoyed reading the newsletter you sent to me. It brought back old memories that I had completely forgotten about after all these years. I enjoyed finding out what happened to Sugamo Prison because I haven't heard what happened to it or to any of my buddies that I spent so much time with.
> I was stationed at Sugamo Prison two different times in 1947 and the summer of 1948. I was there on TDY [temporary duty] with twenty-five troopers from the 188th Parachute Infantry Regiment, 11th Airborne Division. We were under the direct command of the 8th Army, but we all stayed together in one little section of the prison, outside the prison walls. We didn't participate in any of the off duty activities of the regular stationed Army troops. About our only recreation activities were playing poker and going into Tokyo by Army bus to the Ernie Pyle Theatre. I'm sure you've done the same thing. One night my buddy and myself missed the last bus back to Sugamo and we hired a rickshaw to take us back. I don't know how far it was, but it was a long way. It wasn't a bicycle rickshaw, but a man that ran and pulled it. I don't see how he ever pulled us back there, but he did.

We were on duty twenty four hours and off duty twenty four hours. While on duty, we served most of it four hours on and four hours off. While we were on twenty four hour duty, we served our on and off time inside the prison walls. Occasionally we had duty outside the prison walls in the tower and on the walls. Sometimes we were put on alert and we had two men in each tower. They told us the reason for the alerts was that they were going to have an execution, but I never knew for sure.

Shigemitsu was a one-legged man who was not allowed to have his artificial leg in the prison. At times, when he was going out for trial, I got his leg for him. When in the prison, he used crutches. He was a man who never spoke a word to me, although I spoke to him, and he could understand what I was saying.

Taking pictures and cameras were not allowed inside the prison walls. I got a bright idea that I could slip a camera in and take Tojo's picture. I went to Tokyo and bought a small camera, about half the size of a pack of cigarettes, to slip into the prison. I carried it in my pocket, waiting for a chance to get a picture, but in the end, I chickened out and never took one because I was afraid I would get caught. I still have the camera to this day. You were never by yourself when around prisoners. There were always two or more together. Also, we were never allowed to take a gun inside the prison. The only guns were outside the prison walls.

In Bob's last letter he wrote:

> I am returning the information that you sent me, along with a copy of an article I wrote in the Salisbury Post. I used some of the information you sent in the article. It was very helpful. Through the article, I discovered another Sugamo veteran, Dr. Walter Hood of Salisbury, North Carolina. He is a retired professor at Catawba College. He called me the day the article came out, and I gave him your address. He has since informed me that he has heard from you. We plan to get together soon and discuss Sugamo. He has some pictures of the prison that were taken from the inside looking out. He said he slipped the camera into the prison inside his jacket pocket and actually passed inspection with it in there.

James H. Holton from Tennessee served at Sugamo from Feburary of 1948 until April of 1950. He stated:

> Many of the men who served with us were killed in the Korean War. You and I were both wounded, but we made it back. Thank God for that.

James Holton. (Courtesy James Holton)

I was in the guard room the night they hung Tojo and the six other major war criminals. I can remember some things and have forgotten others. I remember one of the hangmen, but not his name. He was a lieutenant. He used to go into the cells and talk with the men who were condemned. These men did not know that he was the hangman until they went to the gallows. After they climbed the thirteen steps, there stood the lieutenant. The sentenced man or men's eyes would open wide and they were surprised to discover that this man was the hangman.

I enjoyed my tour of duty at the prison. The food was good, the E.M. Club was excellent, everyone got along well, and the morale was always high.

In a later letter, Jim wrote: "I've been in the VA Hospital three times since September with my heart. I had open heart surgery, but I'm doing better now. I just turned sixty on the 21st of February [1991]."

Jim was sent before the troop commander, Capt. William Harrigan, on numerous occasions for minor infractions of military rules and regulations. He stated:

> I was real young. I went into the Army when I was sixteen. I remember one time when I was in his office, getting chewed out for something I did or didn't do, and the captain leaned back in his chair, thinking it was near the wall. He fell on the floor and everyone laughed at him. He was mad as hell at me and I was probably the only one who didn't laugh.

Walter K. Hood of North Carolina read the article about Sugamo Prison, written by Robert Hartley, in a Salisbury, North Carolina, newspaper. He called Robert and informed him that he had also served at Sugamo. Both discovered that they had lived in the same area for more than twenty years, practically as neighbors, and weren't aware of it. Hartley informed Hood that he was corresponding with me and then called me and told me of Walter Hood's Sugamo past.

The discovery of Walter has been of immense value to me. While he was stationed at Sugamo, he was an amateur photographer, among other things. He could easily have been court-martialed and sent to prison for taking photographs inside the prison, which was forbidden. But he has made life much easier for me by taking those illegal photographs. He sent me about forty large pictures, along with a diagram of Sugamo Prison. Numbers, circled and with arrows pointing to the location and direction from which the picture was taken, were marked on the diagram, with corresponding numbers on the backs of the pictures. Accompanying the pictures and diagram of Sugamo Prison was an eight-page description of the photographs. Since I had been a so-called outside man at the prison, Walter's diagram and photos made it as easy for me as taking a full-guided tour of the prison.

One photograph showed me that he either knew exactly what he was doing or else was the bravest—or foolhardiest—man at Sugamo. I refer to a photograph of the cells used by the seven condemned major war criminals. Before December 1948 the prison officials would virtually have shot anyone caught taking a picture of those cells. I have concluded that Walter knew exactly what he was doing. He got away with it.

Walter describes the photo mentioned above as follows:

Walter K. Hood. (©Dr. Walter Hood, all rights reserved.)

Photo 29. Corridor B, Cell Block 5, the home of Tojo and other famous prisoners. Of all the secret photographs, this was undoubtedly one of the riskiest to take. At night there would be only one person on each level patrolling the corridor connecting all of the cell blocks. Thus, if the Officer of the Guard or the Officer of the Day should appear (which at odd moments they did, of course), the guard and whatever he might be doing would be seen instantly. But that was not all; the second floor (B level) of Cell Block 5 was one of the most carefully guarded areas of the prison, with at least two jailers in the cell block at all times. [You can see them on the right toward the back.] Jailers on A level below and C level above could have seen into B level too. Fortunately, the barred doors opening from the corridor into the cell block had glass between the bars. While attempting to keep my hovering presence outside the doors from becoming obvious, I considered it necessary to wait until the jailers, in their continuous pacing up and down, should turn away from the doors. After some considerable waiting they did just that. I whipped out my camera from under my uniform, walked instantly to the door, held the lens of the camera against the glass for support, and took a short time exposure. Tojo's cell was on the right, back near the first jailer.

Walter was stationed at Sugamo Prison from January 1947 until March 1948. He informed me:

> During the time that I was stationed at Sugamo, I enrolled in various night classes offered by the Army Education Program (AEP) in central Tokyo. The officers at Sugamo were very cooperative and arranged my guard hours to accommodate my classes. I had done some drawing since I was a child, but the first art classes that I had were in Tokyo in the AEP school. The first art museum that I ever entered was in Tokyo too. I mention this because, after a year of general college work following military service, I went to the Pennsylvania Academy of the Fine Arts, and later to the American Academy in Rome.
>
> Making a living in the so called art world can be an extremely difficult thing, especially if one does not follow the current "isms," is not a leftist, and detests pornography and blasphemy in works of art. In short, despite my years of training, I found it needful to get a handful of degrees. It was not until I had virtually finished my doctorate, a Ph.D. in art history, that I was able to get work as a college professor. I retired this past spring [1990].
>
> When I was at the prison, the enlisted men were, for the most part, in one of two groups—guards or jailers. The jailers, being in the cell blocks, did not carry firearms. Nor did the guards when the post was inside the Red Area, as in the corridors connecting cell blocks. Out-of-doors, as in the old wooden towers which were there at the time (new steel towers were being put up shortly before I left), our weapon was the old semi-automatic 30 caliber carbine. We had training in firing the .45, but enlisted men were not issued side arms.
>
> During my stay at the prison, I think I pulled duty on every guard post there. Interestingly, there was no Jeep patrol at that time, although I sometimes went as a guard in a Jeep when truckloads of sentenced prisoners were taken some miles away on work details. Toward the end of my stay, I worked more with the sentenced prisoners out-of-doors (green relief) than on regular guard posts.

As for my feelings about my assignment to Sugamo, I think it may surprise you if I tell you that it, in retrospect, appears the happiest time of my life. This, of course, is in reference to my total situation. I was young and foolish which made associating with famous (or infamous) people on a regular basis rather exciting. My duties were not oppressive. Many times the schedule amounted to twenty-four hours on, forty-eight hours off. The twenty-four hour tour was divided so that three hours were actually spent on a post, followed by six hours off, repeating the cycle through the twenty-four hour period. Thus, I had much time on my own.

There was some adventure too. Travel was extremely limited since almost everything was off limits, but I managed to visit the wonderfully beautiful area around Mt. Fuji on a number of occasions and climbed the mountain twice. I broke into prison one night by climbing the barbed wire fence after I failed to make a train connection coming back from Fujiyoshida and arrived in Ikebukuro after midnight. The fence was terribly noisy!

Contributing much to the general happiness was a circle of close friends such as I had not had before, and have not had since.

I was one of the first guards to respond to the emergency that occurred August 29, 1947, when the first Japanese suicide occurred at Sugamo.

Robert L. McMahon of New Jersey served with the military police at Ichigawa Heights, Tokyo, where the IMTFE trial of the Class A war criminals was held. After the trial was over, he served at Sugamo. He enlisted in the army in 1947 at the age of seventeen and arrived in Japan in late 1947. He was assigned to the Twenty-fifth Infantry Division and then transferred to the Ichigawa trial in November 1947.

To my knowledge Robert is the first ex-GI to state that the facilities at Sugamo were poor. Apparently, to those of us who did not have the good fortune to serve at the Ichigawa War Ministry Building, everything was relative. What we didn't know didn't hurt us.

He wrote:

The MP detachment at the trials in Tokyo were billeted at the former Japanese Imperial War Ministry Building. The War Ministry was Tojo's headquarters during the war. It was a nice building in Ichigawa, located near the Shinjuku section of Tokyo. It was about a ten minute ride on the bus from downtown Tokyo. The area we were at was untouched by the bombing of Tokyo.

The MP detachment was commanded by Lt. Col. Aubrey Kenworthy who had also held trials in the Philippines at the end of WWII. Some of

Robert L. McMahon. (Courtesy Robert L. McMahon)

the older MP's had served with him at those trials. The detachment (8th Army shoulder patch) consisted of the Lieutenant Colonel, two Lieutenants and about fifty to seventy enlisted men. We lived in the War Ministry Building where the trials were held. The facilities were excellent, compared to the poor facilities you had at Sugamo.

I had always assumed that we were just a bastard unit, but looking at the bumper markings on our jeeps in the attached photos indicates that we must have been attached to the 720 MP battalion in Tokyo.

Also located at the War Ministry Building were the court room and offices for the eleven judges. The judges were from the countries involved in the war with Japan. They were Major Generals or civilians with

Hideki Tojo and Col. Aubrey Kenworthy. (Courtesy Robert N. Shively)

equivalent status. Our job was to provide twenty-four hour security for the complex, security for the prisoners while in court, and crowd control. I was assigned to a ten man team that drove to Sugamo every morning, in two jeeps and a bus with the windows covered, to pick up and return the Class A prisoners.

After all the testimony was given at the trials and the judges were making their decision, the trials were shut down. Approximately half of our unit was sent to Sugamo Prison to assist there. Apparently your unit was under strength, because I recall that they had sent down about thirty troopers from the 11th Airborne Division also to assist. We remained at Sugamo until the trials resumed for the sentencing, at which time we returned to the War Ministry. Once the prisoners were sentenced, we returned to Sugamo until they were executed. We were all then reassigned to the 720 MP Battalion in Tokyo.

Regarding the trials, I remember that Tojo was not very sociable and normally remained apart from the other prisoners. General Muto used to read maps of China and planned to go to China after the trials, to help the Nationalists against the Reds. He was hung. It should be noted that General Muto was one of the few Japanese generals who had his own troops put to death for committing crimes against the peoples in occupied countries. The Russians and another country would not allow the evidence that was in his favor to be admitted for the record.

While at Sugamo, I worked POW work details. We would take a group of sentenced prisoners to a nearby abandoned factory. There they would remove very large vehicle tires stored in one warehouse and stack them in another. Then we would reverse the process.

I also recall working inside the cell blocks. When the female prisoners were returned from their trials each day, the male prisoners became very excited. They all tried to get to a good location so that they could see the females.

I returned to the States in early 1950, prior to the Korean War. I was later sent to Korea with the Rangers and the 187 Regiment. I also returned a second time and served with L Company, 14 Infantry, 25th Division at the time the war ended.

I stayed in the military for eleven years. I was discharged in 1959 and was a New Jersey State Trooper for twenty five years. I'm retired from the troops, but still working.

Richard J. Olguin of Tennessee is a retired master sergeant. He was the NCO/IC of the platoon that was brought down from the Eleventh Airborne Division in northern Japan. This platoon served as guards and jailers at Sugamo during the latter part of the trial of the Class A war criminals and during the executions.

He stated:

> The officer in charge of my platoon was Lt. McCann, a real nice guy — quiet and did not bother anyone.
>
> At the time we were assigned to Sugamo there were several old gallows. There were several new gallows constructed, totaling five if my memory serves me.
>
> We were housed within the prison proper. Our rooms were cell blocks, some four men to a room. Facilities were excellent and I might add the chow was great.
>
> Back in those days the troops at the prison and those from the 11th Airborne didn't get along too well. Before we left Japan in 1949, we had ongoing warfare with the troops from the 1st Cavalry Division and the Tokyo 720 MP Battalion. We were accused of being cocky smart asses, and I guess some of us were. We buddied only with our own people.
>
> One night after Tojo had been condemned to hang, he complained that one of our guys was keeping him awake because his shoes made too much noise as he walked back and forth in front of his cell. I checked it out and reported it to Lt. McMann. The next day there was a rug outside Tojo's cell for the guard to walk on. How about that! It was

Robert Weatherspoon (left), Richard Olguin (right). (Courtesy Richard Olguin)

shocking to see some of the pampering that was extended to these criminals.

When I arrived at Sugamo I had just reached the age of seventeen and had just received a promotion to Buck Sergeant. I told a little lie when I went into the 11th Airborne Division at the age of fifteen. My priorities at that time were the girls in the dance halls down on the Ginza.

Richard later became the equivalent of a soldier of fortune for the U.S. Army. He was selected to train, and often lead, troops in covert operations.

Willis H. Rawlins of California retired as a lieutenant colonel. When he arrived at Sugamo in early 1946, he was a lieutenant. There wasn't anything outside the prison walls at that time. He supervised the building of the Troop Headquarters Building, officers quarters, troop quarters, motor pool building, laundry, rehabilitation building, two wings of the hospital, football and baseball fields, theater, officers' and enlisted men's club buildings, bowling alley, and installed the new boiler that furnished heat for the prison and several other service buildings — kitchen and eating areas, post exchange, service club, and so on.

Willis wrote:

When we took the prison over there were Japanese, Germans and some Italians there. Since these were political prisoners, we released the Japanese prisoners but held on to the German and Italian prisoners for awhile, until we had instructions to ship them to Germany and Italy. I can't remember everything I would like to after all these years, but I think there were American authorities waiting in Germany for the arrival of some of these prisoners.

When we finished building the bowling alley it was the first in Japan. We had five Generals that bowled all afternoon. No one else had a chance at it. We used prisoners as pin setters. They had never seen the game but got very good very soon. In fact, they got better than most GI's.

About the gallows: there was one already there when we took over the prison. I modified it and made the drawings myself for four new ones. I had ordnance make all the iron parts and my carpenters put the things together, in the same spot but in a permanent building. I've drawn a sketch to show where it was located and another one to show you what it looked like. We never used the fifth gallows. We did hang four at a time on several occasions.

When a hanging was scheduled we would call the 8th Army Provost Marshal's office in Yokohama. They always sent a guy up to Sugamo who went straight to the Officer's Club. He would drink all he wanted, until he was smashed, then we would haul him to the hospital area and lock him in a cell for two or three days, or however much time was needed to sober him up, before the hanging. He used an English formula to determine how far the man needed to be dropped — weight, height, age, and condition.

I requistioned the rope to be used in the hangings and they sent me three-ply hemp rope. This was not acceptable since regulations called for four-ply manila rope. There was none in Tokyo so we sent a man to the Philippines to get what was ordered. I ordered five hundred feet. The requisition for the rope was justified by putting "to hang war criminals" on it. The 8th Army G-4 Supply brought sixteen copies back to me and asked me to sign all of them. I asked why there were so many copies and he said, "souvenirs" and off he went. I did not get a souvenir. When I got the rope, I cut the lengths they needed and put the rest in my supply room.

When Tojo and the other six major war criminals were hung, I took the rope used for their executions and locked it up. The next day I burned it in my boilers. I did cut some six inch pieces of another rope for the CO to give away to his friends. They all thought they had a piece of the rope that hung Tojo. Not so! I repeat, no one on earth has a piece of that rope!

Since I designed and built the gallows, I had to be present at all the hangings. The prison commander said that if anything went wrong, I would have to fix it. Nothing went wrong.

One day I asked Tojo when he knew that he had lost the war. He said, "When the marines invaded Guadalcanal." I said, That was in 1942. Why didn't you stop the war? You would have saved millions of lives. He said, "You don't know what it takes to start a war nor what it takes to stop one." He wouldn't talk anymore about it. The other Class A war criminals had very little to do with him.

Once, during my assignment at Sugamo Prison, I got into some kind of trouble. The Prison Commander and I had to go over and get lectured by Sir William Webb, the Chief Judge at the trials. This incident involved Admiral Nagano, the Japanese Admiral in command of the navy and one of the chief planners of the attack on Pearl Harbor in December, 1941. He broke his cell window while closing it. It was about 9:30 pm when the duty officer called me at home and asked me if I would fix it. I said sure, first thing in the morning. I had had a long hard day and wanted to rest. This was in the dead of winter and he caught pneumonia and died. This incident also got me ordered to General MacArthur's headquarters to be personally chewed out by the General's Chief of Staff. He informed me that I had gotten my share of the Class As and that I could not have anymore.

I left Sugamo in early July, 1949 and went to the 2nd Infantry Division at Fort Lewis. From there I was assigned to the Army Ordnance Depot at Chattanooga, Tennessee as Post Engineer. I was there long enough to rebuild a TNT plant, then on to the 3rd Army Headquarters, and on and on until I retired December 31, 1960.

In December 1990 Willis Rawlins called me. He was home for the Christmas holiday but informed me that he had undergone several operations for cancer and had to return to Pendleton Naval Hospital for chemotherapy treatment.

Willis died in August 1991 and was given full military honors.

I can only hope that the colonel understood how much I appreciated his contribution to this book.

Ira Sutterfield of Arkansas was a prison guard from the beginning of the occupation until May 1946. He is the only member of the Sugamo team I've been able to contact who began guarding war criminals before Eighth Army officials took command of Sugamo Prison. Yokohama Prison was used to hold war criminals until it became too crowded and everyone was moved to Sugamo.

Ira sent me a picture of Tokyo Rose walking in the Yokohama

exercise yard. He claims that before they moved to Sugamo, they held two Americans accused of treason. He thinks one was John Powell from Idaho, but he couldn't remember the other American's name. It was John D. Provoo.

In recalling one incident at the Yokohama Prison he wrote: "A German colonel was being sent back to Germany for trial and cut his wrists. I called the Day Officer and he came running to the cell, but didn't bring a key. Colonel Misengers decided he wanted to live by the time they got the cell door opened. They bandaged him up and he was sent to Germany. I don't know what happened to him after that."

Wilfred F. Willert of North Dakota joined the army in April 1946. After basic training and a short assignment at Camp Stoneman, California, he was transferred to Sugamo Prison. He arrived in February 1947. At that time prisoners were still being brought in and confined, while others were being tried for war crimes or released. He wrote:

> We discharged the wrong inmate once. There were two prisoners by the same name. One, a protected witness, was to be sent home. The one sentenced to serve a term in prison was sent to us in error and released. We didn't catch it until cell check. We sent one of our interpreters to the fellow's house and he was there.
>
> While I was at Sugamo we lost our first suspected war criminal to suicide. He was Superior Petty Officer Waichi Ogawa. On Friday August 29, 1947 he knotted his underwear into a rope and strangled himself. Ogawa was put in Sugamo for protective custody and questioning on June 30. After questioning by SCAP's Australian legal section, he definitely became a Class C suspect and was transferred to a war crime cell block. He had beheaded two Australian soldiers on a South Pacific island. He chose to kill himself rather than stand trial and face the penalty for his war crime.
>
> For recreation we climbed Mt. Fuji or went to the beaches and resort hotels. A certain number of us could get a sailboat, with crew, in Tokyo Bay for a small sum of money or play golf, with lessons. We also toured Tokyo, Yokohama and the surrounding area in groups by Army bus. It was pretty good duty.

After being discharged, Will returned to North Dakota, where he had a livestock farm. After ten years of grain, beef, and dairy farming he went to the University of North Dakota and earned his degree in education. After many years of service with the John Deere Company and in the fertilizer, chemical, and seed businesses, Will retired. He now plans to travel with his wife, Sara.

Wilfred F. Willert. (Courtesy Wilfred F. Willert)

Lloyd E. Oler, Sr., wrote:

> I arrived at Sugamo in November of 1948 and was assigned to the guard section. My duties consisted of tower guard around the high perimeter wall, walking the corridors on all three floors of the cell blocks, relaying messages for the prisoners inside the cell blocks to the prison office, and guarding prisoners on work detail or during visitations of relatives.
>
> In April, 1949 I was transferred to the jailer section and was assigned to cell block 5-C — the condemned floor. We walked back and forth in front of four cells every half hour, and then changed with another jailer who sat in front of a cell and watched a prisoner who was likely to commit suicide.
>
> In June I was assigned to cell block 6. All these war criminals were sentenced to life. My duties were to sign prisoners in and out of the block for work details, exercising and visitation, seeing that they were fed and bathed at the proper times, and ensuring them medical treatment when necessary.
>
> In December I was transferred back to 5-C as acting sergeant of the condemned row, and served there until July of 1950 when I left for

Edward J. Capodilupo. (Courtesy Edward J. Capodilupo)

Korea. There I was assigned to Company F, 19th Infantry, 24th Division.
 I found the prisoners most interesting to talk to, and they talked freely about their trials and convictions. They also taught me to speak Japanese rather fluently.

Lloyd retired from the U.S. Army Engineers in October 1988. He has four sons, two of whom are career men in the air force. The oldest is a fighter pilot.

He lost his wife of thirty-seven years to cancer and is currently engaged to Marilyn Rudersdorf, who manages American Legion Post 13 in their home state of Wisconsin.

Edward J. Capodilupo of Maryland joined the army in 1946. He served at Sugamo from May until December 1947. In his last letter he wrote:

At Sugamo, I was appointed to the guard section. I was a tower guard, farm guard, prison guard, and also at times an interrogation guard.
 I remember, during the prisoners' shaving time we checked the razors for broken blades. If we found a broken blade we cleared the cell to search for it. This was to prevent suicides.
 I also remember standing guard over the war criminals and listening to Provost Marshal personnel interrogating them. I recall one specific

Robert Murphy. (Courtesy Robert Murphy)

incident. A Japanese ship, holding Allied women, was shot at by an American plane. Because of this the ship's captain gave the order to line up several women, machine gun them, and throw them into the water. One Filipino woman was rescued by an American submarine. Several years later I was standing guard over a Japanese prisoner in the interrogation room. A Filipino woman sat across from him. She pointed right at him and stated, 'He is the one that gave the order.' This prisoner was the captain of the Japanese ship, and she was the woman rescued by the American submarine.

After my tour of duty at Sugamo, I transferred to the 25th Division in Osaka, Japan. I re-enlisted for a second tour in June, 1950 and served until 1953. I was sent to Korea in September, 1950. There I served with the 1st Cavalry, 8th Regiment, E Company. In 1951 I returned to the States, and was stationed at Fort Jackson, South Carolina. In March, 1952 I went back to Hokkaido, Japan, where I was with the 1st Cav., 27th Ordnance small arms repair.

I was married in 1955. I have four children and one grandson. I have been with Raytheon for over thirty years and recently had the pleasure of being part of the making of the Patriot Missiles.

The last man to write to me was Robert Murphy of Minnesota. He wrote:

I arrived at Sugamo in January, 1948. I was assigned to the jailer section and worked cell block 6 where condemned war criminals were held. Later, I was assigned to cell block 5 where Tojo and his cabinet members were confined. After working there for nine months, I became a cook. Later, I was asked to become Father Ryan's assistant, working with both the catholic priest and the protestant minister. I enjoyed that job very much. I set up all the services for the prisoners, plus the GI's services on Sundays. I also worked with a missionary priest who was in charge of an orphanage. It was fun going out to the orphanage and spending time with all the children. They were very good, and the little ones were so cute.

Shortly after Father Ryan was murdered, I transferred into the gate section where I made sergeant and remained until I came home and was discharged in June, 1950. The soldier who was eventually accused of murdering Chaplain Ryan was W. C. Manis. He was a very quiet fellow who always minded his own business, and was a good soldier. Nobody at Sugamo believed he had anything to do with the murder. I personally think he was just a fall guy that the CID blamed in order to save face.

After spending almost a year at home, I went to work as a fireman for the Milwaukee Railroad. I was promoted to Engineer in 1955, and worked as such until 1986 when I retired. I ran almost every type of engine they have on the rails, including those on Amtrak.

I married my wife, Donna, in May, 1952. We have nine children and, at this time, ten grandchildren.

REFLECTIONS

Since the author played a part, it is easier to discuss reflections after more than forty years have passed than if the history had happened last year. Many things take place in forty-three years.

During the trials, the United States and its allies set precedents for future war crimes trials. At the end of World War II, the world demanded that those responsible for the barbaric atrocities that had occurred be brought to justice. The trial of Nazi war criminals at Nuremberg was better conducted than those in Tokyo. The time consumed by the Tokyo trials — almost two and a half years — with the sanctioned delaying tactics of the defense, almost defeated their purpose. They did not have the desired effect on either the Japanese people or the world.

When we evaluate the impact of World War II war crimes trials on reducing future atrocities, we must admit failure. There are the wartime atrocities of Korea, Vietnam, and Iraq to contemplate. Moreover, Saddam Hussein of Iraq, in addition to butchering innocent people, has massively escalated mindless environmental destruction.

Perhaps the only benefit to be gained from conducting war crimes trials is the psychological moment of restoration it provides for the victors. In Vietnam we experienced the alternative.

General MacArthur, as SCAP, rushed the trials of Generals Tomoyuki Yamashita and Masaharu Homma in Manila. They were tried by military tribunals as Class B war criminals — Homma for the Bataan Death March and Yamashita for the Rape of Manila. Yamashita was charged within three weeks of the surrender, and the trial was scheduled to begin three weeks after that. Both generals were intelligent, respected, and showed themselves to be dignified and honorable men. They were condemned to hang for the crime of not having full control over their subordinates. Both generals claimed that they were not in the area at the time the atrocities were committed. Yamashita, after hearing his sentence of death, composed the following short poem:

> The world I knew is now a shameful place.
> There will never come a better time for me to die.

General Homma was incarcerated in Sugamo Prison on December 8, 1945. His uniform and decorations were taken from him, and, within a week, he was returned to Manila to stand trial. After the trial his wife, Fujiko, appealed to MacArthur to spare him. She failed, but her efforts did accomplish one thing: Homma was executed by firing squad instead of hanging.

On December 20, 1945, a petition was filed with the Supreme Court to test the question of MacArthur's jurisdiction over the trial of Yamashita. The decision was made public on February 4, 1946. The petition was denied: The military had authority to conduct the trial, and the Court lacked jurisdiction even to question the fairness of the trial. Justice Jackson elected to take no part in the decision. Two justices, Murphy and Rutledge, presented some unusually strong and stinging dissents, which ruffled MacArthur, but these dissenting remarks had a considerable effect on both the Tokyo and Yokohama trials. MacArthur made sure that the trials were legal and that the suspects had proper defense representation. He also commuted seventy death sentences.

If the United States and its allies were intent on setting precedents by conducting war crimes trials, they would have accomplished much more had the punishments fitted the crimes. To "slap the wrist" of a war criminal convicted of murder allows the precedent to be quickly forgotten.

None of the Class A war criminals sentenced to life served a life sentence unless he died of natural causes within a very few years. They were all paroled and pardoned by 1958. The last surviving Class A war criminal was Teiichi Suzuki, the army general who helped plan Japan's economy during the war. He was sentenced to life imprisonment in December 1948 but was released on parole from Sugamo Prison in 1955 and was granted a full pardon in 1958. He died of heart failure in 1988 at the age of one hundred.

At the end of the trials, there were almost forty Class A prisoners at Sugamo who had never been indicted. They were released, and all were surprised at the leniency of the sentences handed down. Nobusuke Kishi published his autobiography in 1960. In it he expressed "astonishment that only seven" of the accused Class A war criminals received the death sentence. He believed that if the Americans were being tried in similar circumstances, no Japanese court would have allowed Allied prisoners to defend themselves. Kishi was prime minister of Japan from 1957 to 1960.

One subject that arose only to be quickly swept away during the trial was that of the Japanese 731st Regiment and the bacteriological warfare it conducted in China. It is amazing how supposedly top-secret information seeps out over a period of time. Several years ago a short article appeared in a local (Washington state) newspaper about one of General MacArthur's aides who reported a World War II coverup. Dr. Murray Sanders, a former lieutenant colonel and adviser on biological warfare, admitted that the United States government had been covering up a dark secret for forty years.

In 1945 American military authorities in Tokyo agreed not to prosecute numerous Japanese scientists and researchers who, it was later discovered, had used Chinese, Korean, and Russian civilians and American and Allied prisoners of war as human guinea pigs in bacteriological experiments. The U.S. authorities knew about the human experimentation, but agreed not to prosecute in exchange for Japan's scientific data on germ warfare.

These experiments occurred in Harbin, China, under the direction of Lt. General Shiro Ishii, the leader of the infamous military medical group known as Unit 731. Some of the worst atrocities of the war were committed here, in the name of medical research, at a cost of more than three thousand lives! In the depth of winter, prisoners were placed in cold water and then forced outside to freeze. Later they were carried inside and their frozen flesh was beaten with boards or plunged into hot water to assess its sensitivity. Others were injected with bubonic plague, cholera, syphilis, and other diseases. Several of Ishii's researchers performed vivisections, usually without anesthetics, while others placed prisoners behind metal screens with their buttocks exposed to fragmentation bombs that had been laced with a gas to give them gangrene. The researchers then timed how long it took the prisoners to die.

Han Xiao, deputy director of the Pingfang District Administration Office, spent almost twenty years learning what happened: "At first, the experiments were carried out on the bodies of animals, but later they shifted to using people. These were battlefield prisoners and civilians arrested by the Japanese." Han also reported that most of the human guinea pigs were Chinese, but Koreans, Russians, Mongolians, and, later, Americans and other Allies were used. The researchers wanted to compare the resistance of various nationalities and races to deadly germs.

Some people were tested on several different occasions until they died. They were then transported through a secret tunnel for cremation. The experiments were carefully recorded and documented. The records indicate that some of the experiments went beyond germ research. Some prisoners were exposed to X-rays for long periods. Others had their blood replaced with horse blood to determine if they could survive. Women were infected with syphilis to make vaccines.

The Japanese research on biological warfare, which might have changed the course of the war, stopped when Russia invaded Manchuria in August of 1945. The Japanese researchers gassed the remaining prisoners and blew up the camp in an effort to destroy the evidence before they fled. Only a small wooden plaque now marks the site as a secret germ warfare factory. The yellow brick headquarters building has become a junior high school for Harbin's suburban Pingfang district. Two skeleton chimneys that once were part of the camp furnaces rise above the surrounding homes. The rest of the camp has been destroyed.

A few of the Japanese surrendered to the Russians. They were tried at a Russian war crimes trial in the border city of Khabarovsk and sentenced to fifteen years. However, most of 3,600 men in the 731st Regiment made it back to Japan, where General Ishii made a deal with the American occupation authorities. He and his subordinates were given immunity from prosecution in return for their research papers.

The story of the infamous 731st Regiment was written by Seiichi Morimura and Masaki Shimozato and published in Japan under the title of *The Devil's Gluttony* in 1982. It became a best-seller—an unusual occurrence since many Japanese find sanctuary in not facing unwanted truths. In their book Morimura and Shimozato reported that General Ishii died of natural causes in 1959. Another member of Unit 731, General Masaji Kitano, founded the pharmaceutical company Green Cross, which has pioneered the use of artificial blood. Other officers of the unit became successful doctors and medical researchers in Japan.

Harbin's inhabitants were less fortunate, according to Han. When the Japanese left, they released their diseased laboratory animals. In 1946 bubonic plague, carried by rats and mice, ravaged the Pingfang district, killing more than one hundred people.

Chinese authorities interviewed almost one hundred local laborers who had been forced to work outside the camp. Their testimonies were given further credibility in later reports and in the book published in Japan. Han stated: "It is the duty of us in the district to clarify the history of this period and use it to tell future generations."

The Chinese government raised the case of the germ warfare unit at Harbin in the summer of 1982 to protest the rewriting of Japanese schoolbooks, from which atrocities and many other facts about Japanese involvement in World War II were eliminated.

In 1977 Japan's Education Ministry published guidelines for the basic history textbooks for Japanese schools. At that time the existing history of World War II was more than two hundred pages long. The new guidelines reduced it to six pages. Most of these were filled with photographs of Hiroshima and Nagasaki, a table of Japan's war dead, and photographs of the fire-bombing of Tokyo. Practically every nation that fought against Japan, with the exception of the United States, strongly protested this action. With this change in history textbooks, Japan hoped to become known as a victim of the war, and to cease to be a nation that planned a massive campaign of aggression.

No matter what the American authorities believed those research papers contained, the objectives cannot possibly justify their actions. The research was in any case crude, backward, and barbaric. Any nation that had a monopoly on nuclear power certainly did not need this kind of research information—nor did we need to embarrass ourselves in such a despicable manner.

To top off this whole unsavory mess, a local newspaper published an article prepared by the *New York Times* in August 1990, titled, "Japanese Scientist Not Eager to Solve This War Mystery." In Tokyo construction workers cleared the site of an old government building in order to erect a new National Institute of Health building. They unearthed parts of thirty-five human skeletons that appeared to have been buried forty-five to fifty years ago. When asked to examine the remains and determine their origin, Tokyo's National Museum of Science thought about it and then politely declined. Since then, so have a handful of Japan's leading medical schools and forensic scientists. When officials of Tokyo's Shinjuku Ward, the neighborhood where the skeletons were found, asked the minister of health and welfare for help, they received a curt letter in reply. It read: "The ministry wishes that Shinjuku Ward will cremate and bury the remains without delay."

The remains were found just steps from the site of General Ishii's wartime laboratory. The main camp of Unit 731 was in Harbin, but Ishii also spent a lot of his time at his Tokyo laboratory. A professor at Kanagawa University suspected that the remains found in Tokyo were those of prisoners shipped back from Harbin for study after they died. He stated: "There are many people who think it may be safer not to know."

On the Murder Trial of an American

Pvt. 1st Cl. William C. Manis, a Sugamo guard, was charged with the murder of Chap. Capt. John A. Ryan on April 5, 1948. It was the first such murder charge in U.S. Army history. He was tried by a court-martial in Yokohama, Japan, and found guilty in August 1948.

After Chaplain Ryan was killed, it took the army CID almost three weeks to determine that he had been shot rather than stabbed to death, as they first thought. At first, they accused several Japanese and Korean underworld bosses of the murder, but could not prove it. Later they lined up Sugamo's American guards, jailers, and other personnel in the post theater and — for some unknown reason — inspected their faces and shins. They then secretly searched the footlockers of prison personnel. Two Japanese prostitutes later gave conflicting testimonies at the court-martial. The CID investigators did the "Keystone Kops" in the cartoons a favor — they made them look good.

Several witnesses for Manis, including his commanding officer and first sergeant, testified to his good character and reputation. Four members of the court that tried him, along with 112 residents of Sullivan and Hawkins counties, Tennessee, where his home was located, signed a petition for clemency in his case.

He was sentenced to life imprisonment and served eight and a half years in federal prison before he was paroled. After being imprisoned, Manis enlisted the assistance of Tennessee's former senator Estes Kefauver, who pleaded with the Judge Advocate General to grant Manis's request for a lie detector test. It was repeatedly denied.

Every man from Sugamo with whom I have been able to correspond who knew Manis, claims that he could not and would not hurt a fly.

Having obtained and read Manis's court-martial records, I reached the conclusion that he served more time in federal prisons for something he did not do than some of the Japanese war criminals for some of the worst atrocities committed during World War II.

On returning to Sugamo from pass leave, Manis reported to the main gate guard that he thought he'd heard a shot and a scream. As a result of his mentioning this, Father Ryan's body was found. Manis was charged with the murder three months later. Kept in a Japanese jail, he was allowed no visitors and did not meet or talk with his defense representatives until the trial was under way.

Manis became a trustee early in his confinement and remained so until he was released.

At the reunion two ex-Sugamo men claimed that Ryan told them that he had information regarding a large black-market ring and was going out to have it stopped. Two other ex-Sugamo men related how that evening Ryan told them that if they heard a scream it would most likely be him.

Manis's opinion of the army CID personnel is unprintable.

APPENDIX A
Names of the Accused

Abe, Tatsuo
Abe, Tsunee
Adachi, Fukusaburo
Adachi, Seiichi
Aihara, Kajuro
Aihara, Kazutane
Akaike, Kohei
Akamatsu, Shigeo
Akamatsu, Toranoshin
Akamine, Teruo
Akatsuka, Hanji
Akiba, Genzo
Akira, Hiroshi
Akita, Niro
Akita, Teruo
Akiyama, Fukujiro
Akiyama, Yonesaku
Akutsu, Toshi
Anaguchi, Shozo
Ando, Tetsuo
Anjo, Hiroshi
Aoki, Shoichiro
Aoki, Yuji
Aona, Shigeru
Aoyagi, Jimbei
Arai, Takahisa
Arakawa, Kazuo
Araki, Kuniichi
Aramaki, Sakujiro
Arao, Okikatsu
Ariizumi, Shigeru
Asada, Shigetsuchi

Asaka, Toshinori
Asakura, Todao
Asano, Yukio
Asari, Eiji
Asoma, Nakakichi
Azuma, Hiroshi
Baba, Kensako
Bando, Bunhachi
Beppu, Takeshi
Chigara, Naraichi
Chin, Mo Ei
Chiuma, Sazae
Chuba, Tadayuki
Date, Tatsumi
Deguchi, Taichi
Eato, Shunsuke
Ebi, Yosoichiro
Egawa, Sachio
Eizumi, Shigeo
Emori, Hidetoshi
Enatsu, Tokuji
Enoki, Yoshinori
Enomoto, Muneo
Eto, Shigeki
Fujihira, Naotada
Fujii, Hiroshi
Fujii, Sannojo
Fujii, Shoichi
Fujiki, Fumio
Fujimori, Yasuo
Fujimoto, Minoru
Fujinaka, Matsuo

Fujino, Ranjo
Fujino, Takeji
Fujioka, Hideo
Fujisaki, Seitaro
Fujisaki, Takenosuke
Fujita, Mitsuyoshi
Fujita, Shoshaburo
Fujita, Sietaro
Fujita, Takayashi
Fujita, Tatsuro
Fukami, Kazuo
Fukijima, Keitaro
Fukuda, Katsuma
Fukuda, Kingoro
Fukuda, Shigeru
Fukuda, Tokuro
Fukuhara, Isao
Fukumoto, Norio
Fukumura, Yuetsu
Fukunaga, Kiyozo
Fukunaga, Takeo
Fukushima, Kyusaku
Funaki, Eisaku
Funaki, Kaoru
Furukawa, Tamotsu
Furuno, Masaji
Furushima, Chotaro
Furuya, Tatsuhiko
Furuyama, Mataichi
Fushimi, Mamoru
Goiyama, Shinju
Gomi, Yasuo
Gonda, Masaru
Goshima, Shiro
Goto, Hirozo
Goto, Isamu
Goto, Kinzo
Goto, Toshio
Gunji, Takanosuke
Habe, Toshitaro
Hachiya, Masao
Hada, Kyui
Hada, Masato
Hagido, Morimitsu

Hagihara, Wakado
Hamada, Tomekichi
Hamamoto, Jiro
Hanamori, Tomizo
Hara, Isamu
Hara, Mokichi
Harada, Kichiji
Haraguchi, Kaname
Hasegawa, Wataru
Hashimoto, Chogo
Hashimoto, Hitoshi
Hashimoto, Shigeyoshi
Hashimoto, Takeshi
Hashiyama, Noboru
Hata, Seitaro
Hata, Tatsumi
Hatakayama, Toshio
Hatakeyama, Iseo
Hatano, Kozo
Hattori, Masanori
Hattori, Sho
Hayashi, Junsho
Hayashi, Masao
Hayashi, Shigeaki
Hazama, Kosaku
Hichino, Shinobu
Hida, Usaji
Higashiguchi, Ryoichi
Higuchi, Keiji
Higurashi, Saburo
Hikita, Toyokazu
Hirabayashi, Masajiro
Hirai, Kenshi
Hirako, Goichi
Hiramatsu, Sadaharu
Hirano, Kenji
Hirano, Kurataro
Hirano, Ryuma
Hirano, Yoshimi
Hirao, Kenichi
Hirate, Kaichi
Hitosugi, Yukio
Homma, Nubua
Honda, Hajime

Honda, Hiroji
Hori, Sakuzo
Hori, Yoshio
Horie, Masaichi
Horiuchi, Kiyoma
Hosano, Yoshio
Hosoi, Sutoumon
Hosotani, Yuhei
Hozumi, Eiichi
Hozumi, Masakatsu
Ichiba, Tokuichi
Ichinoe, Kimiya
Ichioka, Hisashi
Ichiyanagi, Noburo
Ieda, Nakazo
Iita, Kakuzo
Iiyama, Toranosuke
Ijitsu, Asao
Ikadazu, Nobuo
Ikeda, Kaneyoshi
Ikeda, Yoshiyuki
Ikegami, Uechi
Ikehara, Shigeichi
Ikemiyagi, Morikaji
Imai, Katsuto
Imai, Kiyomi
Inada, Masazumi
Inagaki, Mitsuzo
Inaki, Makoto
Inami, Yoshiaki
Inanaga, Iwao
Ino, Masaji
Inoue, Katsutaro
Inoue, Mitsushige
Inoue, Otohiko
Inoue, Yoshiyuki
Inouye, Morio
Irie, Yoshiaki
Ise, Chitoku
Ishibashi, Masao
Ishibe, Kiyoji
Ishida, Kitaro
Ishida, Naozo
Ishida, Otogoro

Ishigaki, Kakuji
Ishige, Michiharu
Ishihara, Tazuko
Ishii, Isaburo
Ishikawa, Kenpei
Ishikawa, Tsuneo
Ishimatsu, Matasuke
Ishimori, Hatsuo
Ishiyama, Jammatsu
Ishizaki, Hideo
Ishizaki, Noboru
Ishizawa, Katsuo
Isoya, Goro
Isujiro, Akiyoshi
Itagaki, Kanenobu
Itezono, Tatsuo
Ito, Akiro
Ito, Benji
Ito, Eiichi
Ito, Kenji
Ito, Nobuo
Ito, Shiroji
Ito, Shoji
Ito, Shoshin
Ito, Taichi
Ito, Yosichi
Iura, Shojiro
Iwabuchi, Kiyomi
Iwanaga, Kenji
Iwanami, Shamatsu
Iwanuma, Tsuguo
Iwasaki, Masutaro
Iwata, Yagoheiji
Iwataka, Kenji
Izumi, Toyosuke
Jin, Iichiro
Kageshita, Jiro
Kajiyama, Shin
Kakinoki, Fukujiro
Kaku, Takanobu
Kakuta, Hajime
Kamada, Shuji
Kamae, Kinji
Kambe, Hatsuaki

Kameda, Jirokichi
Kameoka, Yoshio
Kamimoto, Keiji
Kamishinbara, Taneyoshi
Kamiyasumiba, Ryutatsu
Kanamaru, Takeo
Kanayama, Nubuo
Kaneko, Takio
Kanetsuna, Ryugo
Kaneyama, Hisao
Kanno, Masami
Kariya, Yoshiaki
Karube, Yuzo
Kasai, Hyomo
Kasatani, Eiichi
Kasuya, Kunzio
Kataoka, Masao
Kataura, Toshiatsu
Katayama, Goichi
Katayama, Kenge
Kato, Genzo
Kato, Masayoshi
Kato, Rimpei
Kato, Tetsutaro
Katsuki, Kunizo
Katsuta, Haruo
Kawabata, Shimekichi
Kawabe, Nagayasu
Kawaguchi, Shinnosuke
Kawahira, Kenji
Kawai, Shoji
Kawakami, Harushige
Kawakami, Shoichi
Kawakami, Suetaka
Kawamorita, Shojiro
Kawamura, Kameki
Kawamura, Tomohisa
Kawane, Yoshitaka
Kawasaki, Iwao
Kawate, Harumi
Kida, Satohiko
Kihara, Kazuo
Kikuchi, Jutaro
Kikuchi, Kenichi

Kikuchi, Masatomo
Kimoto, Kazuo
Kimura, Goro
Kimura, Makoto
Kimura, Ryunosuke
Kimura, Shigeru
Kimura, Tomotsu
Kimura, Tsutafu
Kimura, Yasushi
Kimura, Yokinaga
Kimura, Yoshiichi
Kinari, Ichiji
Kintaichi, Isami
Kinugasa, Kazuo
Kira, Imajira
Kirishita, Takeo
Kirya, Masauki
Kishi, Tatsuro
Kita, Takeo
Kitada, Mitsuno
Kitamura, Sueharu
Kitashima, Riichi
Kiya, Shigekazu
Kobayashi, Hideichi
Kobayashi, Koei
Kobayashi, Minoru
Kobayashi, Morikado
Kobayashi, Risaku
Kobayashi, Ryoji
Kobayashi, Sadaharu
Kobayashi, Tetsuo
Kobayashi, Yasuo
Kobuke, Mitoku
Kodama, Noboru
Kodama, Takeo
Koga, Akiyoshi
Kohama, Seisho
Kohara, Katsuo
Kohara, Yasuo
Koike, Kaneichi
Koiwa, Zenkichi
Koizumi, Tokiichi
Kojima, Itchisaku
Kokubo, Nobuo

Komatsu, Teruhisa
Komatsu, Tsurugi
Komine, Yoshie
Kondo, Jiro
Kondo, Kanechi
Kondo, Kenichi
Kondo, Kinpichi
Kondo, Kiyoshi
Kondo, Shoogo
Kondo, Tamae
Konishi, Hiroichi
Konishi, Shinpachi
Kono, Hiroaki
Kono, Masatoshi
Kono, Shoji
Koshikawa, Masao
Kotani, Yoshiro
Kozawa, Saburo
Kubo, Hisayoshi
Kubo, Toshiyuki
Kubota, Jutaro
Kuboyama, Hideto
Kumatani, Morimasa
Kumazono, Genosuke
Kunikane, Eihachi
Kunitake, Michio
Kurada, Kuraichi
Kurakawa, Minoru
Kurata, Masanosuke
Kurihara, Yoshio
Kuriyama, Michio
Kuroiwa, Yasuhiko
Kurokawa, Yohachi
Kusaka, Toshio
Kusumoto, Tomenosuke
Kuwabara, Masao
Kuwada, Haruo
Kuwae, Ryoyu
Kuwano, Sahachi
Mabuchi, Masaaki
Maeda, Kazuo
Maeda, Kumaichi
Maeda, Toshioka
Maejima, Yuichi

Maekawa, Kazumasa
Maeuchihara, Takeshi
Maida, Ichiro
Makao, Hajime
Makino, Reiichiro
Makino, Umetaro
Makuda, Minoru
Mano, Junji
Mantani, Umosuke
Mariyama, Gisaburo
Masaki, Kyusho
Matake, Kakutaro
Matake, Shinchiro
Matsuda, Sadaya
Matsuki, Suekatsu
Matsumae, Miso
Matsumori, Hideo
Matsumoto, Inokichi
Matsumoto, Kenshiro
Matsumoto, Shoichiro
Matsumoto, Yoshitaro
Matsumuro, Saburo
Matsuo, Kaiji
Matsuo, Kyujiro
Matsuo, Syokei
Matsuoka, Tomezo
Matsuura, Saburo
Mayeda, Minoru
Michishita, Masanobu
Mikami, Kizo
Mikawa, Masaru
Mikota, Itsuo
Mimura, Taizo
Mimura, Tetsu
Minagawa, Tokio
Minami, Yoshisuke
Minamide, Tahichi
Minemo, Genji
Minemoto, Yoshinari
Mito, Hisashi
Mitsuhashi, Yoshio
Mitsuoka, Yoshio
Miumi, Matsuzo
Miura, Soichi

Miura, Taichero
Miwa, Yoshiatsu
Miyahara, Fusao
Miyakawa, Nobuhiro
Miyatake, Kunio
Miyazaki, Hiroshi
Mizuguchi, Yasutosi
Mizuno, Tatsuo
Mizuno, Tetsuo
Mizuno, Toru
Mizuno, Toshio
Mononobe, Choho
Mori, Bunichi
Mori, Daisaku
Mori, Kiyoichi
Mori, Shigeji
Mori, Takao
Mori, Yasumori
Mori, Yoshio
Morimoto, Iichiro
Morimoto, Kenji
Morimoto, Shigemi
Morimoto, Yasuji
Morimoto, Zenji
Morita, Hiroyuki
Morita, Masaichi
Moritama, Yoshiyotsu
Moriyama, Momoichi
Moro, Hisao
Morooka, Yoshiyuki
Motohashi, Masao
Motoi, Eishi
Motokawa, Sadamu
Motomiya, Unosuke
Motonaka, Sadao
Motyashiki, Shinichi
Mukumoto, Shimpei
Munehiro, Genichi
Munenaga, Kampei
Murai, Masaaki
Murakami, Eiichi
Murakami, Takuji
Murakami, Tetsuya
Murakami, Yoneo

Murase, Akihisa
Murase, Tenjiro
Murata, Masayoshi
Murata, Sadayoshi
Murata, Sotaro
Muta, Hatsuo
Muta, Matsukichi
Muto, Zenichi
Mutsuro, Fujio
Myazaki, Yoshio
Nadahara, Iwayoshi
Nagahara, Keiji
Nagai, Noboru
Naganuma, Seichi
Nagaoka, Masaji
Nagatomo, Tsugio
Naka, Masayuki
Nakagawa, Hajime
Nakagawa, Minoru
Nakagawa, Shintaro
Nakagawa, Tatsuo
Nakagura, Seizo
Nakajima, Heikichi
Nakajima, Hidemaro
Nakajima, Sukeo
Nakamichi, Kanji
Nakamura, Hideji
Nakamura, Minoru
Nakamura, Rokushi
Nakamura, Tomoki
Nakanishi, Masao
Nakanishi, Yoshio
Nakano, Ichitaro
Nakano, Masamoto
Nakao, Umesaku
Nakata, Yoshio
Nakatani, Masataro
Nakayama, Hiroji
Nakayama, Minoo
Nakayama, Tarekichi
Nakazawa, Satoru
Nakazawa, Tasuku
Nakazono, Hirotoshi
Namba, Motoo

Narazaki, Masahiko
Narikawa, Masanobu
Narisako, Tadakuni
Narita, Kikumoto
Nasuno, Yoshizo
Natao, Masatake
Nawa, Tomoya
Neishi, Takashi
Nemoto, Kanji
Nemoto, Ko
Nemoto, Ryoichi
Nemoto, Tsune
Niizuma, Kinzaburo
Ninomiya, Yutaka
Nishi, Masamori
Nishi, Takeyasu
Nishida, Tsugio
Nishikawa, Ko
Nishikawa, Yoshio
Nishimura, Takeki
Nishimura, Tomoe
Nishina, Gontoro
Nishino, Jiro
Nishioka, Shigeru
Nishitani, Manichi
Nishiyama, Kiyoshi
Nizukoshi, Saburo
Nobuta, Hideshi
Noda, Eiichi
Noda, Hidehiko
Noda, Ietoshi
Nogawa, Nobuyoshi
Noguchi, Etsuji
Noguchi, Keizo
Noguchi, Yuzuru
Nojima, Mineo
Nomi, Minoru
Nomoto, Akira
Nonogaki, Shiro
Noto, Kiyohisa
Nozaka, Keiichi
Nozaki, Kenichi
Nozaki, Seiji
Nukata, Hiroshi

Numajiri, Shigeru
Numata, Takazo
Oba, Kojiro
Obara, Toshihiro
Obayashi, Kiyoshi
Obinata, Hiroshi
Oda, Tayuru
Odazawa, Yutaka
Odeishi, Shigemaru
Oga, Tokio
Ogasawara, Kiyoshi
Ogawa, Toru
Ogawa, Zensaku
Ogihara, Kenichi
Ogimoto, Yoshio
Ogiya, Yorio
Ohno, Minehiro
Ohno, Norio
Oikada, Takekazu
Oka, Masahiro
Okabuchi, Yukio
Okada, Haruo
Okada, Miyoroku
Okada, Takaji
Okada, Tasuku
Okamoto, Hitoshi
Okamoto, Junichi
Okamoto, Motomu
Okazaki, Isajiro
Okazaki, Kojuro
Okeda, Shohei
Okida, Sanji
Oku, Mitsumasa
Okuba, Mataishi
Okuba, Mutsuo
Okuda, Hyoichi
Okuda, Sakuichi
Okuma, Kaoru
Okura, Sakae
Omoi, Taikichi
Omori, Shigeru
Onishi, Hajime
Onishi, Soji
Onishi, Tamotsu

Ono, Buichi
Ono, Iwazo
Ono, Takematsu
Ono, Teruo
Ono, Toshihiko
Onodera, Chosuke
Onodera, Shoji
Oota, Narumi
O Ran, Rai
Orito, Denkichi
Osada, Kunihiko
Osako, Ko
Osanai, Shigeru
Osawa, Shigenori
Oshima, Norimasa
Oshiro, Eikichi
Oshiwa, Munehiko
Ota, Koichi
Ota, Tsuzuo
Otahara, Kiyotomi
Otake, Michiji
Otaki, Akira
Otani, Keijiro
Otani, Kiyonori
Otosu, Norifumu
Otsuki, Kaoru
Otsuki, Takahashi
Ouchii, Shintaro
Oya, Hideo
Oyama, Masakatsu
Ozawa, Kichihei
Ozawa, Masaharu
Rikitake, Yaichi
Rin, Ei Hatsu
Ryu, Miki
Ryu, Takaji
Sagae, Yutaka
Saheki, Bunro
Saito, Hiromitsu
Saito, Hiromo
Saito, Kyosuke
Saito, Mitsuo
Saito, Terukichi
Saito, Yoichi

Sakaba, Kaname
Sakagami, Motoichi
Sakaguchi, Kiyofusa
Sakai, Hideo
Sakai, Keichi
Sakai, Seiji
Sakai, Tsuyoshi
Sakai, Yosa
Sakaino, Takayoshi
Sakakibara, Kazuya
Sakakibara, Yasutake
Sakamoto, Yuhichi
Sakano, Sadeo
Sakuma, Hidechika
Sanematsu, Yuzuro
Sano, Sokochi
Sanokawa, Takao
Santo, Hirokichi
Saramoto, Mitsujiro
Saruwatari, Atsutaka
Saruwatari, Kunio
Sasaki, Isamu
Sasaki, James K.
Sasaki, Jukichi
Sasaki, Kishio
Sasaki, Shigeru
Sasaki, Shooichi
Sasazawa, Chuta
Sato, Heikichi
Sato, Isamu
Sato, Isao
Sato, Katsuyasu
Sato, Kazuo
Sato, Kushiro
Sato, Masashi
Sato, Shinichiro
Sato, Shinnosuki
Sato, Tadashi
Sato, Taichi
Sato, Torao
Sato, Yoshinao
Sawa, Tomisaburo
Sawamura, Masatoshi
Sawano, Yoshikazu

Seino, Kiyoshi
Seki, Noburo
Sekihara, Masaji
Senba, Yoshitaka
Seyama, Tadayuki
Shiba, Tsutomi
Shibano, Tadao
Shibata, Saburo
Shibata, Teruo
Shibuya, Masanari
Shiina, Michizo
Shiinoki, Hisayoshi
Shimabara, Niichiro
Shimamoto, Kyugoro
Shimano, Sheijiro
Shimizu, Masao
Shimizu, Shigeji
Shimizu, Shuichi
Shimizu, Tsuruzo
Shimoda, Chiyoshi
Shimodaira, Naoza
Shimode, Ryoichi
Shimomi, Tadashigo
Shingo, Yoshio
Shinjo, Morizo
Shinkae, Takayoshi
Shinoda, Shuichi
Shinohara, Masakiyo
Shinya, Fusao
Shioiri, Rikio
Shirai, Ryoei
Shirakata, Yoshio
Shirakawa, Matsusaburo
Shirasaya, Kiichi
Shiro, Toshio
Shiroshita, Takeji
Shito, Rinsaburo
Shiuchi, Ikoma
Shizawa, Mamoru
Shuraki, Takeo
Someya, Masonori
Song, Kap Chin
Suda, Kiyamatsu
Suda, Takesi

Sudo, Yoshio
Suematsu, Kazumoto
Sugai, Yasui
Sugasawa, Iju
Sugasawa, Kiyotaka
Sugeta, Chikayoshi
Sugi, Masafumi
Sugihara, Eiichi
Sugiura, Ryuzaburo
Sugiyama, Nobuyasu
Sugo, Shotaro
Sukegawa, Misao
Sumitoko, Shizuo
Sunobe, Rokuro
Susuki, Yoshihiro
Suyenaga, Aiijaku
Suzuki, Akira
Suzuki, Hideo
Suzuki, Hikari
Suzuki, Keizo
Suzuki, Ken
Suzuki, Koji
Suzuki, Kunji
Suzuki, Masao
Suzuki, Satoji
Suzuki, Tomoichi
Tadaki, Nobuyuki
Taguchi, Yasumasa
Taguchi, Yoshio
Tagusari, Sukeo
Taika, Seizo
Taike, Nobuyuki
Tajima, Isaburo
Taka, Toichi
Takagano, Mitsuo
Takagi, Masayoshi
Takahashi, Chojuro
Takahashi, Fukuji
Takahashi, Hasanoru
Takahashi, Izou
Takahashi, Koichi
Takahashi, Shingo
Takahashi, Shozo
Takahashi, Takao

Takahashi, Yukio
Takaku, Masaji
Takami, Shunishiro
Takamoto, Tsutomu
Takamura, Naoichi
Takamura, Tokuichi
Takano, Shusaku
Takano, Tadashi
Takasago, Yasushi
Takasaki, Iku
Takashima, Tezio
Takashita, Toraichi
Takata, Shuichi
Takayama, Hiroaki
Takeda, Chikara
Takeda, Nobumasa
Takeda, Sadamu
Takenaka, Kazuo
Takeshita, Toshio
Takeuchi, Hiroshi
Takeuchi, Jiro
Takeuchi, Minoru
Takeuchi, Tsunetaro
Takeyoshi, Munehei
Takezoe, Tamotsu
Takizawa, Masaji
Takuma, Masatara
Tamura, Chomatsu
Tamura, Hijime
Tamura, Ippei
Tamura, Sotojiro
Tanabe, Kiyoshi
Tanabe, Mitsuo
Tanabe, Toshisuke
Tanaka, Hirokazu
Tanaka, Hiroshi
Tanaka, Kazuo
Tanaka, Kumataro
Tanaka, Ryohei
Tanaka, Shinichi
Tanaka, Tokizo
Tanaka, Tokuichi
Tanaka, Yoshinari
Tanifuji, Nisa

Taniguchi, Gosuke
Taniguchi, Tetsuo
Tanimoto, Shunichi
Tanno, Sanzo
Tanoue, Suketoshi
Tarodachi, Miki
Tashiro, Jiro
Tashiro, Tomoki
Tashiro, Toshio
Tateno, Ryoichi
Tauchi, Yoshio
Tenabe, Tadao
Tendo, Jiro
Terada, Seiichi
Terada, Takeo
Teraoka, Masao
Terashima, Seichi
Terashita, Yoichiro
Teshima, Fusataro
Tezuka, Takashi
Tobita, Tokio
Toda, Toshio
Toji, Kentaro
Tokuda, Hisakichi
Toma, Seisaku
Tomioka, Kikuo
Tomita, Mitsuo
Tomomori, Kiyoharu
Tonomura, Okuji
Tonozuka, Kinzo
Torisu, Taro
Toshino, Junsaburo
Toyama, Fusao
Toyama, Masaichi
Toyama, Toshio
Toyama, Yahei
Tsuchiya, Hichiro
Tsuchiya, Tatsuo
Tsuchiyama, Keishi
Tsuchiyama, Tokuzo
Tsuda, Koju
Tsuda, Tahei
Tsuda, Tsunesuke
Tsuji, Hideo

Tsuneyoshi, Yoshio
Tsuno, Kazuyoshi
Tsuruda, Yoshitaka
Tsurumaru, Hironaga
Tsutsui, Hajime
Tsutsui, Shizuko
Uchida, Goro
Uchida, Kanemasu
Uchida, Manemasu
Uchida, Masayuki
Uchida, Techiharu
Uchikura, Masonori
Uchiyama, Eitaro
Uda, Shuzo
Ueda, Fumio
Ueda, Jiro
Uishiki, Eiichi
Umeda, Makoto
Umehira, Masao
Umino, Hajime
Uno, Hiroichi
Urayama, Tameichi
Ushihara, Tatsumi
Ushioda, Hiroshi
Uwamori, Masao
Wachi, Nobushige
Wachi, Takaji
Wada, Shusuke
Wada, Tsuneji
Wada, Yasuo
Wakamatsu, Manzo
Wakamatsu, Tadakazu
Waki, Toshihara
Wako, Yusei
Washimi, Seitaro
Watanabe, Eisuke
Watanabe, Fukuichi
Watanabe, Katsunosuke
Watanabe, Saburo
Watanabe, Sadao
Watanabe, Shohei
Watanabe, Takeo
Watanabe, Tokio
Watanabe, Tomikuni

Watanabe, Zentaro
Yadoiwa, Isao
Yagi, Yoshika
Yakamaru, Katsuya
Yamada, Asao
Yamada, Kenzo
Yamada, Tomio
Yamagishi, Masakazu
Yamaguchi, Fukuma
Yamaguchi, Mitsunari
Yamaguchi, Nishio
Yamaji, Koseki
Yamakawa, Kuramatsu
Yamakawa, Yoji
Yamamoto, Eijiro
Yamamoto, Fukuichi
Yamamoto, Hiroshi
Yamamoto, Juso
Yamamoto, Kichiji
Yamamoto, Masaji
Yamamoto, Seijiro
Yamamoto, Takeo
Yamamoto, Tanimori
Yamamoto, Toshihisa
Yamamoto, Tsunehiko
Yamamoto, Yasumasa
Yamamura, Yoshio
Yamanaka, Goro
Yamanaka, Koichiro
Yamanaka, Norio
Yamanaka, Takanori
Yamanaka, Toshitsuga
Yamasaki, Tateo
Yamashita, Sai
Yamata, Rikio
Yamauchi, Kunimitsu
Yamauye, Hitoshi
Yamazaki, Hashiyuki
Yamazaki, Kiichi
Yanabe, Motohide
Yanagizawa, Akira
Yanagizawa, Kenichi
Yanagizawa, Tojiro
Yasaru, Tetsotoshi

Yasuda, Katsuyoshi
Yasuda, Kishiro
Yasuda, Naofumi
Yasuda, Zenichiro
Yasue, Kiyoshi
Yasukawa, Masakiyo
Yasukawa, Shinryu
Yasutake, Hideo
Yatagai, Kiyoshi
Yokoyama, Isamu
Yokoyama, Kanzaburo
Yokoyama, Otokichi
Yokoyama, Yutaka
Yokura, Sashizo
Yonemaru, Masakuma
Yonemura, Tokuji
Yoritsune, Shuji
Yoshida, Hideo

Yoshida, Hisao
Yoshida, Kanji
Yoshida, Kiichi
Yoshida, Masato
Yoshida, Masayoshi
Yoshihara, Tsuyoshi
Yoshimura, Asaichi
Yoshinaga, Shishitaro
Yoshio, Tetsuro
Yoshitsuga, Seiichiro
Yoshizawa, Kunio
Yuasa, Torao
Yui, Kiyoshi
Yukino, Koshi
Yumita, Kyogzo
Yuri, Kei
Yutani, Seiichi

APPENDIX B
Potsdam Proclamation Defining Terms for Japanese Surrender, July 26, 1945

(1) We—The President of the United States, the President of the National Government of the Republic of China, and the Prime Minister of Great Britain, representing the hundreds of millions of our countrymen, have conferred and agree that Japan shall be given an opportunity to end this war.

(2) The prodigious land, sea and air forces of the United States, the British Empire and of China, many times reinforced by their armies and air fleets from the west, are poised to strike the final blows upon Japan. This military power is sustained and inspired by the determination of all the Allied Nations to prosecute the war against Japan until she ceases to resist.

(3) The result of the futile and senseless German resistance to the might of the aroused free peoples of the world stands forth in awful clarity as an example to the people of Japan. The might that now converges on Japan is immeasurably greater than that which, when applied to the resisting Nazis, necessarily laid waste to the lands, the industry and the method of life of the whole German people. The full application of our military power, backed by our resolve, will mean the inevitable and complete destruction of the Japanese armed forces and just as inevitably the utter devastation of the Japanese homeland.

(4) The time has come for Japan to decide whether she will continue to be controlled by those self-willed militaristic advisers whose unintelligent calculations have brought the Empire of Japan to the threshold of annihilation, or whether she will follow the path of reason.

(5) Following are our terms. We will not deviate from them. There are no alternatives. We will brook no delay.

(6) There must be eliminated for all time the authority and influence of those who have deceived and misled the people of Japan into embarking on world conquest, for we insist that a new order of peace, security and justice will be impossible until irresponsible militarism is driven from the world.

(7) Until such a new order is established and until there is convincing proof that Japan's war making power is destroyed, points in Japanese territory to be designated by the Allies shall be occupied to secure the achievement of the basic objectives we are here setting forth.

(8) The terms of the Cairo Declaration shall be carried out and Japanese sovereignty shall be limited to the islands of Honshu, Hokkaido, Kyushu, Shikoku and such minor islands as we determine.

(9) The Japanese military forces, after being completely disarmed, shall be permitted to return to their homes with the opportunity to lead peaceful and productive lives.

(10) We do not intend that the Japanese shall be enslaved as a race or destroyed as a nation, but stern justice shall be meted out to all war criminals, including those who have visited cruelties upon our prisoners. The Japanese Government shall remove all obstacles to the revival and strengthening of democratic tendencies among the Japanese people. Freedom of speech, of religion, and of thought, as well as respect for the fundamental human rights shall be established.

(11) Japan shall be permitted to maintain such industries as will sustain her economy and permit the exaction of just reparations in kind, but not those (industries) which would enable her to re-arm for war. To this end, access to, as distinguished from control of, raw materials shall be permitted. Eventual Japanese participation in world trade relations shall be permitted.

(12) The Occupying forces of the Allies shall be withdrawn from Japan as soon as these objectives have been accomplished and there has been established in accordance with the freely expressed will of the Japanese people a peacefully inclined and responsible government.

(13) We call upon the government of Japan to proclaim now the unconditional surrender of all Japanese armed forces, and to provide proper and adequate assurances of their good faith in such action. The alternative for Japan is prompt and utter destruction.

APPENDIX C
IMTFE Charter

CHARTER OF THE
INTERNATIONAL MILITARY TRIBUNAL FOR THE FAR EAST

SECTION I
CONSTITUTION OF TRIBUNAL

ARTICLE 1. Tribunal Established. The International Military Tribunal for the Far East is hereby established for the just and prompt trial and punishment of the major war criminals in the Far East. The permanent seat of the Tribunal is in Tokyo.

ARTICLE 2. Members. The Tribunal shall consist of not less than six members nor more than eleven members, appointed by the Supreme Commander for the Allied Powers from the names submitted by the Signatories to the Instrument of Surrender, India, and the Commonwealth of the Philippines.

ARTICLE 3. Officers and Secretariat.

    a. President. The Supreme Commander for the Allied Powers shall appoint a member to be President of the Tribunal.

    b. Secretariat.
        (1) The Secretariat of the Tribunal shall be composed of a General Secretary to be appointed by the Supreme Commander for the Allied Powers and such assistant clerks, secretaries, interpreters, and other personnel as may be necessary.
        (2) The General Secretary shall organize and direct the work of the Secretariat.
        (3) The Secretariat shall receive all documents addressed to the Tribunal, maintain the records of the Tribunal, provide necessary clerical services to the Tribunal and its members, and perform such other duties as may be designated by the Tribunal.

ARTICLE 4. Convening and Quorum, Voting, and Absence.

a. <u>Convening and Quorum.</u> When as many as six members of the Tribunal are present, they may convene the Tribunal in formal session. The presence of a majority of all members shall be necessary to constitute a quorum.

b. <u>Voting.</u> All decisions and judgements of this Tribunal, including convictions and sentences, shall be by a majority vote of those members of the Tribunal present. In case the votes are evenly divided, the vote of the President shall be decisive.

c. <u>Absence.</u> If a member at any time is absent and afterwards is able to be present, he shall take part in all subsequent proceedings; unless he declares in open court that he is disqualified by reason of insufficient familiarity with the proceedings which took place in his absence.

SECTION II
JURISDICTION AND GENERAL PROVISIONS

ARTICLE 5. Jurisdiction Over Persons and Offenses. The Tribunal shall have the power to try and punish Far Eastern war criminals who as individuals or as members of organizations are charged with offenses which include Crimes Against Peace. The following acts, or any of them, are crimes coming within the jurisdiction of the Tribunal for which there shall be individual responsibility:

a. <u>Crimes Against Peace.</u> Namely, the planning, preparation, initiation or waging of a declared or undeclared war of aggression, or a war in violation of international law, treaties, agreements or assurances, or participation in a common plan or conspiracy for the accomplishment of any of the foregoing;

b. <u>Conventional War Crimes.</u> Namely, violations of the laws or customs of war;

c. <u>Crimes Against Humanity.</u> Namely, murder, extermination, enslavement, deportation, and other inhumane acts committed before or during the war, or persecutions on political or racial grounds in execution of or in connection with any crime within the jurisdiction of the Tribunal, whether or not in violation of the domestic law of the country where perpetrated. Leaders, organizers, instigators and accomplices participating in the formulation or execution of a common plan or conspiracy to commit any of the foregoing crimes are responsible for all acts performed by any person in execution of such plan.

ARTICLE 6. Responsibility of Accused. Neither the official position, at any time, of an accused, nor the fact that an accused acted pursuant to order of his government or of a superior shall, of itself, be sufficient to free such accused from responsibility for any crime with which he is charged, but such circumstances may be considered in mitigation of punishment if the Tribunal determines that justice so requires.

ARTICLE 7. Rules of Procedure. The Tribunal may draft and amend rules of procedure consistent with the fundamental provisions of this Charter.

ARTICLE 8. Counsel.
  a. Chief of Counsel.nThe Chief of Counsel designated by the Supreme Commander for the Allied Powers is responsible for the investigation and prosecution of charges against war criminals within the jurisdiction of this Tribunal and will render such legal assistance to the Supreme Commander as is appropriate.

  b. Associate Counsel. Any United Nation with which Japan has been at war may appoint an Associate Counsel to assist the Chief of Counsel.

SECTION III
FAIR TRIAL FOR ACCUSED

ARTICLE 9. Procedure for Fair Trial. In order to insure fair trial for the accused the following procedure shall be followed:

  a. Indictment. The indictment shall consist of a plain, concise, and adequate statement of each offense charged. Each accused shall be furnished, in adequate time for a defense, a copy of the indictment, including any amendment, and of this Charter, in a language understood by the accused.

  b. Language. The trial and related proceedings shall be conducted in English and in the language of the accused. Translations of documents and other papers shall be provided as needed and requested.

  c. Counsel for Accused. Each accused shall have the right to be represented by counsel of his own selection, subject to the disapproval of such counsel at any time by the Tribunal. The accused shall file with the General Secretary of the Tribunal the name of his counsel. If an accused is not represented by counsel and in open court requests the appointment of counsel, the Tribunal shall designate counsel for him. In the absence of such request the Tribunal may appoint counsel for the accused if in its judgement such appointment is necessary to provide for a fair trial.

  d. Evidence for Defense. An accused shall have the right, through himself or through his counsel (but not through both), to conduct his defense, including the right to examine any witness, subject to such reasonable restrictions as the Tribunal may determine.

  e. Production of Evidence for the Defense. An accused may apply in writing to the Tribunal for the production of witnesses or of documents. The application shall state where the witness or document is thought to be located. It shall also state the facts proposed to be proved by the witness or the document and the relevancy of such facts to the defense. If the Tribunal grants the application, the Tribunal shall be given such aid in obtaining production of the evidence as the circumstances require.

ARTICLE 10. Applications and Motions before Trial. All motions, applications, or other requests addressed to the Tribunal prior to the commencement of trial shall be made in writing and filed with the General Secretary of the Tribunal for action by the Tribunal.

SECTION IV
POWERS OF TRIBUNAL AND CONDUCT OF TRIAL

ARTICLE 11. Powers. The Tribunal shall have the power:

a. To summon witnesses to the trial, to require them to attend and testify, and to question them.

b. To interrogate each accused and to permit comment on his refusal to answer any questions.

c. To require the production of documents and other evidentiary material.

d. To require of each witness an oath, affirmation, or such declaration as is customary in the country of the witness, and to administer oaths.

e. To appoint officers for the carrying out of any task designated by the Tribunal, including the power to have evidence taken on commission.

ARTICLE 12. Conduct of Trial. The Tribunal shall:

a. Confine the trial strictly to an expeditious hearing of the issues raised by the charges.

b. Take strict measures to prevent any action which would cause any unreasonable delay and rule out irrelevant issues and statements of any kind whatsoever.

c. Provide for the maintenance of order at the trial and deal summarily with any centumacy, imposing appropriate punishments, including exclusion of any accused or his counsel from some or all further proceedings, but without prejudice to the determination of the charges.

d. Determine the mental and physical capacity of any accused to proceed to trial.

ARTICLE 13. Evidence.

a. Admissibility. The Tribunal shall not be bound by technical rules of evidence. It shall adopt and apply to the greatest possible extent expeditious and non-technical procedure, and shall admit any evidence which it deems to have probable value. All purported admissions or statements of the accused are admissible.

b. Relevance. The Tribunal may require to be informed of the nature of any evidence before it is offered in order to rule upon the relevance.

c. Specific Evidence Admissible. In particular, and without limiting in any way the scope of the foregoing general rules, the following evidence may be admitted:

(1) A document, regardless of its security classification and without proof of its issuance or signature, which appears to the Tribunal to have been signed or issued by any officer, department, agency or member of the armed forces of any government.
(2) A report which appears to the Tribunal to have been signed or issued by the International Red Cross or a member thereof, or by a doctor of medicine or any medical service personnel, or by an investigator or intelligence officer, or by any other person who appears to the Tribunal to have personal knowledge of the matters contained in the report.
(3) An affidavit, deposition or other signed statement.
(4) A diary, letter or other document, including sworn or unsworn statements, which appear to the Tribunal to contain information relating to the charge.
(5) A copy of a document or other secondary evidence of its contents, if the original is not immediately available.

d. Judicial Notice. The Tribunal shall neither require proof of facts of common knowledge, nor of the authenticity of official government documents and reports of any nation or of the proceedings, records, and findings of military or other agencies of any of the United Nations.

e. Records, Exhibits, and Documents. The transcript of the proceedings, and exhibits and documents submitted to the Tribunal, will be filed with the General Secretary of the Tribunal and will constitute part of the record.

ARTICLE 14. Place of Trial. The first trial will be held at Tokyo, and any subsequent trials will be held at such places as the Tribunal decides.

ARTICLE 15. Course of Trial Proceedings. The proceedings at the trial will take the following course:

a. The indictment will be read in court unless the reading is waived by all accused.

b. The Tribunal will ask each accused whether he pleads "guilty" or "not guilty."

c. The prosecution and each accused (by counsel only, if represented) may make a concise opening statement.

d. The prosecution and defense may offer evidence, and the admissiblity of the same shall be determined by the Tribunal.

e. The prosecution and each accused (by counsel only, if represented) may examine each witness and each accused who gives testimony.

f. Accused (by counsel only, if represented) may address the Tribunal.

g. The prosecution may address the Tribunal.

h. The Tribunal will deliver judgement and pronounce sentence.

SECTION V
JUDGEMENT AND SENTENCE

ARTICLE 16. Penalty. The Tribunal shall have the power to impose upon the accused, on conviction, death, or such other punishment as shall be determined by it to be just.

ARTICLE 17. Judgement and Review. The judgement will be announced in open court and will give the reasons on which it is based. The record of the trial will be transmitted directly to the Supreme Commander for the Allied Powers for his action. Sentence will be carried out in accordance with the Order of the Supreme Commander for the Allied Powers, who may at any time reduce or otherwise alter the sentence, except to increase its severity.

By command of General MacArthur,

Richard J. Marshall
Major General,
General Staff Corps.
Chief of Staff.

APPENDIX D
Full Text of General MacArthur's Review of the War Crimes Sentences

No duty I have been called upon to perform in a long public service replete with many bitter, lonely and forlorn assignments and responsibilities is so utterly repugnant to me as that of reviewing the sentences of the Japanese War Criminal defendants adjudged by the International Military Tribunal for the Far East. It is not my purpose, nor indeed would I have that transcendent wisdom which would be necessary, to assay the universal fundamentals involved in these epochal proceedings designed to formulate and codify standards of international morality by those charged with a nation's conduct. The problem indeed is basically one which man has struggled to solve since the beginning of time and which may well wait complete solution till the end of time. In so far as my own immediate obligation and limited authority extend in this case, suffice it that under the principles and procedures prescribed in full detail by the Allied Powers concerned, I can find nothing of technical commission or omission in the incidents of the trial itself of sufficient import to warrant my intervention in the judgements which have been rendered. No human decision is infallible but I can conceive of no judicial process where greater safeguard was made to evolve justice. It is inevitable that many will disagree with the verdict, even the learned justices who composed the Tribunal were not in complete unanimity, but no mortal agency in the present imperfect evolution of civilized society seems more entitled to confidence in the integrity of its solemn pronouncements. If we cannot trust such processes and such men we can trust nothing. I therefore direct the Commanding General of the Eighth Army to execute the sentences as pronounced by the Tribunal. In doing so I pray that an Omnipotent Providence may use this tragic expiation as a symbol to summon all persons of goodwill to a realization of the utter futility of war — that most malignant scourge and greatest sin of mankind — and eventually to its renunciation by all nations. To this end on the day of execution I request the members of all congregations throughout Japan of whatever creed or faith in the privacy of their homes or at their altars of public worship to seek Divine help and guidance that the world keep the peace lest the human race perish.

APPENDIX E
U.S. Army
Sugamo Prison
APO 181/500, Tokyo, Japan
1945-52
Personnel Roster

1. Abovoun, Edward E.
2. Achtyl, Edmund S.
3. Adams, James D.
4. Adams, Lonnie B., Sr.
5. Adams, Samuel
6. Aday, Charles K.
7. Addis, Jack R.
8. Adkins, James
9. Adkins, Raymond A.
10. Adler, Armake
11. Adler, Arnold
12. Aguirre, Salvador S.
13. Ahart, Carmen D.
14. Ahearn, W. E.
15. Alamond, James C.
16. Albanese, Eugene W.
17. Alden, Orian B.
18. Aldridge, Thomas R.
19. Alford, Jack B.
20. Aliff, William E.
21. Allbritton, James
22. Allen, Everett C.
23. Allen, Marvin D.
24. Allen, Norman L.
25. Allen, Pat
26. Allen, Stuart V.
27. Allen, William C.
28. Allgeier, Richard F.
29. Allison, James H.
30. Almerico, Pat
31. Alonzo, Martin
32. Altman, Peter
33. Amaral, Frank J.
34. Amendola, John S.
35. Ames, Donald D.
36. Andariese, Robert W.
37. Anderson, David W.
38. Anderson, Harry W.
39. Anderson, Jeff
40. Anderson, John
41. Anderson, Keith
42. Andores, Gus
43. Andres, Alex C.
44. Andrews, Melvin
45. Anekduke, Nicholas R.
46. Anglin, William B.
47. Anthony, Billy G.
48. Apland, James J.

49. Aponte, Carlos
50. Armel, Parker L., Jr.
51. Armstrong, Obediah P.
52. Arnett, J. B.
53. Ashburn, Roosevelt J.
54. Ashby, Lloyd C.
55. Ashcroft, Walter
56. Ashley, Hotie S., Jr.
57. Aumon, John
58. Axtell, Bud
59. Baethke, LeRoy F.
60. Bagley, Maurice
61. Bailey, Charles H.
62. Baja, Morris
63. Baker, Andre R.
64. Baker, Dayton E.
65. Baker, Harold W.
66. Baker, James K.
67. Baker, Richard L.
68. Bakowski, Joseph J.
69. Ballard, Clifford A.
70. Ballard, Clyde
71. Ballard, William J.
72. Ballosh, William
73. Baltozer, George R.
74. Banks, William R.
75. Bannister, Bob
76. Barass, Wesley G.
77. Barbarick, Lewis J.
78. Barber, Francis C.
79. Barber, Lloyd E.
80. Barela, Meulin
81. Baribault, Arthur J.
82. Barkdull, Delynn
83. Barker, Cleatus A.
84. Barnhart, Charles
85. Barrett, Obert
86. Barrett, Roger W.
87. Barrix, Samuel D.
88. Barros, John B.
89. Barwise, Frederick A.
90. Bates, Elmore
91. Baum, Victor L.
92. Baumgardner, Albert
93. Baxter, Don
94. Bayless, Gilbert G.
95. Bayman, Harry F.
96. Beach, Bob
97. Beach, Kenneth
98. Beal, Allan H.
99. Beard, Charles R.
100. Beaty, Byron
101. Becker, Charles C.
102. Beckner, Francis M.
103. Becvar, Edward V.
104. Beiber, Max K.
105. Belback, Arthur
106. Belcher, Robert I.
107. Belderson, Donald D.
108. Bell, James H.
109. Belloth, Richard
110. Beltinck, Thomas D.
111. Benicky, Edward
112. Benitou, Richard J.
113. Bennett, Donald E.
114. Bentley, William E.
115. Berg, Leo O.
116. Berg, Rodney O.
117. Bergeron, Romeo A.
118. Bergstrom, Loren E.
119. Berlew, Ziba S.
120. Bettencourt, George
121. Betz, Gerard G.
122. Bianchini, Arthur
123. Bickford, Robert J.
124. Bickwermert, William B.
125. Biggs, Jack C.
126. Billings, Sidney A.
127. Billingsley, John E.
128. Birnell, John M.
129. Biscoe, Robert A.
130. Bistram, John
131. Blair, Billy D.
132. Blair, Calvin T.
133. Blair, James R.
134. Blakesly, Harold
135. Blankenship, Talmadge L.
136. Blankenship, William H.

Appendix E

137. Blessing, Edwin B.
138. Blower, Robert C.
139. Bock, Fritz S.
140. Bogonovich, Eli
141. Bohler, Calvin W.
142. Boles, Billy D.
143. Bolin, Billy J.
144. Bonilla, David J.
145. Bonneau, Roland D.
146. Booker, Harry C.
147. Borake, Andrew N.
148. Borushko, John A.
149. Bovay, Richard C.
150. Bowers, William A.
151. Bowie, Oscar M.
152. Bowling, William R.
153. Bowman, Donald P.
154. Bowman, Eugene B.
155. Bowman, William J.
156. Boyd, Kenneth T.
157. Boyd, Richard L.
158. Boykin, German N.
159. Boyle, Raymond P.
160. Bozik, Frank
161. Braden, Herbert
162. Bradshaw, Eugene R.
163. Bragg, Elton P.
164. Brain, Kenneth R.
165. Brake, Elmer J.
166. Branch, Samuel C.
167. Brandy, Charles E.
168. Brannen, Robert L.
169. Brannen, Virgil W.
170. Brask, Harlan
171. Braunsberg, Richard E.
172. Breaux, Leo A.
173. Brewer, Eugene L.
174. Bridenbrouge, Richard
175. Bried, Alfred E.
176. Brightbill, Leon R.
177. Britt, Vernon G.
178. Brocious, Milfred A.
179. Brock, Harland C.
180. Brock, Robert L.

181. Brocklehurst, Charles A.
182. Broderick, Col.
183. Bromwell, Arthur R.
184. Brooks, Charles E.
185. Brooks, James H.
186. Brooks, Phillip A.
187. Broome, Charles, Jr.
188. Broussard, Louis
189. Brown, Alvin H.
190. Brown, Clarence M.
191. Brown, Hugh J.
192. Brown, James E.
193. Brown, Johnnie C.
194. Brown, Keith
195. Brown, Peter A.
196. Brown, Richard K.
197. Brown, Robert M.
198. Brown, Wilfred W.
199. Brown, William T.
200. Browning, James B.
201. Bruder, Floyd N.
202. Brumley, John H.
203. Bruton, Ted E.
204. Bryant, Jesse L.
205. Bryer, Edward J.
206. Buchanan, Charles W.
207. Buck, Richard W.
208. Buck, Thomas
209. Budas, Edward F., Jr.
210. Buhet, Paul H.
211. Bullock, Ray T.
212. Burcham, Gordon R.
213. Burgess, Carlton M.
214. Burgess, Marvin D.
215. Burk, Edward J.
216. Burke, John G.
217. Burke, Tom B.
218. Burnett, Paul F., Jr.
219. Burr, George C., Jr.
220. Burts, James H.
221. Busby, James E.
222. Bushaw, Andrew
223. Busiamonte, Albert H.
224. Bustard, Carl L., Sr.

225. Butler, Harold R.
226. Byce, Gene A.
227. Byrd, Glenn
228. Cabaong, Mamerto G.
229. Cabrera, Johnny R.
230. Cail, Herman R.
231. Cain, William E.
232. Caitnamer, Fred E.
233. Calabria, Joseph A.
234. Calaway, Robert
235. Callaway, Cecil
236. Calvert, Alfonso
237. Campbell, George G.
238. Campbell, Lyle L.
239. Campbell, Wade
240. Campion, Thomas
241. Cantineri, Michael L.
242. Caphton, Donald
243. Capodilupo, Edward J.
244. Cappellano, Roland D.
245. Capps, Logan V.
246. Cardenas, Daniel
247. Carlson, Glenn N.
248. Carnell, Robert E.
249. Carney, Francis J.
250. Carnialbe, Manuel
251. Carr, Frank J.
252. Carr, Lester V.
253. Carrell, Robert F.
254. Carrethere, Dallas L.
255. Carrillo, Thomas
256. Carter, David
257. Carter, Hugh L.
258. Carter, John W.
259. Carter, Thomas J.
260. Cash, Donald E.
261. Cassell, Leonard
262. Cassity, Ervin N.
263. Castle, Jesse O.
264. Cataldo, Fredrick
265. Caudill, Roland D.
266. Caulder, Carson
267. Caulfield, Richard E.
268. Cavallon, Joe E.
269. Caven, William D.
270. Cedeno, Gilberto
271. Celentano, Ralph A.
272. Cellucci, Antonio
273. Chandler, Edward C.
274. Chandler, Leland F.
275. Chaplin, Fredrick
276. Chapman, William G.
277. Chiaro, Reese D.
278. Chiemingo, Alexander
279. Childress, James R.
280. Chinen, Shomei
281. Chitwood, Birnell L.
282. Choby, Edward J.
283. Chrietzberg, William
284. Chrisman, Roscoe R.
285. Christenson, Virgil
286. Church, Karl H.
287. Churray, Francis J.
288. Cihal, Gerald J.
289. Clark, Daniel H.
290. Clark, Donald R.
291. Clark, Randall N.
292. Clark, Robert L.
293. Clark, Walter F.
294. Claxton, Lawrence P.
295. Clement, Ray R.
296. Clements, Donald R.
297. Clementson, William S.
298. Clettenberg, Robert J.
299. Cline, Raymond R.
300. Cobb, Clinton W.
301. Coby, Gerald L.
302. Coffill, James
303. Coker, Ellis C.
304. Coleman, Jack D.
305. Coleman, James T.
306. Coleman, John J.
307. Coleman, Lewis B.
308. Coleman, Michael J.
309. Collins, Charles H.
310. Collins, Herman E.
311. Collins, Lewis P.
312. Collins, Richard E.

Appendix E

313. Collins, Robert L.
314. Collins, Thomas S.
315. Comer, Herman P.
316. Compton, Arnold L.
317. Compton, Raymond T.
318. Conn, Riley
319. Connell, Hershel C.
320. Connelly, Edward P., Jr.
321. Conner, James D.
322. Conner, John A.
323. Conner, Robert K.
324. Conner, Roger R.
325. Conner, William H.
326. Connerty, James L.
327. Connolly, James J.
328. Connors, Lawrence P.
329. Conwell, Stanton B.
330. Cook, Alden H.
331. Cook, Carroll M.
332. Cook, Joseph P.
333. Cook, William A.
334. Coombe, Norman
335. Cooper, Alfred B.
336. Cooper, Billy J.
337. Cooper, Eldon
338. Cooper, Velton
339. Copeland, James A.
340. Cordova, Marion T., Jr.
341. Cordray, James L.
342. Corkadel, Norman L.
343. Corley, John A.
344. Cormier, Richard M.
345. Cornelison, Donald E.
346. Corns, William R.
347. Cosner, Robert E.
348. Costa, Edmund J.
349. Coulter, Carl H.
350. Covert, Lewis A.
351. Cox, Junior W.
352. Cozad, Gene R.
353. Craft, Howard D.
354. Craig, Phillip H.
355. Crary, Francis W.
356. Crawford, Edward G.
357. Crawford, Frederick W.
358. Creamer, Ed R.
359. Creel, Clarance W.
360. Crockett, Frank M.
361. Crossley, John A.
362. Crossman, Franklin W.
363. Crow, William F.
364. Csaszar, Andrew M.
365. Csicsay, Walter
366. Cullen, Vincent J.
367. Cummings, Theodore R.
368. Cummings, Walter T.
369. Cunningham, Herbert L.
370. Cunningham, James R.
371. Cunningham, Roy L.
372. Curcio, George F.
373. Czaja, Victor A.
374. Czikowsky, Albert O.
375. Dabney, Eugene A.
376. Dande, Charles J., Jr.
377. Danielson, Harry H.
378. Darling, Clarence G.
379. Darnell, Billy H.
380. Davey, Richard N.
381. Davila, Daniel, Jr.
382. Davis, Elmer W.
383. Davis, Harold
384. Davis, James W.
385. Davis, Jimmie J.
386. Davis, Richard M.
387. Davis, William R.
388. Day, Vernon
389. Dearman, Alfred V.
390. Decker, John
391. Decker, Merle R.
392. Dedloff, Edward P.
393. DeGrange, Roscoe
394. DeLapp, Bernard T.
395. DeLong, Harold T.
396. DeLozier, Ellie E.
397. Dennis, Lloyd M.
398. Denny, John E.
399. DeSilva, Manuel
400. Desjardins, Pierre

Appendix E

401. Detroit, Maurice E.
402. Dettling, Charles F.
403. Deuble, John J.
404. Devine, William J.
405. Devore, James A.
406. Dewald, Ralph E.
407. Diaz, Ignas P.
408. Dicarlo, Pat
409. Dickerson, William E.
410. Dickson, Alvin D.
411. Dierking, Edward R.
412. DiFalco, Virgil T.
413. DiGilermo, Anthony V.
414. Dillehay, Robert L.
415. Dixon, Herman
416. Dobbs, Jerry F.
417. Dolzodolia, Valdo C.
418. Donaldson, William H.
419. Dooley, Dick W.
420. Dorio, Michael J.
421. Doty, LaVere S.
422. Douglas, George N.
423. Douglas, Verle R.
424. Dowling, James E.
425. Dowty, Harold D.
426. Doyle, Jack A.
427. Drehniel, Earl
428. Drinnon, Roy C.
429. Driver, Grady M.
430. Drouhard, Larry J.
431. Drown, Howard E.
432. Druelinger, Donald R.
433. Drury, Ray E.
434. Drury, W. D.
435. Ducca, Teddy P.
436. Duckworth, George U.
437. Duke, Ray A.
438. Dumas, Stewart N.
439. Duncan, Thomas W.
440. Dunlop, Charles K.
441. Dunn, Harry L.
442. Durbin, William C.
443. Durham, Samuel I.
444. Dyals, Witmer A.
445. Eddy, Neil M.
446. Edmonds, Donald K.
447. Edwards, James B.
448. Edwards, John M.
449. Edwards, Robert J.
450. Ehlert, Robert C.
451. Einwechter, Russell
452. Elam, Gerald
453. Elder, A. M.
454. Eldridge, Dan F.
455. Ellingwood, Thomas J.
456. Elliott, Jesse M.
457. Ellsworth, Leonard K.
458. Elrod, Wallace C.
459. Elwood, James L.
460. Ely, Jacob
461. Emerson, Donald
462. Emmert, Cecil L.
463. Emmett, Robert E.
464. Endsley, John P.
465. Endsly, Patrick
466. English, John J.
467. Ensor, Charles H.
468. Epley, Albert P.
469. Erdman, David
470. Ericson, Jewel C.
471. Ernandis, Andrew
472. Estee, Louie H.
473. Estrada, Francisco
474. Eubank, Clifford P., Jr.
475. Eudy, Robert H.
476. Eustler, Rex T.
477. Evans, Arnold D.
478. Evans, Donald D.
479. Evans, George W.
480. Evans, John M.
481. Evans, Walter R.
482. Ewell, Stockton W.
483. Ewing, Eldon E.
484. Faivre, Donald L.
485. Fallind, Daniel, Jr.
486. Farmer, Richard L.
487. Farr, Gerald E.
488. Farris, Vernon R.

489. Feltner, Lynn
490. Fendrych, Charles F.
491. Feragren, Clarence A.
492. Ferazzi, Paul
493. Ferguson, Monroe
494. Ferry, Charles R.
495. Fields, Fred T.
496. Fignar, Francis E.
497. Fillis, Richard A.
498. Fish, Lesley
499. Fishburn, William
500. Fisherd, Rolland J.
501. Fleming, Flo F.
502. Flener, William D.
503. Flikkema, Albert
504. Flint, Francis
505. Foehr, James
506. Foltz, Robert F.
507. Fonda, Charles M.
508. Forbes, Edward J.
509. Ford, Marvin E.
510. Ford, Richard H.
511. Fortunato, Giacomo M.
512. Fossett, John J.
513. Foster, George C.
514. Foster, James
515. Foster, Thomas T.
516. Fowler, Elmer
517. Fox, Cyril C.
518. Fox, Theodore
519. Frame, Michael
520. Frank, Ernest L.
521. Frazier, Charles J.
522. Freeman, Clifford H.
523. Freeze, Bobby J.
524. Friedman, Allan D.
525. Friedman, Cyrus R.
526. Friedman, Gerald O.
527. Friend, John M.
528. Friend, Olbert N.
529. Frisch, Leroy A.
530. Fry, Charles E.
531. Fukumitsu, George
532. Fullmer, Albert
533. Furtado, Gilbert P.
534. Furtick, Clyde B.
535. Galipeau, Maurice A.
536. Gallegos, Abedon O.
537. Galloway, George L.
538. Galm, Edward W.
539. Galvin, John E.
540. Gandy, William W.
541. Gannon, William H.
542. Garcia, Nicanor
543. Garcia, Ray L.
544. Garcia, Reuben
545. Garde, Eugene E.
546. Garland, Donald R.
547. Garrett, Franklin P.
548. Garry, William W.
549. Garten, Fred E.
550. Garvin, Harry R.
551. Gaskin, Joe H.
552. Gautreaux, Lester
553. Gay, Jack L.
554. Gay, James D.
555. Gaynor, Michael J.
556. Gender, Donald L.
557. Gengemback, Don
558. Gennaro, Harry C.
559. Germait, Elmer J.
560. Gerner, Robert J.
561. Ghirozi, Robert G.
562. Gibson, Jacob L., Jr.
563. Gildea, Thomas J.
564. Gildry, John
565. Giles, Nicholas S.
566. Gilley, Calvin C.
567. Gillian, Fred L.
568. Gilliland, John M.
569. Ginn, Alver H.
570. Ginn, John L.
571. Giordino, George
572. Gipson, Freddie M.
573. Gipson, Tony C.
574. Glasgow, Charles M.
575. Gleiforst, Roy D.
576. Glendening, Dan H.

577. Godding, Walter E.
578. Goff, Jerry R.
579. Goins, George K.
580. Gonzales, Clarence
581. Goode, William C.
582. Goodman, Bennie
583. Goodrich, John W.
584. Goodrich, Max E.
585. Gordon, Barry T.
586. Gordon, Lewis P.
587. Gore, Virgil E.
588. Gottschalk, Donald C.
589. Graaff, Vincent M.
590. Gracey, James
591. Gradick, Joseph S.
592. Graham, Edward P.
593. Graham, Lee
594. Graham, Melvin L.
595. Grant, Donald A.
596. Grantham, Thomas W.
597. Gray, Frank M.
598. Green, Carl C.
599. Green, John
600. Green, Pascal B.
601. Greenlee, Ralph I.
602. Gregory, Roy J.
603. Griewahn, William R.
604. Griffith, Jerry
605. Grimes, Richard A.
606. Gromaski, Donald J.
607. Grubbs, Darward
608. Guglielmo, John R.
609. Gullion, Melvin A.
610. Gunnels, Herman L.
611. Gurwell, Ralph W.
612. Guyor, Norman F.
613. Haas, Harvey F.
614. Hadgolon, John K.
615. Hager, James R.
616. Hagney, Kenneth C.
617. Halberstadt, Roy W.
618. Hale, Gordon R.
619. Hall, Exus J.
620. Hall, James R.

621. Halterman, Olen L.
622. Hamilton, David C.
623. Hamilton, Delmar E.
624. Hamlyn, John H.
625. Hammerness, Oscar
626. Handwerk, Col.
627. Haney, Don C.
628. Hanges, Peter J.
629. Hannah, Grover L.
630. Hansen, Martin A.
631. Happel, Richard G.
632. Hardy, Robert
633. Harenza, Joseph G.
634. Harkins, Lloyd
635. Harlan, Clarence L.
636. Harlow, Jack E.
637. Haroartz, Austin
638. Harper, John H.
639. Harper, Ray J.
640. Harrell, Edward
641. Harrell, Johnny C.
642. Harrend, James E.
643. Harrigan, William F.
644. Harris, Morgan
645. Harrison, Frank D.
646. Harrison, Sydnor W.
647. Hartley, Robert
648. Hartman, Aloys P.
649. Hartman, Earl R.
650. Haskins, David
651. Hastings, Buford C.
652. Hathaway, Harry D.
653. Hawkes, George R., Jr.
654. Hawkes, Hal J.
655. Hawkins, Ronald E.
656. Hawthorne, Elliott
657. Hay, Paul E.
658. Hayden, Hayden C.
659. Hayhurst, Gerald S.
660. Haynes, Norman L.
661. Hazelwood, Lewis C.
662. Hearne, David, Jr.
663. Heath, James L.
664. Heaton, Charles W.

665. Heckman, Albert E.
666. Hedgepath, William E.
667. Heindel, James P.
668. Helmick, Elmer L.
669. Henderson, Elwood
670. Hendricks, Dick
671. Henneke, Charles H.
672. Hepner, Donald C.
673. Herman, Paul R.
674. Hern, Jesse J.
675. Herrera, Reuben
676. Herring, John
677. Hesser, James R.
678. Hestley, Claude L.
679. Heup, Robert R.
680. Heynig, Charles A.
681. Hibbs, Charles L.
682. Hickey, Joseph L., Jr.
683. Hicks, Richard G.
684. Higashi, Yoshitatsu
685. Higgins, Fred
686. Hight, Tommy M.
687. Hikawa, George
688. Hill, Hale T.
689. Himelhan, Richard E.
690. Hinis, Sylvester J.
691. Hinman, Henry A.
692. Hirsch, Kenneth A.
693. Hoar, John B.
694. Hocking, Raymond J.
695. Hodgdon, John K.
696. Hogg, Cecil
697. Hoggard, Arthur B.
698. Holland, John H.
699. Holland, Paul E.
700. Hollenbeck, James F.
701. Holman, Richard C.
702. Holton, Charles G.
703. Holton, James H.
704. Hood, Walter K.
705. Hoonan, Robert
706. Hoover, Robert E.
707. Hopson, Travis
708. Horita, Wayne T.

709. Horn, Arvil B.
710. Horn, Jesse J.
711. Hoskins, David W.
712. House, Robert M.
713. Howell, Victor L.
714. Howie, William R.
715. Howze, Charles F.
716. Hruaka, John C.
717. Huddart, Harry
718. Hudson, Bill J.
719. Huff, Jack G.
720. Huff, James F.
721. Huffman, John F.
722. Huffmaster, Marvin L.
723. Huggins, Shirley J.
724. Hughes, John
725. Hughes, Sylvester, Jr.
726. Hughey, Jay B., Jr.
727. Hulberstad, Roy
728. Hull, Joe
729. Hulsey, Harold E.
730. Hume, Thomas R.
731. Hummel, Ronald J.
732. Hutchinson, Floyd F.
733. Hyser, Ervin
734. Hytha, Bob
735. Ibe, Carl
736. Ihnat, George J.
737. Imler, Ross E.
738. Ingram, Billie E.
739. Irby, Grover P.
740. Isenberg, Wilbur M.
741. Ishibashi, Tommy M.
742. Iverson, Merle D.
743. Iverson, William D.
744. Ivey, Roy W.
745. Iwamoto, George
746. Jackman, Walter M.
747. Jackson, George F.
748. Jackson, M. A.
749. Jakubowski, George
750. James, Don L.
751. Jerun, Frank
752. Jervah, Howard R.

753. Jesionek, John J.
754. Jesseman, Winston C.
755. Jessup, Warren B.
756. Jimeney, Rosie A.
757. Johnson, Alfred M.
758. Johnson, Beverly S.
759. Johnson, George B.
760. Johnson, Harold F.
761. Johnson, Leonard H.
762. Johnson, Maurice L.
763. Johnson, Merrill G.
764. Johnson, Richard T.
765. Johnson, Robert H.
766. Johnson, Roger S.
767. Johnson, Russell
768. Johnson, Virgil N.
769. Johnson, William J.
770. Johnson, Willie E.
771. Jones, Charles
772. Jones, Donald D.
773. Jones, Donald L.
774. Jones, John P.
775. Jones, Maynard
776. Jones, Robert F.
777. Jones, Robert L.
778. Jones, William
779. Jordan, Lewis P.
780. Joy, Donald M.
781. Joyce, James P.
782. Judd, Billy E.
783. Judson, George B.
784. Kading, Delbert C.
785. Kaeider, James
786. Kajihara, Hiroshi R.
787. Kamada, John
788. Kampher, George
789. Kanada, James Y.
790. Kane, Robert J.
791. Karras, George
792. Kasunic, Joseph
793. Kazarnowicz, Edward J.
794. Kazubski, Edmund A.
795. Keeble, Thurman M.
796. Keever, Ermon B.
797. Keliska, Joseph
798. Keller, David L.
799. Kelly, George V.
800. Kelly, James W.
801. Kelnhofer, Roger L.
802. Kennedy, Glen M.
803. Kennedy, John C.
804. Kennedy, Lucian
805. Kennedy, Robert M.
806. Kerby, Otto J.
807. Kerns, John A., Jr.
808. Kerns, John R.
809. Keys, George D.
810. Kidd, Thomas W.
811. Kikuchi, Yoshio
812. Kindig, Richard N.
813. King, Fred S.
814. King, Jay S.
815. King, Norman A.
816. Kinney, Robert A.
817. Kinsey, Richard L.
818. Kinsman, Arthur F.
819. Kipp, Karl J.
820. Kirby, Lamar
821. Kisko, Frederick J.
822. Klatt, Carl F.
823. Klesko, Joseph M.
824. Kleysteuber, Junior R.
825. Klippel, Frank E.
826. Klott, Anthony A.
827. Knisley, Elmer W.
828. Knowles, Wayne A.
829. Koblinski, Raymond J.
830. Koeplin, Elmer
831. Konkle, Howard E.
832. Konoplistsy, Thomas
833. Korgie, Leonard F.
834. Kortze, Charles W.
835. Kostha, Arthur
836. Koth, James E.
837. Koyama, Richard Y.
838. Kozak, Peter
839. Kreider, James A.
840. Krikelas, Nicholas L.

841. Krueger, Vern E.
842. Krutul, John
843. Kubota, Ryo
844. Kueber, Leonard J.
845. Kugler, Frank J.
846. Kunsmeiler, Theodore R.
847. Kuprian, William F.
848. Kurata, Harry H.
849. Lab, Ralph E.
850. LaBarr, Raymond
851. Labram, Ronald R.
852. Lacey, Rolland L.
853. Lackman, Richard C.
854. Lacy, Harry M.
855. LaFace, Alfred
856. LaFavor, Donald C.
857. Lain, Delbert L.
858. Lainberger, Edward H.
859. Laird, Brooks H.
860. Laliberte, Maurice R.
861. LaLone, Leo H.
862. Lamar, John B.
863. Lamson, Marvin
864. Landau, Marvin
865. Lane, Donald R.
866. Langdon, Bernard A.
867. Lanphear, Frederick E.
868. Lansford, Ernest E.
869. LaPorte, Donald E.
870. LaRosa, Alfred C.
871. LaRose, Jack W.
872. LaSerge, Lewis M.
873. Lasley, Merrill E.
874. Lathram, Bernard H.
875. Latty, Lloyd E.
876. Lauderdale, Dell W.
877. Lauderdale, Leonard D.
878. Laughrun, Roy A.
879. Laus, Paul C.
880. Lavala, Harold
881. Lavinski, Frank J.
882. Lawrence, David R.
883. Lawrence, Vardie L.
884. Lawson, Elbert
885. Lawson, John P.
886. Lawson, Richard A.
887. Layer, Kenneth
888. Lazarou, Lazaros
889. Leach, Henry C.
890. Lee, Basley
891. Lee, Robert H.
892. Leffers, Murray J.
893. Lefferson, Leonard
894. Leighty, Eldridge D.
895. Lersch, Milton F.
896. Leslie, Edward J.
897. Lester, William H.
898. Leverett, Ralph
899. Lewis, Darwin C.
900. Lewis, George R.
901. Lewis, James E.
902. Libby, Ray
903. Liberman, L. E.
904. Lickert, Fred W.
905. Lickun, Joseph F., Jr.
906. Lifechutz, Seymour
907. Light, Doyle W.
908. Lindsey, Marcus H.
909. Link, Robert I.
910. Linstrom, Lennert
911. Lipke, Walter C.
912. Lipscomb, Melvin E.
913. Lipscomb, Thurman L.
914. Lister, Marshall
915. Little Bear, Robert F.
916. Little, David T.
917. Lloyd, George T.
918. Lloyd, Joseph R.
919. Locke, Edward C.
920. Long, Stanley L.
921. Long, William G.
922. Longbottom, John H.
923. Longmore, Donald G.
924. Lopez, Fernando L.
925. Lorange, Robert F.
926. Lord, Dick
927. Lorenz, Ernest E.
928. Lotzer, Eldred R.

929. Lounsbury, Arthur E.
930. Louviere, Joseph
931. Lowe, Harold
932. Lowe, James O.
933. Lucero, Noah
934. Lumpkins, Lewis H.
935. Luna, Fred S.
936. Lunn, James E.
937. Luther, Martin E.
938. Luty, Edward S.
939. Lutz, Stanley W.
940. Lynch, Jack
941. Lynch, Joseph F.
942. Lynch, Thomas
943. Lynch, William E.
944. Lynn, Clyde F.
945. Lyons, Charles E.
946. McAllister, Hubert M.
947. McAnich, Richard L.
948. McCabe, Joseph R.
949. McCann, Gene L.
950. McCauley, David C.
951. McClure, James
952. McConnachie, George H.
953. McCool, Kenneth
954. McCormick, Francis W.
955. McCraney, George E.
956. McCurry, Leslie
957. MacDonald, Brendan J.
958. McDonald, Eugene M.
959. McDonald, Ralph
960. McFarland, Charles
961. McGregor, Art L.
962. McGuire, Charles V.
963. McIntyre, Robert K.
964. McIsaac, John F.
965. McKeen, Calvin C.
966. McKenna, Richard A.
967. McKenzie, Regis
968. McKibbin, J. C.
969. McKinnon, Harvey
970. McLaughlin, James P.
971. McLean, Julian N.
972. McLeod, Harry N.
973. McMahon, Robert L.
974. McManus, John A.
975. McNeish, Paul M.
976. McRae, Bert
977. McSwain, Campbell S.
978. Maddox, William H., Jr.
979. Madison, Robert W.
980. Magbual, Felecisimo
981. Maher, Robert J.
982. Makowsky, John F.
983. Malkiewicz, Robert D.
984. Malkisch, Stephen
985. Malone, Coleman
986. Manis, William Carson
987. Mann, Russell L.
988. Mannino, Anthony V.
989. Marcum, Millard D.
990. Mardstorn, Clyde E.
991. Marker, Franklin J.
992. Marlow, Glenn H.
993. Marshall, Alvin R.
994. Marshall, Robert A.
995. Martin, Billie C.
996. Martin, David B.
997. Martin, Russell G.
998. Maskevich, John F.
999. Massengale, Lloyd J.
1000. Massey, Hildred T.
1001. Masters, Myrl W.
1002. Mather, Howard G.
1003. Matthews, Charles L.
1004. Mauldin, James N.
1005. Max, Ernest W.
1006. Mayden, Howard E.
1007. Mayeda, Charlie
1008. Mayne, Charles
1009. Mays, Paris L.
1010. Meador, Kenneth
1011. Meadors, Grandville H., Jr.
1012. Mefford, Thomas J.
1013. Meliet, Robert L.
1014. Melvin, Duane T.
1015. Mendenhall, Jim
1016. Mercer, Dwayne

1017. Meredith, Robert E.
1018. Messier, William R.
1019. Messina, John S.
1020. Metkowski, Edward
1021. Meyer, Edward R.
1022. Meyer, Jack B.
1023. Meyer, Leroy A.
1024. Meyer, LeRoy A.
1025. Meyers, Kenneth B.
1026. Meyers, Richard N.
1027. Michalowski, Casimer
1028. Michlinski, Benjamin S.
1029. Mickle, John E.
1030. Millarch, John
1031. Miller, Curtis
1032. Miller, Donald S.
1033. Miller, Earl E.
1034. Miller, Frank
1035. Miller, Glenn T.
1036. Miller, Morris
1037. Miller, Neil
1038. Miller, R. H.
1039. Miller, Ray E.
1040. Miller, Robert E.
1041. Miller, William T.
1042. Millican, Charles F.
1043. Milligan, Alan L.
1044. Million, Samuel
1045. Mills, Paul W.
1046. Mincey, Raymond
1047. Minmaugh, James J., Jr.
1048. Mitchell, William D.
1049. Mitiporich, Alix
1050. Miyaji, Nobuo
1051. Mock, Thomas M.
1052. Molish, Frank M.
1053. Mollere, Alex J.
1054. Monteleone, Vincent T.
1055. Moomaw, Stanley O.
1056. Moore, Bernon A.
1057. Moore, Harold B.
1058. Morales, Albert L.
1059. Morekami, Takashi S.
1060. Moretti, Dezonie F.
1061. Morgan, David K., Jr.
1062. Morgan, Theo
1063. Mori, Tadashi
1064. Morris, Junior R.
1065. Morris, Solomon
1066. Morrison, Franklin D.
1067. Morton, Jack
1068. Movsesian, Movses
1069. Mulay, Samuel, Jr.
1070. Mullen, William J.
1071. Mumpowers, Herbert
1072. Muncilly, John R.
1073. Murdock, John L.
1074. Murphy, Carleton H.
1075. Murphy, Charles E.
1076. Murphy, Christopher M.
1077. Murphy, John M.
1078. Murphy, Robert J.
1079. Murray, Francis R.
1080. Murray, James M.
1081. Murray, Robert E.
1082. Myers, Donald E.
1083. Myers, Gerald
1084. Mysliwski, Raymond T.
1085. Nagamine, Yasuyei H.
1086. Nakashita, Kelly S.
1087. Nakayama, Shizuo
1088. Naone, Philip R.
1089. Nash, Eugene C.
1090. Nason, Richard H.
1091. Nathan, Aaron
1092. Nave, John W.
1093. Neeson, David T.
1094. Nelson, George J.
1095. Nelson, Kenneth R.
1096. Nelson, Laurin R.
1097. Nelson, Wilson R.
1098. Neman, Dudley N.
1099. Newman, William A.
1100. Nichoct, Keikhi
1101. Nichols, Dewey J.
1102. Nichols, Rayburn C.
1103. Nissen, Jack W.
1104. Nissen, James P.

1105. Nivens, Harry E.
1106. Noes, Raymond J.
1107. Nogarity, Andrew L.
1108. Nogueria, Antonio R.
1109. Norton, Willie E.
1110. Null, Hugh D.
1111. Nuzzi, Henry A.
1112. Oberlin, Benjamin G.
1113. Ogden, Glenn B.
1114. Ogle, Lloyd J.
1115. O'Grady, Thomas J.
1116. Okimoto, Henry H.
1117. Olasci, Byron
1118. Oldham, Freddie D.
1119. Oler, Lloyd E., Sr.
1120. Olguin, Richard
1121. Olienyk, Steve
1122. Oliver, William J.
1123. Olson, Robert
1124. O'Malley, John
1125. O'Neal, George A., Jr.
1126. O'Neal, Luther B.
1127. O'Neil, Raymond F.
1128. O'Parman, James, Jr.
1129. Orr, Alexander P.
1130. Osborne, Bill M.
1131. Osborne, S. G.
1132. Oshiro, Mitsuo
1133. Ostgarden, Floyd R.
1134. Overfelt, Charles W.
1135. Ovsanik, Andrew N.
1136. Owens, John A.
1137. Owens, John K.
1138. Owens, Roy
1139. Owens, Travis H.
1140. Owens, William C.
1141. Ownbey, Arthur D.
1142. Ownbey, Bill
1143. Pacific, Elso C.
1144. Page, Charles E.
1145. Page, Jesse L.
1146. Paige, Gerald F.
1147. Painter, Edward J.
1148. Palke, Robert J.
1149. Palmer, Glenn A.
1150. Paolini, Mario G.
1151. Paretta, Joseph
1152. Parham, Charles
1153. Parker, Earl O.
1154. Parks, Kenneth R.
1155. Parrett, Edward
1156. Pasley, Edward J.
1157. Pate, Melvin E.
1158. Patrick, Jack E.
1159. Patrick, Wendell E.
1160. Patterson, Bernie J.
1161. Patterson, Charles W.
1162. Paul, Lelan F.
1163. Payne, Frank E.
1164. Peabody, George B.
1165. Pearce, Earl
1166. Peay, Albert A.
1167. Peel, Robert J.
1168. Penca, Anthony R.
1169. Pendall, Carl E.
1170. Pendarvis, William
1171. Pennise, Santo
1172. Perfidio, Louis P.
1173. Perkins, Robert E.
1174. Permett, Lewis J.
1175. Perry, Bill R.
1176. Perry, Douglas R.
1177. Perry, Hubert J.
1178. Perry, Ralph
1179. Perry, Raymond H.
1180. Perry, Robert
1181. Personett, William, Jr.
1182. Peters, Daniel G.
1183. Peterson, Larenz
1184. Petrige, Pasquale J.
1185. Petterson, Norman F.
1186. Phifer, George F.
1187. Phillips, Grover J.
1188. Phillips, Leland H.
1189. Phillips, Teddy R.
1190. Picard, George
1191. Pickett, Leslie M.
1192. Pifer, William C.

1193. Pikoluas, James A.
1194. Pilch, Norbert
1195. Pinali, Frank
1196. Piskering, Russell S.
1197. Poe, Earl F.
1198. Poliziana, Joseph
1199. Pollock, Frank E.
1200. Pontello, Patrick M.
1201. Pontier, Chester E.
1202. Poorman, Jack E.
1203. Pope, Jesse
1204. Poretta, Joseph
1205. Porter, Harley L.
1206. Potter, Charles L.
1207. Powell, Don M.
1208. Powell, Elzie C., Jr.
1209. Powerautz, S.
1210. Powers, Robert A.
1211. Powers, Roy R.
1212. Pratt, Donald
1213. Pratt, Donald L.
1214. Preece, Edward M.
1215. Preston, Shirley H.
1216. Pretakiewicz, Anthony E.
1217. Price, Edmund P.
1218. Price, Thomas H.
1219. Prinzo, Anthony L.
1220. Pritikin, Neil
1221. Prout, Edward L.
1222. Puccini, Leslie E.
1223. Pullen, Charles W.
1224. Pye, John J.
1225. Qucici, John F.
1226. Quellete, Conrad
1227. Quenette, Donald F.
1228. Quick, Howard
1229. Raden, Edward P.
1230. Ragland, Dale E.
1231. Railer, Roy F.
1232. Rainwater, Claude L.
1233. Rake, Robert
1234. Ramberg, Harlen L.
1235. Ramirez, Roberto
1236. Ramos, Alfredo
1237. Ramsever, Charles
1238. Randazzo, Samuel J.
1239. Randzo, Edward K.
1240. Rape, Carl L.
1241. Rarelazzo, Manuel
1242. Rasmussen, Harold E.
1243. Rathbone, Frank
1244. Rawlins, Willis H.
1245. Ray, R. B.
1246. Raymer, Arthur T.
1247. Raynolds, Jessie R.
1248. Reaves, Ira
1249. Reber, Alfred R.
1250. Redepenning, Harold
1251. Reed, Kenneth P.
1252. Reed, Russel S., Jr.
1253. Reeves, Robert L.
1254. Reilly, John J.
1255. Reilly, Joseph G.
1256. Reimer, George L.
1257. Remaly, William M.
1258. Remmert, Roy W.
1259. Render, Dalton L.
1260. Retzloff, Roy
1261. Rhoden, Clifford
1262. Rice, Harry P.
1263. Rice, Melvin C.
1264. Rich, Charles
1265. Rich, Robert I.
1266. Richards, Franklin L.
1267. Richardson, Leon D.
1268. Rickard, James R.
1269. Ridens, James H.
1270. Riggen, Walter E.
1271. Riley, Donald W.
1272. Riley, Johnnie G.
1273. Rindels, Raymond M.
1274. Riojas, Lorenz C.
1275. Ritchie, Ernest E.
1276. Rivers, Donald E.
1277. Rizzi, Charles J.
1278. Robbins, Clement
1279. Roberts, Clifton J. C.
1280. Roberts, Howard D.

1281. Roberts, Stanley A.
1282. Robinson, John R.
1283. Robinson, Leland S.
1284. Robinson, Rufus E.
1285. Robison, Lester N.
1286. Roche, Edwin J.
1287. Rocheleau, Joseph M.
1288. Rogers, Burr M.
1289. Rogers, Elmo M.
1290. Rogers, Marvel L.
1291. Rorland, Robert M.
1292. Rorman, Edward
1293. Rosen, Irwin E.
1294. Rosenblatt, Norman
1295. Rosier, Harlan E.
1296. Ross, John M.
1297. Ross, Norman A.
1298. Roth, John
1299. Rothstein, Marshall
1300. Roupp, Richard D.
1301. Rowe, Carleton N.
1302. Ruddock, Jules B., Jr.
1303. Ruppel, Albert F.
1304. Russell, Carroll L.
1305. Russell, Elbert L.
1306. Russell, John J.
1307. Russell, Kenneth N.
1308. Rutland, Alsie L.
1309. Ryan, James J.
1310. Ryan, John A.
1311. Ryan, Joseph F.
1312. Saars, Ernest E.
1313. Sabol, Paul
1314. Sakauwe, Elichi
1315. Sakowicz, John J.
1316. Saladak, John E.
1317. Saladino, Mario A.
1318. Sallee, Bobby S.
1319. Samarjia, Steve S.
1320. Sample, William W.
1321. Sams, Raymond L.
1322. Sanchez, Eugene E.
1323. Sanders, Warren D.
1324. Sansom, James F.
1325. Sansom, John G.
1326. Santee, Joseph
1327. Saullo, Gaetano A.
1328. Savoy, Cledus P.
1329. Sawyer, Dwayne N.
1330. Sceusa, Carlo
1331. Schiling, John T.
1332. Schmahl, Dana C.
1333. Schmidt, Frederick M.
1334. Schmidt, Lyle E.
1335. Schmidt, Richard J.
1336. Schmus, Eugene
1337. Schneider, John
1338. Schumacher, Glenn
1339. Schumm, Edward C.
1340. Schumsa, Robert L.
1341. Schut, James T.
1342. Schwartz, Burton
1343. Scott, Robert D.
1344. Scott, Thomas A.
1345. Scuder, Walter A.
1346. See, Wayne
1347. Seeber, Edward H., Jr.
1348. Seibolt, Victor L.
1349. Seifort, Raymond E.
1350. Seitz, Herman J.
1351. Selander, Edgar D.
1352. Self, Farrell H.
1353. Semanchick, Frank
1354. Shackelford, Edward
1355. Sharp, Carl M.
1356. Sharp, William D.
1357. Shebalin, Alexander I.
1358. Shelton, John S.
1359. Shenkel, Willard F.
1360. Shepherd, Lewis A.
1361. Sherfield, Lt.
1362. Sheruleim, Floyd
1363. Shigemura, Bert S.
1364. Shimer, Charles L.
1365. Shimizu, Willie
1366. Shively, Robert N.
1367. Short, Ode L.
1368. Short, Vernon C.

1369. Shreve, Eugene N.
1370. Shultz, Talmadge
1371. Sieta, Takeshi
1372. Sigafus, Delbert
1373. Siler, Charles L.
1374. Simmons, Edgar M.
1375. Simmons, Harry
1376. Sinda, William
1377. Singh, William
1378. Singleton, Eugene A.
1379. Sistare, Tom B.
1380. Skelton, Leo R.
1381. Slagle, Harvey L.
1382. Slatton, James E.
1383. Sleeth, Herbert N.
1384. Slinker, Kenneth E.
1385. Slomanski, Henry
1386. Smedley, Charles F.
1387. Smelcer, Edward M.
1388. Smith, Anthony
1389. Smith, Bernard A.
1390. Smith, Charles E.
1391. Smith, Charles M.
1392. Smith, Edgar E.
1393. Smith, Edward F.
1394. Smith, Francis G.
1395. Smith, Frank C.
1396. Smith, Gordon A.
1397. Smith, Noble
1398. Smith, Richard F.
1399. Smith, Robert U.
1400. Smith, William J.
1401. Snearer, Karl F.
1402. Snuggs, Charlie O.
1403. Snustad, George L.
1404. Snyder, Deo B.
1405. Snyder, Kenneth E., Jr.
1406. Soaree, Norman A.
1407. Socebee, John J.
1408. Sofelkamich, Charles G.
1409. Solari, Robert J.
1410. Sopke, Joseph B.
1411. Sorenson, Keith R.
1412. Soto, Joe
1413. Soto, Leopold
1414. Sparks, Darrell L.
1415. Sparks, Wayne C.
1416. Spence, George E.
1417. Spencer, Nathan L.
1418. Spieler, Robert E.
1419. Spitz, James D.
1420. Spring, William V.
1421. Sprout, James E.
1422. Stacy, William A.
1423. Stafford, Darrell L.
1424. Stahley, Robert M.
1425. Staley, James L.
1426. Stanfel, Joseph
1427. Stanton, Raymond B.
1428. Stark, Harry A.
1429. Starkey, Jack W.
1430. Starkey, John N.
1431. Starnes, Donald L.
1432. Starring, Harry, Jr.
1433. Statton, James
1434. Staudenmayer, Charles
1435. Steck, Robert L.
1436. Stelmachowski, Eugene J.
1437. Stephens, Billy
1438. Stepnick, George
1439. Stevens, D. A.
1440. Stiles, Almond D.
1441. Stimpson, George W.
1442. Stipe, Eldridge E.
1443. Stock, Everett F.
1444. Stodola, Roland W.
1445. Stohler, Donald M.
1446. Stone, Billy
1447. Stone, James R.
1448. Stone, Kenneth
1449. Stone, Kenneth L.
1450. Stoner, Jacob R.
1451. Stonko, Andy
1452. Stormer, Lester J.
1453. Stout, Arthur V.
1454. Stout, Cicero C.
1455. Straub, Carl E.
1456. Strem, Walter

1457. Stretman, Donald L.
1458. Strong, Casey
1459. Strong, Clark E.
1460. Struss, Walter W.
1461. Stuart, Donald L.
1462. Stuart, Everett C.
1463. Stulick, James
1464. Sturges, Richard M.
1465. Sullivan, Albert J.
1466. Sullivan, George G.
1457. Sullivan, Robert C.
1468. Sullivan, Robert G.
1469. Surcey, David F.
1470. Surratt, Eugene N.
1471. Susice, Norman G.
1472. Sutcliffe, Lee A.
1473. Sutterfield, Ira
1474. Sutterfield, James L.
1475. Sutton, Harold R.
1476. Swain, Fred M.
1477. Swain, George L.
1478. Swain, Julian
1479. Swain, Weaver D.
1480. Swanson, Austin
1481. Swanson, Martin
1482. Swearengin, Carl J.
1483. Sweeney, Ambrose
1484. Sweeney, Benjamin L.
1485. Sweetland, John
1486. Swiger, Carl E.
1487. Szulcyewski, George J.
1488. Tabor, Marshall E.
1489. Tagalos, George
1490. Takahashi, Hiroki
1491. Takate, Henry K.
1492. Taketa, Tatsuo
1493. Tallman, Wayne A.
1494. Tanabe, James
1495. Tanaka, James K.
1496. Taniguchi, Harry H.
1497. Tannian, Martin J., Jr.
1498. Tarangelo, Donato
1499. Tasoe, Jiro M.
1500. Tatman, Edward
1501. Taylor, Jack T.
1502. Taylor, James E.
1503. Taylor, John Y.
1504. Taylor, Odis T.
1505. Taylor, Robert W.
1506. Tetzlaff, Arlyn E.
1507. Tewis, Walter
1508. Thamke, Joe
1509. Thevenin, William M.
1510. Thom, George
1511. Thomas, James L.
1512. Thomas, Murrell
1513. Thomas, Ralph P.
1514. Thomason, Elmer F.
1515. Thompson, Charles R.
1516. Thompson, Donald V.
1517. Thompson, James D.
1518. Thompson, William
1519. Thooft, Amandus S.
1520. Thorson, Norbert L.
1521. Thurman, James
1522. Tibbitts, Boyden C.
1523. Tipton, Thomas J.
1524. Tischler, Morris
1525. Titone, Vincent R.
1526. Todd, John T.
1527. Togerson, James E.
1528. Toone, Guy T.
1529. Tortella, Alexander J.
1530. Tourville, Robert R.
1531. Toutaint, Oscar J.
1532. Trace, Richard N.
1533. Travers, David T.
1534. Twigg, Harry B.
1535. Udell, Robert L.
1536. Urban, John J.
1537. Uyeda, Robert
1538. Valdez, Louie L.
1539. Valencta, Donald M.
1540. Valentine, James
1541. VanHorn, Howard G.
1542. VanHorn, Virgil
1543. VanSickle, Kenneth D.
1544. Vasapolli, Alfred A.

1545. Vatawick, Edward
1546. Veesey, George J.
1547. Venegoni, Robert
1548. Vialpando, Jose D.
1549. Victorine, Harry
1550. Viera, Dewey H.
1551. Vincent, Lee P.
1552. Vinciale, Patrick J.
1553. Vines, Paul R.
1554. Vitanko, Samuel
1555. Vlymen, William
1556. Vogel, Max M.
1557. Vogt, Silverius H.
1558. Vopalacky, Charles F.
1559. Wacker, Earl J.
1560. Waddell, Jesse E.
1561. Wages, Edmund W.
1562. Wagner, John F.
1563. Walker, Ivan N.
1564. Walker, John B.
1565. Walker, Oscar L.
1566. Wallace, Loren P.
1567. Waller, Earl T.
1568. Wallin, Kenneth D.
1569. Walsh, Patrick J.
1570. Ward, Charles J.
1571. Ward, Elbert P.
1572. Ward, Ernest E.
1573. Ward, John F.
1574. Warmsdorfer, Jerdon E., Jr.
1575. Warner, Clarence L.
1576. Warner, Paul W.
1577. Warner, William L.
1578. Warnick, Clyde C.
1579. Washburn, Wilbur M.
1580. Watson, Edwin G.
1581. Watson, Robert K.
1582. Watts, Albert D.
1583. Weatherbee, Richard I.
1584. Weatherford, Phenix C.
1585. Weaver, William E.
1586. Webb, George M.
1587. Webb, James Hoyt
1588. Webber, Richard N.
1589. Welahan, John M.
1590. Welker, Ivan
1591. Wells, Kelly W.
1592. Werkmeister, Melvin E.
1593. Wessels, Rudolph V.
1594. West, Roland R.
1595. Whitaker, James C.
1596. White, Ancal
1597. Wicks, Richard
1598. Wilbert, Wilferd F.
1599. Wilcock, George Y.
1600. Wiley, Luther D.
1601. Wiley, William T.
1602. Wiley, William W.
1603. Wilkin, Robert
1604. Willert, Will
1605. Williams, Bob F.
1606. Williams, Clayton O.
1607. Williams, Curtis C.
1608. Williams, Donald R.
1609. Williams, Thomas A.
1610. Williams, Thomas B.
1611. Williamson, Hugh
1612. Willis, Edward
1613. Wilson, George C.
1614. Wilson, Glen D.
1615. Wilson, Hilleard
1616. Wilson, Irvin G.
1617. Wilson, John C.
1618. Wilson, Rex J.
1619. Wilson, Truman H.
1620. Wimer, Lawrence W.
1621. Winklepleck, Wade H.
1622. Winter, Robert F.
1623. Wise, Howard K.
1624. Wolfe, Edward
1625. Wolford, Samuel H.
1626. Woller, Leo
1627. Wolter, Fred A.
1628. Wolter, Leo F.
1629. Wood, Bunyan D.
1630. Wood, Eddie L.
1631. Woodland, Rolind R.
1632. Woodrum, John K.

Appendix E

1633. Wooten, Paul V.
1634. Wright, George H.
1635. Wright, John
1636. Wright, Joseph R.
1637. Wright, Mobley
1638. Wright, Wilbur G.
1639. Wroblonski, Sylvester F.
1640. Wurm, Wayne W.
1641. Wyatt, Deloy E.
1642. Yamada, George
1643. York, Willie M.
1644. Young, Everett A.
1645. Young, Harry P.
1646. Young, Orland
1647. Young, Poy G.
1648. Young, Richard L.
1649. Yount, Dick T.
1650. Zabrecky, Ray T.
1651. Zalud, William J.
1652. Zamay, Paul E.
1653. Zamos, Mike
1654. Zerflieh, Don

BIBLIOGRAPHY

Axelbank, Alex. *Black Star Over Japan: Rising Forces of Militarism.* New York: Hill & Wang, 1972.
Bergamini, David. *Japan's Imperial Conspiracy.* New York: Pocket Books, 1971.
Blair, Clay, Jr. *MacArthur.* New York: Pocket Books, 1977.
Boyle, Martin. *Yanks Don't Cry: A Marine's Eye View of Four Years in a Japanese Prison Camp.* New York: Bernard Geis Association, 1963.
Brackman, Arnold C. *The Other Nuremberg: The Untold Story of the Tokyo War Crime Trials.* New York: Quill-William Morrow, 1987.
Breuer, William B. *Retaking the Philippines.* New York: St. Martin's Press, 1986.
Browne, Courtney. *Tojo: The Last Banzai.* New York: Holt, Rinehart and Winston, 1967.
Coffey, Thomas M. *Imperial Tragedy: Japan in World War II.* New York: Pinnacle Books, 1970.
Craig, William. *The Fall of Japan.* New York: Dial Press, 1967.
Craigie, Sir Robert. *Behind the Japanese Mask.* London: Hutchinson, 1945.
Dover, John W. *War Without Mercy.* New York: Pantheon Books, 1986.
Duus, Masayo. *Tokyo Rose: Orphan of the Pacific.* Tokyo: Kodansha International, Limited, 1979.
Eichelberger, Robert L. *Our Jungle Road to Tokyo.* New York: Viking Press, 1950.
Fahey, James J. *Pacific War Diary 1942-1945.* New York: Zebra Books, 1963.
Feis, Herbert. *Japan Subdued.* Princeton, N.J.: Princeton University Press, 1961.
_____. *The Road to Pearl Harbor.* Princeton, N.J.: Princeton University Press, 1950.
Fussell, Paul. *Wartime.* New York: Oxford University Press, 1989.
Garfield, Brian. *The Thousand Mile War.* New York: Ballantine Books, 1969.
Gilbert, G. M. *Nuremberg Diary.* New York: Signet Books, 1961.
Grew, Joseph C. *Ten Years in Japan.* New York: Simon and Schuster, 1944.
Hanayama, Shinso. *The Way of Deliverance: Three Years with the Condemned Japanese War Criminals.* New York: Charles Scribner's Sons, 1950.
"Historical Abstract: Chaplain Oscar W. Schoech: Missionary to War Criminals." *Concordia Historical Institute Quarterly.* 1984.
Hoyt, Edwin P. *Closing the Circle.* New York: Van Nostrand Reinhold Company, 1982.
_____. *Japan's War, The Great Pacific Conflict.* New York: McGraw-Hill Book Company, 1986.

---. *War in the Pacific.* 2 vols. New York: Avon Books, 1990.
"Illustrated Story of WWII." *Reader's Digest.* 1969.
International Military Tribunal for the Far East Command. Documents furnished by Crosby Library, Gonzaga University, Spokane, Washington, 1989.
James, David H. *The Rise and Fall of the Japanese Empire.* London: George Allen & Unwin, 1951.
Johnson, Chalmers. *An Instance of Treason: Ozaki Hotsumi and the Sorge Spy Ring.* Stanford, Calif.: Stanford University Press, 1964.
Kenworthy, Aubrey Saint. *The Tiger of Malaya.* New York: Exposition Press, 1953.
Kerr, Bartlett E. *Surrender and Survival, The Experience of American POWs in the Pacific.* New York: William Morrow and Company, 1985.
Kodama, Yoshio. *Sugamo Diary.* Tokyo: Radiopress, 1960.
Manchester, William. *American Caesar.* New York: Dell Publishing Co., 1978.
Manning, Paul. *Hirohito—The War Years.* New York: Bantam Books, 1989.
Morison, Samuel E. *The Rising Sun in the Pacific, History of the United States Naval Operations in World War II.* Vol. 3. Boston: Little, Brown, 1948.
National Archives, Technical Service Branch. *Review of Yokohama Class B and C War Crime Trials by the US 8th Army Judge Advocate 1946–1949.* Washington, D.C.: Microfilm Publications, Government Printing Office.
Newcomb, Richard F. *Iwo Jima.* New York: Bantam Books, 1982.
Prange, Gordon W., with Donald Goldstein and Katherine V. Dillon. *Target Tokyo, the Story of the Sorge Spy Ring.* New York: McGraw-Hill Book Company, 1984.
Reel, Frank. *The Case of General Yamashita.* Chicago: University of Chicago Press, 1949.
Reischauer, Edwin O. *Japan, Past and Present.* New York: Alfred A. Knopf, 1964.
---. *The Japanese.* Cambridge, Mass.: Harvard University Press, 1978.
Sebald, William. *With MacArthur in Japan.* New York: W. W. Norton & Co., Inc., 1965.
Shapiro, Michael. *Japan.* New York: Henry Holt & Co., 1989.
Shigemitsu, Mamoru. *Japan and Her Destiny.* New York: E. P. Dutton, 1958.
Shiroyama, Saburo. *The Life and Death of Koki Hirota.* Tokyo: Kodansha International Limited, 1974.
Spector, Ronald H. *Eagle Against the Sun.* New York: Free Press, 1985.
Stewart, Sidney. *Give Us This Day.* New York: Avon Books, 1990.
Taylor, Lawrence. *A Trial of Generals: Homma, Yamashita, MacArthur.* Icarus Press, 1981.
Time-Life Books, Editors of. *World War II.* New York: Prentice Hall Press, 1989.
Togo, Shigenori. *The Cause of Japan.* New York: Simon & Schuster, 1956.
Toland, John. *But Not in Shame: The Six Months After Pearl Harbor.* New York: Random House, 1961.
---. *Infamy—Pearl Harbor and Its Aftermath.* New York: Doubleday and Company, 1982.

———. *The Rising Sun.* New York: Random House, 1970.

Tsunetomo, Yamamoto. *The Book of the Samurai.* Tokyo: Kodansha International Limited, 1979.

Turnbull, S. R. *The Samurai—A Military History.* New York: Macmillan Publishing Company, 1977.

Ward, Robert E., and Frank Joseph Shulman. *The Allied Occupation of Japan 1945-1952.* Chicago: American Library Association, 1972.

Warner, Dennis, and Peggy Warner, with Commander Sadao Seno. *The Sacred Warriors.* New York: Van Nostrand Reinhold, 1982.

Young, Peter. *The World Almanac Book of World War II.* New York: World Almanac Publications, Enterprise Association, 1981.

INDEX

Adams, Lonnie B. 10, 11, 13, 201-204
Africa, Bernabe 123
Aihara, Kajuro 92-101, 164
Aihara, Kazutane 76-87, 150, 193
Akira, Hiroshi 92-101, 164
Allied Council 189, 190
Allied POWs 58, 60, 63, 74-75, 79-84, 87-93, 97, 102, 103, 105, 111-116
Anaguchi, Shozo 108-119, 171
Anami, Korechika 16
Anderson, Harry 203, 205-206
Anthony, Bill 206-207, 217, 218
Aoki, Yuji 218-220
Araki, Sadao 17-18, 37, 124, 136
Ascot 109, 113
Azabu, Regiment Headquarters 186

Barwise, Fred 13, 207-208, 216
Bataan Death March, Case #304 31, 48, 52, 101-105, 122, 138, 166, 241
Berezhkov, V. 53
Berlew, Ziba 216
Bernard, Henri 41
Bickwermert, William B. 208-215
Blakney, Ben Bruce 46, 54
Blankenship, Talmadge 200
Blue Prison 3, 34, 36, 206, 210
Bowman, Don 220
Brackman, Arnold 24
Brazil Maru 78, 80, 81, 82, 83, 85
British Chivalry 109, 114-115
Broome, Charles 188, 206
Buddhism 178, 180, 181, 182, 183, 186, 187, 190, 191
Burr, Robert L. 198
Bushido Code 65, 66, 67
Bustard, Carl 215-218

Camp Drake 186, 215
Capodilupo, Edward J. 238-240
Carr, E. L. 9
Chakravarty, B. N. 123
Chen, Shang 123, 189
Choeji Shinto Temple, Case #25 63-67, 142
Churchill, N. E. 63
Churchill, Winston 47
Class A charges 6, 40-41, 137
Class B charges 6
Class C charges 7, 57, 138
Class C sentences by case number 141-175
Clavell, James 50
Coleman, Beverly 43, 48
Coleman, Jack 218-220
Comyns-Carr, Arthur 42, 44, 54
Cramer, Myron C. 42, 49
Crary, Francis W. 9, 216

D'Aguina, Phillip 34
Daisy Moller 109, 115-116
Derevyanko, K. N. 123, 189, 191
Doihara, Kenji 18, 37, 122, 126, 136, 177, 178, 189, 191
Donovan, William of O.S.S. 4
Duus, Masayo 36
Dyer, Fredrick E. 74-75

Egawa, Sachio 73-76, 147, 193
Eichelberger, Robert L. 2, 8, 56, 62, 67, 188
8th Army 2, 5, 8, 33, 34, 56, 57, 85, 92, 199, 234
8th Army Stockade 2, 11, 12

11th Airborne 199, 203, 223, 231, 232, 233
Ellingwood, Tom 217
Enoura Maru 78, 80, 81, 82
Eramwell, Donald 64
Evans, Walter 217
Executions, Class C 192-193

Fihelly, John 55
1st Cavalry Division 186, 198, 232, 240
Ford, Gerald 36
Foster, George C. 220-221
Fujihira, Naotada 105-108, 169
Fujimori, Yasuo 108-119, 170
Fukuaka POW Camp #18, Sasebo, Case #94 73-76, 147
Fukuda, Tokuro 73-76, 147
Fukumoto, Menjiro 60-61
Fukushima, Kyusaka 92-101, 164

Gascoigne, Alvary 123
Geneva Convention 45, 121, 177
Goiyama, Shinju 92-101, 164
Golunsky, S. A. 42, 44
Gonzaga University 197
Goodrich, Max 207, 217, 221-223
Gordon, Barry 209, 211, 212
Goring, Hermann 26, 51
Goshima, Shiro 92-101, 164
Gradick, Joseph 220
Guam, attack on 46
Guilder, John W. 43, 48

Hague Accord 45
Hamana, Arimi 90
Hanai, Tadashi 48
Hanayama, Shinsho 9, 177-183, 185-191, 198, 206
Handwerk, Morris 188, 189, 190, 191
Harbin, China 243-245
Harrigan, William F. 207, 226
Hartley, Robert E. 223-224, 226
Hashida, Kumihiko 17
Hashimoto, Kingoro 18-19, 37, 131, 136

Hata, Shunroku 19, 123, 125, 136
Hattori, Masonori 108-119, 171
Hattori, Sho 77-87, 150
Hayashi, Goro 66
Hellships, Case #154 76-87, 150
Higgins, Carlisle 52
Higgins, John P. 42, 49
Hirako, Goichi 92-101, 164
Hirano, Kurataro 101-105, 166, 193
Hiranuma, Kiichiro 19, 21, 37, 55, 135, 136
Hirao, Kenichi 92-101, 164
Hirohito, Emperor 21, 22, 37, 47
Hirota, Koki 19-20, 48, 122, 123, 130, 136, 177-179, 182, 188, 191
Hitler, Adolf 23, 26, 110, 118
Holton, James H. 224-226
Hondo, Shijeru 16
Hong Kong, attack on 24, 46
Homma, Masaharu 33, 38, 102, 104, 105, 139, 241, 242
Hood, Walter K. 5, 224, 226-229
Hoshino, Kaoki 20, 29, 130, 136
Hsiang, Che-chun 41
Hull, Cordell 2, 46

Ichioka, Hisashi 108-119, 170
IMTFE 15, 18, 37, 38, 39, 40, 42, 44, 45, 46, 47, 50, 51, 52, 55, 56, 57, 121, 122, 137, 138, 177, 178
Inada, Masazumi 92-101, 164
Inukai, Tsuyoshi 19, 26, 29
Ishii, Isami 71
Ishii, Shiro 243, 244, 245
Ishizaki, Noboru 108-119, 170
Itagaki, Seichiro 20-21, 39-40, 122, 127, 136, 179-180, 191
Ito, Shoshin 92-101, 164
Iura, Shojiro 108-119, 170
Iwanmura, Tsusei 5

Japan Urban Development Company 13
Jaranilla, Delfin 42, 48
Jean Nicolet 109, 111
John A. Johnson 109
Johnson, William 217

Kambe, Hatsuaki 68-73, 145
Kamikaze 16
Kamimoto, Keiji 68-73, 145
Kawakami, Shoichi 108-119, 170
Kawane, Yoshitaka 101-105, 166, 193
Kawasaki, Genichiro 64
Kawate, Haruni 59
Kaya, Okinori 21, 124, 136
Keenan, Joseph B. 42-46, 48, 49, 55, 197
Kefauver, Estes 246
Kempeitai Police 45, 46, 64, 65, 72, 98
Kenworthy, Aubrey 229, 231
Kerns, John 217
Kido, Koichi 16, 21-22, 47, 131, 136, 177
Kikuchi, Jutaro 63-67, 142
Kimura, Heitaro 22, 39, 40, 122, 126, 136, 180, 191
Kimura, Taro 180
Kimura, Tomatsu 59
Kishi, Nobusuke 208, 242
Kitano, Masaji 244
Kiyose, Ichiro 43, 54
Kleiman, Samuel J. 49
Kodama, Hiroshi 76
Koiso, Kuniaki 22, 127, 136
Koizumi, Chikahiko 17
Komatsu, Teruhisa 108-119, 170
Konoye, Fumimaro 16, 17, 29
Koshikawa, Masao 68-73, 145
Kota Bharu, attack on 24, 46, 47
Kuba, Toiso 65
Kubo, Toshiyuki 93-101, 165
Kukuoka, POW Camp #3, Case #15 59-62, 141
Kusaka, Toshio 108-119, 170
Kwantung Army 16, 18, 20, 22, 23, 30, 32, 38, 44, 45
Kyushu Imperial University Hospital, Case #290 92-101, 164-165

Leonard, David 208
Logan, William 54
Lopez, Pedro 42, 52

Mabuchi, Masaaki 63-67, 142, 192
MacArthur, Douglas 15-17, 25, 39, 41-43, 47-49, 56, 57, 102, 105, 122, 123, 136, 177, 189, 208, 235, 241-243
McCormick, Francis 35
McDougall, Edward S. 41
McMahon, Robert L. 229-232
McNeish, Paul 188
Maddox, William 197, 198, 217
Mahoney, Daniel 197
Mahoney, William 197
Makino, Reiichiro 92-101, 164
Manchuckuo 18, 20
Manila, Philippines 24, 38, 48
Manila, Rape of 52, 241
Manis, William C. 240, 245-246
Mansfield, A. J. 41
Marco Polo Bridge 21, 32
Masumoto, Shinichi 1
Matsui, Iwane 22-23, 122, 128, 136, 181-182, 190-191
Matsuoka, Yosuke 23
Matsusaki, Yoshiki 59
Matsuzaki, Hiromasa 5
Mei, Ju-ao 41
Meiji University 43
Menon, Govinda 41
Minami, Jiro 23, 129, 136
Mito, Hisashi 108-119, 170
Mitsuchima POW Camp, Case #1 58-59, 141
Mori, Yoshio 93-101, 165
Morimoto, Kenji 93-101, 165
Morimura, Seiichi 244
Moriyama, Minoru 64, 65
Motonaka, Sadao 108-119, 170
Mukden, Manchuria 15-17, 20, 26
Mulder, W. G. F. Boegerhoff 41
Muramatsu, Tsuneo 88
Murphy, Robert 239-240
Muto, Akira 24, 122, 125, 136, 182-183, 190-191, 231
MV Scotia 109
MV Sutlej 109, 112

Nagano, Osami 24-25, 235
Nakadate, Kyuhei 90
Nakagawa, Hajime 108-119, 170
Nakamura, Kiyoteru 75

296 Index

Nakazawa, Tasuku 108-119, 170
Nancy Moller 109, 113-114
Nanking, Rape of 18, 20, 22-23, 52, 122, 137, 182
Nashimoto, Morimasa 47
National Archives 58, 197
Nellore 109
Nishima, Yokichi 59
Nogawa, Nobuyoshi 93-101, 165
Nolan, H. G. 41
Nomura, Kichisaburo 2, 46
Norman, Herbert E. 123
Northcroft, Erima H. 42
Noto, Kiyohisa 105-108, 169
Nuremberg Trials 37, 40, 51

Odazawa, Yutaka 105-108, 169
Ogawa, Waichi 236
Oie, Satoshi 183, 186, 187
Oka, Takasumi 25, 128, 136, 177
Okada, Kikusaburo 51
Okawa, Shumei 25-26
Okubo, Mataishi 68-73, 145
Okuma, Kaoru 105-108, 169, 193
Oler, Lloyd E., Sr. 2, 237-238
Olguin, Richard J. 232-233
Omori Prison 2
Oneto, Robert 41
Onishi, Takijiro 16
Orito, Denkichi 73-76, 147
Oryoku Maru 78, 79, 81, 84, 85
Oshima, Hiroshi 26-29, 110, 118, 129, 137
Ott, Eugen 3
Ouchi, Hyoe 49
Ozaka, Hotzumi 3

Pal, Radha M. 41
Patrick, Lord 42
Pearl Harbor, attack on 18, 24, 27, 30, 46, 47, 121, 235
Pechkoff, Z. 123
Percival, Arthur 47
Potsdam Declaration 40, 177
Powell, John 236
Provoo, John D. 236

Quick, Howard 206
Quilliam, R. H. 42

Rawlins, Willis H. 233-235
Reimer, George 201
Ribbentrop, Joachim Von 26, 110, 118
Richard Hovey 109
Rikitake, Yaichi 59-62, 141
Roling, B. V. A. 41
Ryan, John A. 8, 240, 245, 246
Ryu, Miki 93-101, 165

Sanders, Murray 243
Sato, Kenro 25, 27, 77, 135, 137
Sato, Yoshinao 93-101, 139, 165
SCAP 15, 16, 40-43, 46, 48, 51, 56, 57, 76, 87, 88, 91, 92, 100, 122, 140, 236, 241
Schmahl, Dana C. 51, 206
Sebald, William 122, 123, 136, 189-191
Senba, Yoshitaka 93-101, 165
Shanghai Bund, attack on 46
Shaw, Patrick 123, 189
Shigemitsu, Mamoru 27-28, 44, 122, 123, 132, 137, 200, 224
Shimada, Shigetaro 28, 77, 133, 137
Shimozata, Masaki 244
Shinagawa Hospital Camp, Case #186 87-92, 153
Shinto Religion 46, 63, 65, 66, 67, 178, 181, 183, 185
Singapore, attack on 46
Shiratori, Toshio 28-29, 55, 134, 137
Shively, Robert N. 199-202, 231
Siam-Burma Railway 21, 22, 27, 31, 39, 52, 122, 138
Smith, David 48
Sorge, Richard 3, 4
South Manchurian Railroad 16, 23
Stars and Stripes Review 7
State-War-Navy-Coordinating Committee 15
Stepnick, George 35
Submarine Warfare, Case #339 108-119, 170-171
Sudeo, Nakajima 59
Sugamo Prison 1-13, 16, 25, 30, 33,

Index

34, 36, 38, 39, 44, 49, 51, 62, 76, 87, 88, 92, 95, 100, 101, 105, 107, 108, 122, 139, 177-180, 184, 186-189, 192, 195-201, 203, 206-211, 215-224, 226, 228-238, 240, 242, 245, 246
Sugiyama, Hajime 17
Sutterfield, Ira 235-236
Suzuki, Teiichi 29-30, 132, 137, 242

Tadaki, Nobujuki 108-119, 170
Tadao, Shibano 183
Takahashi, Chojuro 108-119, 170
Takahashi, Masaru 76
Takahashi, Masonori 65
Takayanagi, Kenzo 43
Tanaka, Shizuichi 17
Tanoue, Suketoshi 76-87, 150
Tashiro, Jiro 93-101, 165
Tashiro, Tomoki 93-101, 165
Tashiro, Toshio 67-73, 145
Tavenner, Frank 54
Thailand, attack on 46
Tjisalak 109, 111-112
Tochima, Dr. 11
Togo, Shigenori 24, 30, 122, 123, 133, 137
Toguri, Iva 34, 36
Tojo, Hideki 2, 9, 16, 18, 20, 21, 24, 26, 28, 29, 30-32, 34, 37, 43, 54, 55, 122, 137, 177, 183, 184, 185, 188, 189, 190, 191, 200, 207, 220, 221, 225, 227, 228, 229, 231, 232, 234, 235, 240
Tokuda, Hisakichi 87-92, 153, 203
Tokyo Military Prison, Case #78 67-73, 145
Tokyo Rose 34-36, 100, 198, 200, 206, 210, 235
Tomekichi, Nomura 76
Tomioka, Sadatoshi 117
Torisu, Taro 93-101, 165
Toriyama, Tadashi 64
Toshino, Junsaburo 76-87, 150, 193
Tourat, Francis 63, 64
Toyama, Mitsuru 20
Toyotama Prison 12
Truman, President 47
Tsuchiya, Tatsuo 58-59, 141
Tsutsui, Shizuko 93-101, 165

24th Infantry Division 209, 215
27th Special Naval Base, Kairiru Island, New Guinea, Case #329 105-108, 169

Ueda, Jiro 77-87, 150
Umezu, Yoshijiro 28, 32-33, 44, 55, 123, 134, 137, 207
U.N. War Crimes Commission 15
Uzawa, Somei 43

Van Aduard, Lewe 123
Vincent, Lee P. 206

Wada, Shusuke 76-87, 150
Wainwright, Jonathan M. 102
Walsh, Patrick 186, 188, 190, 191
War Crime Trials, other 33, 34, 57
Watanabe, Fukuichi 73-76, 147
Weatherspoon, Robert 233
Webb, Sir William 25, 41, 49, 50, 53, 54, 55, 56, 235
William K. Vanderbilt 109
Willert, Wilfred F. 236-237
Willoughby, Charles A. 25

Xiao, Han 243, 244

Yakamura, Katsuya 93-101, 165
Yamamoto, Chikao 117
Yamamoto, Isoroku 37
Yamamoto, Tsunehiko 105-108, 169
Yamaoka, George 48
Yamashita, Tomoyuki 24, 33-34, 38, 139, 241, 242
Yanabe, Motohide 108-119, 171
Yokohama, Isau 53, 186
Yokohama trials 2, 33, 34, 56, 57, 92, 101, 242
Yokoyama, Isamu 93-101, 165

Zaryanov, Ivan M. 42, 44

www.ingramcontent.com/pod-product-compliance
Lightning Source LLC
Chambersburg PA
CBHW030102170426
43198CB00009B/468